AF270081

HOW ISAIAH BECAME AN AUTHOR

HOW ISAIAH BECAME AN AUTHOR

Prophecy, Authority, and Attribution

DAVID DAVAGE

FORTRESS PRESS
Minneapolis

HOW ISAIAH BECAME AN AUTHOR
Prophecy, Authority, and Attribution

All Scripture quotations are the author's own translation unless otherwise noted.

Scripture quotations marked (NRSV) are from the New Revised Standard Version
Bible, copyright © 1989 National Council of the Churches of Christ in the United
States of America. Used by permission. All rights reserved worldwide.

Cover image: Kristin Miller
Cover design: Kristin Miller

Print ISBN: 978-1-5064-8106-7
eBook ISBN: 978-1-5064-8107-4

CONTENTS

Part III
The Prophet Isaiah as a Mesopotamian Author

Part IV
Negotiations in the Second Temple Period

PREFACE

Do we really need another book on Isaiah? As is expected from an academic author, I will here attempt to do what the French literary scholar Gérard Genette says is the task of all prefaces: to get the book *read* and to get it read *properly* by presenting my reasons for writing it and my intentions with it. At the same time, I am aware that contrary to what scholars have usually emphasized for the understanding of *biblical* texts—that for a passage to be correctly interpreted, one needs to read it in its literary context with an awareness of the historical circumstances in which it came to be—most of my readers will interact with this book in a fragmentary way, skimming through many parts (especially this preface) while reading more carefully one or two chapters that are seen as relevant for their own work. If I have done a good job, some of these pieces will then be extracted and put to use in different contexts to serve the purposes of other arguments. In contrast to the habits of the scribes from Qumran, however, most will probably reveal from where they got these pieces—"my" book.

I thus want to start this preface by acknowledging (and embracing) the fact that the theories we hold about authorship do not always coincide with our reading practices. In fact, this is one of the reasons why I have written this book—to highlight how our own way of dealing with books and their authors have often made us miss the fact that ancient writers were not always thinking along the same lines. As but one example, most will likely deal with the main argument of this book as if it is my intellectual property. After all, this is the way we have been taught and the way one must proceed in light of current copyright laws. However, this has not always been the case. In fact, author constructs have varied over time, and the notion of intellectual property has not always been attached to them. Some would say that this is indeed one of the main differences between the "ancient world" and "our time," but this is not entirely correct.

In fact, a second reason for writing this book has been to highlight the complexity of both ancient and contemporary constructions of authorship: neither is uniform, but both bear witness to continuous negotiation over time. As it turns out, the notion of intellectual property is not as clear-cut even in our days, since the underlying dichotomy between creativity and imitation is not always consistently upheld. Can it really be said, for example, that the observations in this book are truly mine? Would it not be the case that if the many individual observations would be disassembled, it would be possible to find scholars elsewhere who have made similar observations? And is it not likely that I have missed some of them (although I hope that I have been able to track down and credit as many as possible)?

At the same time, is it not equally true—as Enheduanna said a couple of thousands of years ago—that "that which has been created here no one has created before"? Is not the way previous observations have been *stitched together* in this book into a pattern—an argument—in fact new? To borrow the distinction argued by some of the German scholars debating the notion of intellectual property at the end of the eighteenth century, while the ideas ("die Gedanken") may not all be new, their expression ("die Form dieser Gedanken") hopefully is and thus may stimulate further conversation and help us think about these topics in fresh ways.

So what about the 'book' called *Isaiah*? If you have picked up this book because you are interested in knowing more about a certain prophet named Isaiah ben Amoz who supposedly lived in the eighth century BCE and how much of the 'book' that bears his name he has in fact written, you will be disappointed. This is not that kind of a book. What interests me here is not the possible relating of undemarcated bits and pieces of the 'book' called *Isaiah* to various unnamed individuals in narrowly defined time frames. Other scholars have done that with much more success than I could ever do, and for that, I am grateful. Many observations in this book build on their insights. What interests me is, instead, another set of historically oriented questions.

Briefly put, it will be the thesis of this book that the relation between the prophet and the 'book' has been constructed in several different ways from the time of the composition of the 'book' up until the initial centuries CE and that these contrasting constructs are best understood in light of changes in the way authorship has been understood. It is well known that while the 'book' called *Isaiah* was originally transmitted anonymously and composed over a large period of time so that much of the material in the 'book' cannot be dated to the eighth century, the prophet Isaiah ben Amoz would nonetheless eventually be seen as the originator of the entire work. How can this be? Were the scribes who added the superscription in Isa 1:1 misinformed? Or perhaps worse: Were they intentionally misleading? In previous studies, scholars have either attempted to defend the "historicity" of the paratext or looked for ways to make sense of it, not least in terms of pseudepigraphy. I will show how both these explanations are insufficient in that they proceed from author concepts not likely shared with the scribes who added the superscription.

In sum, the focus of this book will be an unpacking of this transformation by asking how the relationship between the prophet and the 'book' has been perceived from the time of its composition through the centuries that followed. This will be achieved by situating the discussion in relation to two contrasting author concepts of the ancient world—a Mesopotamian trajectory and a Greek one—and it will be seen that these trajectories were intensely negotiated at the very time when the prophet Isaiah started to be seen as the originator of the whole 'book.' In other words, one of the main emphases of this study will be that authorship is historically contingent and that when readers (ancient or contemporary) are not aware of this, they may suggest interpretations of the relationship between the 'book' and the prophet that are anachronistic retrojections of their own presuppositions.

Why, then, is this a topic worth pursuing? The obvious answer to such a question would be that while similar work has been done on the relation between, most significantly, Moses and the Pentateuch and David and the Psalms, there is still no such book-length study on the prophet Isaiah and the 'book' that bears his name. Given that the 'book' called *Isaiah* is one of the most quoted in the late Second Temple period, it is a vacuum that needs to be filled.

However, I think that this topic also has the potential to appeal not only to experts on the 'book' called *Isaiah* but to those interested in thinking further about such notions as *authority* and *interpretation*. As I will argue in this book, changes in author concepts affect not only the way we understand how books are believed to have originated but also the way authority is constructed, and a focus on such changes can therefore make us reflect on the relation between *creativity* and *imitation*, *inspiration* and *skill*, and perhaps also on our search for—and placing value in—"originals." If successful, this book will perhaps even make us appreciate—rather than see as problematic—the fact that most of the 'books' of the Hebrew Bible are, in fact, anonymous.

Before turning to these issues, a few words on terminology are needed. Since I want to highlight that the relation between the prophet and the 'book' is continuously negotiated, using the common designation for the 'book'—the book *of* Isaiah—is problematic, since it may implicitly convey a connection between the two that cannot be taken for granted. Therefore, I have chosen to refer to the prophet as "the prophet Isaiah" (or simply as Isaiah, if the context is clear enough) and to the 'book' as either the 'book' called *Isaiah*, the 'book' *Isaiah*, or simply *Isaiah*. I hope that this use will be clear enough and cause as little confusion as possible. As in my work on the 'book' of Psalms, I have chosen to use single quotation marks around 'book' to emphasize it as historically contingent.

As is appropriate in a preface, I want to conclude by expressing my gratitude to individuals and communities without whom this book would be far from what it is. First of all, I want to thank my wife, Samantha, for all of the support she has provided during these two years of intense writing and my two boys, Samuel and Elias, for all the joy and good times.

Second, I would like to thank my colleagues at Umeå University who have given good feedback along the way and, more importantly, have welcomed me as a postdoc in the best way possible. Thank you, Prof. Tomas Lindgren; Drs. Karin Berber Neutel, Stefan Gelfgren, Thomas Girmalm, Tord Larsson, Niclas Lindström, Mikael Lundmark, Jonas Nilsson, Elisabeth Raddock, Olle Sundström, Leif Svensson, Mats Wahlberg, and Mikael Winninge; and doctoral students Jacob Astudillo, Johan Eriksson, Mimmi Norgren Hansson, Johan Runemark Brydsten, Hannes Sonnenschein, and David Wiljebrand. I only wish that I had had the chance to see you more in person—most of this book was written from a temporary office in my bedroom during the Covid-19 pandemic.

I also want to thank the Old Testament research seminar at Lund University, where I was appointed Reader (Swedish "docent") in May 2020. It is great to be part of a continuing conversation with such brilliant minds. Special thanks go to my *Doktorvater*, Prof. (recently emeritus) Fredrik Lindström, as well as to Prof. em. Erik Aurelius; Drs. Katharina Keim, Dag Oredsson, Blaženka Scheuer, and Ola Wikander; and doctoral students Elisabet Nord and Sara Järlemyr. I am also grateful for the input from my colleagues at the Academy of Leadership and Theology: Profs. Greger Andersson, Lena-Sofia Tiemeyer, and Tommy Wasserman; Drs. Lennart Boström, Stefan Green, Niklas Holmefur, and Mikael Tellbe; as well as Dan Elofsson, Joel MacInnes, and Ludvig Nyman.

Needless to say, tracking down and finding all the books I needed during a pandemic has not been easy, so a special thanks also goes to all of the incredible people in the Facebook group "Hebrew Bible Resources in the Times of Corona," who have managed to find all kinds of obscure books and articles for me faster than I thought was possible. A huge thank-you also goes to the team at Fortress Press, especially Carey Newman, Elvis Ramirez, and Danny Constantino—it has been a joy working together on this volume!

Last but not least, I want to thank my Lord and Creator, Jesus Christ, for guidance and for being a constant source of hope and inspiration. "Let me hear of your steadfast love in the morning, for in you I put my trust" (Ps 143:8).

PART I

FRAMING THE TASK AT HAND

Chapter 1

ON BOOKS AND ELUSIVE AUTHORS

The Author That Did Not Die

"Death to the author!" If one was to formulate the main message of the brief but widely influential article of Roland Barthes into a slogan, such an imperative would seem quite fitting.[1] In his article, this French nineteenth-century literary scholar—who at the time of his tragic death in 1980 had established himself as a leading and internationally renowned voice on authorship issues—attempted to sideline (if not completely obliterate) the recurring scholarly idea that "the *explanation* of a work is always sought in the man or woman who produced it, as if it were always in the end, through the more or less transparent allegory of the fiction, the voice of a single person, the *author* 'confiding' in us."[2] In light of the observation that a text "is not a line of words releasing a single 'theological' meaning (the 'message' of the Author-God) but a multi-dimensional space in which a variety of writings, none of them original, blend and clash,"[3] or put more bluntly, that "the text is a tissue of quotations drawn from the innumerable centers of culture,"[4] the scholarly inquiries were deemed as ultimately futile:

> Once the Author is removed, the claim to decipher a text becomes quite futile. To give a text an Author is *to impose a limit on that text*, to furnish it with a final signified, to close the writing. Such a conception suits criticism very well, the latter then allotting itself the important task of discovering the Author (or its hypostases: society, history, psyche, liberty) beneath the work: when the

---

1. This chapter was first published in English in the journal *Aspen* 5–6 as "The Death of the Author" in 1967 and then came out in French in the journal *Manteia* 5 a year later ("La mort de l'auteur"). Below, when I quote from Barthes, it will be from the 1977 reprint of the English article (Barthes 1977).
2. Barthes 1977, 143 (emphasis in the original).
3. Barthes 1977, 146.
4. Barthes 1977, 146.

Author has been found, the text is "explained"—victory to the critic. Hence there is no surprise in the fact that, historically, the reign of the Author has also been that of the Critic, nor again in the fact that criticism (be it new) is today undermined along with the Author.[5]

The possible implications of the notion of these authorial limitations—what I will call paratextual tamings—will be further unpacked below, but first, a more fundamental observation must be made. By choosing to introduce Barthes as above—that is, with a brief biographical note—and framing quotes from the article as "his" ideas, a tension is highlighted in the way scholarly discussion on authorship is often carried out.

On the one hand, it is not difficult to agree with Barthes that an author cannot be easily accessed by studying her/his texts. Even when combined with information about her/his life, it is still an elusive task to map an author's possible intentions. Barthes is also certainly in the right when claiming that a text is always a combination of sources and influences that can be traced to a plethora of cultures, genres, and traditions.[6] No text (or author) can claim originality in any absolute sense.[7] It thus seems reasonable to loosen the grip the author has had on the text, and although Barthes somewhat overstates his case,[8] it remains a perfectly valid line of inquiry to emphasize the reader in the processes of making sense of texts.

On the other hand, it is easy to see that Barthes ultimately failed—is it not the case that when reading "The Death of the Author," critics such as myself are still occupied with understanding not so much the article on its own terms but rather the article as an expression of the ideas of Barthes? Is it not recurrently stressed that Barthes (and other academic

---

5. Barthes 1977, 147 (emphasis added).

6. See also Barthes 1974, 10.

7. I will return to this issue below, in the discussion of the Romantic author, but it should be stressed already here that although it is clear that Barthes critiques a view of the author as creator and sole originator of a work (cf. Bertens 2019, 186), this is not in total contrast to the Romantic author (since the author is not viewed as an isolated island there either). However, a clear contrast is found in that Barthes sidelines the author *in the actual interpretive work* ("It is language which speaks, not the author"; Barthes 1977, 143), while the Romantic ideal puts the author in the center.

8. See, for example, the way he creates an unnecessary dichotomy when he claims that "a text is made of multiple writings, drawn from many cultures and entering into mutual relations of dialogue, parody, contestation, but there is one place where this multiplicity is focused and that place is the *reader*, not, as was hitherto said, the author" (Barthes 1977, 148; emphasis added).

authors) needs to be read in proper context—in dialogue with other texts penned by him, with the historical environment in which he lived, and with philosophical paradigms influential at this time, such as structuralism and poststructuralism, the Romantic author ideal, and Marxism, to name but a few? The more Barthes is loosened from these historical entanglements, the higher the risk of misunderstanding his argument, so the logic goes.[9] Briefly put, it can be observed that to understand the theories about the death of the author, scholars tend to put an author and her/his intentions at the center of the discussion.

Now, it would be possible to object by saying that it is not necessarily the *actual* Roland Barthes that is subject to these inquiries. He rather performs an "author function" à la Michel Foucault. Such a perspective is indeed interesting and will be further explored below, but the main point still stands: in modern-day literary scholarship, the author is far from dead.[10]

DEATH TO THE PROPHET?

Turning to biblical studies in general and studies on the 'book' called *Isaiah*[11] in particular, similar observations can be made. Being a discipline with roots deeply embedded in historical inquiries about the genesis of texts—when were they written, by whom, and for what purpose?—it should come as no surprise that a significant amount of scholars are occupied with questions surrounding the formation of the 'book' called *Isaiah* and that such a task has been oriented toward finding proper historical contexts for the various bits and pieces that have been joined to form this anthology of prophetic voices.[12] Along the paths of discovery, various authors have been killed off, while others have taken their place. More specifically, the prophet Isaiah himself, who had been

---

9. Similar observations can be made in popular culture, where the "death of the author" has not dampened public interest in biographical information on authors. On the contrary, biographies, memoirs, and similar works have continued to be sold and are deemed crucial for a book's success (cf. Bertens 2019, 189). The interest is so big that authors are often required to come up with a second narrative—the story about how (and why) the book came into being.

10. For a brief overview, see also Berensmeyer, Buelens, and Demoor 2019.

11. On my use of "the 'book' called *Isaiah*" for the 'book' and "the prophet Isaiah" for the prophet, see the preface.

12. A brief overview of research on the "historical" Isaiah can be found in Sweeney 2016a, 298–301. For an extensive historical survey, see Moser 2012. See also Williamson 2009; Berges 2010a; Schultz 2015, 19–27; Kratz 2015, 110–52.

understood as an author, came to be placed in the back seat quite soon.[13] Taking his place were instead several anonymous authors or tradent groups (Ger. *Trägerkreise*), and when arranging the products of these skilled scribes diachronically, various models of how the 'book' called *Isaiah* was given its "final" shape could be presented.[14] In a sense, then, *Isaiah* ceased to be "author literature" and was increasingly understood as "tradition literature."[15] Acknowledging that several individuals were involved in the transmission, what was envisaged was thus a kind of coauthorship.[16] Needless to say, this shift in the scholarly approach to the 'book' called *Isaiah* also came to reconfigure the role played by the prophet *Isaiah*. Instead of an "author," he was seen as an authority figure, a brand name of sorts, anchoring the anthology firmly in a specific prophetic tradition.

Now, although it is certainly correct that many agents have been involved in the composition and transmission of the 'book' called *Isaiah* and although the notion of tradent groups has been very helpful

---

13. This is almost unanimously true if focusing on research on the 'book' called *Isaiah* in its received, "final" form(s), although discussion regarding the possibility of relating certain parts of the 'book' to the prophet Isaiah is still ongoing. For an example of a scholar who understands the 'book' to be assembled by individuals other than the prophet Isaiah while still arguing that most of the words themselves can be traced back to him, see Oswalt 1986, 1998. More common, however, are approaches such as the one by Blenkinsopp 2000, 73–74, who argues that "the tendency among many critical scholars in recent decades is to assume that both the Pentateuch and the book of Isaiah are essentially Second Temple compilations, literary constructs put together by the intellectual and religious elite during the Persian period . . . or even later. . . . But I see no reason to disallow a significant eighth B.C.E. Isaian substratum." A common theory has been to see (parts of) chapters 6:1–9:6 constituting an old core, a *Denkschrift* (sometimes also called an *Immanuelschrift*; see, e.g., Berges 2012b, 7) that contains personal memoirs of the prophet Isaiah from the period of the Syro-Ephraimite crisis (so first Budde 1928, although the contours of the idea had been developed by him in several previous publications, including Budde 1920, 1923). Although the theory has been largely abandoned, the quest for traces of this figure has continued up until today, even if the rhetoric of "freeing" *authentic* utterances of the prophet Isaiah (his *ipsissima verba*) from *spurious* passages coming from other hands (so, e.g., Becker 1968) is becoming less frequent (it is still proposed, however, in some recent work, such as in many of the contributions in Block 2015).

14. Needless to say, similar observations were also made in relation to other "traditional authors," such as Moses for the Pentateuch, David for the 'book' of Psalms, or Solomon for Ecclesiastes.

15. See, e.g., Berges 2011; 2017, 17. Cf. Berges 2012b, 1: "These writings are verbal expressions of living traditions, passed on and developed by knowledgeable tradents utilizing the medium of text." However, Berges is himself nonetheless one of the scholars who use the 'book' called *Isaiah* as a tool to reconstruct a biography of the prophet Isaiah (see esp. Berges 2012b).

16. Cf. the observation by Helle 2020a, 56, in relation to literary studies.

in framing the dynamics of textual composition and transmission, there is an aspect in the shift from author to tradition that has so far remained largely unexplored—namely, how authorship is constructed *in the texts themselves*. Without such a focus, scholars will always run the risk of working with anachronistic ideas about the relation between 'authors' and 'books,' and this can perhaps be illustrated by the fact that the common understanding of the superscription in Isa 1:1 creates a paradox—Why would the name of a certain prophet make a text not written by him authoritative in a culture where most traditions were circulated anonymously? The question begs an answer, and it will be the task of this study to attempt to provide one. Put differently, it will be shown that research on the 'book' called *Isaiah* is still in many ways proceeding from the author concept critiqued by Barthes above. The desire to in some way identify (and distinguish) original and subsequent prophetic voices has not been tamed,[17] and the question of who (pl.) wrote the 'book' called *Isaiah* is still very much at the center of discussion,[18] although it is done in tandem with more synchronic foci:

> Despite this shift away from the individual originator, cultural contextualizations of literary works rely on authors, for it is only by way of the author that a text can be culturally positioned (nationally, ethnically, regionally, historically or ideologically). Thus, although the concept of "author" might be one of the most contested categories in literary theory, it is far from dead in the practice of literary scholarship. . . . Where authorship is assumed to be collective and successive, the reader who is aware of this is likely to construct not one, but several, authorial images on the basis of the text in question. Layers or selected aspects of the text might then be ascribed to individual (hypothetical) authors. They might also be ascribed to groups of authors . . . [which] allows for assumptions about the social group from which a text emerges and to whose identity formation it contributes.[19]

---

17. Although it can also be noted with Becker 2020, 40–41, that the general scholarly shift has been one that moves away from the person of the prophet and toward an interest in the 'book' as a "whole."

18. Cf., e.g., Nissinen 2019, 2: "The ongoing debate about the degree of historicity of the Hebrew Scriptures and the quest for authentic prophetic words within the heavily edited prophetic books and narratives of the Hebrew Bible have made many scholars seek arguments from related phenomena in the surrounding cultures."

19. Heinen 2019, 10, 16–17.

Consequently, even if the prophets have been killed off, the authors are far from dead. They remain essential, since it is believed that the creative minds behind the text anchor it not only in a tradition but in specific historical settings that are crucial for the interpretive task. Nonetheless the texts from which scholars construct the authors are no more than

> a series of clues, or enigmas, whose decipherment is supposed to reveal the author's time and identity. . . . Scholars now rely on linguistic, literary, and historical information to try and place the author . . . instead of traditions and texts connected with an assumed author. But the contexts derived from this historical data are just as much constructed as the biography . . . that readers built out of ancient textual traditions. It is also, like the constructed . . . biography, used to interpret the text.[20]

Now, although it should not be denied that research on the formation of the 'book' called *Isaiah* has advanced our understanding of these processes in very significant ways—there is indeed no reason to diminish the importance of asking these questions—it is notable that the 'book' itself shows show little interest in identifying its authors. Why is that?

Native Constructs

In this study, the elusive question about who wrote the 'book' called *Isaiah* will be approached from a slightly new direction. The common impulses to search for clues that can point to historical circumstances in which texts were "penned" will be avoided. Portraits of authors will not be painted; neither will new theories of composition be formulated. Instead, the focus will be on the fact that the texts themselves have so little to say about questions that have been so central to biblical scholarship, and it will be suggested that a fundamental reason for this is that different author concepts are in play. The main question to be answered in this study is thus not "Who wrote the 'book' *Isaiah*?" but "In what ways have early tradents constructed the relation between the prophet and the book?" For this dynamic to be successfully described, native author constructs will need to be identified, unpacked, and put in relation to author discourses produced in both the 'book' *Isaiah* itself and its early

---

20. Bolin 2017, 36, speaking on Ecclesiastes and Solomonic authorship.

transmission. Moreover, in relation to the observation above that author designations can be understood as imposing *limits* on texts, it will be necessary to trace the impact of paratextual activity. Understanding paratexts as belonging to a set of overlapping transtextual relationships, they have been described by the French literary scholar Gérard Genette as the following:

> A literary work consists, entirely or essentially, of a text, defined (very minimally) as a more or less long sequence of verbal statements that are more or less endowed with significance. But this text is rarely presented in an unadorned state, unreinforced and unaccompanied by a certain number of verbal or other productions, such as an author's name, a title, a preface, illustrations. And although we do not always know whether these productions are to be regarded as belonging to the text, in any case they surround it and extend it, precisely in order to *present* it, in the usual sense of this verb but also in the strongest sense: to *make present*. . . . More than a boundary or a sealed border, the paratext is, rather, a *threshold* . . . an "undefined zone" between the inside and the outside, . . . "a fringe of the printed text which in reality controls one's whole reading of the text."[21]

Understanding author designations as paratexts thus highlights their taming function. They are added to limit interpretive options and suggest certain ways in which the text ought to be read and used—they mark the "boundaries between acceptable and forbidden interpretations."[22] The notion of control and taming should not be understood as static, however. While the paratext attempts to tame the text, it is also true that the paratexts will be understood differently in various historical and cultural settings, since readers also (often unknowingly) tame the paratext. It will thus be important to study not only when and why paratexts are added but also how they are interpreted.[23]

To carry out the investigation in as lucid a way as possible, the study is structured into fifteen chapters arranged in six main parts.

The first part of the book will be concluded by chapter 2, where an overview of how author concepts are negotiated today will be provided.

---

21. Genette 1997, 1–2, quotes Philippe Lejeune in the last sentence.

22. Bolin 2017, 9. See also Heinen 2019, 13, who talks about "limiting the potential meanings of a text by giving more plausibility to some interpretations than to others."

23. Elsewhere, I have analyzed these processes in relation to the 'book' of Psalms (see, e.g., Willgren 2016a, 2019a, 2020; Willgren Davage 2020a).

The purpose of including such a discussion is twofold: (1) to show that at any given time, multiple concepts are likely to be in play—it is thus to be expected that the ancient sources reveal a similar complexity—and (2) to provide a framework for understanding much of the contemporary research on biblical authorship.

Proceeding from this general introduction, part 2, "Searching for Native Authorship Theories," will provide the theoretical framework for the study. Here, two contrasting ancient author constructs will be identified and presented. Chapter 3 will focus on what will be called a Mesopotamian trajectory, while chapter 4 introduces a Greek trajectory.

Then the ways in which the relation between the prophet Isaiah and the 'book' that now bears his name have been constructed will be analyzed from a diachronic point of view. Part 3, "The Prophet Isaiah as a Mesopotamian Author," will focus on the earliest phases of this history—namely, on how authorship is constructed in *Isaiah* itself. Chapter 5 will look at texts that relate a prophet to writing, chapter 6 will focus on how more agents than the first recipient of divine revelation have been intertwined anonymously in the transmission of the 'book,' and chapter 7 will unpack the ways in which the 'book' has been paratextually framed.

Part 4, "Negotiations in the Second Temple Period," constitutes somewhat of a bridge, where some of the first indications of the relation between the prophet and the 'book' being affected by the negotiation between the Mesopotamian and the Greek trajectories will be presented. Chapter 8 will look at how the prophet is related more explicitly to acts of writing in 1–2 Chr, and the picture will then be broadened in chapter 9 to similar indications of change in the 'book' of Psalms and the 'book' called *Ben Sira*, while chapter 10 will survey the ways in which the relation between the prophet and the 'book' are constructed in the Dead Sea Scrolls.

The fifth and final analytical part, "The Prophet Isaiah as a Greek Author," will then show how the prophet Isaiah is reimagined as a Greek author by looking first at the works of Josephus and the New Testament in chapter 11 and then at early Christian writers and the development of author biographies in chapter 12. The last chapter in this part of the book, chapter 13, will provide examples of further negotiations in rabbinic literature.

Last, in part 6, "The Book 'of' Isaiah," the results will be summarized in a diachronic overview of the history of the transformation of Isaianic authorship in chapter 14, followed by a brief discussion in chapter 15 of some possible areas for future studies.

Chapter 2

Functions and Geniuses

The Author Function

Even if Barthes was unsuccessful in delivering the text from its author, his work did sideline the actual *individual* in critical studies, and this was further elaborated by Foucault in his 1969 article "Qu'est-ce qu'un auteur?"[1] Rather than excluding the "author" from the critical inquiry altogether, Foucault introduces the notion of an author function:

> We should reexamine the empty space left by the author's disappearance; we should attentively observe, along its gaps and fault lines, its new demarcations, and the reapportionment of this void; we should await the fluid functions released by this disappearance.[2]

This has much in common with Barthes not only by overlapping with the latter's notion of "limits" that are "imposed" on the text but also because Foucault understands the "author" as a projection of "our way of handling texts."[3] More specifically, according to Foucault, the author function

> is not formed spontaneously through the simple attribution of a discourse to an individual. It results from a complex operation whose purpose is to construct the rational entity we call an author. Undoubtedly, this construction is assigned a "realistic" dimension as we speak of an individual's "profundity" or "creative" power, his intentions or the original inspiration manifested in writing. Nevertheless, these aspects of an individual, which we designate as an author (or which comprise an individual as an author), are

---

1. Foucault 1969. Below, when quoting from this work, I will use the English translation of this article, reprinted as Foucault 1977.
2. Foucault 1977, 121.
3. Foucault 1977, 127.

projections, in terms always more or less psychological, of our way of handling texts: in the comparisons we make, the traits we extract as pertinent, the continuities we assign, or the exclusions we practice. In addition, all these operations vary according to the period and the form of discourse concerned.[4]

Authorship is thus underlined as historically contingent, as has been suggested in the previous chapter, and Foucault suggests that the name of the author serves as a means of classification—"a name can group together a number of texts and thus differentiate them from others. A name also establishes different forms of relationships among texts"[5]—and, quite importantly, "characterizes a particular manner of existence of discourse."[6] In fleshing out the theoretical framework of such a discourse-oriented approach, Foucault makes an interesting observation: on the one hand, there has often been a need for authors; on the other hand, there exist authorless texts:

> The "author-function" is not universal or constant in all discourse. Even within our civilization, the same types of texts have not always required authors; there was a time when those texts which we now call "literary" (stories, folk tales, epics, and tragedies) were accepted, circulated, and valorized without any question about the identity of their author. . . . The "author-function" is tied to the legal and institutional systems that circumscribe, determine, and articulate the realm of discourses; *it does not operate in a uniform manner in all discourses, at all times, and in any given culture*; it is not defined by the spontaneous attribution of a text to its creator, but through a series of precise and complex procedures; it does not refer, purely and simply, to *an actual individual* insofar as it simultaneously gives rise to *a variety of egos* and to *a series of subjective positions* that individuals of any class may come to occupy.[7]

---

4. Foucault 1977, 127.

5. Foucault 1977, 123.

6. Foucault 1977, 123. Needless to say, the discussion here thus focuses on authors as they relate to specific texts, although Berensmeyer, Buelens, and Demoor 2019, 6–7, are certainly correct to point out that authorship and the act of writing are not identical, as made clear in, for example, posthumous publications (including prequels, sequels, fan fiction, etc.) and the fact that authors can often keep their status as authors despite the fact that they have stopped writing—their reputation even sometimes grows "because of the 'mystery' of their silence" (7).

7. Foucault 1977, 125, 130–31 (emphasis added).

Note then that Foucault briefly sketches the contours of processes where texts are situated within authorial discourses: "Speeches and books were assigned real authors, other than mythical or important religious figures, only when the author became subject to punishment and to the extent that his discourse was considered transgressive."[8]

The first observation to be made is thus that it is possible to imagine contexts where texts are transmitted without any need to name authors. For a biblical scholar, this means that there is a constant need to evaluate the interpretive horizon from which authorship is viewed, as these concepts are constantly changing. In fact, Foucault's work on the author function has proved a valuable resource in biblical studies, not least the way he introduces the notion of discourses tied to a founder ("initiators of discursive practices").[9] To exemplify this notion, he talks about the way the works of Karl Marx and Sigmund Freud "established the endless possibility of discourse"[10] in a way that future texts could participate in these discourses by both analogy and contrast. The works are, so to speak, foundational, and to participate in the discourse entails placing oneself within the influence of these works in a way that indicates that it is always necessary to "return to the origins" (i.e., to straighten out possible distortions accumulated over time). This also means that the discourses are dynamic and unstable, since a potential discovery of a new text by Marx, for example, can fundamentally alter the "foundation."[11]

Second, the development of author concepts seems to be intrinsically connected to developments in book history and thus highlights the importance of historically sensitive analysis of paratextual activity and the need to stay close to the scribal and material cultures in which the biblical texts were composed.

Moreover, the attempt to move away from what Foucault calls "tiresome repetitions"[12] such as "Who is the real author?" or "Have we proof of his authenticity and originality?" and toward more discourse-oriented questions such as "Where does it [the discourse] come from; how is it circulated; who controls it?" is welcome and overlaps substantially with the focus chosen for this study. But although the work of Foucault will

---

8. Foucault 1977, 124.

9. Foucault 1977, 132. A good example of how this notion can be applied to biblical studies is found in Najman 2003. She traces the development of a Mosaic discourse, which she understands as a discourse tied to a founder (Moses) from its origin in Deut and further on in the Second Temple period.

10. Foucault 1977, 131.

11. Foucault 1977, 135–36.

12. Foucault 1977, 138.

be an important conversation partner, it is still clear that his work retains a named figure (even if s/he is not to be identified with an actual individual) at the center of the study of texts, and it will thus be important to keep a critical eye on the fact that there is not always a "space left by the author's *disappearance*," as per the quote above. Instead, the opposite scenario can just as well be imagined, one where texts were originally transmitted without any named author, only to be provided with such a name along the way. This means that the idea of a discourse tied to a *founder* needs to be treated with some suspicion, and in some tension to the understanding of the author function as a means of *classification*—a kind of boundary marker or "fence" around a discourse.

THE ROMANTIC GENIUS

If, per the overview above, the author is to be seen primarily as a function, not an individual, why is there still such a public interest in individual authors? The answer is quite straightforward: author concepts are never fully consistent but under constant negotiation. In this case, it means that current ideas about authors are as much indebted to Barthes and Foucault as they are to other author constructs—most significantly the Romantic genius.

When Johann Wolfgang von Goethe (1749–1832) writes that authorship entails "the reproduction of the world around me by means of the internal world which takes hold of, combines, creates anew, kneads everything and puts it down again in its own form, manner,"[13] he summarizes in a concise manner an ideal picture of a creative process that took shape in the Romantic era, an ideal centered on a clear value-laden dichotomy between *originality* (good) and *imitation* (bad). According to Edward Young (1683–1765),

---

13. Quoted from Woodmansee 1984, 447. The quote (and the discussion below) makes clear, however, that Woodmansee's claim that Goethe "departs sharply from the older Renaissance and neoclassical conception of the writer as essentially a vehicle of ideas to describe him not only as transforming those ideas, but as transforming them in such a way as to make them an expression of his own—unique—mind" (447) is somewhat overstated, since Romantic authors also describe themselves as vehicles to some extent (see Goethe's notion of reproducing the world around him, cf. n. 24 below). Nonetheless, the comment captures the often recognized tension in the "postclassical era" between the author "as divinely inspired, as sacred, as a seer, on the one hand, and as a craftsman of words whose allegiances and influence extend only to his power over language, story, and rhetoric itself, on the other," noted by Bennett 2005, 36.

> *Originals* are, and ought to be, great favorites, for they are great benefactors; they extend the republic of letters, and add a new province to its dominion: *Imitators* only give us a sort of duplicates of what we had, possibly much better, before; increasing the mere drug of books, while all that makes them valuable, *knowledge* and *genius*, are at a stand. The pen of an *original* writer, like *Armida's* wand, out of a barren waste calls a blooming spring: Out of that blooming spring an *Imitator* is a transplanter of laurels, which sometimes die on removal, always languish in a foreign soil.[14]

Behind this idea is evidently a complicated process where earlier author ideals are negotiated, and to understand the main contours of this process—since it has the potential to shed light on similar processes in relation to the 'book' called *Isaiah*—three aspects that played a significant part will be mentioned: the printing press, commercialization, and copyright.

The Printing Press

The first aspect influencing the development of the Romantic author concept is the transition from a manuscript culture to a print culture and the observation that the printing press would fundamentally affect not only the way books were produced but also how they were interpreted.[15] The very fact that books could now be disseminated broadly in exact copies was a game changer and has deeply affected both the notion of textual stability (What does it mean for a book to be "fixed" and have a "final form"?) and the interpretation of differences between various text forms (Are they to be seen as *variants*—that is, deviations from an original—or are we rather to speak about an intrinsic *variance*?).[16] Since the printing press would make the production of a book much cheaper,

---

14. Young 1759, 10–11 (emphasis in the original).

15. See especially Eisenstein 1980; cf. the later Baron, Lindquist, and Shevlin 2007. The groundbreaking work of Eisenstein has been critiqued by, for example, Margaret J. M. Ezell for generalizing the impact and effects of the printing press. In her work, Ezell shows, for example, that in Ireland and Iceland, manuscript culture coexisted with print culture for some time (Ezell 2019; see also Johns 1998). However, and although this critique is well put, it still remains a valid point that the printing press would eventually (and despite resistance; see, e.g., Eisenstein 2011) fundamentally impact the way books were conceived of. This also underscores the more basic observation that technological developments are intrinsically intertwined with cultural change.

16. For this distinction, see especially Cerquiglini 1989 (for an English translation, see Cerquiglini 1999), whose work became significant in what is now often called the "new philology" or "material philology" (cf. Nichols 1990). For an introduction related to

authors would soon proliferate, as lamented by (the fictitious) Martinus Scriblerus in the preface to Alexander Pope's *The Dunciad*:

> We shall next declare the occasion and the cause which moved our poet to this particular work. He lived in those days, when (after Providence had permitted the invention of printing as a scourge for the sins of the learned) paper also became so cheap, and printers so numerous, that a deluge of authors covered the land; whereby not only the peace of the honest unwriting subject was daily molested, but unmerciful demands were made of his applause, yea of his money, by such as would neither earn the one, nor deserve the other.[17]

Needless to say, this development, when combined with the "manuscript culture's aura of exclusivity,"[18] where "originals" were starting to be coveted, since they came to represent "the literal mark of the author as an individual rather than a mass-produced commodity,"[19] also affected biblical scholarship, where a lot of time and effort was invested in attempts to remove corruptions and variants that had accumulated over time and so reconstruct the text as close to the "original" autographs as possible.[20]

Commercialization

A second aspect, which is related to the first, is that the Romantic emphasis on the original genius also developed as a contrast to the emergence of a new guild that was occupied with filling the needs of the printers, a guild skilled in adjusting their writing to the various types of texts requested.[21] Being the next logical step in the commercialization of print, it gave rise to polemical binaries where originality, genius,

---

biblical studies, see Lied and Lundhaug 2017 or Willgren 2020, where I discuss possible consequences for the study of the formation of the 'book' of Psalms.

17. Quoted from Rogers 2006, 420–21. For a discussion of the possible implications of this lament for the understanding of Alexander Pope's relation to the printing press, see Eisenstein 2011.

18. Ezell 2019, 122.

19. So Latham 2019, 171.

20. For this, see, e.g., Aurelius 2014, 357, who lists some of the terms used to designate these corruptions: "Zutat, Zuwachs, Auswuchs, Wuscherung." Although this would change—and Aurelius points to Lothar Perlitt as an example of a scholar assessing these variants more positively (e.g., "Juwel")—the fundamental task to trace various portions of the text to various authors or tradent groups has remained, as noted above.

21. For a discussion, see Schellenberg 2019, 134–38. To this observation should be added a caveat—namely, that other factors played a part as well, such as the earlier tendency

and creativity came to be seen as opposite to disinterest, hackwork, and imitation:[22]

> An *Imitator* shares his crown, if he has one, with the chosen Object of his Imitation; an *Original* enjoys an undivided applause. An *Original* may be said to be of a *vegetable* nature; it rises spontaneously from the vital root of Genius; it *grows*, it is not *made*; *Imitations* are often a sort of *Manufacture* wrought up by those *Mechanics*, *Art*, and *Labour*, out of pre-existent materials not their own.[23]

In these words by Young, there is also a construction of the genius as someone working alone ("undivided applause") and that the creations emanating from him were indeed "his." Young thus "raises issues of property: he makes a writer's ownership of his work the necessary, and even sufficient condition for earning the honorific title of 'author,' and he makes such ownership contingent upon a work's originality."[24] As the author takes center stage, information about that author also becomes important to the interpretive task, and the writing of

---

to emphasize "the mastery of rules extrapolated from classical literature" (so Woodmansee 1984, 430).

22. See also the discussion in Easley 2019, 150–51.

23. Young 1759, 11–12 (emphasis in the original).

24. Woodmansee 1984, 431. While this is true and central to the way critics often interact with texts, Sophus Helle has argued that there is some ambiguity in the way inspiration is described that implies a potential self-effacement aspect even in the genius-centered Romantic author ideal (see esp. Helle 2019b, 133, where he quotes William Blake, who speaks of writing *against his will*—that is, conceptualizing inspiration as something that sometimes eludes the author, despite being internal to her/him). The notion that the Romantic author also describes inspiration as externally conditioned (e.g., by divine inspiration, dreams, etc., thus overlapping with what will be seen below in relation to both Mesopotamian and Greek trajectories, contra Woodmansee 1984, 427, who speaks of it only as an internalization of previous modes of inspiration) or that authorship can in a sense be understood in terms of medial agency (so Helle) should not, however, obscure the fact that the named author is still at the center of the interpretive activity here. As observed by Biagioli 2011, 1848n2, the Romantic author can be understood as "a figure of irreducible expressive individuality rather than a creator *ex nihilo*" (emphasis in the original). But the issue is still interesting and can be formulated with Berensmeyer, Buelens, and Demoor 2019, 5: "Is the poem that derives from inspiration the experience that the poet has before writing it down, so that the written text is only a copy of the experience, or is the linguistic expression identical to the poet's inspiration, and thus something given to the poet by a higher power than his/her 'own voice' not an act of self-expression at all? In that case, 'genius' would be defined as heteronomous rather than autonomous, and characterized by 'impersonality' rather than a unique and original personality."

biographies becomes necessary. Put differently, the author's work becomes closely related to her/his life.[25]

Copyright

This also leads to a third and final important factor influencing the development of the Romantic author concept that needs to be mentioned here: the negotiations surrounding copyright.[26] An illustrative example would be the Statute of Anne, which in 1710 granted the rights to a work to its author for a renewable period of fourteen years, provided that the author was still alive.[27] Laws such as these evidently also raised the issue of piracy, which was intensely debated in the latter part of eighteenth-century Germany. Consider, for example, the defense of piracy by Christian Sigmund Krause (1758–1829):

> Most people buy books precisely to use the intellectual material in every way, . . . reprinters [i.e., the literary pirate] excepted—they do it only for the sake of fun. But we keep coming back to the question *So I am allowed to read, learn, abbreviate, expand, teach, translate, write about, laugh about, scold, and mock the intellectual content of the book—basically do with it whatever I want, good and evil—but I am not allowed to copy or print it?* If authors really could prohibit the latter because it impairs their advantage, why shouldn't they just as well forbid that someone makes a good book out of ten bad books of theirs because it harms their honor? Where do you want to draw the line? . . . By what right can someone have more ownership of his written ideas than of his spoken ones? By what right can a preacher forbid the reprinting of his sermons when he cannot prevent any of his listeners from taking notes on all of them? Would it be more ridiculous if a professor wanted to demand of his students that they never use to their advantage a certain new proposition he had taught them than if he demanded the same from all the booksellers—who had no obligations to him in comparison with his students—regarding a new

---

25. Cf. Berensmeyer, Buelens, and Demoor 2019, 5.

26. See, e.g., Woodmansee 1984 (cf. Easley 2019, 147) but also the more recent Biagioli 2011, 1847: "A figure of radical individuality, genius was mobilized between the end of the eighteenth century and the middle of the nineteenth century to conceptualize a new kind of property authors could claim in their texts and other works deemed expressive."

27. For a detailed discussion of the background and consequences of the statute, see Deazley 2004 (cf. Schellenberg 2019, 139–41).

book? No, no, it is too obvious that the concept of intellectual property is useless.[28]

Noteworthy is that although the author criticizes the possibility of legally prohibiting piracy, Krause still adheres to an author concept similar to the Romantic. The problem is not that there is no originator but that one cannot satisfactorily regulate between different kinds of uses—to distinguish reprint from other uses was deemed too arbitrary. His view would not triumph, however. It was rather the dichotomy between idea ("die Gedanken") and expression ("die Form dieser Gedanken") formulated by, for example, Johann Gottlieb Fichte that paved the way for a legal notion of intellectual property:[29]

> We can distinguish two things about a book: the *physical* aspect, the printed paper, and the *intellectual* one. . . . This intellectual aspect is . . . to be further divided into the *material*, the content of the book, the ideas it brings about, and into the *form* of those ideas, the manner and connection in which the phrases and words are presented. The first [the *material*] obviously does not become our property simply by a transfer of the book to us. . . . We must read the book . . . and thus incorporate it into our own connection of ideas. . . . But what nobody can ever appropriate, because

---

28. Krause 1783, 416 (emphasis added). My translation of the German: "Gerade um den geistigen Stof auf alle Art zu benutzen, kaufen die mehrsten die Bücher, . . . Nachdrucker ausgenommen, doch leztere nur des Spases wegen. Und nun kommen wir immer wieder auf die Frage zuruck: ich kan den geistigen Stof des buchs lesen, lernen, abkürzen, erweitern, lehren, übersezen, darüber schreiben, lachen, ihn tadeln, verspotten, gut und bös anwenden, kurz, damit machen, was ich nur immer will; und nur abscheiben oder abdrucken sollte ich ihn nicht dürfen?—und wenn die Verfasser lezteres wirklich unterfagen könnten, weil es ihren Vortheil Abbruch thut, warum solten sie nicht eben sowol verbeiten dürfen, das man aus zehn schlechten Büchern von ihnen Ein gutes macht, weil es ihrer Ehre schadet? Wo will man ihnen die Grenze ziehen? . . . Mit welchem Rechte will ein Mensch mehr Eigenthum an seinen geschriebenen, als an seinen gesprochenen Gedanken haben? Mit welchem Rechte will ein Prediger den Nachdruck seiner Reden verbieten, da er nicht verhindern kan, daß jeder seiner Zuhörer seine ganzen Predigten nachschreibt? Wäre es lächerlicher, wenn ein Professor von seinen Jüngern verlangen wolte, sie solten einen gewissen neuen Saz, den er sie gelehrt hatte, nie zu ihrem Nuzen anwenden, als wenn er eben das von allen Buchhändlern, die ihm doch in Vergleichung mit seinen Jüngern gar keine Verbindlichkeiten haben, in Ansehung eines neuen Buchs verlangt? Nein, nein, es ist zu auffallend, daß der Begriff des geistigen Eigenthums unbrauchbar ist."

29. For an analysis of Fichte, see, e.g., Biagioli 2011, who states, among other things, that "the romantic genius is seen as the direct ancestor to the foundational notion of 'personal expression' in modern copyright" (1847–48). Similar arguments were proposed in British debates.

this remains physically impossible, is the *form* of these ideas, their connection, and the signs with which they are presented. . . . The latter always remains his [the author's] *exclusive property*.[30]

Similar distinctions were made in British debates. Here, for example, is Francis Hargrave (1741–1821):

Every man has a mode of combining and expressing his ideas peculiar to himself. . . . A strong resemblance of stile, of sentiment, of plan and disposition, will be frequently found; but there is such an infinite variety in the modes of thinking and writing as well as in the extent and connection of ideas, as in the use and arrangement of words, that a literary work *really* original, like the human face, will always have some singularities, some lines, some features, to characterize it, and to fix and establish its identity; and to assert the contrary with respect to either, would be justly deemed equally opposite to reason and universal experience.[31]

In sum, then, it is no overstatement to say that during the Romantic era, the (named)[32] author was given a central place, not least in the

---

30. The article was first published as Fichte 1793, here quoted from Fichte 1846, 225–28 (emphasis in the original). My translation from the German: "Wir können an einem Buche zweierlei unterscheiden: das *körperliche* desselben, das bedruckte Papier; und sein *geistliges*. . . . Dieses Geistiges ist . . . wieder einzutheilen: in das *Materielle*, den Inhalt des Buches, die Gedanken, die es vorträgt; und in die *Form* dieser Gedanken, die Art wie, die Verbindung in welcher, die Wendungen und die Worte, mit denen es sie vorträgt. Das erste wird durch die bloße Uebergabe des Buches an uns offenbar nich nicht unser Eigenthum. . . . Wir müssen das Buch lessen . . . und so ihn in unsere eigene Ideenverbindung aufnehmen. . . . Was aber schlechterdings nie jemand sich zueignen kann, weil dies physisch unmöglisch bleibe, ist die Form dieser Gedanken, die Ideenverbindung in der, und die Zeichen, mit denen sie vorgetragen werden. . . . Die letztere also bliebt auf immer sein *ausschliessendes Eigenthum*."

31. Quoted from Biagioli 2011, 1850 (emphasis in the original), originally published in 1774. Cf. the later comment by Eliot 1982, 36–37: "One of the facts that might come to light in this process is our tendency to insist, when we praise a poet, upon those aspects of his work in which he *least* resembles anyone else. In these aspects or parts of his work we pretend to find what is individual, what is the peculiar essence of the man. We dwell with satisfaction upon the poet's difference from his predecessors, especially his immediate predecessors; we endeavor to find something that *can be isolated* in order to be enjoyed. Whereas if we approach a poet without this prejudice we shall often find that not only the best, but the most individual parts of his work may be those in which the dead poets, his ancestors, assert their immortality most vigorously" (emphasis added).

32. Here should be mentioned that the practice of naming authors varied, especially in relation to types of publications. As summarized by Easley 2019, periodical publications were, for example, often anonymous, and had collaborative models of authorship.

interpretive task. Author intention and intellectual property were to be guiding principles, and the notion that Barthes polemicizes against is seen clearly.

Contrasts or Continuums?

When describing the shifting waves on the ever-changing sea of author-ship, scholars often emphasize contrasts. It has, for example, been claimed that for an author to be seen as responsible for her/his works, "the nature of writing would have to be completely rethought. And that . . . is exactly what eighteenth-century theorists did."[33] However, even if the noted changes can be seen as radical within a limited con-text of negotiation, there are continuities that stretch back far beyond modern times, and it will be seen as this study proceeds that there are in fact similarities between ancient author concepts and both Romantic ideals and poststructuralist critiques that should be neither understated nor overly emphasized.[34] As but one example, despite being often repeated as contrasting the "ancient world," continuities do in fact exist in relation to notions of *originality* and *imitation* on the one hand and the idea of *intellectual property* on the other. However, as will be seen, these views are not shared by all, thus making the notion of an "ancient world" in the singular misguided. Ultimately, this underlines the his-torical contingency of specific author concepts and the importance to search for native author theories, even though history has a tendency to repeat itself.

As a final observation, it can be remarked that one of the features central to the discussion of Barthes, Foucault, and the Romantic author ideal—namely, the distinction between the role and function of authors as *originators* and readers as subsequent *interpreters*—presumes author hierarchies that are also historically contingent. In fact, this may indicate

---

However, and perhaps as a consequence, these authors were often viewed as "lacking creativity, originality, imagination and taste," especially when related to the practice of scissors-and-paste journalism (148).

33. Woodmansee 1984, 442.

34. Cf. Helle 2019b, 115: "The modern emphasis on originality came about not as a radical break with the common premodern focus on transmission but as a gradual rearrangement of already existing terms and tensions within the concept of authorship." He then goes on to suggest that "a model of authorial agency as mediating, nonbinary, and partial is a better starting point for writing the history of authorship than the now-dominant model of authorship as original creation, since it takes in more variation, com-plexity, continuity, and change." He makes several important observations, and I will return to his arguments in my discussion of the Mesopotamian and Greek trajectories below.

that there is still considerable influence from the Romantic ideal on the discourses of Barthes and Foucault. To clarify, while Barthes and Foucault disagree with the Romantic ideal on the authority of the author as compared to the authority of the reader, they are not arguing in a way that gives readers the authority to *change* the (words of the) text.

In our days, such hierarchies are, however, starting to be redefined, as anonymous collaborative authorship is resurfacing in electronic publications such as Wikipedia (where texts are sometimes even automatically generated by bots),[35] where the boundaries between the author and the reader are almost effaced, since there are no "final" or "stable" texts. Designated as Web 2.0, it has urged scholars to introduce new terms, such as "wreaders" or "prosumers."[36] As the focus will now be on author constructs in the ancient world, these current negotiations can thus serve as a reminder of the need to pay attention not only to the relation between authors and text but to the relation between originators and subsequent tradents.

35. See, for example, the bot Lsjbot, created by Sverker Johansson from Sweden, who is responsible for the majority of articles on the Swedish Wikipedia (as well as the Cebuano Wikipedia), apparently creating them at a pace of around ten thousand articles per day (https://en.wikipedia.org/wiki/Lsjbot). Pseudonymity has also become common praxis when creating screen names (cf. Latham 2019, 180).

36. Cf. the overview in van der Weel 2019, where a number of consequences are outlined. For example, a consequence of *wreadership* is that "it has never been easier to appropriate and repurpose the writings of others" (226). Van der Weel also mentions that reading is becoming more fragmented (on this, see also Siker 2017), that access to the means of publication has been further democratized, that there are no quality barriers—which effectively diminishes the authority of an individual author (for a discussion on the dynamic relation between an expansive mass culture and a restrictive economy of prestige, see Latham 2019)—and that writing is often made public by default. It can also be recognized that the above-discussed notions of copyright are also currently being negotiated with concepts such as, for example, Creative Commons (van der Weel 2019, 223).

Part II

SEARCHING FOR NATIVE AUTHORSHIP THEORIES

CHAPTER 3

THE MESOPOTAMIAN TRAJECTORY

Turning to the two trajectories, the Mesopotamian[1] and the Greek, it will be clear that since they are both quite complex, ideas related to different periods of time will necessarily be somewhat simplistic in presentation. The focus will not be on explaining these trajectories in detail—the aim is rather to get a better understanding of what native authorship theories in these contexts may have looked like so that they can be used as a background for exploring the constructions of authorship in the composition and transmission of the 'book' called *Isaiah* and trace major cultural changes that may have impacted these constructions. Although it would be tempting to present the two trajectories as constructing completely contrasting views of authorship and argue for their uniqueness, it would not do justice to the material at hand. As will be seen, the trajectories are to be understood not as binary poles but rather as separate clusters on a spectrum with much interaction over time.[2] They are also not the only ones, nor does the notion of them being trajectories imply a neat and streamlined evolution of authorial ideas. Conceptions similar to both early and late stages often resurface throughout time, although in somewhat reshaped form.

---

1. Needless to say, the Sumerian, Babylonian, and Assyrian (Akkadian) cultures are not one and the same, but as will be clear from the survey below, they have enough similarities to enable me to treat them as related to a Mesopotamian trajectory in contrast to a Greek one.

2. That these cultures interacted over time is common knowledge (see, e.g., Wikander 2017), and it is thus reasonable to assume that this would also have affected author concepts in various ways in various geographical areas. The observations made by Loprieno 2019 in relation to Egyptian sources, for example, shows that Egypt may have developed author concepts similar to the ones that will be presented in the discussion of the Greek trajectory quite early (see, e.g., the discussion of Khakheperreseneb; cf. Parkinson 1997, 144–50).

In this chapter and the next, a wide range of different texts will be surveyed. To formulate native theories of authorship, it will be crucial to study how the texts themselves talk about their authors not primarily as sources of historical information but as examples of shared understandings ("implied poetics")[3] of the relation between authors and texts.[4] It will also be necessary to look at paratextual activity: to what extent do texts have author designations (*peritexts*), how are authors referred to in other texts (*epitexts*), and how are authorship issues settled? The primary focus will thus be the relationship between the "author" and the "text." What role is s/he described to have in the text's interpretation, and what control is s/he claimed to have over the text?

Historical studies of authorship often begin with Homer. This survey will, however, focus first on the Mesopotamian trajectory.[5] The reason is quite simple: it has what many Assyriologists would refer to as the first named author in history—a woman named Enheduanna. The journey thus starts not with a man but with a woman.

Dying Authors Birthing Texts

Starting an investigation on author concepts in Mesopotamia with a named author needs, however, to be put in proper context. It was seen in the previous chapter that Foucault could "easily imagine a culture where discourse would circulate without any need for an author,"[6] and this is indeed what is found in ancient Mesopotamia. As noted by most scholars, literary texts are predominantly (almost exclusively) anonymous,[7] and this remained the case for hundreds of years. A clear example is found in the catalogs of incipits from as early as the Ur III period (ca. 2100–2000 BCE) and up to the Neo-Babylonian period (625–539 BCE). In these catalogs, a range of literary works are listed and arranged, and the point of reference is never a named *individual*

---

3. So Beecroft 2010, 2.

4. A similar approach is taken by Helle 2019b, 122 (cf. Helle 2020a, 58), building on the insights of Graziosi 2002 and Beecroft 2010.

5. Cf. Helle 2020a, 56. The recently published *Cambridge Handbook of Literary Authorship* is a welcome exception to this trend.

6. Foucault 1977, 138.

7. The list could be made long; see, e.g., Hallo 1962, 1963; Foster 1991; Michalowski 1996; Glassner 2001; Veldhuis 2004; van der Toorn 2007, 27–50; Brisch 2010; Frahm 2011; van de Mieroop 2016, 19–20; and Foster 2019.

but always the *incipits* of the works—that is, their first word(s).[8] No interest is shown in anything resembling an "author." How is this to be understood? Are authors nowhere to be found? A colophon preserved in a collection of temple hymns provides the first clue:[9]

> The compiler of the tablet (is) Enheduanna. | My lord, that which has been created (here) no one has created (before).[10]

That Enheduanna is named here, as well as in the text of other compositions, one of which will be in focus below,[11] has led to her being given the designation referred to above—the first named author in world history.[12] In line with what would be expected from critical inquiries,[13] this has also led scholars to ask a series of historically oriented questions—Who was she?[14] When did she live? Did she really author these hymns?[15]—and some answers have been provided. It has been concluded that she was the daughter of Sargon of Akkad, priestess of the moon god Nanna at Ur,[16] and that some of the hymns may

---

8. For an overview and discussion of these catalogs, see Willgren 2016a, 395–403. Only occasionally do these incipits overlap with names (see, e.g., Hallo 1963, 174–75).

9. For an introduction and translation of the temple hymns, see Sjöberg and Bergmann 1969. Colophons—that is, "eine vom Text getrennte Notiz des Schreibers am Ende einer Tafel literarischen Inhalts, die Aussagen über diese Tafel und über Personen, die mit dieser Tafel zu tun haben, enthält" (so Hunger 1968, 1)—are well studied, not least by the just mentioned Hermann Hunger.

10. Sjöberg and Bergmann 1969, 49.

11. According to Helle 2020a, 57, a total of five poems feature Enheduanna's name. Apart from the Sumerian Temple Hymns and the *Exaltation of Inanna*, which I will discuss here, she is also mentioned in three other hymns, one to Inana and two (fragmentary) to Nanna.

12. See, e.g., Hallo and van Dijk 1968; Hallo 1996, 266—"the first non-anonymous, non-fictitious author in world history—and a woman"—and most recently Helle 2019a.

13. As but one example, consider how Hallo and van Dijk 1968 spend considerable time sketching the portrait of Enheduanna, relating other compositions to her based on style (3), calling her a "systematic theologian" and a "passionately involved author," suggesting that "her poetic efforts must have served as a model for much subsequent hymnography" (4), and so on, concluding that there is therefore "little reason to deny the claim" to authorship (the last quote is from Hallo 1976, 185).

14. Some have even questioned whether Enheduanna is a name or if it may rather be a generic term "indicating any high priestess of the god of the city of Ur" (see Glassner 2002, 87).

15. The question is also raised in relation to other compositions where she is named. For a discussion, see, e.g., Civil 1980, 229; Zgoll 1997; Black 2002.

16. See, e.g., Hallo and van Dijk 1968, 1–11; Sjöberg and Bergmann 1969, 150.

not have originated with her.[17] But what does the colophon itself indicate? A first observation to be made relates to the wording. In this text, Enheduanna is conceived of as a "compiler." Behind this translation is found an important metaphor not foreign to scholars of literary history—namely, the notion of "weaving."[18] In brief, Enheduanna is described as the "weaver" of the tablets. This could be understood as a contrast to the notion that something was created that *no one had created before*, but the metaphor in fact provides an illuminating solution: while the act of weaving combines *already existing threads*, the result is a *pattern* that had not existed before. The authorship of Enheduanna is thus not conceived of as a creation ex nihilo but as providing inherited tradition with a new shape.[19]

An additional observation should also be made that sheds light on the relation between Enheduanna and the collection: her name does not feature in the catalogs that list the Temple Hymns. In three catalogs from the Old Babylonian period, it is instead its incipit *é-u₆-nir* that is listed, without any reference to Enheduanna (N2, or P255993,[20] reverse col. 1,

---

17. It has been noted, for example, that at the end of the ninth hymn, the words "additional hymn" are found. Different versions of the collection also exist (see, e.g., Zimmern 1930; Sjöberg and Bergmann 1969, 14–16), and it has been argued that hymns 8, 9, 12, and 20 address kings and temples historically later than Enheduanna (Wilcke 1972, 48–49).

18. For a brief historical overview of the metaphor, see Helle 2019b, 123–28.

19. As to the question of why Enheduanna is mentioned here, Helle suggests that it relates to the function of the collection: "The figure of the author served to guarantee the underlying unity of the text, and with it, the unity of the culture depicted in that text.... The figure of Enheduana thus transformed Sumerian from a heterogeneous congeries of traditions into a singular entity that others could appropriate and use" (2019a, 2). Similar observations as to the function of the collection have been observed before. Claus Wilcke, for example, suggested that it was compiled in order to favor and facilitate the restitution of temple worship disrupted during Sargon of Akkad's campaign against Lugalzaggesi in the Sumerian South (1972, 48), and William W. Hallo and Johannes J. A. van Dijk connected it to an attempt by Sargon to provide the theological foundations for a united empire by instituting "a cultic union of their chief priestly offices in the person of his daughter Enheduanna, the devotee of Inanna," as well as equating the Sumerian Inanna with the Akkadian Ištar (1968, 9–10). As more hymns were subsequently added, the collection would have performed other functions (see, e.g., Wilcke 1972, 49).

20. This text was first published in Kramer 1942, with some corrections in Bernhardt and Kramer 1956, 393n3. It was subsequently discussed by Civil 1975; and Hallo 1963, 1975; and later by, e.g., Weitemeyer 1990, 382–83; Black 1998, 24–27; Tinney 1998, 1999; Vanstiphout 2003; Veldhuis 2004, 58–66; Rubio 2009, 25–28; and Delnero 2010.

line 13; U2, or P346208,[21] obverse line 21; and L or P345372,[22] obverse col. 2, line 9). Noteworthy is also that all of these catalogs feature in the discussion of what scholars have come to designate as "the Decad,"[23] a list of works used in school settings. Evidently, then, Enheduanna was not considered as important for the interpretation of the work, nor was she seen as central to its continued transmission by subsequent scribes. The contrast to what Barthes referred to as the task of the "critic" could not be greater.

A look at another text featuring Enheduanna highlights this dynamic further—namely, the *Exaltation of Inanna*, a composition that was part of the Decad mentioned above, thus to be recognized as a widely known composition with significant cultural impact.[24] In the poem, which addresses the goddess Inanna, Enheduanna recounts in first-person speech (see, e.g., the repeated "I, Enheduanna") how she has been expelled by a man named Lugalanne from the temple and her office as high priestess; that she prayed to the moon-god Suen/Nanna, who did nothing; and that she now turns to Inanna (the "Exalted Lady") with her plea. What is interesting is that the making of the text seems to be recounted on lines 138–44:

"This filled me, this overflowed from me, Exalted Lady, as I gave birth[25] for you. | What I confided to you in the dark of night, a

---

21. This text was first published in Gadd and Kramer 1963, and a transliteration and partial translation were provided by Kramer 1961. It was discussed by Hallo 1966; and Civil 1975; and subsequently by, e.g., Tinney 1999, 168; Vanstiphout 2003; Robson 2003; and Delnero 2010.

22. This text was first published in de Grenouillac 1930 and discussed in, e.g., Kramer 1942, 16–19; Bernhardt and Kramer 1956, 393n3; Flückiger-Hawker 1996; Weitemeyer 1990, 382; Tinney 1999, 168; Black et al. 2004, 299; and Delnero 2010.

23. The term was introduced by Tinney 1999, who expanded on a reconstructed "beginners level" of scribal training proposed by Niek C. Veldhuis ("the Tetrad"). According to Tinney, "the Decad" would be the next stage in the training, and as the name reveals, it consisted of ten compositions. Although featured on these lists, the Temple Hymns are not included in the Decad (see also Robson 2001; Veldhuis 2004; Delnero 2006, 2010). Vanstiphout 2003, 10, refers to all three as the "major curricular catalogues." For an introduction and translation of these compositions, see Black 2004, 299–352. A discussion and general overview are also found in Willgren 2016a, 39–41.

24. Cf. the somewhat anachronistic but telling assessment by Zgoll 1997, 40, that the poem, which is preserved on a total of seventy-seven manuscripts, can be seen as the "erste Bestseller der Weltliteratur."

25. Helle 2020a, 63, notes that the use of the syllable /du/ could be intentionally ambiguous—it can be understood as to give birth (*du₂*; cf. Attinger 2019, 11n105: "je te l'ai [le chant] 'enfanté'"; this translation is preferred by most scholars), to create (*du₃*), to speak (*du₁₁*; this alternative is preferred by Attinger), or to release (*du₈*). The birth

singer shall perform for you in the bright of day! | Because of your assaulted wife, because of your assaulted child, | Great was your fury, remorseless your heart." | The almighty queen, who presides over the priestly congregation, | She accepted her prayer.[26]

The text is fascinating, not least due to the birth metaphor. Earlier in the poem, on lines 51–55, a city (possibly) is described as unable to conceive, a city where women no longer converse with their husbands at night:

Your sacred order having been communicated to the city that had not said "The Country for you" to those that had not said "Your father!" (that) territory returned to your feet, | and *became incapable of procreating.*[27] | The woman there no longer speaks of love with her husband, | she no longer talks with him *at night,* | nor *reveals to him* her most secret desires.[28]

Reading these two parts (lines 51–55 and 138–44) in light of each other, it can be suggested that while the malfunctioning womb in lines 51–55 leads to a breakdown in nightly communication between lovers, the successful dialogue between Enheduanna and Inanna (a dialogue with possible sexual undertones?)[29] leads to a metaphorical birth—the text[30]—and it is also here that her prayer is heard. She has creative labor pains, and the poetic outcome is not the result of her own genius but of a divine-human interaction. As a channel of divine revelation, the human recipient will, however, soon be sidelined: "As the text is born and released into the world, it is also separated from

---

metaphor would strengthen the parallel to lines 51–55 but does not affect my main argument here.

26. Translation from Foster 2016, 335.

27. There are several possible ways to understand the phrase. For a discussion, see Attinger 2019, 6n45, who notes that a literal translation would be something like "les pieds ont glissé de sa matrice," thus explicitly mentioning a womb, a translation followed by Helle 2020a, 63 ("The womb [of the city] is out of order"), while Foster 2016, 333, for example, translates it as "No one, indeed, had set foot in its *sheepfolds*" (emphasis added).

28. My translation of Attinger 2019, 6 (emphasis added), from the French: "Ton ordre sacré ayant été communiqué à la ville qui n'avait pas dit: 'Le Pays pour toi!,' à ceux qui n'avaient pas dit: 'Ton père!,' (ce) territoire est retourné à tes pieds, | *et est devenu incapable de procréer.* | La femme là-bas ne parle plus d'amour avec son époux, | elle ne s'entretient plus la nuit avec lui | ni ne lui révèle ses *désirs les plus secrets*" (emphasis in the original).

29. Cf., e.g., Hallo and van Dijk 1968, 33, who translate line 137 as "the nuptial chamber awaits you."

30. I follow the analysis of this text in Helle 2020a, 64.

the body of its parent."[31] More specifically, Enheduanna is sidelined in favor of the singer, the *gala*, who performs the song. Enheduanna no longer has control over its continuing transmission, and the poem also switches from first- to third-person speech. The "I" disappears, and it is notable that the *gala* is regularly associated with funerals. If significant, the creation of the text could thus be seen as leading to the death of the author.[32] That the first-person speech returns in the last line need not take away from this conclusion. Instead, it can be interpreted as if additional voices are now subsumed under the first person,[33] and so in light of the observation that the poem's ending makes Enheduanna a model of prayer, an example to follow ("She accepted her prayer"), the final exhortation is voiced by them all: "To Inanna be praise!" (line 153). When the voices mix, it also becomes more difficult to distinguish Inanna from Enheduanna:[34]

> Inanna's sublime will was for her restoration. | It was a sweet moment for her, she was arrayed in her finest, she was beautiful beyond compare, | She was lovely as a moonbeam streaming down. (145–47)

Ultimately, then, what is envisaged in this poem is an author conception that sidelines Enheduanna. She neither is understood as a creative genius originating the poem nor has any significance in the continuing transmission. Instead, authorship is conceived of as a creative interaction between several agents—a deity, a first human recipient, and subsequent human recipients—that are ultimately intertwined.

---

31. See Helle 2020a, 64, who also notes that the separation is emphasized by the structure of line (Helle 2020b, 104):

(a) what	(a') a singer
(b) in the dead of night	(b') at midday
(c) I spoke to you	(c') will repeat to you

32. Following Helle 2020a, 65.

33. Cf. Helle 2020a, 57 ("The authorial self is not contained within one person but is distributed across a number of voices that either speak it into existence or come to embody it"); van der Toorn 2007, 13.

34. Hallo and van Dijk 1968, 62–63. Helle 2020a, 61, also notes a similar ambiguity on line 151, concluding that "when Enheduana becomes an author and composes the hymn to Inana, Inana is simultaneously speaking back, so that their two voices become virtually indistinguishable."

NAMING AUTHORS ANEW

After Enheduanna follows centuries of silence regarding authors. This indicates that her naming needs to be seen as somewhat of an exception. But as names were again starting to accompany texts in Neo-Assyrian times, especially in relation to the collecting of literature for libraries by Ashurbanipal,[35] a picture similar to the one just observed can be painted, indicating that the author concept itself was indeed no anomaly.

Consider first a catalog found in Ashurbanipal's libraries that dates to the seventh century BCE and has been designated by Wilfred G. Lambert as "A Catalogue of Texts and Authors."[36] The list is significant for the mapping of the Mesopotamian trajectory, not least since it seems to indicate that the development of new paratextual practices was connected to changes in material cultures. In this case, the first systematically organized library in Mesopotamia coincides with the first catalog relating names to compositions[37] as well as with an increasing spread of the practice of adding names to compositions.[38] Designated as a catalog of texts and authors and seen in light of the increasing practice of adding names, one may think that what the list contains is something like a compilation of names of individuals that were thought to have composed specific works in the sense that they were now theirs, but only a cursory reading will make clear that the names cannot be taken as authors in any Romantic sense of the word.[39] The catalog mentions not only humans but also gods and legendary kings, and they are all said to have "spoken" these texts. In one place, the "author" is a horse(!). The relation between these names and the texts they are juxtaposed to thus needs further scrutiny, and three examples will show that

---

35. For an overview, see Fincke 2003; cf. Heeßel 2010, 139.

36. Lambert 1962. He notes that it was "probably not much older than Ashurbanipal," in whose library all three known copies were found (76).

37. Cf. Helle 2020b, 209.

38. See similarly Helle 2020b, 210.

39. This is often recognized, but the names are still evaluated on the basis of modern ideas. As an example, in his evaluation of the list, Foster 2019, 20, claims that "certain people in the list . . . were not so much authors—in the sense that they created a work that had not existed before—as they were compilers or editors who integrated disparate swatches or strands of related material into a new text with such success that the resulting product was generally adopted thereafter as standard." Formulated in such a way, it provides quite a contrast to how the Sumerian Temple Hymns speak about Enheduanna and thus underscores the need for native theories of authorship.

the pattern sketched so far in relation to Enheduanna is in fact quite consistent.[40]

Interwoven Agency

Consider first the *Erra Epic*. The catalog mentions the incipit *[King of All Habitations, Creator of] the World Region*, followed by "[This is what] was revealed to [Kabti-ilāni-Marduk, son of Dābibi], and which he spoke."[41] Interestingly, the *Erra Epic* itself concludes with a similar statement:

> The praise-(song) of the great lord Nergal (= Erra) and hero Ishum– | how Erra went into a rage and set out to lay the lands low and destroy their people, | but his counsellor Ishum calmed him so sparing a remnant– | the *compiler* of his tablets was Kabti-ilāni-Marduk, son of Dābibu: | he *revealed it to him in a nocturnal vision* and, just as he declaimed it while wakeful, | so he left nothing out, he added to it not a single line. (V, 39–44)[42]

As translated here, the passage first gives a summary of the contents of the poem and then moves to a discourse on its creation. Here, a human is mentioned as the "compiler of his tablets" (*kāṣir kammīšu*)—literally

----

40. Apart from the examples quoted here, which provide more lengthy expositions, names of "authors" are also occasionally found in other places. They have been included when asking for a blessing at the end of a poem, they are sometimes hidden in acrostics, and at one point, a name is even found at the end of a manuscript. The name Saggil-kênam-ubbib is, for example, featured in an acrostic work where the first syllable of each stanza together form the sentence *a-na-ku Sa-ag-gi-il-ki-[na-am]-ub-bi-ib ma-ash-ma-shu ka-ri-bu sha i-li u shar-ri*, which Glassner 2002, 86, translates as "I am Saggil-kênam-ubbib, the exorcist, who gives thanks to the gods and to the king." Important in this context is that the inclusion of the name is related not to writing but to exorcism—Saggil-kênam-ubbib identifies himself as a worshipper, not a writer (cf. similarly van der Toorn 2007, 40, but on *Ludlul*). This is also the case for many of these paratexts, which will not be analyzed in detail here (for a recent overview, see Foster 2019), although the Mesopotamian trajectory, as analyzed here, will provide an interesting framework for future studies on these names and paratexts. This is also true for the observation that some genres, like letters and royal inscriptions, were always related to specific named individuals (so Helle 2020b, 211; cf. Michalowski 1996, 185) and that collections of instructions often have a narrative frame where some legendary figure is mentioned (on this, see Vayntrub 2018). As but one example, see, e.g., the first thirteen lines of the Sumerian *Instructions of Shuruppak*, where Shuruppak is introduced by an anonymous voice as a wise man of old who passes on instructions to his son (see also Loprieno 2019 on Egypt).
41. Lambert 1962, 65.
42. Translation from George 2013, 61 (emphasis added).

"weaver," using the same metaphor as in the Sumerian Temple Hymns—and the line following this identification conveys that the composition is a result of a nighttime vision, as was also the case in the *Exaltation of Inanna*.[43]

As with the *Exaltation*, the voices are also somewhat elusive. They intermingle, as is seen in the scholarly discussion of the line reading "*he* revealed it to *him* . . . just as *he* . . . *he* added." While most scholars have understood the first "he" as referring to the deity, who is thus revealing something to Kabti-ilāni-Marduk,[44] no straightforward case can be made,[45] and the translations of Benjamin R. Foster provide a good example of this. When translated and commented upon in *Before the Muses*, the line is interpreted as indicating that Kabti-ilāni-Marduk wrote down a revelation discoursed by Ishum as Kabti-ilāni-Marduk was waking up, omitting nothing at all: "He revealed it at night, and, just as he (the god?) had discoursed it while he (K.) was coming awake, he (K.) omitted nothing at all."[46] However, in a 2019 discussion, Foster changed his mind, instead arguing that the entire line refers to Kabti-ilāni-Marduk: "He let him see it at night, and, just as he put it in words while he was coming awake, he omitted nothing at all."[47] In this scenario, then, it would be Kabti-ilāni-Marduk who disclosed his idea to the god rather than the other way around, and the reason for Foster's change of mind is based on the analogy to the nighttime experience retold by Enheduanna. This then brings us back to the observation made there—that the divine and human voices intermingle: "As shown by the parenthetical insertions needed to make sense of the text in translation, Kabti-ili-Marduk's description of his own authorship oscillates back and forth between two 'he's,' god and poet, obscuring the distinction between them."[48]

---

43. One should not, therefore, distinguish sharply between the weaver metaphor and the dream scene, as is done by, e.g., Helle 2019b, 114.

44. See, e.g., Michalowski 1996, 186; or more recently Helle 2020a, 62.

45. Although the logic of the passage could favor an understanding where it is the god who reveals things to Kabti-ilāni-Marduk. At least, the part mentioning that nothing is left out or added would not make sense if the point is to stress human agency and creativity. Rather, it seems to convey that something has been revealed to a human recipient who faithfully puts it into writing. This would also be supported by the catalog of "authors," which understands it in this way.

46. Foster 1996, 2:788; see also Foster 1991, 19–20.

47. Foster 2019, 14.

48. Helle 2020a, 62.

Consequently, instead of here seeing a "tacit admission that the wording did not originate with him,"[49] the intertwining of divine and human agency in the Mesopotamian trajectory is further emphasized, and the result is that, as in the *Exaltation of Inanna*, the original human recipient is eventually sidelined. Ultimately, the source of inspiration resides neither in the text itself nor in the human writing it down but rather in the (revelatory) *interaction* between divine and human agents. The poem is, so to speak, not understood as the intellectual property of Kabti-ilāni-Marduk, and he will therefore not be considered relevant when subsequent readers interpret the poem.

This could be further underscored by the statement that nothing is omitted, a common trope (rather than a factual statement of textual fixation)[50] claiming that the human recipient is not her-/himself creating new content but rather provides a container for a faithful preservation and continued transmission of the revelatory interaction. This is also how the act of writing is made part of the events described. Being a faithful copy of the outcome of the divine-human interaction, the text becomes divinely approved and widely disseminated, and the poem proceeds by involving other agents in the production and transmission of it:[51]

> When Erra heard it he approved. | What pertained to Ishum his vanguard satisfied him. | All the gods praised his sign [i.e., his poem]. | Then the warrior Erra spoke thus: | "In the sanctuary of the god who honors this poem, may abundance accumulate, | but let the one who neglects it never smell incense. | Let the king who extols my name rule the world. | Let the prince who discourses the praise of my valor have no rival. | Let the singer who chants (it) not die from pestilence, | but his performance be pleasing to king and prince. | The scribe who masters[52] it shall be spared in the enemy country and honored in his own land, | in the sanctum of the learned, where they shall constantly invoke my name, I shall grant them understanding. | The house in which this tablet

---

49. Lambert 1957, 1. This is followed by, e.g., Hallo 1962, 15 ("The reference to divine inspiration is simply a way of denying Kabti's authorship of the epic and implying that he received it from an earlier authority") and van der Toorn 2007, 41 ("The author, in other words, is not the real author").

50. Cf., e.g., Cancik-Kirschbaum and Wagensonner 2017, 43.

51. Helle 2020b, 224, understands the lines that follow in a hierarchical way, but such a reading is not necessary.

52. Cancik-Kirschbaum and Wagensonner 2017, 44, and Helle 2020b, 124, have "memorizes" (Ger. "memoriert").

is placed, though Erra be angry and the Seven be murderous, | the sword of pestilence shall not approach it, safety abides upon it. | Let this poem stand forever, let it endure till eternity, | let all lands hear it and praise my valor, | let all inhabitants witness and extol my name." (V, 45–61)[53]

As the quote shows, there is an explicit connection between writing and performance. For the textually transmitted divine-human interaction to be successful, it could not stay with the first human tradent.[54] Nor could it stay as a single textual artifact. It needed instead to be disseminated more broadly, both in space (cf. "all the gods," "all lands," "all inhabitants," etc.) and in time ("forever," "till eternity"), and this included performances in various contexts.

Interestingly, *the clay tablet itself* also becomes a blessing to the house in which it is placed. As containers of a divine-human revelatory interaction transmitted by human tradents, texts were given important roles in the interaction between gods and humans, and the containers of these texts—the tablets—were invested with life-giving powers. Copying the *Erra Epic* was, then, a means of extending this blessed presence, and the scribe undertaking such an activity is promised protection in enemy land and honor in his own land. Why? Because it was considered a faithful copy of divine-human interaction that called for a certain response—to extol the valor and name of the deity.

If a correct interpretation, it follows that there is no fundamental conceptual distinction between a "scribe"—that is, a subsequent tradent—and the first human tradent other than one of diachrony: the first human tradent (who is sometimes also a scribe) is simply the first one to channel the divine-human revelatory interaction, only to be followed by subsequent scribes who similarly partake in the channeling and interpretation of revelation. As Enheduanna, Kabti-ilāni-Marduk functions as a channel, a weaver (thus effacing any dichotomy between originality and imitation) who is ultimately marginalized in the subsequent transmission.

Embodied Interaction

A second example proceeds from the observation that the "Catalogue of Texts and Authors" mentions the *Epic of Gilgamesh* together with a

---

53. Translation from Foster 1996, 2:788.

54. I will use the terms *recipient* and *tradent* synonymously to reflect the way they are intertwined in the sources.

certain Sîn-lēqi-unninnu. It is well known that this epic enjoyed popularity over an extended period of time and that it existed in various versions and went through a series of major changes.[55] From consisting of individual narratives about Gilgamesh in Sumerian in the third millennium BCE to existing in several different compilations in the second millennium, an Akkadian standard version came to be established in the first millennium BCE, a version that was found in the libraries of Ashurbanipal. Whereas the earlier versions were anonymous, the standard version was now related to a named individual: Sîn-lēqi-unninnu. This observation alone, that the name is related to a version that builds on a long process of transmission, illustrates quite clearly what the weave metaphor conceptualized above, but yet another observation can be made in relation to the underlying author concept: The epic was provided with a new prologue in Neo-Assyrian (possibly Middle Babylonian) times that includes a notion of revelation and writing:[56]

> [Him who] saw everything, let me [make kno]wn to the land, | [Who all thing]s experienced, [let me tea]ch i[t] ful[ly]. . . . [The hi]dden he saw, the undisclosed he discov[ered]. | He brought back information from before the flood, | Achieved a long [j]ourney, exhausted, but at peace. | All his toils he (or "were"; my comment, see the discussion below) [engra]ved on a (stone) stela / an inscription. (1–2, 5–8)[57]

Gilgamesh, who embodies the earlier noted interaction between a deity and a human recipient by being half a god himself, is here told to be a transmitter of wisdom from before the flood[58] as well as disclosing and possibly engraving the hidden things he had seen,[59] although the

---

55. A detailed discussion can be found in Tigay 1982. According to van de Mieroop 2016, 27, changes continued to be made well into the late second century BCE.

56. Tigay 1982, 244.

57. Translation from Tigay 1982, 141.

58. Tigay 1982, 143, notes that this is in some contrast to what would have been expected themes in a prologue.

59. As noted by Tigay, this engraving would—in line with the purpose of royal inscriptions—grant Gilgamesh some kind of immortality, although it should be added that it is not as author but as legendary figure (1982, 144–45). A comparison to a royal inscription also indicates that a blessing from future rulers is sought, and many scholars have pointed to the *Cuthean Legend* as a possible inspiration for the Gilgamesh prologue, a legend that in its Middle Babylonian version recounts how Enmerkar does not leave a similar inscription behind and that the result is that Naram-Sin does not "bless him before Shamash" (quoted from Foster 1996, 1:261; cf. Tigay 1982, 145–46; Westenholz 1997, 280–93). Then in the Standard Babylonian version, it is mentioned that

latter is unclear, since there is ambiguity regarding who is actually doing the engraving.[60] By now, such an ambiguity should not surprise, as it was also clear in the *Exaltation* and the *Erra Epic*, and further emphasizing this is that the ambiguity continues in the epic, since the prologue reframes the voices in the narrative in a way that radically changes it: "The whole 'epic' is third person, but the narrator is really the main protagonist."[61] Consequently, although narrated in the third person and ascribed to Sîn-lēqi-unninnu, it has been suggested to be a "third-person autobiography of Gilgamesh,"[62] thus ultimately blurring their roles, and that, in the flood story, "a new wrinkle appears: an intrusive narrator, whose voice is transmitted by the overall storyteller, appears in the person of Uta-napishtim, survivor of the great flood and the winner of eternal life. This voice is the voice that Gilgamesh aspires to but never attains."[63]

To be observed is also that in the prologue, the pattern where a human recipient sees something (which has in some way been revealed to her/him)[64] that is first written down and subsequently performed[65] is again visible. The epic thus places Gilgamesh as the first recipient in a long chain of transmission.[66] Yet it is not Gilgamesh that is mentioned in the catalog but Sîn-lēqi-unninnu.[67] The Mesopotamian distributive

---

Naram-Sin himself has written an inscription "[for] all time" that is now to be read (Foster 1996, 1:263; cf. Helle 2020b, 165–66) and that those who read his inscription will get out of trouble: "You who have read my inscription | and thus have gotten yourself out (of trouble), | you who have blessed me, may a future (ruler) | Bless you!" (177–180, Westenholz 1997, 331).

60. Cf. Helle 2020b, 168n44.

61. Michalowski 1996, 188.

62. Michalowski 1996, 188.

63. Michalowski 1996, 188.

64. In the *Epic of Gilgamesh*, this is emphasized by "the frequency of the verbs 'see' and 'know,' and the nouns 'wisdom,' 'secret(s),' 'hidden thing(s)'" (quote from Tigay 1982, 143, who makes a similar observation).

65. "[Take out] and read aloud from the lapis-lazuli tablet | [How/that] Gilgamesh went through all hardships . . ." (lines 25–26), translation from Tigay 1982, 141.

66. It is thus partially correct to say that Gilgamesh is "turned . . . into an author" (van der Toorn 2007, 34)—that is, only if understood in the Mesopotamian, distributive sense as including more agents.

67. Cf. Lambert 1962, 77. van de Mieroop 2016, 21, understands this naming as "crucial for the author function, that is, the interaction with the discourse," but as will be seen below, this is indeed *not* the case, as commentaries interact with the discourse without any deference to a named tradent.

author concept, sidelining the first human tradent, is shining through with full force.[68]

The "First One"

It has so far been noted that authorship in the Mesopotamian trajectory is conceived of as a divine-human interaction that draws several human agents into the process of transmission and that the first recipient is often sidelined. This notion of a "first" human tradent (i.e., a tradent chronologically prior to subsequent ones) is made explicit in the third and last example—the epilogue to *Enuma Elish* (tablet VII, lines 145–62):

> They (the fifty names of Marduk) must be grasped: let the "first one" explain (them). | Let the wise and knowledgeable discuss (them) together. | Let the master repeat (them) to make the pupil understand. | Let him open the ears of the "shepherd," the "herdsman," | He must not neglect the Enlil of the gods, Marduk, | So his land may prosper and he himself be safe. | . . . | The explanation

---

68. I find this to better reflect the sources than the view that "the authorial claim of the scholars often came at the expense of kings" (Helle 2020b, 162, building on the work of Paul-Alain Beaulieu) so that the naming of Sîn-leqi-unnennu would in some way transfer the epic from Gilgamesh to Sîn-leqi-unnennu. Although it may be true that there was competition between royal figures and scribal guilds, the idea presupposes a notion of intellectual property that is not seen in the sources themselves. Another observation relating to the problems caused when author concepts alien to the sources are imported can be made in relation to Tigay's discussion, where a clear Romantic author concept is used as a point of reference. When talking about the Old Babylonian version, he states that "the plan of the integrated epic thus testifies to the working of a single artistic mind, and the work of this person is so creative that he deserves to be considered an *author*, rather than an editor or compiler" (1982, 42; emphasis in the original). Then when focusing on the late version, he says, "In wording and plot, then, the late version represents a revised form of the Old Babylonian version, not a new composition, and the writers responsible for these revisions will therefore be described as *editors* or *redactors*" (56; emphasis in the original), and even later, as he evaluates the contribution by Sîn-leqi-unninnī, he states that "the very fact that the epic is attributed to him indicates that Sîn-leqi-unninnī must have made some important, perhaps definitive, contribution to its formulation. It is certainly possible that he was the editor of the late version, but this is not necessarily the case" (247). Similar views have been expressed by other scholars as well (see, e.g., Hallo 1962, 15; Foster 2019, 20) and in relation to other Mesopotamian sources (cf. the discussion on the scribe Ilimilku by Wyatt 2015, 401: "Does it mean that Ilimilku was a copyist, writing out a text either under dictation [oral] or from a *Vorlage*, an *Ur-Text* [written], with no individual input [apart of course from his own errors!]? Or does it mean that in some sense he had at least an editorial, at most an authorial, role?"), but to be noted is that this is not how the epic itself is framed.

(of the names) which the "first one" discoursed before him (Marduk).[69] | He wrote down and preserved[70] for those in the future to hear. | [The prais]es of Marduk, he who created the Igigi-gods. | Let them . . . , let them invoke his name. | Let them noise abroad the song of Marduk, | He who subdued Tiamat and took kingship.[71]

Here again, a divine-human interaction—this time between Marduk and someone described as the "first one"—results in a text. The designation "first one" is quite interesting and goes well in line with what has been observed so far, although it is somewhat elusive, since this figure is claimed to *explain* the divine revelation, *discourse it, write it down*, and *preserve it* for future generations. Do we here have a condensed story of textual production and authorship? If so, it is clear that the human recipient is again somewhat sidelined. As in the examples above, the passage underlines that the human is not the *source* of inspiration and authority but that these notions rather involve several agents. The inevitable consequence is that what is actually central to the interpreter is the *revelation itself*—or, perhaps better, the revelatory interaction. It is as such that the designation "first one" makes sense: that the channeling of revelation into textual form is done through a(n unnamed) "first one" indicates that this act is neither the end of the interaction nor the goal of the revelation. It needs to continue beyond both the production of a text and the first one. It is not surprising, then, to find that the first human recipient shares a purpose with the text: to explain the fifty names of Marduk, a purpose extended beyond the "first one" to other named groups—most significantly the "wise and knowledgeable" and the "master"—who are supposed to discuss and generate further knowledge on the subject, hence creatively continuing the transmission of the revelation channeled through the "first one." They become, as it

---

69. The adding of the name of Marduk here underscores the observation that was made in relation to the *Erra Epic*—namely, that there is potential ambiguity here—although the mentioning of the "first one" makes the sentence much more straightforward and can thus be translated without the clarification, as in Foster 2019, 15 ("The revelation that the first one put in words in his presence"), although in his comment, he anachronistically identifies the "first one" as "the author."

70. Cf. the new translation in Foster 2019, 15, where he comments that the notion of preservation (which he now translates as "established it") could be understood as the creating of text with nothing added or deleted (cf. the *Erra Epic* above).

71. Translation from Foster 1991, 21–22. The *Enuma Elish* is not mentioned in Lambert's catalog. It has been suggested that it may have featured in relation to the mentioning of Oannes-Adapa, to be reconstructed instead of Lambert's "The Lunar Crescent of Anu [and] Enlil," but some deem it unlikely (for a discussion, see Helle 2020b, 308–9).

were, the "second ones," "third ones," "fourth ones," and so on, in the chain of transmission. The puzzling anonymity of Mesopotamian literature is starting to make more sense, and the emerging paratextual habit of relating names to Neo-Assyrian texts has been given its proper context:[72] these names are not to be understood as references to creative geniuses with ownership rights whose intentions are important for the interpretive task, nor are they understood as founders of discourses; more precisely, they are understood as the "first ones" or "subsequent ones" in a process of transmission. A consequence of this is that scholarly categories such as authors, compilers, redactors, and even scribes are blurred in the sense that they are all understood as equal partakers (recipients and tradents) in the chain of transmission.[73] The "first one" does not have more authority than the "subsequent ones," nor does s/he have more control over the text and its contents. If correct, the literature of Mesopotamia suddenly becomes much less anonymous, since colophons regularly include the name of the scribe,[74] with their marginal importance for the interpretation of texts neatly illustrated by the physical location of the paratexts.

That the activity of scribes and the "first ones" are not to be seen as distinct can be illustrated further with an interesting "colophon-like passage"[75] at the end of a catalog that features the scribe Esagil-kīn-apli and provides a glimpse of how the standardizing of texts in Neo-Assyrian times was perceived:

> Concerning those which from old time [*sic*] were not held together "as a new weave" (SUR.GIBIL) but tangled like threads, with no duplicate to be had— | in the reign of Adad-apla-iddina (1068–1047 BCE), King of Babylon, in a new way . . . |

---

72. Cf. somewhat similarly Helle 2020b, 46: "The cuneiform scribes saw themselves as links in a chain of textual transmission, where a scribe would receive a manuscript, copy it, and pass it on to another scribe, who would then do the same. But the first link in that chain was not particularly important; what mattered was only that it was kept going." See also Lambert 1957, 1, although proceeding from a different author concept: "Successive generations of storytellers and scribes have all shared in fashioning the final product, and an original hand can no longer be traced."

73. Cf. a similar observation in relation to Egyptian literature by Loprieno 2019, 27–28, who first observes, "Egyptian literature was . . . among the *least* authorial ones in human history," and then states that "the Egyptian evidence does not provide an answer to the question whether the composer of an Egyptian text only wrote it *down* or also *wrote* it" (emphasis in the original).

74. See, e.g., Hunger 1968 or the Late Babylonian practice of mentioning a scribe following a clear scheme of X, son of Y, son of Z (so Lambert 1957, 1).

75. So Frahm 2011, 326. Wee 2015, 253, calls it *Esagil-kīn-apli's Manifesto*.

> Esagil-kīn-apli, son of Asalluḫi-mansum, sage of Ḫammurabi the king | . . . deliberated with himself, and Sa-gig (entries) from the crown to the feet | were held together "as a new weave" (SUR.GIBIL). . . . Sa-gig (is) a compilation of (forms of) sickness and a compilation of (forms of) distress. | *Alamdimmû* (concerns) physical features (and) external form, (which reveal) the human's fate | that Ea and Asalluḫi/Marduk(?) decreed. Concerning the two series, their (method of) compilation is the same.[76]

As can be seen, the work of Esagil-kīn-apli is described using the same metaphor as the one used in the Sumerian Temple Hymns. He weaves the disordered threads of tradition into something new[77]—that is, compiling ancient sources relating to the diagnostic series Sa-gig, which lists various forms of sickness and distress, into a new whole with a clear arrangement (from head to foot).[78] Again, it is seen how "originality and tradition are not opposite forces but are composed of each other,"[79] and moreover, it can be observed that the mention of Esagil-kīn-apli does not dictate that the work is therefore carried out by him only. In fact, the name Esagil-kīn-apli is associated with a "large number of incantation, medical, and omen texts, in a list of more than a hundred compositions,"[80] which indicates that "the precise role of Esagil-kin-apli remains unclear, since it is unlikely that he could have been *personally responsible* for the edition of so many works. The likelihood is that Esagil-kin-apli was head of a scribal school which collected and copied numerous texts, and perhaps was *ultimately responsible* for new text editions. There are, however, no surviving autographs *from Esagil-kin-apli himself,* but only later references to him in colophons, etc."[81]

---

76. Translation from Wee 2015, 253 (emphasis in the original). See also Finkel 1988, 143–59; cf. Frahm 2011, 326; Foster 2019, 20–21. The text is also discussed in, for example, Lambert 1957.

77. As argued by Wee 2015, 253–54; cf. the discussion in Frahm 2011, 328. Helle 2020b, 348, also points to *Uruana*, a "bilingual lexical list compiling the various names of plants used for medical purposes," which uses similar vocabulary and names Ashurbanipal.

78. Cf. Heeßel 2010, 142. Scholars also often point to another text that mentions a series that "Esagil-kīn-apli has *not* unraveled" (translation by Wee 2015, 254; emphasis added; cf. Frahm 2011, 330; Helle 2020b, 227). While Heeßel 2010, 154, understands this as indicating that Esagil-kīn-apli's version had not been accepted in Assur, Frahm argues that it should instead be understood in terms of Esagil-kīn-apli not having provided explanations for the old version (Frahm 2011, 330).

79. Helle 2019b, 124.

80. Geller 1990, 212.

81. Geller 1990, 212n25 (emphasis added).

Although the notion of "personal responsibility" is quite beside the point (it rather reflects a notion of authorship that includes the idea of intellectual property), it is noteworthy that the paratextual activity described—adding a name to a text—does not efface ambiguity. A chorus of voices over time is still heard, and another important observation can be made—namely, that the name that is added is not necessarily that of the "first one" but could be anyone in the chain of transmission.

Commenting on Texts

Returning again to *Enuma Elish*, it was noted above that the first human recipient shared the purpose to explain the fifty names of Marduk with the text and that subsequent ones were encouraged to take up this task in the continuing transmission of the text. Interestingly, this is exactly what is found in a new genre of texts that is starting to appear in the eighth century BCE—text commentaries.[82] With precursors in the late second millennium (the tradition itself claims that the content goes back to the beginnings of history),[83] the earliest known examples are from a scribe active between 716 and 683 BCE. The genre then reaches full bloom in the libraries of Ashurbanipal and the centuries that followed,[84] and in all, almost nine hundred clay tablets have been discovered that date up until the second century BCE.[85] More than half are from Nineveh, and more than half are omen commentaries.[86] Curiously, in a text that may preserve the first (at least the oldest surviving) explicit reference to the use of commentaries, the above-mentioned scribe Esagil-kīn-apli is referred to on line 27,[87] and the tablet then describes the genre as the following:

---

82. These have been studied in particular by Frahm 2011.

83. For a discussion of the possible origins of this genre, see also Johnson 2013, who among other things points to the *Zà-mì Hymns* as "scholastic commentaries concerned with the orthography, etymology and meaning of the names of various deities." I have discussed other aspects of these hymns elsewhere (see Willgren 2016a, 50–51, 56, 60–61, with references).

84. Frahm 2011, 24–27.

85. Frahm mentions the possibility that these commentaries were eventually written on parchment so that the genre may have lived on for quite some time after the last remains (Frahm 2011, 26).

86. For a tabulated overview, see Frahm 2011, 405–6.

87. See Geller 2000, 248.

> Afterwards, you will learn how to investigate, (*through the use of*)
> *ṣâtu*-lists, *translations*, and (monolingual?) *lišānu*-lists(??), the ritu-
> als (written in) Sumerian and Akkadian.[88]

Since these commentaries provide a firsthand view of how scholars in the Mesopotamian trajectory interacted with texts and thus
can shed light on what role and function authors were believed to
have, the characteristics of these commentaries will need some more
elaboration.[89]

A first observation is that the comments almost never deal with texts
in their entirety[90] but most often explain features in an atomistic fashion by quoting individual lemmas, words, or short phrases (of different
lengths) from a single base text (although some deal with more than one
base text).[91] The quoted lines can differ in several ways from the text as
found elsewhere, which may indicate that they have been written down
from memory,[92] and the fact that they were then subsequently retained
as the commentaries were copied testifies to an intrinsic variance in the
textual transmission. The base text was regularly introduced by some
kind of quotation formula (or cola), like, for example, *libbū* ("as in")[93]
or *ša iqbû* ("[this is] what *he* said"), although it is unclear whether "he"
refers to "the word of a teacher, to the stream of tradition in general,
or maybe to another written source. They often seem simply to be
used as quotation-marks, to introduce quotations from other scholarly
literature—or some other external source."[94]

Second, the commentaries are found structured in three basic
forms: (1) tabular lists with two columns where the base text is quoted
to the left and the explanation given to the right, (2) running texts with
the explanation sections intended (this is the most common form), and
(3) running texts with lemmas and explanations separated by cola.

---

88. Translation from Frahm 2011, 329, who also provides a discussion of both text and
translation.
89. The overview follows Frahm 2011, 28–58.
90. Frahm 2011, 79, mentions that a few omen commentaries deal with larger
sections.
91. Frahm 2011, 28.
92. Frahm 2011, 107.
93. For example, see Frahm 2011, 187: "Thickness" (means) "strength," (as in) "If the
Narrow Place of the Gallbladder is thick, the son will become more powerful than his
father."
94. Koch-Westenholz 2000, 32. It thus resembles the use of אשר אמר in the pesharim
of Qumran. As shown by Brown-deVost 2019, there are many similarities between these
two kinds of commentaries.

Third, two types of explanations can be observed: literal explanations and nonliteral ones. Consider the following *Sa-gig* commentary, where this distinction is made explicit:

> "If he (the exorcist on his way to the patient's house) sees a kiln-fired brick (*agurru*), the patient will die."—(The brick can have its) usual meaning (*kayy(am)ān*); secondly, (it can denote) a man who turned back [from] the river ordeal, | (because) [a (means) "water"] and gur (means) "to return"; thirdly, (it can be) a pregnant woman, (because) a (means) "son" and GUR$_4$, (when read) kir$_{(3)}$, (means) "to nip off."[95]

As seen here, a commentary can offer more than one explanation of the same passage. Moreover, the explanations are regularly either lexical or factual (explanations can also be psychological or theological—at times updating the pantheon), and sometimes, the commentators admit that they do not know the meaning of a certain text or word. As to how explanations are provided, several techniques are used. One way is to have a lemma explained by providing a synonym or a chain of synonyms, but the commentaries also explain logograms, provide figurative interpretations, paraphrase, provide etymological discussions, specify the pronunciation of words, use gematria, and so on.[96] See, for example, KAV 46, obverse 10:

> (The theonym) ^{d}*pap-sukkal*, (pronounced) *papšukkal* (and written with the signs) *pap* (and) *šukallu*, (represents) the god Ilabrat [(and) . . .].[97]

Fourth, it can be observed that the commentators themselves are never mentioned by name. Sometimes, it is stated that the explanation can be traced back to a scholar ("according to the scholar[s]," *ša pî ummâni*) or to several scholars ("according to a second scholar," *ša pî ummâni šani*), but they are not named either.[98] This is to be expected in line with what has been shown above regarding the centrality of the

---

95. Frahm 2011, 38.

96. For a detailed discussion of all these features, see Frahm 2011, 60–79.

97. Frahm 2011, 256.

98. See also Finkel 1988, 149n56. Sometimes, though, a comment can expand on a narrative's character's speech or acts, like in a comment on the exorcistic treatise *Marduk's Address to the Demons*, where the line "(I am) Asalluḫi, who is clothed with radiance and full of fearsomeness" is explained as "He (Marduk / some scholar?) said (this) because

transmitted content in comparison to the "first one," and so when referring to a text (which is rarely done), it is by means of its incipit, not by means of its "first one," as can be seen in the following quote, referring to *Ludlul bēl nēmeqi*:

> *ši-pir* DUḪ DU DU (is to be read and interpreted as) "He will *walk* (in) the 'work of abundance'" (*šipir ṭuḫdu illak*); (this means), "triumphantly," as in: "My far-reaching arms were kept continually covered, holding each other; I, who walked in a princely fashion, learnt slinking"—(this) is said in *Ludlul bēl nēmeqi*.[99]

What do these commentaries say about *Enuma Elish*, then? Consider the following two examples. The first is from a one-column tablet with fairly long lines:

> "The gods shall bring in their presents before him" (quotation from *Enuma Elish* VII 110)—(This refers to) the presents that are given in the month of Nisannu from the sixth day to the twelfth day; (it is) because of Zababa, as *it is* said.[100]

The other is more intriguing, since it is a comment on the fifty names of Marduk. The commentary "seeks to demonstrate that the names and epithets are without exception intimately related to each other," and the comment on the passage calling Marduk ᵈ*Tu-tu-*ᵈ*zi-kù . . . il šāri ṭābi bēl tašmê u magāri* ("Tutu-ziku, the god of the fair breeze, lord who hears and accedes") looks like the following:[101]

dingir	*i-lum*	dingir (means) "god"
ᵗᵘIM	*šá-a-ri*	tu$_{[15]}$[IM] (means) "breeze"
ᵈᵘḪI	*ṭa-a-bu*	du$_{[10]}$[ḪI] (means) "fair"
dingir	*be-lum*	dingir (means) "lord"
zi	*še-mu-ú*	zi (means) "to hear"
zi	*ma-ga-rum*	zi (means) "to accede"

What can be seen here is thus a clear example of how a divine-human interaction transmitted by a "first one" finds new arenas and is

---

(*aššu*) of the exorcist who is equipped with a garment (*made of*) *a red head cow*." The radiance is hence related to the garment of the priest (Frahm 2011, 82).

99. Quoted from Frahm 2011, 102. Other examples are found on 88 and 97.

100. Frahm 2011, 113.

101. Frahm 2011, 115.

taken up and further discussed by "subsequent ones" without centering either the "first one" or the "subsequent one" in the interpretation proper. Even if names have started to be attached to texts, the "first one" does not provide interpretive lenses through which the texts can be read. The intentions of individuals are nowhere to be found, and no authority is invested in "first ones." Barthes is probably smiling in his grave at the thought of authors so dead, where the persons mentioned are not seen as originators but as weaving the threads of tradition into ever-new shapes with the decentralization of the first weaver as a consequence, even when s/he is mentioned by name:

> The anonymity of scholarship and literary creativity at first may disorient if we aim for a traditional history of thought, but it puts us in a privileged position; we do not have to kill off the author: he or she is already dead. We are forced into a close reading of the text, as the author has disappeared. Social and marital status, professional preoccupation, and the relationship to grand historical events are of no importance. Even if we wanted to, we could not recover them.[102]

LOCATING THE AUTHOR

The overview of the construction of authorship in the Mesopotamian trajectory has provided some interesting results. It has been observed as a recurring feature that authorship is conceived of as an intertwining of divine and human agency that eventually draws more humans into the picture and so decentralizes not only the "first one" but also (even visually) the "subsequent ones."[103] In light of the survey above, it may thus seem fair to conclude that the recurring absence of an author's name "may lie . . . in recognition that performer, traditor, or auditor of the text play roles no less important than that of the author himself"—since without the dissemination and understanding of the text, it is

---

102. van de Mieroop 2016, 30.

103. More examples could be provided of this chain of transmission, not least from the "Catalogue of Texts and Authors." See, for example, col. I, lines 6–7: "[These are what was *revealed to*] Oannes-Adapa and *which he spoke*" (Lambert 1962, 73; emphasis added), or col. VI, lines 15–17: "[Texts and recipes] from before the Flood [which Ea *spoke* and Ada]pa *wrote at his dictation* [and which NN] *wrote down from the mouth of* Anšekurra" (following the restoration of van der Toorn 2007, 342; emphasis added).

"lost, and the author's achievement nullified"[104]—or that in this trajectory, humans are not seen as authors at all:

> Were the gods then, as the Mesopotamians claimed, the real authors of the works which men just reproduced? Let us not be deceived. All knowledge, in Mesopotamia, was the product of a revelation, which usually took the form of a dream. To the idea of revelation the Mesopotamians also added the idea of a quest, such as the journey of Gilgamesh which led him "down a very long road by which the sun came out," or the brief descent into Hell of an Assyrian prince.[105]

The problem with both these suggestions, however, is that they presuppose an understanding of authorship that is not supported by the material. It is not quite to the point to call the gods authors simply because all texts above portray *a divine-human interaction that intertwines the agency of both*.[106] Neither is it to the point to distinguish the "author" from the performer, traditor, or auditor, since authorship is distributed onto them all. The fact that the first human recipient performed important functions in the creation of the text—s/he proclaims, repeats,[107] explains, and preserves it—does not place her/him in any *exclusive* relation to the text but rather relates her/him to the ones *coming after*, who are invited into this dynamic to do likewise.

Needless to say, this also reframes the issue of textual stability and faithful transmission. If the "first one" is not perceived as an autonomous

---

104. Foster 1991, 31. See also, e.g., Helle 2019b, 135; or van de Mieroop 2016, 25, who identifies three people as together "fulfill[ing] the author-function": (1) the "original creator, whom in modern times would be considered the author," which "was given little prominence"; (2) the manuscript owner, who brought texts together; and (3) the "scribe," who "could do much more than faithfully copy of [*sic*] the text, although the colophon asserted that this was the sole aim." Cf. Helle 2020a, 69, who somewhat overstates his case when he then concludes that the Mesopotamian distributive author concept has consequences for the study of authorship in general (so that one should abandon notions of coauthorship, etc.). As will be seen below, in relation to the Greek trajectory, such a position would risk blurring features of other cultural constructions of authorship.
105. Glassner 2002, 87–88 (originally Glassner 2001, 113).
106. Cf. the observation by Helle 2020b, 157, about Oannes-Adapa (esp. in relation to Berossus's account): "A creature of the gods and a teacher of humans, Oannes cannot be placed in either group, but constitutes a strange blend of beings. As the mythical paragon of a Babylonian author, Oannes fully demonstrates that the creation of literature ideally belongs to the fishy space between gods and men."
107. Cf. the recurring formulation "They gave the command, I have repeated it" in the catalog of texts and authors discussed in Lambert 1962, 72–73.

creative genius and if s/he channels divine revelation by textualizing it in a way that the text itself now becomes a vessel, it would become an object for study only insofar as it connects the reader to the divine realm intertwined with the "first one." Consequently, when scholars interpret the statement of faithful transmission in the *Erra Epic* as if "Mesopotamian poetic tradition" had "a clearly defined notion . . . of a pristine text that had not been added to or taken away from,"[108] it is only partially correct, since it conflates divine revelation and text. That divine revelation has been transmitted without being altered does not mean that the *text* therefore cannot be altered.[109] In fact, a hymn ascribed to Assurbanipal implicitly reveals an opposite situation:

> He who abandons this song to obscurity, who does not extol Shamash, light of the great gods, | or who makes substitution for the name of Assurbanipal, whose assumption of kingship Shamash commanded by oracle, | and who names some other king, | may his string-playing be painful to people, | may his joyful songs be the gouge of a thorn![110]

Implied in the urge *not to make the hymn about someone else* is likely a reality where songs *were* in fact subject to change, and this is quite clear once examples of textual transmission such as the *Epic of Gilgamesh* are taken into consideration. So even though authorship was constructed as involving divine revelation, this interaction was not necessarily related to the earliest possible form of the text. The recurrent use of the weaving metaphor illustrates this with all clarity.

It follows, then, that textual fixation was not a central issue in the transmission process, a conclusion that underscores the above-mentioned observation that no sharp divide existed between "originator" and "scribe" in the sense that an "author" would have created an *original*, with the scribe becoming his *imitator* à la Young.[111] Such a divide rather presupposes notions of textual stability and authorship that are based on an idea of intellectual property and a dichotomy between original (creative) work and later (repetitive) polishing of a work (that ultimately

---

108. Foster 1991, 31; 2019, 23.

109. Cf. the example given in van de Mieroop 2016, 25: "The series should be revised. Let the king command: two 'long' tablets containing the explanations of antiquated words should be removed, and two tablets of the extispicy series, *bārûtu*, should be put (instead)."

110. Translation from Foster 1991, 29.

111. Cf. Helle 2019b, 114–15; or Ingold 2010.

belongs to someone else) that are alien to this context.[112] Instead of being related to a specific individual, faithful transmission and explanation are features shared with future generations.[113] Anchored in the authority of divine-human interaction and sanctioned by the gods, the written copy of the revelation would become an important source for performative use and scribal transmission, invested with a derived authority that ultimately would make the "first one" sidelined as but one of many points of contact between the divine and the human, a place where inspiration overflowed. Although the "first one" is thus an important part of the story of text in both space and time, s/he would soon lose that importance. In the end, then, the question of who the author "really" is in the Mesopotamian trajectory has been answered in quite surprising ways.

---

112. See, for example, Bonaventure's classic exposition, which underlines the notion of intellectual property needed for these distinctions to be meaningful: "For someone writes out the words of other men without adding or changing anything, and he is called the scribe [*scriptor*] pure and simple. Someone else writes the words of other men, putting together material, but not his own, and he is called the compiler [*compilator*]. Someone else writes the words of other men and also his own, but with those of other men comprising the principal part while his own are annexed merely to make clear the argument and he is called the commentator [*commentator*], not the author. Someone else writes the words of other men and also of his own, but with his own forming the principal part and those of others being annexed merely by way of confirmation, and such a person should be called the author [*auctor*]" (quoted from Kraebel 2019, 98). It may need to be stressed here that by saying this, I am not invalidating these categories in contemporary research. I am only pointing out that if we are searching for native theories of authorship, they are less relevant.

113. Cf. Foster 2019, 23: "Authors in Mesopotamian civilization well know and were wont to recall in their texts that composition was an ongoing, contributive enterprise, in which the author, or 'first one,' was present only at the beginning."

CHAPTER 4

THE GREEK TRAJECTORY

Turning now to the Greek trajectory, it will be seen that its constructions of authorship often are in some contrast to the observations made in relation to the Mesopotamian trajectory. As a reminder that the two trajectories are not to be seen as distinct and binary poles and that there is constant negotiation also within the two trajectories, this investigation will begin with a text that has overlaps with the Mesopotamian trajectory. As in the texts surveyed above, it speaks of authorship as the result of divine-human interaction, albeit with a twist. The passage, which will be quoted in some length below, is from Plato's *Ion* and centers on Socrates, who in a rather lofty way provides a critique of poets by disputing the claim by Ion, a professional rhapsode (from the Greek ῥαψῳδεῖν, literally "to sew songs [together]"; cf. the weaving metaphor above), that his performance is based on skill and knowledge:[1]

> **Soc.** I must say I have often envied you rhapsodes, Ion, for your
> art: for besides that it is fitting to your art that your person
> should be adorned and that you should look as handsome as
> possible, the necessity of being conversant with a number of
> good poets, and especially with Homer, the best and divinest
> poet of all, and of apprehending his though and not merely
> learning off his words, is a matter of envy; since *a man can
> never be a good rhapsode without understanding what the poet
> says*. For the rhapsode ought to make himself an *interpreter
> of the poet's thought* to his audience; and to do this properly
> without knowing what *the poet* means is impossible. So one
> cannot but envy all this.

---

1. The translations of *Ion* below are all from Fowler and Lamb 1925 (all emphases are mine).

Ion. What you say is true, Socrates: I at any rate have found this the most laborious part of my art; and I consider I speak about Homer better than anybody, for neither Metrodorus of Lampsacus, nor Stesimbrotus of Thasos, nor Glaucon, nor any one that the world has ever seen, had so many and such fine comments to offer on Homer as I have.

Soc. That is good news, Ion; for obviously you will not grudge me an exhibition of them.

Ion. And indeed it is worth hearing, Socrates, how well I have embellished Homer; so that I think I deserve to be crowned with a golden crown by the Homeridae.

Soc. Yes, and I must find myself leisure some time to listen to you, but for the moment, please answer this little question: are you skilled in Homer only, or in Hesiod and Archilochus as well?

Ion. No, no, only in Homer; for that seems to me quite enough. (*Ion* 530b–531a)

Read after an overview of the Mesopotamian trajectory, this passage may seem to constitute a clear contrast (if only by the fact that *Ion* is clearly related to a named individual—Plato), and there is indeed truth to that. Most significantly, Ion seems to adhere to a view where the rhapsode, if wanting to be successful, needed to understand what the *poet* (not the poem)—in this case, Homer—says. It is the *thoughts of the poet* that are to be interpreted, and this requires skill. However, as the conversation develops, Plato's Socrates will attempt to deconstruct this idea in what can best be understood as "a complex negotiation, or a struggle, with the traditional myths [about poetic inspiration] of his time."[2] Central in his critique is the observation that Ion can only interpret Homer, not Hesiod or the other poets, despite the fact that many of the things of which Homer speaks are the same as the other poets. Socrates thus concludes the following:

Soc. . . . anyone can see that you are unable to speak on Homer with art and knowledge. For if you could do it with art, you could speak on all the other poets as well; since there is an art of poetry, I take it, as a whole, is there not? (*Ion* 532c)

2. Mualem 2012, 157.

Ion agrees and asks Socrates to explain how this can be, which he does:

> Soc. As I was saying just now, this is not an art in you, whereby you speak well on Homer, but a divine power, which moves you like that in the stone which Euripides named a magnet, but most people call "Heraclea Stone." For this stone not only attracts iron rings, but also imparts to them a power whereby they in turn are able to do the very same thing as the stone, and attract other rings; so that sometimes there is formed quite a long chain of bits of irons and rings, suspended from one another; and they all depend for this power on that one stone. In the same manner also the Muse inspires men herself, and then by means of these inspired persons the inspiration spreads to others, and holds them in a connected chain. For all the good epic poets utter all those fine poems not from art, but as inspired and possessed, and the good lyric poets likewise. . . . If they had fully learnt by art to speak on one kind of theme, they would know how to speak on all. And for this reason God takes away the mind of these men and uses them as his ministers, just as he does soothsayers and godly seers, in order that we who hear them may know that it is not they who utter these words of great price, when they are out of their wits, but that it is God himself who speaks and addresses us through them. (*Ion* 533d–534d)

In this passage, Socrates speaks of poetry as the result of a divine-human interaction carried further by subsequent performers to spectators, forming a long chain of tradents that somewhat resembles the Mesopotamian trajectory. Socrates's claim is that the literature of the poets is not the result of someone's genius or skill but is inspired by the divine (Muse).[3] However, in contrast to the Mesopotamian trajectory and indeed with Greek tradition before him,[4] he speaks of the poets

---

3. On the invocation of Muses in the construction of authority in Greek literature by both poets and philosophers, see Marincola 1997, 3–5.

4. As argued by Bingham 2016, 221–23 (cf. Marincola 1997, 3–5), in early Greece, "the Muse is an inspiring presence, but apparently only in an auxiliary capacity, one that promotes almost an autonomous poetic spirit. . . . Early Greek conceptions of inspiration differed, then, from those that Plato would later set forth. Inspiration was not understood, in the main, to place the poet into a state of unconscious passivity. Instead, by his own spirit and mind, he composed his song with the aid of the deity in such a way that the song conveyed truth."

as "out of their wits"—having had their minds taken away (see also, e.g., Plato, *Meno* 99a–c).[5] In the Mesopotamian trajectory, the human and divine were intertwined in a way that distributed agency to them both. Here, the human becomes a vessel that is completely governed by divine agency. The humans are not crafting poems but channeling revelation like mantic seers (cf. Plato, *Apol.* 22c).[6] This becomes even clearer as Socrates unpacks his ring metaphor a bit more:

> Soc. And are you aware that your spectator is the last of the rings which I spoke of as receiving from each other the power transmitted from the Heraclean lodestone? You, the rhapsode and actor, are the middle ring; the poet himself is the first; but it is the god who through the whole series draws the souls of men whithersoever he pleases, making the power of one depend on the other. And, just as from the magnet, there is a mighty chain of choric performers and masters and under-masters suspended by side-connexions from the rings that hang down from the Muse. One poet is suspended from one Muse, another from another: the word we use for it is "possessed," but it is much the same thing, for he is *held*. And from these first rings—the poets—are suspended various others, *which are thus inspired, some by Orpheus and others by Musaeus*; but the majority are possessed and held by Homer. Of whom you, Ion, are one, and are *possessed by Homer*; and so, when anyone recites the work of another poet, you go to sleep and are at a loss what to say; but when someone utters a strain of your poet, you wake up at once, and your soul dances, and you have plenty to say: for it is not by art or knowledge about Homer that you say what you say, but *by divine dispensation and possession.* (*Ion* 535e–536c)

In the choice between craft and inspiration, Socrates thus argues in favor of the latter, and while the ring metaphor distributes that inspiration to further agents—performers such as the rhapsode but also the audience, who Socrates argues can be inspired by the performance so that they laugh or cry—it is clear that the attaching of rings creates a

---

5. Cf. Mualem 2012, 158–59.

6. On the distinction between mantic seers and prophets, see further Wyrick 2004, 181–82; cf. Mualem 2012, 154–57.

distance to the original inspiration.[7] To unpack this a bit further, consider the beginning of the dialogue again, where Socrates rather sarcastically praises the skill of the rhapsode in interpreting the poet. Although it is now clear that Socrates in fact does *not* believe that the rhapsode is skilled—he is indeed rather a "fool"[8]—the dispute that follows is not around whether or not *a specific individual has created a poem* but rather *by what means*. This creates a crucial contrast to the Mesopotamian trajectory, since both Socrates and the position he critiques understand the poet as a point of origin for the poem in a way that makes her/him the focal point of attention. Put differently, although Socrates attempts to reduce the poet as somewhat of an "empty vessel"[9] and although what shines through is ultimately a negative view on inspiration, the logic of the passage is still that since the poets were inspired, inspiration was required to interpret them. How this is played out is clear in the last paragraph quoted above, where Socrates argues that Ion is possessed by *Homer himself*. In this sense, then, just as Homer was inspired by the Muse, so does the rhapsode need to be inspired by Homer to understand his poetry. Consequently, although describing the poet as possessed, Socrates still places her/him at the center of the interpretive activity. Needless to say, although their authority is implicitly attacked by Socrates,[10] Homer, Hesiod, and Archilochus were all held in high esteem as significant cultural personages in the passage above.

A preliminary and fundamental observation about the Greek trajectory is, then, that while the Mesopotamian trajectory revealed a distributive concept where a first (often unnamed) recipient is immediately sidelined, the Greek trajectory rather conveys an idea where a *specific* (named) individual and her/his (divinely inspired?) intentions are placed at the center of the interpretive activity, which is also competitive in nature—the entire dialogue between Socrates and Ion starts with Ion telling Socrates he had just won a competition (530a). Having thus set the stage, in what follows, these intertwined and debated characteristics will be further unpacked, starting with the elusive notions of authority and intent.

---

7. This can be seen in the fact that Plato also elsewhere (see, e.g., *Leg.* 669c, 719c; *Resp.* 382e) claims that the problem with poets is that they reproduce the Muse's words in a flawed manner so that ultimately, they end up contradicting themselves (so Bingham 2016, 218; cf. Mualem 2012, 158).

8. Cf. Mualem 2012, 160: "Plato skillfully manages here to create a new meta-myth in which the 'hero' is the god and the 'fool' is the poet."

9. This endeavor may thus relate to the "'ancient quarrel' between philosophy and poetry" (so Mualem 2012, 162).

10. So Mualem 2012, 161.

Interpreting the Author

As implied above, an important observation to be made is that the Greek trajectory differs from the Mesopotamian one by means of paratextual practice. In contrast to the practice of referring to texts by means of their incipits, in the Greek trajectory, texts are often quoted and referred to by means of naming an individual.[11] S/he is seen as an originator of a certain work, and since the written text was conceived of as a witness to this source, it was important that the interpretation was guided by an understanding of her/his intent.[12] The way this plays out can be seen clearly in Aristotle's *Poetics*. Here, the author is described as fundamental to the construction of literary works, and the notion that the poets are the creative sources responsible for their works is constantly assumed, not least in the way Aristotle himself quotes and refers to other works as he maps out his literary theory (cf., e.g., "Aeschylus, *in his Philoctetes*, wrote," Αἰσχύλος μὲν γὰρ ἐν τῷ Φιλοκτήτῃ ἐποίησε; *Poet.* 1458b; emphasis added).[13] Although Plato (and Aristotle) can speak of these authors as (divinely) inspired, narratives of literary production in the Greek trajectory nonetheless often assume the craft and skill of poets in a way that places them in the center of interpretation. This idea is so permeating that even works with unknown authors are referred to in light of their human author. As but one example, consider Aristotle's comparison of the works of Homer with an anonymous poet of the Epic Cycle:

---

11. As for the latter, it should be noted that it need not always have been the case (i.e., that works were only rarely transmitted anonymously). As has been discussed by experts on Homer, it is not certain that "he" ever existed—the name may have been constructed by a group of rhapsodes called the Homeridai. Understanding the *-idai* as indicating descendance, it came to be interpreted as pointing to an individual, and in light of what will be observed in relation to Greek author trajectory, the creation of such an individual would make good sense. Speaking in favor of such a view is also the possibility that the title "Homeridai" was originally a Greek translation of a Phoenician *benê 'ōmerîm* ("the sons of speakers")—that is, a name for "the tale-tellers as a professional class" (see West 1997, 622–23). It would thus provide an interesting example of how a title was reinterpreted in light of an author concept alien to the original context.

12. A good example of this is the marginal exegetical commentary to the *Iliad*, which recurrently explains what the *poet* means and teaches (Scodel 2019, 47). Cf. somewhat similarly Wyrick 2004, 395 (although not speaking of intent): "Authorship is the product of a classical and especially Hellenistic Greek literary discourse that sought to account for and explain the nature of a given text by linking its features to the circumstances of its origin, namely, to the life of its creator."

13. Translation from Halliwell 1995. The common use of ποιεω for the composition of poetry in post-Homeric Greek may in itself underline the creative human achievement.

56

As regards narrative mimesis in verse, it is clear that plots, as in tragedy, should be constructed dramatically, that is, around a single, whole, and complete action, with beginning, middle, and end, so that epic, like a single and whole animal, may produce the pleasure proper to it. . . . That is why, as I said earlier, Homer's inspired superiority over the rest can be seen here too . . . but the others build their works round a single figure or single period, hence an action of many parts, as with *the author of* the *Cypria* and the *Little Iliad* (οἷον ὁ τὰ Κύπρια ποιήσας καὶ τὴν μικρὰν Ἰλιάδα). (*Poet.* 1459a–b)[14]

Aristotle thus refers to texts by means of their author, and similarly, when speaking of the effect a lecture has on the listener, Aristotle notes that

some people will not accept the statements of a speaker unless he gives a mathematical proof; others will not unless he makes use of illustrations; others expect to have *a poet* adduced as witness (οἱ δὲ μάρτυρια ἀξιοῦσιν ἐπάγεσθαι ποιητήν). (*Metaph.* 995a)[15]

To be able to interact with other texts, one thus needed to know their (human) source.[16] Consider, for example, the words of a sixth-century poet:

Cyrnus, as I perform my skill let a seal [σφρηγὶς] lie upon these words, and they will never be stolen unnoticed, nor will anyone trade something worse for the good that is available; and everyone will say: "These are the verses of Theognis, the Megarian, known by name throughout all humanity."[17]

The notion of intellectual property and the search for the intention of an author can thus not be claimed to be alien to the ancient world,

---

14. Translation from Halliwell 1995 (emphasis added).

15. Translation from Tredennick 1996; cf. Scodel 2019, 47.

16. It could also be mentioned here that, as noted by Marincola 1997, 4–5, "part of the philosopher's claim to authority is an emphasis on their own knowledge and innovation," and the same goes for historians, who emphasized "that the work before the reader rested on the author's personal inquiry and investigation" (5).

17. Quote from Scodel 2019, 55. Interesting is that although a clear notion of authorial ownership of the collection of poems is expressed, some of the poems themselves have been argued to in fact not originate from Theogonis (see Scodel 2019, 55). For an extensive discussion, see Selle 2008. .

an ex nihilo creation of Romanticism. Note how Plato (who was noted above to speak of divine inspiration) speaks of authorial intention in *Protagoras*, which preceded these discussions by two millennia:

> The opening of the ode [of Simonides] must at once appear crazy if, *while intending to say* that it is hard for a man to become good, he inserted "indeed." There is no sort of sense, I imagine, in this insertion, *unless we suppose that Simonides is addressing himself to the saying of Pittacus as a disputant*: Pittacus says—It is hard to be good; and the poet controverts this by observing—No, but to become good, indeed, is hard for a man, Pittacus, truly— not truly good; he does not mention truth in this connexion, or imply that some things are truly good, while others are good but not truly so: *this would seem silly and unlike Simonides. (Prot. 343)*[18]

The quote illustrates clearly that knowledge about the ideas of an author was essential when attempting to understand literary works in the Greek trajectory. Since the relation between the originator and the work itself was so strong, poets could also be praised or blamed for things that their characters said as if it was their own words,[19] and the content of a poem was regularly judged in relation to what was known about the author from elsewhere. Consequently, it is not surprising that the Greek trajectory also has a growing interest in the biographies of authors.[20]

The logic behind this development is quite clear: if authorial intent is important, it follows that information about an author's life can both inform the reading of a text and, at the same time, be extracted from the author's texts (see, e.g., the relation between the idea that Homer was blind and the blind singer Demodocus in the *Odyssey*).[21] Authors could also become the subject of new poems, be honored with statues, and so on (see, e.g., the notion of a statue of Homer in Smyrna: "There is a library and the Homereion, a square stoa with a shrine of Homer and a wooden statue"; Strabo 14.1.37).[22]

---

18. Translation from Lamb 1967 (emphasis added).

19. See Scodel 2019, 47–48, for some examples.

20. Cf. Wyrick 2004, 291. See also the discussion of the later development of autobiographies in Badura and Möller 2019.

21. Cf. Wyrick 2004, 291. As noted by Helle 2020a, 58, the discussion of Homer's blindness may also be understood as a debate about "whether epic poetry was fundamentally oral or written, since a blind man could not have composed his poetry in writing."

22. Quoted from Graziosi 2002, 74.

Nothing similar is found in the Mesopotamian trajectory. Even in cases when "first ones" were mentioned by name, their lives and achievements were never used to interpret texts, even the instances where such achievements were recounted, as with, for example, Lu-Nanna, who is juxtaposed with the "Series of Etana" in the "Catalogue of Texts and Authors" and who is described in the third tablet of the incantation series *Bit Meseri* as being "two-thirds of a sage and [the one who] drove a dragon out of E-Ninkarnuna, Shulgi's temple to Ishtar."[23]

COMPETITION AND THEFT

The practices of interacting with other poets noted above are not to be seen as confined to written discourse; they also permeate the performative settings where the poems had their primary locus, as was seen in the passage quoted first in this chapter.[24] An author was thus not necessarily related to a *written* product but could be seen as either the first performer or the supervisor of the initial performance.[25] This performative aspect is shared with the Mesopotamian trajectory, and although it is here configured by the characteristics of Greek authorship, it underlines that textual fixation could not be expected in this trajectory either:[26]

> Authors, as opposed to performers of traditional material, would hope to be re-performed in situations remote from themselves both in space and time. Such re-performance would make them authors only if their texts were relatively stable—absolute fixity only became a reasonable expectation much later, and although scholars could try to establish precisely correct texts, these were often impossible under ancient conditions of transmission.[27]

However, the strong connection between authorial intent and the text itself resulted in an expectation that the integrity of a work would

---

23. Quoted from Helle 2020b, 372. On the catalog entry, see Lambert 1962, 67.

24. See also Scodel 2019, 49–53.

25. Scodel 2019, 50. Cf. Wyrick 2004, 17: "Prior to the fifth century B.C.E., composers were not differentiated from performers."

26. Cf. Peirano 2012, 68, especially her discussion of imitation and the notion of *anaplerosis*—"a type of composition that specifically elaborates on the text by addressing missing pieces of a story and expressing the point of view of characters and their reactions to specific events that are glossed over in the master-author's narrative" (19).

27. Scodel 2019, 50.

be maintained when copied. Even though marginal comments would eventually fill the manuscripts, they were regularly not provided with author designations and could thus easily be added to or omitted.

The combination of the named author being central to the interpretation of texts and the competitive performative settings also made theft possible, as indicated in Theognis's act of sealing above.[28] This is almost a truism but should not be overlooked, as it has quite far-reaching consequences not only for the understanding of an author but also for scholarly studies of authors and their texts. When Homeric epics and other texts were explicitly related to named individuals and when these individuals became indispensable for the interpretation of their texts while at the same time providing authority to the text,[29] anonymous texts would increasingly be regarded as a problem—they were in acute need of authors.[30] At the same time, in light of biographical knowledge of authors and their texts, some texts were starting to be judged as wrongly attributed, and so the notion of *pseudepigraphy* was born, both as a way of indicating mistakes in the transmission and to designate intentional forgeries, which could have been motivated by the fact that large sums of money were paid to get a hold of classical works, as indicated by some later writers:[31]

---

28. For an insightful discussion of how the origins of this kind of literary theft were conceived in the Greek trajectory as related to Ptolemy II and Peisistratus, see Wyrick 2004, 203–80. Not surprisingly, these discussions featured economic (esp. related to book trade, as will be seen below), psychological (e.g., the wish to enter a closed system of authoritative authors), personal (e.g., the desire for fame), and political (e.g., altering authoritative texts so that they would promote a certain agenda) motives. In this context, theft is primarily to be understood as "literal copying," in contrast to the creative imitation of previous authors (*mimesis*), which was held in high esteem. As argued by Marincola 1997, 12, "The literary tradition of classical antiquity . . . was conservative and, for many centuries, consciously classicizing, with appeal made to a few unchanging models of acknowledged mastery. . . . One should imagine how the masters . . . would have said the same thing" (13; cf. also Pitts 2013, 233, 233n12, on historiographic works).

29. In this sense, in the Greek trajectory, authority and anonymity came to be seen as two opposites, and it was therefore necessary to provide an author to every text (cf. somewhat similarly Wyrick 2004, 4).

30. Cf. the discussion in Speyer 1971, 111, and Peirano 2012, 45–46, pointing, among others, to a lament by Galen (*De libris propriis* 19.10.4–5): "I know, dear Bassus, the reason why many publish my work as their own: for it was given to friends and students without ascription (*epigraphē*), because they were not intended for publication, but in response to those who asked to have my lecture notes on what they heard." See also the comments on the development of these aspects in Roman times in Badura and Möller 2019, 66–67.

31. Cf. Speyer 1971, 112.

> If at any place I will insert the name of Aesopus, to whom I already paid the debt that I owed, let it be known that I do so for the sake of authority, as some artists do in our age *who fetch a greater price for their newly made artifacts if they ascribe the name of Praxiteles to their statue, that of Mys to smooth silver, that of Zeuxis to a painting.* To such an extent biting envy is more favorable to adulterated ancientness than to the good works of the present. (Faidros, *5 Praef.*)[32]

In a similar vein, Galen of Pergamon would even use this idea as an authenticity criterion, claiming that prior to the book trade, no books were ever falsely attributed:

> But since Plato wrote thus, let someone show us in which book of Hippocrates other than "On the Nature of Man" it is possible to find this method or, if it is not possible, let it be found that no one is a more trustworthy witness than Plato as to whether this book is authentic. For among other things Plato was closer in time to the disciples of Hippocrates and if the book was of one of theirs, it would have been inscribed with the very name of the writer. *For before there were kings in Alexandria and Pergamum who were competing for the acquisition of ancient books, no book was ever falsely inscribed. Those who were procuring the books having begun to accept payment, they used to bring many books having inscribed them falsely with the name of some ancient author.* But these kings lived after the death of Alexander, while Plato had written these things before the rule of Alexander when titles had not been adulterated yet but each book was displaying the name of its real writer on the title. (Galen, *Commentaria in Hippocratis De Natura Hominis* 15.104–5)[33]

The accuracy of such a theory is, of course, to be doubted,[34] but it illustrates that book trade likely played a role in the development of paratextual practices, and if compared to the Mesopotamian trajectory, although there is evidence that tablets were acquired for both major libraries and personal ones, there was no proper trade of tablets between

---

32. Quote from Peirano 2012, 51 (emphasis added). See a similar example in Speyer 1971, 112.
33. Quoted from Peirano 2012, 41.
34. Cf. the discussion in Wyrick 2004, 236.

individuals,[35] as is supposed by the quote above and seen throughout the Greek trajectory, at least from the fifth century BCE, where "some individuals began accumulating books in quantity."[36] Consider as an additional example the description of Euthydemus that introduces a dialogue between him and Socrates:

> Euthydemus, the handsome, *had formed a large collection of the works of celebrated poets and thinkers* and therefore supposed himself to be a prodigy of wisdom for his age and was confident of surpassing all competitors in power of speech and action. (Xenophon, *Mem.* 4.2.1; emphasis added)[37]

Returning to the risk of having text transmitted under a "false name," it would soon necessitate criteria by which an attribution could be evaluated, and when detected, an act of wrong attribution could have dire consequences. A case in point would be the activity of the chresmologues and how the work of Onomacritus is evaluated. Onomacritus was from Athens and lived sometime in the fifth century BCE. He is said to have "set in order" the oracles of Musaeus, but because of this work, he was banished from Athens. Why? He had been "caught by Lasus of Hermione in the act of inserting (*empoieōn*) into the writings of Musaeus an oracle, according to which the island of Lemnos should disappear into the sea."[38] His mistake was that he altered the words of "authenticated oracles" by adding material to it that did not come from the Musaeus.[39]

Here is also where the *sphragis* mentioned above by Theognis fills its paratextual function. It would contain information about the author, such as "place and year of birth, along with background information on family and financial means and sometimes also containing encoded

---

35. Cf. van der Toorn 2007, 18: "Tablet collectors did not purchase texts for money." For a brief summary, see Willgren 2016a, 400. An interesting colophon gives a window into this activity as it first provides a list of balag lamentations and then states, "I have these (out of) 21 balag lamentations. The ones I do not have, send (those) balag lamentations to me!" (for this tablet, see Gadotti and Kleinerman 2011).

36. Scodel 2019, 59.

37. Translation from Marchant and Todd 2013. There is also a mention in unassigned fragment 327 of Eupolis's works of a place "where books are for sale" (οὖ τὰ βιβλί᾽ ὤνια; Storey 2011).

38. Translation from Nissinen 2017, 141.

39. See Nissinen 2017, 141–42, who also mentions the theory of John Dillery that Lasus's comments could also have been motivated by a competitive performative setting where he recurrently polemicized against Onomacritus.

specifics only accessible to insiders,"[40] and was intended to serve as a kind of "copyright statement *avant la lettre*."[41] As an example, the *sphragis* in Vergil's *Georgica* reads as the following:

> So much I sang in addition to the care of fields, of cattle, and of trees, while great Caesar thundered in war by deep Euphrates and bestowed a victor's laws on willing nations, and essayed the path to Heaven. In those days, I, Virgil, was nursed by sweet Parthenope, and rejoiced in the arts of inglorious ease—I who toyed with shepherds' songs, and, in youth's boldness, sang of you, Tityrus, under the canopy of a spreading beech.[42]

Evidently, this paratextual practice could also contain fictional information, and a *sphragis* could be used "to give credibility to a forged set of lines."[43]

The focus on authenticity can also be seen in a work that is sometimes called the first "library catalog" (a designation possible only if sidelining the extensive Mesopotamian material)—namely, *Pinakes*, the bibliographical work of Callimachus that was supposedly written across a staggering 120(!) scrolls and systematically cataloged 'books' present in the Alexandrian library.[44] Since the actual tablets are unfortunately lost, their contents are possible to recover only by means of later references and the few fragments that remain. But even if no firm conclusions can be drawn regarding the actual system(s) used when cataloging, enough material has been gathered to paint the picture of some of its content. More specifically, when listing books, Callimachus did include not only their titles, incipits, and number of lines but also bibliographical information (books were arranged alphabetically within generic categories such as rhetorical works, laws, etc.); biographical sketches of the authors, who seem to have been arranged alphabetically within defined classes (such as philosopher, rhetor, etc.); and even discussions of dating

---

40. Badura and Möller 2019, 68.

41. So Badura and Möller 2019, 67, who also discuss the language used for "stolen" books and note that "in Martial's *Epigram* 1.52, the book stolen by a literary competitor is likened to a manumitted slave, the rival author is a *plagiarius*, a slave trader or kidnapper" (71).

42. Quoted from Badura and Möller 2019, 69.

43. Badura and Möller 2019, 70.

44. For a detailed discussion, see Blum 1991.

and authenticity.[45] Consider, for example, the following two passages, where the *Pinakes* is quoted:[46]

> Eudoxos, son of Aischines, of Knidos, astronomer, geometer, physician, legislator. He studied geometry under Archytas, and medicine under the Sicilian Philistion, as Kallimachos says in the *Pinakes*. But Sotion says in his *Successors* [of the philosophers] that he had [also] heard Plato. . . .

> He [Parmenides] philosophizes in verse, just as Hesiod, Zenophanes and Empedokles . . . and it seems that he was the first to discover that the Evening star and the Morning star are the same; but others say it was Pythagoras. Kallimachos, however, says that *the work was not by him* [i.e., not by Pythagoras].

Behind these evaluations were criteria developed by the Alexandrian grammarians into what has been designated as *Echtheitskritik*.[47]

ECHTHEITSKRITIK AND PSEUDEPIGRAPHY

The first observation to be made is that although the emanating discussion of the authenticity of author designations (*Echtheitskritik*), which became commonplace in the third century BCE (its roots are likely to be found earlier), was likely related to the grammarians' cataloging of texts in the new libraries of, for example, Pella, Antioch, Pergamon, and Alexandria as well as their editing of texts,[48] where individual lines needed authentication, it does not suffice as an explanation, since no such discussions followed similar needs in the Mesopotamian trajectory and the libraries of Ashurbanipal. This is indeed a crucial observation: in the

---

45. Cf. Scherbenske 2013, 42–46; Scodel 2019, 61. Spurious works may even have been distinguished from the genuine ones by being placed at the end, in a separate list (so Blum 1991, 234). According to Wyrick 2004, 289–90, the list was necessary because "the works of a given author might not necessarily be shelved together, since sometimes scrolls might contain works of more than one author and were shelved according to the author of the first work in the scroll."

46. Quote from Blum 1991, 152, 158 (emphasis added), where more examples are found.

47. The term *Echtheitskritik* is Speyer's. Other suggestions include "attribution analysis" (so Blum 1991; Wyrick 2004) and more plainly "literary criticism" (so Pfeiffer 1968). The Greek term related to this critical work is found in Dionysius Thrax as the sixth and "fairest" of the grammarian's task: κρίσις ποιημάτων.

48. So Speyer 1971, 115; cf. Najman 2014, 38.

Mesopotamian trajectory, there are *no discussions of false attributions*—a direct consequence of the fact that authors were conceived of along quite different lines. Only in the Greek trajectory did libraries and editorial work lead to authenticity discussions, and only here is it plausible to argue that these two factors could have been decisive in the development of this practice.[49]

As for the actual system, the grammarians developed three categories of classification, with the first two most regularly used: (1) "legitimate" writings (γνήσια), (2) "bastard" writings (νόθα), and (3) "ambiguous" writings (employing different terms such as ἀμφίβολα, ἀμφιδοξούμενα, or ἀμφιβαλλόμενα).[50] Among the things inquired into to assess authenticity were *style, vocabulary, teaching, contradictions*, and *anachronisms*, alongside such things as what *alphabet, dialect* (language), or *writing material* was used as well as a possible lack of *quotations* in sources where they would have been expected.[51]

Moreover, a system of critical signs was developed in the early third century, probably starting with Zenodotus of Ephesus and then expanded by Aristarchus of Samothrace in the Library of Alexandria.[52] These signs were placed in the margins and were intended to indicate whether the editor saw the text as genuine or not (the *obelos*), if lines were also found in other parts of the poem (*asteriskos*), and if two consecutive lines were interchangeable (*sigma* and *antisigma*).[53] Some examples, not limited to the Alexandrian grammarians, will paint the picture of the widespread nature of these discussions. Consider, for example, Herodotus, who questioned whether Homer was the author of the Cyprian poems:[54]

---

49. Thus the argument by Peirano 2012, 38, that libraries "forced the librarians to decide between genuine and spurious works" and that the editing of texts "demanded evaluation of the authenticity of individual lines and expressions" (39) is only true for the Greek trajectory.

50. Speyer 1971, 122. Cf. the similar distinction in Eusebius's *Hist. eccl.* 3.25: "recognized writings," "disputed writings," and "rejected writings." The interesting fact that familial terms are used to describe the status of texts will be further discussed below. See also the discussion in Peirano 2012, where she, among others, notes that "metaphorical usage of the lexicon of paternity in the Greek exploits the commonly found notion that an author is in a sense the father of his own writings" (38).

51. See the overview in Speyer 1971, 112–28, 152–55, 179–210. See also the discussions in Peirano 2012; and Najman and Peirano 2019.

52. So Peirano 2012, 39; cf. Speyer 1971, 116; Wyrick 2004, 260.

53. Following the overview in Peirano 2012, 39, who also shows how this practice continued with the Romans.

54. Cf. also the note in *History* 4.32, where he is not certain that Homer wrote the *Epigonean epic*. Speyer 1971, 114, calls Herodot "der erste Echtheitskritiker."

In these verses [referring to a passage from the *Odyssey*] the poet shows that he knew of Alexandrus' wanderings to Egypt; for Syria borders on Egypt, and the Phoenicians, to whom Sidon belongs, dwell in Syria. *These verses and this passage prove most clearly that the Cyprian poems are by the hand not of Homer but of another.* For the Cyprian poems relate that Alexandrus reached Ilion with Helen in three days from Sparta, having a fair wind and a smooth sea; but according to the Iliad he wandered from his course in bringing her. (*Hist.* 2.116–17)[55]

See also Diogenes of Laertius's *Lives of the Philosophers*, where it is recounted how

Favorinus in the first book of his *Memorabilia* declares that the speech of Polycrates against Socrates *is not authentic* (Φαβωρῖνος δέ φησιν ἐν τῷ πρώτῳ τῶν Ἀπομνημονευμάτων μὴ εἶναι ἀληθῆ τὸν λόγον τὸν Πολυκράτους κατὰ Σωκράτους); for he mentions the rebuilding of the walls by Conon, which did not take place till six years after the death of Socrates. And this is the case. (2.39)[56]

Or see Dionysius of Halicarnassus's discussion of Dinarchus's works:

I said nothing about the orator Dinarchus in my writings on the ancient orators because he was neither the inventor of an individual style, as were Lysias, Isocrates and Isaeus, nor the perfecter of styles which others had invented, as I judge Demosthenes, Aeschines and Hyperides to have been. But I observe that many have thought that this man also deserves renown for the brilliance of his oratory; I observe too that he left both public and private speeches which are inconsiderable neither in number nor in quality. Therefore I have decided that he should not be passed over, but that for serious students of rhetoric, who do not wish merely to don the trappings of the art, it is imperative, or at any rate a matter of high priority, *to examine his life and style and to distinguish between his genuine and spurious speeches.* At the same time, however, I saw that neither Callimachus nor the grammarians from Pergamum had written any detailed study of him, and that through this failure to examine him in greater detail *they had committed errors which have resulted not only in many falsifications*

---

55. Translation from Godley 1920.
56. Translation from Hicks 1925a. See also, e.g., 6.80 and 8.8.

but also in the ascription to Dinarchus of many speeches which are not his at all, and to others of speeches which were written by him. . . .

After these prefatory remarks there still remains one very necessary task, to determine his life-span, in order to be able to say something definite on *the matter of which speeches are genuinely* (γνησίων) *his and which are not.* Now we assume that he returned from exile at the age of seventy, as he himself says when he calls himself an old man; since it is from this age onwards that we most commonly call men at this time of life old. If we base our calculations upon this general approximation (for we have no other precise information), he would have been born during the archonship of Nicophemus. If anyone says that he was born earlier or later than the date stated he will, in addition to adopting an unsound argument, also be depriving him of many of his speeches, or rather all except five or six; for he will be saying that he was too old to have written some and too young to have written others. What is more, we should not be wrong if we were to say that he began to write speeches at the age of twenty-five or twenty-six, especially since Demosthenes and his party were at the height of their power at that time. Pythodemus is the twenty-sixth archon after Nicophemus. Therefore if anyone assumes as genuine any speeches that we find to be earlier than the year of this archon, we may reasonably disbelieve him; and again we might similarly include in the list of spurious speeches those completed between the archonships of Anaxicrates and Philippus: for nobody would have sailed to Chalcis for speeches, either public or private: they were not so completely at a loss for speeches. (*Din.* 1, 4)[57]

Dionysius then continues with a discussion of the style of Dinarchus and provides a comprehensive overview of his works, where spurious works are discussed in detail. Regarding *On Behalf of the Athmoneis*, for example, he concludes that it is falsely ascribed (i.e., by mistake) to him (ψευδεπίγραφοι εἰς αὐτὸν λόγοι εἰσὶν οἵδε, *Din.* 11), since it would have been written when Dinarchus was only twenty-one years old.[58] Another speech is deemed as not by him, since it critiques the oligarchy, while Dinarchus was "a friend of those who had established the oligarchy" (*Din.* 11), and yet another was deemed as written in a style different

---

57. Translation from Usher 1985. In *Roman Antiquities*, he also claims that there are "interpolations among the genuine Sibylline oracles, being recognized as such by means of the so-called acrostics" (4.62.6).

58. Najman and Peirano 2019. See also *De. Din.* 13, where many private speeches are deemed as spurious on similar grounds, and the discussion in Speyer 1971, 119.

from Dinarchus's: "One can find in it, if nothing else, much that is silly and quibbling, characteristics which are far removed from those of Dinarchus" (*Din.* 11).

What this discussion shows is that although what is today labeled as "literary fraud"—that is, *intentionally* false attribution—certainly existed (cf. Theognis and Galen above), most discussions are attempts to identify mistakes (some caused by, e.g., homonymy, either of authors or of works).[59] Pseudepigraphy can thus fundamentally be described as "texts that are suspected, and in many cases proven, not to be the work of the author to whom they are ascribed"[60]—that is, without specifying if the false attribution was intentional or not.[61] Moreover, it should not be automatically concluded by these discussions that such attributions were always deemed problematic.[62] Instead, there is ample evidence that texts could be attributed to important figures of the past, despite being written by disciples of that figure,[63] a practice well in line with what Foucault labeled a *discourse tied to its founder*.[64] Diogenes of Laertius, for

---

59. Cf. the quote from Philoponus in Wyrick 2004, 230–33, where these two unintentional misattributions are mentioned together with a third—intentional fraud motivated by economy.

60. Peirano 2012, 1. See a further example in, e.g., Athenaeus, *Deipnosophists* 12.11.

61. Peirano 2012, 43. See the illuminating discussion of *imitation* in Najman and Peirano 2019: "Humans are continually invited to emulate through exemplars and by being godlike. Similarly, in the work of pseudepigraphy, the expansion, refinement, and extension of new texts (processes of editing and interpretation) is not a practice of transgression but one of ethical formation."

62. This has been argued in particular by Najman and Peirano 2019 in their analysis of the language used in authenticity discussions, a language that often speaks of texts in terms of "familial" relations. See also Peirano 2012, 32, who underscores that "notions of authenticity—the investigation and assessment of the legitimacy and truth of authorial attributions—are inextricably connected with a culture's understanding of 'truth,' 'reality,' and 'fiction,' all concepts that are culturally specific."

63. Najman and Peirano 2019. Cf. Peirano 2012, 6: "In the cases of Orpheus, Musaeus, and, later, Hippocrates and Pythagoras, authorial attribution, far from being the formulation of a traceable authorial source, is a required marker of discourse that wants to impose itself as 'truth.'"

64. This is therefore often argued to be a good way to understand ancient pseudepigraphy—that is, not to see it as "fraud" but as a common practice. To a high extent, this is true, although the material above has shown more nuances and, most importantly, a contrast to the Mesopotamian trajectory. An often cited example is from later Christian tradition, where Tertullian defends the authority of the Gospel of *Luke* by relating it to Paul: "On the whole, then, if that is evidently more true which is earlier, if that is earlier which is from the very beginning, if that is from the beginning which has the apostles for its authors, then it will certainly be quite as evident, that that comes down from the apostles, which has been kept as a sacred deposit in the churches of the apostles. . . . The same authority of the apostolic churches will afford evidence to the other Gospels also, which we possess equally [as Luke's] through their means, and according to their usage—I mean

example, describes how, according to Ion of Chios, Pythagoras "in his *Triagmi* . . . ascribed some poems of his own making to Orpheus" (*Lives* 8.1.8).[65] This also points to the observation that ancient literature

the Gospels of John and Matthew—whilst that which Mark published may be affirmed to be Peter's, whose interpreter Mark was. For even Luke's form of the Gospel men usually ascribe to Paul. *And it may well seem that the works which disciples publish belong to their masters*" (*Adv. Marc.* 4.5, quoted from Roberts and Donaldson 1965; emphasis added; see also, e.g., Speyer 1971, 34–35; Meade 1986, 10; Najman 2003, 13; on the note of Mark interpreting Peter, cf. Plato above). The point made, as is clear from his argument earlier in the text, is based on the argument that the teaching of the church is coherent and consistent, and that is why the attribution of these texts to a person that was not part of the apostles does not pose a problem: "Luke, however, was not an apostle, but only an apostolic man; not a master, but a disciple, and so inferior to a master—at least as far subsequent to him as the apostle whom he followed (and that, no doubt, was Paul) was subsequent to the others; so that, had Marcion even published his Gospel in the name of Saint Paul himself, the single authority of the document, destitute of all support from preceding authorities, would not be a sufficient basis for our faith. There would be still wanted that Gospel which Saint Paul found in existence, to which he yielded his belief, and with which he so earnestly wished his own to agree" (*Adv. Marc.* 4.2). In Tertullian's view, then, "the designation of the correct *auctor* for each gospel is essential to the authority of the gospels" (Wyrick 2004, 300; emphasis in the original). This is clearly a hierarchy in the transmission of texts foreign to the Mesopotamian trajectory. A final example is Peirano, who points to Origen, who approves relating the epistle to the Hebrews to Paul (ὡς Παύλου), "despite the fact that 'the thoughts are those of the apostle, but the diction and phraseology are those of someone who remembered the apostolic teachings, and wrote down at his leisure what had been said by his teacher' (6.25.13). Origen approves of those who call the epistle the work of Paul since it chimes with the *noemata* of the apostle" (Najman and Peirano 2019).

65. Quoted from Hicks 1925b. He also compiled lists of homonymous authors (see Blum 1991, 202). See also Clement of Alexandria's *Strom.* 1.131.4; Iamblichus, *De vita Pythagorica* 198–99; or Aristotle, who probably doubted that Orpheus was the author of the Orphic poems (*Gen. an.* 2.1; *De an.* 1.5; cf. John Philoponus commentary on Aristotle's *De an.*): "He says 'in the so-called poems,' since the poems do not seem to be by Orpheus, as Aristotle himself says in *On Philosophy*. For the doctrines are his (Orpheus') but they say that Onomacritus put them into verse" (quoted from https://livingpoets.dur.ac.uk/w/Iohannes_Philoponus,_Commentary_on_De_Anima_1.5,_410b27). Somewhat related is also the statement by Plato, *Ep.* II.314b–c (a letter sometimes argued to be pseudepigraphic; see Najman 2003, 13n27), that "the greatest safeguard [against the abandonment of sound doctrine] is to avoid writing and to learn by heart; for it is not possible that what is written down should not get divulged. *For this reason I myself have never yet written anything on these subjects, and no treatise by Plato exists or will exist, but those which now bear his name belong to a Socrates become fair and young.* Fare thee well, and give me credence; and now, to begin with, read this letter over repeatedly and then burn it up" (translation from Bury 1929; emphasis added). The statement may be related to *Ep.* VII.341c–d: "There does not exist, nor will there ever exist, any treatise of mine dealing therewith. For it does not at all admit of verbal expression like other studies, but, as a result of continued application to the subject itself and communion therewith, it is brought to birth in the soul on a sudden, as light that is kindled," where the notion of inspiration discussed above is also mentioned.

was often held in higher esteem than contemporary texts[66] so that an act of false attribution may have been motivated by both economic factors (as seen above) and the desire to be read.[67]

CENTRALIZED AUTHORS

Although there are things that unite the two trajectories surveyed so far, it has hopefully been sufficiently clear that they deal with authorship in quite distinct ways. The Mesopotamian trajectory was seen to be largely anonymous, and when it related a name to a text, the individual was quickly sidelined, pointing to a fundamentally distributive notion of authorship where the named individual was best understood as someone in a series of tradents partaking in the transmission of the overflow of a divine-human revelatory interaction to ever-new recipients. Nowhere did authors play any role in the interpretation of texts, and discussions about intentions and authenticity were not found so that ultimately, the named ones could be seen not as indicating the *founder* of a discourse but rather as providing a (possible) way of *demarcating* a discourse.

The Greek trajectory, however, regularly related texts to named individuals and understood these individuals as important for the interpretation of the text (to be underscored again is that what has been surveyed in these chapters are native descriptions, and as such, they should be taken not as historically accurate statements of the formation of certain texts but as testimonies to ways authorship has been constructed). Although they could also be understood as divinely inspired, the emphasis was less on the divine-human interaction (as in the Mesopotamian trajectory) and more on the inspiration of an individual that would then be seen as responsible for her/his works. To understand the work, one thus needed to situate oneself as close as possible to the originator (as illustrated by Socrates's "Heraclea Stone"). This points to an author hierarchy where authority is distributed in a way different from the Mesopotamian one (see figure 1). The Mesopotamian trajectory located authority in the *text* so that "first" and "subsequent" tradents were not suspended from one another to form a long chain where the last ring was farther away from the stone than the first but rather were all suspended on the stone itself. In contrast, the Greek trajectory located

---

66. Cf. Peirano 2012, 51.
67. Cf. Peirano 2012, 53.

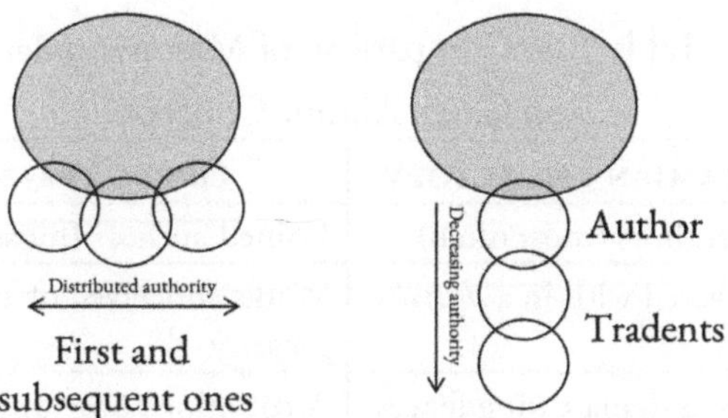

Figure 1. Authority in the Mesopotamian (left) and Greek (right) trajectories

authority in the originator of a text or founder of a discourse so that the text derived authority through her/him.

A final observation is that, as a paratextual habit of naming texts became commonplace and as ancient texts were increasingly coveted and valued, the author concept of the Greek trajectory also made authenticity discussions necessary. In all, this points to the centrality of the author in the Greek trajectory.

HELLENISTIC NEGOTIATIONS

What happens, then, when the two trajectories meet? A few examples pertaining to the intersection between the Mesopotamian and Greek trajectories in Hellenistic times will be provided here to set the stage for the ensuing discussion of the 'book' called *Isaiah*. A fuller discussion including *Isaiah* and other Second Temple texts will be provided in parts 4 and 5. To aid the identification of features from the different trajectories, a general overview is provided in table 1.

The first example of traces of Greek influence upon Mesopotamian literature to be presented here is one of the last preserved catalogs, a single-column tablet from Uruk. Dated to the second century BCE[68]— that is, at the very end of cuneiform culture—it provides a curious list of famous kings combined with the names of famous scribes (*um-man-nu*) that is organized by dividing lines into three major epochs of Mesopotamian history.[69] Presented in such a way, it stands in quite some contrast to earlier catalogs[70] so that the tablet

---

68. The tablet was first published in Dijk 1962. The colophon specifies the tablet to the tenth day of the month Ayyar, year 147, King Antiochos IV (45).

69. Helle 2018, 222.

70. Helle 2018, 220, calls it a "fundamental break with the tradition of the time."

Table 1. A Comparison of Mesopotamian
and Greek Author Concepts

MESOPOTAMIAN TRAJECTORY	GREEK TRAJECTORY
No named authors (most often)	Named authors (most often)
Works interacted with in a *distributive* way	Works conceived of as somebody's *property*
Attributions as demarcating fences to *distinguish* a work from other works	Attributions providing texts with authority by pointing to *originators* or *founders* of discourses
No conceptual difference between the "first ones" and the "subsequent ones" in the transmission of texts; no clear distinction between originator, redactor, scribe, etc.	Conceptual difference between originators and later tradents in the transmission of texts; originators are distinguished from tradents (redactors, scribes, etc.)
Authority located in the *text*	Authority located in the *author*
No concept of pseudepigraphy	Many examples of pseudepigraphy (both *mistaken* and *intentional*)
Texts as the result of divine-human interactions—two spheres that are difficult to distinguish	Texts as the result of divine-human interactions—two spheres that can often be distinguished
Interpretive activity focuses on the *text*	Interpretive activity focuses on *both text and author*
An "author" is best understood as a *tradent*	An "author" is best understood as an *originator*

tells a miniature history of the city of Uruk, its gods, temples, and scholars. It functioned as a form of "historical autobiography" for Anu-belshunu, outlining the origins of his professional and local identity—and did so at a point in time when that identity was at its most fragile.[71]

The named scholars are thus seen as authors who are highlighted as important cultural figures and serve as signposts in a literary landscape—they have become discourse markers for the gathering of

---

71. Helle 2018, 224.

cuneiform classics. Interestingly, the presence of Kabti-ilāni-Marduk, for example, evokes the *Erra Epic*.[72] All this indicates that the Mesopotamian trajectory had changed in some significant respects, and if understanding the list as an attempt to argue cultural superiority in a Hellenistic world, it is not surprising that the changes in fact overlap with the Greek trajectory. One example from the list shows this with all clarity—the observation that Gilgamesh is mentioned in combination with Sîn-lēqi-unninnu:

> [In the time of] king? [Gilgam]esh?: the scholar was Sin-leqi-unninni.[73]

It was noted in the discussion of the *Epic of Gilgamesh* in chapter 3 that the epic, after having circulated without any author designation for a long time, was eventually associated with Sîn-lēqi-unninnu in the "Catalogue of Texts and Authors." Such an association was then understood in light of the Mesopotamian trajectory sketched so far—namely, that Sîn-lēqi-unninnu was named a "subsequent one," a tradent who created "a new weave" (in this case a "standard edition"; cf. Esagil-kīn-apli). It was also noted how such paratextual information did not have any significant impact on the interpretation of the text itself. It is in relation to this observation that the Uruk list reveals a fundamental change. First, it can be observed that names are not mentioned *alongside* texts but rather serve as metonymic *replacements* for the latter.[74] Second and more importantly, the list indicates that paratextual information such as the one found in the "Catalogue of Texts and Authors" has been *reinterpreted in light of a Greek understanding of authorship*, with the consequence that Sîn-lēqi-unninnu is projected back to the time of Gilgamesh(!).[75] He was no longer a subsequent one but the founder of a discourse.

---

72. Helle 2018, 226. Cf. Hallo 1963, 175.

73. Quoted from Helle 2018, 222. The tablet also features Esagil-kīn-apli in relation to a king whose name is not possible to reconstruct, Kabti-ilāni-Marduk in relation to (possibly) Naram-Sin (see also Hallo 1963, 174–75), and also gives the name of the scholar related to Esarhaddon in three languages: Aba-Enlil-dari, Ahiqar, and Achiacharus (cultural appropriation?). Clear overlaps can be seen with the "Catalogue of Texts and Authors" discussed above. Noteworthy is also that in the colophon, the scribe of the tablet traces his heritage to Sîn-lēqi-unninnu.

74. Cf. Helle 2018, 230.

75. Cf. Frahm 2011, 319. As explained by Hallo 1963, 174n58, "That the link implies an attempt to 'date' these authors follows from the plausible restoration [*ina tarṣi*] at the head of each entry by van Dijk" (see van Dijk 1962, 46). See also Helle 2020b, 65: "The authorial attribution anachronistically projects a textual stability that was only

Another indication of the influence of the Greek trajectory on the Mesopotamian one is that fraud was starting to be discussed. As argued above, the way these discussions were shaped in the Greek material presupposed a Greek notion of authorship. So when similar arguments are made in the Mesopotamian trajectory in Hellenistic times, it is not far-fetched to assume a Greek influence. Consider, for example, the *Uruk Chronicle concerning the Kings of Ur*, also from the Seleucid era (the copy is dated to August 14, 251 BCE), where Šulgi, king of Ur, and Lu-Nanna, a scholar (*um-ma-nu*), are accused of tampering with rites:

> The divine Šulgi, son of a daughter of King Utu-ḫegak of Uruk, with the blind Lu-nanna, the scholar, [.?.]—there was [spiteful]ness in their hearts!—improperly tampered with the rites of the cult of Anu, Uruk's regulations, [the] secret [know]ledge of the wise, [and] put down in writing the forced labor exacted by Sîn, lord of Ur. [During] his [rei]gn, he *composed untruthful stelae, insolent writings*, [(concerning) the rites of pur]ification for the gods, and *left them to posterity*.[76]

Although this text is not strictly discussing false attribution, it does mention writing in a prominent place as to negatively evaluate the meddling with the rites by Šulgi and Lu-Nanna, and this is seen more clearly if compared to the way in which the questionable acts of Šulgi is understood in some earlier texts, such as the *Chronicle of the Esagila* (no earlier than 1100 BCE) and the *Chronicle of Ancient Kings* (late Babylonian period):

> (Then Marduk) entrusted the kingship over all their lands to Šulgi, son of Ur-Namma, but he did not perform his rites in their totality, contaminated his cleansing ceremonies, and his mind [*was deranged* (?)].[77]

> Šulgi, son of Ur-Namma, abundantly provided food for Eridu that is on the seashore. However, full of bad intentions, he carried away as booty the wealth of the Esagila and Babylon. Bēl . . . and made to consume (?) his corpse, . . . destroyed him.[78]

---

achieved at a later stage in the epic's development onto a mythical time before this development had ever begun."

76. Quoted from Glassner 2004, 289.

77. Glassner 2004, 269 (emphasis in the original).

78. Glassner 2004, 271.

Although these texts may not refer to the same event, it is noteworthy that the tampering with the cult is directly related to the writing of fraudulent texts in the *Uruk Chronicle*, while no such connection is made in the earlier texts. However, it is also clear that the notion of fraud is not anywhere near the more explicit discussion pertaining to Greek *Echtheitskritik*, and so they need not necessarily be interpreted as very dissimilar to recurring discussions about the truthfulness of political speech in Mesopotamian discourse.[79]

In the end, the two Uruk texts cannot serve as more than possible hints of Greek influence upon the Mesopotamian trajectory, since they are but small ripples on the vast sea of ancient literature—some of the last contributions of a disappearing cuneiform culture—but they indicate that as the focus will now be on the 'book' called *Isaiah*, it will be relevant to keep an eye on the characteristics of both trajectories and the possible effects that author negotiations in Hellenistic times may have on how the relation between the prophet and the 'book' is constructed, not least regarding reinterpretations of paratextual material in line with Greek authorship ideals and discussions of possible fraud.

So with these two different native authorship theories outlined, the time is now ripe to take a closer look at how the relation between the prophet Isaiah and the 'book' called *Isaiah* is constructed in the 'book' itself.

---

79. For an overview, see Pongratz-Leisten 2002. See also Liverani 2010.

Part III

THE PROPHET ISAIAH AS A MESOPOTAMIAN AUTHOR

CHAPTER 5

THE FIRST ONE

In the 'book' called *Isaiah*, a couple of places mention writing explicitly. Notably, these are not Isa 1:1; 2:1; and 13:1. Although the three well-known paratexts introduce sections of prophetic material, they do not mention writing per se but rather frame the 'book' as in some way related to the prophet. To inquire into the question of how this relation is conceived, the investigation thus needs to start elsewhere.

In what follows, the focus will first (in chapter 5) be on the parts of the 'book' called *Isaiah* where written texts or acts of writing are found. Then in chapter 6, the observation that the surveyed writing activity overflows beyond a single individual will be explored, a discussion that, in turn, provides the basis for a diachronically sensitive analysis of the paratexts and their function in chapter 7.

Presented in such a way, it should be emphasized again that the focus of this part of the study is not on the formation of the 'book' called *Isaiah*. Various sources or layers of redaction will not be discussed in any length, nor will the historical accuracy of the studied texts be inquired into. The focus will instead be on unpacking how a tradition identifying prophetic discourse with a prophet called Isaiah is taking shape. However, since the development of such a tradition over time is of importance, the survey needs to be diachronically sensitive and in this sense relate to issues of formation.

PROPHETS WITHOUT BOOKS

Before looking at the 'book' called *Isaiah*, two preliminary clarifications are in place regarding the relation between prophets and prophetic literature. The first relates to the fact that in both ancient Mesopotamia and ancient Greece, prophets were rarely seen as authors. The second is that in contrast to the anonymous transmission of literature in the Mesopotamian trajectory, prophetic oracles were often transmitted together with the names of the prophets. How is this to be understood?

Starting with the first, it can be observed that although the construction of authorship around a divine-human interaction creates clear conceptual overlaps with the task of a prophet,[1] a connection between prophets and written texts is not always evident. In fact, prophecy most often appears in oral contexts and is only rarely written down.[2] Nonetheless, it is often suggested that the compilation of the prophetic 'books' of the Hebrew Bible, if understood as collections of separate oracles, may be understood in light of Neo-Assyrian oracle collections—archival tablets on which oracles were gathered by scribes and stored away—although these were very limited in size,[3] and not many have been found.[4] If correct, it would point to a general disconnect between prophets and prophetic literature, since the written transmission was created by agents *other* than the prophets, who were most often illiterate.[5]

This then leads to the second observation, that on those occasions where individual prophetic oracles were indeed written down (regularly in letters; cf., e.g., 2 Chr 21:12–15), especially in ancient Near Eastern contexts, it was not unusual to name the prophet in question together with information regarding the place of origin for the prophecy.[6] A few examples will paint the picture. Consider first the Mari letters, where prophets are regularly related to specific deities:[7]

> A prophet of Adad, lord of Kallassu. . . . A prophet of Adad, lord of Aleppo, came [with Abu-]ḫalim and spoke to me. . . . This is what the pr[ophet of] Adad, lord of Aleppo, said in the presence of Abu-ḫalim. (no. 1)

> Abiya, prophet of Adad, the lord of Alep[po], came to me and said: "Thus says Adad . . ." (no. 2)

1. Cf. Nissinen 2019, 1, who defines prophecy as a "human transmission of allegedly divine messages," so that the prophets can be seen as acting as "direct mouthpieces of gods whose messages they communicate." Prophecy is thus basically "a process of transmission."
2. So especially Nissinen 2003 and Nissinen 2017; cf. Kratz 2015, 28.
3. See, e.g., van Seters 2000, 85–88; van der Toorn 2009, 123.
4. See Parpola 1997, lxii–lxiv.
5. For a thorough and updated discussion of these issues, see especially Nissinen 2017.
6. Sometimes these scribal notes also included time (see Hilber 2015, 155). For a discussion of the letter genre and its possible relation to written prophecy, see Schniedewind 2019, 95–119.
7. Numbers and translations are from Nissinen 2019.

S[peak t]o Zimri-L[im]: Thus the prophet of [Ša]maš: Thus says Šamaš . . . (no. 4)

In the temple of Ḫišamitum, a [pr]ophet called Iṣi-aḫu arose and said . . . (no. 5)

Lupaḫum, prophet of Dagan, arrived here from Tattul. The message that my lord entrusted him in Sagaratum . . . (no. 9)

Several observations can be made. The first is that although not all of these in fact mention the *name* of the prophet, it is clear that the intertwined divine and human agency noted in the discussion of the Mesopotamian trajectory is present here (see above, chapter 3), indicating that the prophetic *message* (not the prophet) is the focal point. Second, it is equally clear that the (named) prophets in some way provide authorizing frameworks for the divine discourses, which in the Mari letters (and the ancient Near East in general, in contrast to Greek sources) most often concerned the kings. It is not clear, however, how this dynamic plays out. Third, the examples imply that the written versions of the orally delivered prophecies are not created by the prophets themselves, in line with the observation above. In circumstances when the written medium was needed to deliver a prophecy, more agents than the prophet her-/himself were activated.[8]

To unpack the notion of an authorizing framework a bit further, consider the Nineveh oracles, where prophetic authority was often bound to an "affiliation with the temples of Ištar,"[9] indicating that "the divine authority of their messages . . . weighted more than their personalities."[10] If correct, it would emphasize further that the naming of a prophet was ultimately not concerned with her/him but rather intended to show "that the oracle in question was really spoken in an appropriate context."[11] Put differently, the name was included to guarantee that the words did in fact *not* originate with the prophet but with the *deity*. Consider the following examples:[12]

---

8. Evidently, prophets could be both male and female and everything in between (see, e.g., the interesting formulation in letter no. 71, quoted below). On this issue, see further the contributions in Stökl and Carvalho 2013.

9. So Nissinen 2019, 108.

10. Nissinen 2019, 108.

11. Nissinen 2019, 110; cf. Nissinen 2017, 98: "The colophons serve the purpose of demonstrating that the oracles were really spoken and that they have an accredited background."

12. Quoted from Nissinen 2003.

By the mouth of Issar-la-tašiyaṭ, a man from Arbela. (no. 68)
By the mouth of Sinqiša-amur, a woman from Arbela. (no. 69)
By the mouth of the woman Bayâ, a man from Arbela. (no. 71)
Tašmetu-ereš, the p[rophet], prop[hesied this i]n Arbela. (no. 91)

In all these cases, the deity speaks *through* the prophet, by her/his mouth, thus constructing prophecy along the lines of oral performance while indicating that the written versions are in some sense *removed* from the prophets, as noted above. It can thus be suggested that an important reason for including the name was to bridge this gap between the original performative context and the written substitute, but how does this bridging work?

It is well known that in the Hebrew Bible and the cultures surrounding it, names were often seen as related to reality,[13] personality,[14] and—most significant for the discussion here—presence.[15] Put differently, when, in the Hebrew Bible, YHWH proclaims his name, his presence is manifested (Exod 33:18–23; Deut 4:7). In light of what has been said above, the fact that prophetic utterances were transmitted with a "name tag" can thus be understood as ensuring prophetic presence and divine authority at that remote location in which the oracle was delivered. It is the means by which the prophet, so to speak, tags along. This is further underscored by the fact that regularly, the prophet's hair and threads from her/his garment would also be included.[16] The primary function of the name thus is not as a discourse marker of prophetic speech but is related to a specific performative context.

This focus on performative contexts is even further underscored by the observation that when seen from the perspective of legal acts (see, e.g., Ps 49:12 or Jer 15:16), the inclusion of the name of the prophet also ensured that s/he would be awarded:[17]

One shekel of silver, according to the market weights, to Lupaḫum, prophet (*āpilum*) of Dagan, when he went to Tuttul.

---

13. As an example, *Enuma Elish* begins by talking about a time before the heavens and the earth had been named (cf. Gen 2:19; see, e.g., Foster 2003, 391).

14. See, for example, how the names Jacob and Nabal are used in biblical narratives (cf. ואדעך בשם in Ex 33:17), so Mettinger 1987, 18–19.

15. See especially Mettinger 1987, 17–20 (translated into English as Mettinger 1988).

16. As suggested by Malamat 1998, 78–79, the inclusion of these items may have functioned as an "identity card." At the very least, they enforce the notion of the presence of the prophet (cf. also Durand 1988, 40; and the overview in Nissinen 2000, 258).

17. Quotes from Nissinen 2017, 63, 65.

6 minas (of copper to) the pro[p]he[t] at the [city] gate.
1 mina of c[oppe]r (to) the au[gu]r.
[1 (?)] mina to the house [of the god].
[2 (?) m]inas to [. . .].
T[otal], 10 minas.

Returning to the observation made above that several agents would have been involved in those cases where prophetic oracles were delivered in writing and that this would create a disconnect between the prophet and prophetic literature, it can be further noted that when oracles were made part of a literary transmission, the names were often dropped. Looking at the three Neo-Assyrian oracle collection tablets that have been preserved, for example, it is noteworthy that in one of them, some of the oracles are listed without a name.[18] This is also often the case when several oracles are combined in reports, as in, for example, the following words concerning the Elamites, where the name of the prophet is not included:[19]

> [*God*] says as follows: | "I have go[ne and I ha]ve come." | He s[ai]d (this) five, six times, and then: | "I have come from the [m]ace. I have | pulled out the snake which was inside it, I | have cut it in pieces, and I have broken the mace." | And (he said) "I will destroy Elam; its | army shall be levelled to the ground. In this | manner I will finish Elam."[20]

It thus seems as if the literary transmission would sideline the name, and this can be further substantiated by the observation that on those (rare) occasions when prophetic oracles had been stored away in archives by (anonymous?) scribes whose names have not been preserved and later scribes reused them by quoting them in new compositions,[21] the names of the prophets seem to have had little significance.[22] These quotes also indicate that the scribes were not bound by the "original" wordings but could rephrase the prophecies quite freely.[23] All this points to the conclusion that while the name of the prophet performed a function in the

---

18. Parpola 1997, lxiii–lxiv.

19. On these issues, see especially Nissinen 2000, 248–54.

20. Translation from Parpola 1997, 40 (emphasis in the original).

21. See Parpola 1997, lv.

22. In fact, none of the examples provided in Nissinen 2000, 263–68, include the names of prophets, who are rather referred to as *āpilum*, *ḫzyn*, etc.

23. So Nissinen 2000, 267.

initial performative setting, once the oracle had been delivered (either in person or by letter, etc.), the name was no longer important and thus not necessary to include in subsequent literary transmission. The logic seems clear enough: since the name had served to guarantee that the prophecy originated not with the prophet but with the deity, once it had been delivered, there was no need to keep the name.

Ultimately, this goes well in line with the sidelining of the "first one" observed in the transmission of texts in the Mesopotamian trajectory, and it could thus be expected that in those cases when prophetic oracles were transmitted as prophetic literature in the Hebrew Bible, the names of "first ones" would not necessarily be included.

WRITTEN DOWN FOR LIFE

Turning now to the 'book' called *Isaiah* and moving through it synchronically, writing is first encountered in Isa 4:3:[24]

והיה הנשאר בציון והנותר בירושלם קדוש יאמר לו כל־הכתוב לחיים
בירושלם

And it shall come to pass that whoever is left in Zion and remains in Jerusalem will be called holy, everyone who has been written down for life in Jerusalem.

In this passage, writing is given a sense of future orientation, with the mentioned 'book' serving as a record of things that are to come.[25] The premise seems to be that a text has been produced that has the names of remnants written down and that this content will safeguard

---

24. Apart from the passages surveyed here, writing is also mentioned in Isa 10:1–2; 34:4; 44:5; and 50:1, but none of these passages concern the writing down of prophecy. Isa 10:1–2 speaks of the writing of oppressive statutes so that justice is kept from the needy and poor, Isa 34:4 depicts the end-times as the rolling up of a scroll, Isa 44:5 talks about writing on the hand as one way of showing that one belongs to the redeemed of the people, and Isa 50:1 speaks of a divorce document.

25. Whether or not the common suggestion that the passage may be postexilic is correct does not matter here (see most notably Duhm, Kaiser, and Wildberger 1991, 163–65; cf. some critical voices in Oswalt 1986, 147; and Roberts 2015, 67–68; and the discussion in Williamson 2014, 305–6), since the fundamental (rhetorical) orientation of the text remains the same (as observed by Childs 2001, 34–35).

their continued presence in Zion after God's purging of the city.[26] So put, the inclusion of one's name in God's 'book' "implies God's protection,"[27] and the passage can be seen in light of, for example, Exod 32:32,[28] where Moses asks YHWH to either forgive the sins of the people or erase him from the 'book' that YHWH has written. That an Exodus tradition is relevant here is also supported by Isa 4:5, which mentions that a cloud by day and flaming fire by night will be over the new Zion. Similar concepts of a 'book' of the living are also found in Ps 69:29 (ספר חיים), where it is related to the judgment of the enemies of the psalmist, and perhaps Mal 3:16, where a "'book' of remembrance" (ספר זכרון) contains names that are remembered for future protection (cf. also Dan 12:1).[29]

In the 'book' called *Isaiah*, this function of writing can also be seen in 34:16 and 65:6. In the former, a 'book' is mentioned that apparently recorded wild creatures and demons that would possess the land forever after its judgment,[30] and in the latter, the sins of the people are written down so that God can judge them.[31] What these texts have in common, then, is that writing has a future-oriented function—something is

---

26. Cf. Roberts 2015, 68. For a discussion of the possible "origins" of this notion, see Wildberger 1991, 169–70, and, in more detail, Paul 1973, who discusses a wide range of texts.

27. Watts 2004, 76. I see this as a better understanding of the dynamic than the otherwise common notion of "assurance" (Smith 2007, 158). As pointed out by Oswalt 1986, 147, reading the verse as "predestination" (as Wildberger 1991, 169–70, argues, and Kaiser 1983, 86–87, leaves open; cf. also Beuken 2003, 126) somewhat misses the point. For an insightful discussion of whether the remnants are spared because they were faithful or if they become faithful because they are spared, see Goldingay 2014, 117–20.

28. Cf. Oswalt 1986, 145; Motyer 1999, 60; Smith 2007, 158; Williamson 2014, 311.

29. Thus in some contrast to, e.g., Blenkinsopp 2000, 204, who points to passages like Ezra 2:62; 8:1, 3; and Neh 12:22–23, as a background—that is, the recording of names of the new inhabitants of a city (see a similar point in Smith 2007, 157–58). For a discussion, see also Williamson 2014, 311.

30. Wildberger 2002, 316–17, 319–20, 338, understands this verse as a very late gloss so that the notion of a 'book' of YHWH would in fact be a reference to the 'book' called *Isaiah* itself (so also Kaiser 1980, 359). According to Wildberger, it was added in an attempt to "prove that 'the Bible is right,' right down to the last detail" (338). The verse is elusive, and although the idea that "the reader is urged to find confirmation to the prophecy of Edom's destruction by looking elsewhere" in the written transmission of prophecies (Childs has "scripture") is likely valid (so Childs 2001, 257; cf. similarly Blenkinsopp 2000, 454) and thus indicates that this verse may be an example of the intertwining of subsequent voices with the voice of the "first one" that will be noted below (see chapter 6), Roberts 2015, 437, is certainly correct that "precisely what that document might have been remains unclear." Oswalt 1986, 617–18, suggests it refers to a heavenly "Book of Destiny," while Seitz 1993, 237, thinks it refers to a 'book' in which the story about Noah was found. Both suggestions are quite unlikely, however.

31. For a discussion of this passage, see recently Green 2020, 78–80.

written down for later use, either to confirm what has happened or as a reminder of what should happen. In none of these texts are the acts of writing related to the prophet Isaiah, however.

Writing as Symbolic Action

The observed future orientation of the function of writing is developed further in the next passage to be considered, Isa 8:1–2. Here, an unnamed prophet moves to the center, recounting in the first person that things are to be written down to serve as a witness of the trustworthiness of his prophecies:[32]

Isa 8:1–2	ויאמר יהוה אלי	1	And YHWH said to me:
	קח־לך גליון גדול		"Take a large cutting of papyrus
	וכתב עליו בחרט אנוש		and write on it with a red pen:
	למהר שלל חש בז		'Concerning Maher-shalal-hush-baz,'
	ואעידה לי עדים נאמנים	2	and I will take[33] as reliable witnesses
	את אוריה הכהן		Uriah the priest
	ואת־זכריהו בן יברכיהו		and Zechariah, son of Jeberechiah."

Although the verse mentions writing, the specifics are quite uncertain. For one, the vocabulary surrounding the writing material and tools are unclear. It is regularly suggested that גליון refers not to a scroll but

---

32. The notion of an "unnamed" prophet is contrary to how the passage is explained by many commentators, who read it in light of the paratextual framing of the 'book' called *Isaiah* and the fact that the prophet Isaiah has been named in chapter 7 (see, e.g., Williamson 1994, 94–95, who notes that this passage belongs to three passages, "all widely believed to go back to Isaiah of Jerusalem himself, in which he refers to the writing down of certain parts of his message"; cf. Williamson 2018, 208). The text itself, however, does not make this explicit. In fact, in chapter 7, it is quite clear that the prophet Isaiah is *not* the speaker—he is rather included in a narrative where he is *spoken of* in the third person (see further "Sidelining the 'First One,'" chapter 6; the suggestion by Clements 2000, 98–99, that chapter 7 was originally composed in the first person is unpersuasive). Read independently of chapter 7, then, what is presented in chapter 8 is the first-person speech of an anonymous prophet (the same would be the case if read instead as a continuation of chapter 6, as suggested by Williamson 2018, 208, since the speaker in that chapter is also unidentified). To be fair, my observation is, as stated in the introduction to this chapter, not to be taken as a comment on the *origin* of the passage. It only makes clear what information is actually given in the text. While the passage may very well be dated to the time of the prophet Isaiah, the point I make here is simply that if the words are related to him, they seem to have been circulating not with his name attached to them but anonymously.

33. Cf. Beuken 2003, 213.

some kind of stone or metal surface.[34] It is only used twice in the Hebrew Bible, the second time in Isa 3:23, where it is listed among garments of the daughters of Zion. There, it is perhaps to be translated as "mirror,"[35] hence indicating some kind of reflective surface.[36] This would be reasonable in light of one of the meanings of the root of the word גלה: "to reveal." The root also means "to remove" and "to exile," however, and when reading the verse in relation to the papyrus culture in which it belongs, a case has been made to understand גליון as a "cutting"—that is, a piece removed from a supply roll.[37] Hence the translation "cutting of papyrus" above. Such an understanding could then also cast light on the "man's stylus" (חרט אֱנוֹשׁ). As regularly noted, is not straightforward what the notion of "man" indicates. Is it just a way of saying a "common stylus";[38] should it be amended to "a stylus of sickness" (חרט אָנוּשׁ)— that is, a stylus that writes disaster; or is it a stylus with "indelible script" (חרט אָנוּשׁ)?[39] If related once again to scribal habits in papyrus cultures, it has been suggested that it refers to the second of two pens used by scribes, a red pen often used to highlight passages.[40] Last, the preposition ל could be translated as both "concerning" and "[belonging] to."[41]

---

34. This is often supported by the observation that חרט is an engraving tool (Williamson 2018, 194, 199–200).

35. Cf. Smith 2007, 221.

36. Cf. Motyer 1999, 80; Millard 2010, 115–16. For a discussion including early versions, see Watts 2004, 147–48. See also the discussion of the LXX in Katz 1946. A detailed, updated discussion can be found in Williamson 2018, 193–98.

37. This translation, as well as the translation "red pen," is based on the argument presented by Elizabeth VanDyke in her paper "The Pens of the Prophets: The Materiality of Scribal Practice in Isaiah 8," presented at the SBL Annual Meeting in San Antonio in 2021. It overlaps partly with Roberts 2015, 128–29, who reads 8:1 in continuation with his understanding of 8:16 so that a sealed document is implied here too, thus necessitating a material—a piece of papyrus or leather—that could be rolled up. As will be seen below, however, the notion of a sealed document does not capture the dynamics of 8:16 properly.

38. So Motyer 1999, 80; Smith 2007, 221. Cf. van der Toorn 2007, 180, who points to the fingers of a human hand in Dan 5:5.

39. For a discussion including more possibilities, see Williamson 2018, 200–203, who himself argues for keeping it as a "human stylus." Wildberger 1991, 331–32, opts for "disaster stylus" by pointing to 1QM 12 3 (בחרט חיים) and is followed by, for example, Kaiser 1983, 178, and Watts 2004, 148. It is difficult, however, to see how such a reading fits with the logic of the passage (cf. Blenkinsopp 2000, 237; Williamson 2018, 201). Other positions include Stade 1906 and Talmage 1967.

40. So VanDyke 2021. Such a use is found regularly in Egyptian sources but also in, e.g., Dead Sea Scrolls like 2Q14 or 4QNum[b].

41. Williamson 1994, 95n5, argues for the latter, referring to "the common use of *l* before personal names on seals." Smith 2007, 221n290, does not decide between the two. As noted by Watts 2004, 149, the ownership view does not quite fit here, and so

Although these suggestions are only tentative, some conclusions can nonetheless be drawn. The first is that it is clear from the command that what is to be written does not originate with the unnamed prophet but comes from YHWH, thus making the prophet the recipient of a divine revelation supposedly transmitted in writing.

Second, although the prophet is given the command to write, it is not necessarily an indication that he did the actual writing himself.[42] An interesting example from the Mari letters could be instructive here. Among them, one letter introduces a prophet as a sender:

Speak to Zimri-Lim: thus the prophet (*āpilum*) of Šamaš.[43]

In line with the *Isaiah* passage, this could be taken as an indication that the prophet himself had written the letter, had not the circumstances by which it was produced been revealed in another letter:

Another matter: Atamrum, prophet of Šamaš, came to me and spoke to me as follows: "Send me à discreet scribe! I will have him write down the message which Šamaš has sent me for the king." This is what he said to me. So I sent Utu-kam and he wrote this tablet. This man brought witnesses and said to me as follows: "Send this

---

"concerning" is probably to be preferred (so also Wildberger 1991, 335; Blenkinsopp 2000, 238).

42. Nonetheless, this is often presumed. It is, for example, among the three biblical references in which van der Toorn 2007, 179, finds a preexilic prophet writing down oracles (the other being Hab 2:2 and Jer 29:1). Similarly, Watts 2004, 149, refers to Anderson 1960 and states that this passage indicates that "of all the prophets, Isaiah is the one most likely to have known how to write." Anderson's argument, which is based on, among others, 2 Chr 26:22, is that the prophet Isaiah would have been a scribe who also served as a counselor to the king. This is not convincing, however, and the problems with this view will be apparent in my discussion of the 'books' of Chronicles (chapter 8). Quite speculative is also the view of Gevaryahu 1989, 64–65, who argues that the references to "scrolls" and what he understands as the "end of illiteracy" in passages like Isa 10:19; 29:11–12, 18, 24, indicate that *the prophet Isaiah himself* was literate, and more so, "the leader of a circle of young intelligentsia called יודעי ספר." I will return to the notion of a school below ("Authorizing New Carriers"), but it can be noted here that there is nothing in this text that supports such a reconstruction. The notion in Blenkinsopp 2000, 237, that the passage can be seen as "a *literary construct* not a stenographic report of an episode in the life of Isaiah" (emphasis in the original) is to the point, although it may have been taken too far (see the case made in Millard 2010). The point I want to make, however, is not whether or not an individual may have had the skills to write things down but to unpack what the text actually says about how prophecies have been transmitted into writing—and to this end, it is essential to recognize that the prophet is in fact *anonymous*.

43. Translation from Nissinen 2017, 77.

tablet quickly and let the king act according to its words." This is what he said to me. I have herewith sent this tablet to my lord.[44]

So although the prophet initiated a writing process, he is himself not necessarily the one holding the stylus.[45] At the very least, this should be considered an open question in Isa 8.

Third, it is clear that the *purpose* of writing is so that it could be shown later that the prophecy was correct.[46] This is also why two witnesses are summoned,[47] a practice also paralleled in the Mari text (cf. also Deut 17:6; 19:15).[48] In both cases, witnesses are supposed to testify that the prophecy was correctly transmitted, perhaps also confirming its proper origins,[49] and, most importantly, that it had been written *before* the events.[50]

---

44. Translation from Nissinen 2017, 85.

45. Cf. Nissinen 2017, 93.

46. Cf. Oswalt 1986, 222; Wildberger 1991, 336; Watts 2004, 149; Williamson 1994, 97; contra van der Toorn 2007, 182.

47. It can be noted that the names given to the witnesses fit quite well in the context and seem to anticipate some core aspects of later periods of transmission (notably Isa 40–55), since emphasis is placed on "light" and "remembrance" (cf. אור in Isa 9:1; 42:6, 16; 45:7; 49:6; 51:4; etc.; see also the discussions in Williamson 1993, 103; and זכר in 44:21; 46:9; 49:1; 54:4; etc.). For Uriah as "YHWH is light" and Zechariah as "YHWH has remembered," see also Wildberger 1991, 336; Watts 2004, 150. It may thus be that these names are invented, just as Maher-shalal-hush-baz (cf. Beuken 2003, 220, on the latter, which he does not see as a proper name), and that it would be unnecessary to try to identify them, as is done by most commentators. Speaking against this view could be that Jeberekiah—"May YHWH bless"—is also mentioned, since ברך is not prominent in the 'book' called *Isaiah*. It is prominent in the 'book' of Psalms, however, which is heavily influential in Isa 40–55. Regardless, the main point is still that they are reliable (נאמנים).

48. Consequently, it is not as puzzling as argued by some commentators (e.g., Oswalt 1986, 222), and the suggestion by Wolf 1972 that 8:1–4 would be a marriage ceremony, with the writing performing legal functions, is both unlikely and unnecessary. The speaker in v. 2 is, however, a bit unclear. עוד is found in the *hiphil*, "and I will cause to witness/take as witness," indicating that YHWH is still the one speaking (so, e.g., Smith 2007, 221n292). Regarded as improbable, many have favored readings in line with some of the early versions (only the Targum may support the MT; cf. Wildberger 1991, 332–33; Williamson 2018, 205–6). This unclarity is not, however, necessarily a problem. As will be shown later (in the discussion of Isa 8:16 but also in chapter 6), divine agency and human agency are often intertwined in a way that makes them difficult for the modern scholar to distinguish, and keeping the MT as an older reading could then indicate that the versions attempt to clarify the text (see more below, n. 48, chapter 11). Consequently, the objection by Williamson 2018, 205, that "if the text be retained at this point, we have to assume an unexpressed change of subject at the start of v. 3" loses force.

49. See the observations made above, in the section "Prophets without Books"; cf. the discussion in Svärd 2013, 274.

50. Roberts 2015, 128; cf. Williamson 2018, 214–15.

Fourth, the content of the writing is very limited. It consists of one name only, and taken together with the unusual גליון—understood as an act of writing on a large piece of papyrus—as well as the possible use of the red pen, it would not be unreasonable to suggest that this is to be understood as a prophetic symbolic action (cf. perhaps Hab 2:2–4), similar to the one enacted by Ezekiel, who scratches "Jerusalem" into a clay tablet (Ezek 4:1–8; cf. 37:16).[51] The brevity of the content should, then, not surprise, and it can also be added that it is well known from ancient Near Eastern sources that prophetic messages were condensed in such a way.[52] A similar short prophetic message is transmitted in writing in a text close in both time and space, the Lachish Ostracon 3:

> Now it has been told to your servant: "The commander of the army, Coniah son of Elnathan, has gone down to Egypt. He has sent (orders) to take Hodaviah son of Ahijah and his men from here." As for the letter of Tobiah the servant of the king, which came to Shallum the son of Jaddua from the prophet (*hnb*), saying, "Beware!": your servant has sent it to my lord.[53]

Such short messages, which needed to be properly interpreted, inevitably also led to varying interpretations—see, for example, the oracle "Beneath straw water runs!" which is quoted three times in three different contexts in the Mari letters.[54]

---

51. Cf. Kaiser 1983, 179; Childs 2001, 72; Blenkinsopp 2000, 238; Roberts 2015, 129. The notion that it was to be large has often (and sometimes in combination with the notion of a "common" or "human" stylus) been interpreted as an indication that it was written for public display (cf. Oswalt 1986, 221; Wildberger 1991, 330–31, 334–35; Blenkinsopp 2000, 237–38; Childs 2001, 72; Williamson 2018, 203, 211; cf. Eaton 1959, 144. The suggestion by van der Toorn 2007, 180, that this poster would have been hung in the temple is unfounded, however), thus reinforcing this interpretation. Also possibly relevant here is the use of חרט in Exod 32:4, which VanDyke argues is used to make a "blueprint" (of the calf). Watts 2004, 149, notes that the "formulas of narratives of symbolic actions" are used (first argued by Wildberger 1991, 334; cf. Williamson 2018, 210; see also Hos 1:2; 1 Kgs 11:31; Jer 13:4; 25:15; 36:2, 28; 43:9; Zech 11:15) but suggests that the symbolic act is primarily the actions that follow the writing. Why the writing would be excluded is, however, not clear (esp. in light of Jer 36:2, 28). Wildberger also sees the writing as a symbolic action, a "sign which prepares for the actual sign" (334).

52. There is thus no need to suggest with Roberts 2015, 130, that the name would have been only a "tag written on the outside" of a scroll that had more substantial contents on the inside. See, e.g., the discussion in Millard 2010, 111–12.

53. Quoted from Nissinen 2017, 92–93.

54. For a discussion, see Kratz 2015, 16; Nissinen 2017, 83–84.

Authorizing New Carriers

Moving along a few verses, a set of imperatives is found in Isa 8:16 that has commonly been understood as speaking of written prophecies,[55] although the verse does not feature any explicit references to writing apart from the mentioning of an act of sealing:

| Isa 8:16 | צור תעודה 16 | Bind up the testimony, |
| | חתום תורה בלמדי | preserve the teaching in my disciples! |

The grammar of this verse—as well as its relation to the surrounding context in which it is currently found—has caused a lot of trouble. One of the main problems is the identification of the speaker, which is related to the question of whether or not the verbs should be taken as imperatives or as infinitive absolutes.[56] Is it YHWH, the same unnamed prophet as in 8:1, or somebody else? Put differently, to whom do the disciples belong, YHWH or the anonymous[57] prophet?

The Disciples

Given that the verse seems to depict a transmission of teaching and given that this seems to be conceptualized in terms of transmission of writing, would it not have been expected that the voices were clearly distinguishable? Reading the passage in light of a Mesopotamian authorship concept, the answer would be a clear no. In fact, a

---

55. Verses 16–18 have often been seen as an original conclusion to a memoir (so, e.g., Clements 1980, 100; Kaiser 1983, 195). See also the discussion of an Isaianic *Denkschrift* above, n. 13, chapter 1.

56. The popular reading of the verbs as infinitive absolutes was suggested by Wildberger 1991, 364, as a way of solving a perceived problem with the transition to first-person speech in v. 17. According to Wildberger, then, the imperatives would indicate that YHWH is the speaker in v. 16 and that the disciples are his, only to abruptly change to the prophet in v. 17, while the infinitive absolutes indicate that the speaker is the same throughout (see, however, Oswalt 1986, 230, who reads even the infinitive absolutes as "emphatic imperatives," or Williamson 2018, 302, who suggests that it may be the same speaker throughout even with the imperatives when arguing that the command is directed to a third unnamed party, "presumably a professional scribe"). In light of the discussion below, however, this transition was likely not perceived as a problem in the period of time when this text was composed. For the differences in the LXX, see especially van der Kooij 1997 and below, n. 48, chapter 11. To be noted is that some take the disciples as belonging to the prophet even when the speaker is considered to be YHWH (see Uhlig 2009, 121–22).

57. As with Isa 8:1, no name is provided for the prophet (or the disciples), and as with Isa 8:1, most scholars would nonetheless infer that the prophet is in fact Isaiah and that these verses "come from" him (e.g., Wildberger 1991, 365; Berges 2012a, 95).

similar intertwining of divine and human agency was noted in, for example, the *Erra Epic*, and that prophetic voices are often difficult to distinguish from the divine voices they are representing is indeed not a new observation.[58] The verse should thus not be interpreted as relating disciples to *either* YHWH *or* the prophet. In fact, their identities are not presented as significant. Focus is instead on a transfer of the task of transmission of testimony (תעודה) and teaching (תורה; cf. Isa 1:10; 2:3; 5:24; 30:9) originated in a divine-human interaction—note that both terms lack a suffix and thus do not relate this tradition to any specific agent—to subsequent ones.[59]

Seen in light of what was said about the "first one" in the Mesopotamian trajectory—that the intentions of the first (unnamed) human recipient were nowhere essential to the interpretation of the text but that s/he was rather described as proclaiming, repeating, explaining, and preserving the received revelation so that it was faithfully transmitted to the subsequent ones, who were invited to do likewise—this verse then provides an important clue to how the transmission of prophecy in the 'book' called *Isaiah* is constructed.[60] Possibly adding to this picture is also the fact that the verse specifies the content as "testimony" (תעודה)—that is, as a reiteration of something received.[61] Consequently, when this reiterated revelatory interaction is bound up in (ב) the

---

58. On this, see more below, "Voices Intertwined," chapter 6.

59. The lack of suffix is sometimes overlooked in translations. Consider the Swedish Bibel 2000 as an example, which translates to "I want to bind up my teaching, I want to hide my message under a seal in my disciples" (Swedish: "Jag vill knyta in min undervisning, jag vill gömma mitt budskap under sigill i mina lärjungar"). To be noted is also that תעודה and תורה do not refer to two distinct entities (contra Gevaryahu 1989, 66; Uhlig 2009, 126n230) but stand parallel to each other, describing the same revelation in two different ways.

60. This overlaps slightly with the idea of Childs 2001, 76, who speaks of a "canon consciousness" and that "the prophetic witness that was not received when first proclaimed has been collected and preserved in faith for another generation," although the notion of "canon" in this context is unwarranted. What is envisaged is not the demarcation of a *specific set of writings* (Childs is probably correct earlier, on 75, when he claims that what is envisaged in v. 16 is not necessarily a *written* testimony) but a transmission of revelatory tradition that could be represented in various ways and forms, only one of which being writing.

61. Cf. Wildberger 1991, 366–67. It is thus related to עד and derived from עוד ("to go about," or "to repeat"; cf. Ruth 4:7, where it is used to designate a sandal as a witness to a transaction). Somewhat similar is also Blenkinsopp 2000, 243—"a text validated by witnesses"—although the verse does not mention any written text.

disciples, they are inevitably participating in the act of testifying—they become witnesses.[62]

No Actual Writing

Noteworthy is, then, that *no actual writing* is taking place in Isa 8:16, but since this has been a quite contested issue, the main contours of the scholarly discussion of whether or not the statement is literal or metaphorical need to be rehearsed.

According to the literal view, the passage depicts how a prophet "wrote down his oracles on a scroll"[63] and how he called this "his *torah*, perhaps in order to compare the scroll with the written priestly *torah*," and testimony, "not only because it was a witness to God's instructions in the present but also because it witnessed to his plans in the future. Therefore it was bound and sealed and committed to his disciples."[64] Such a view is not persuasive, however, not least since it is based on a notion of the "writing of oracles" and intellectual property not supported by the text. The verse does not describe any writing down of torah belonging to a certain prophet on a scroll. It mentions neither writing (that notion would require that תורה or תעודה are used to convey *written texts* in v. 16, contrary to how the terms are used elsewhere; see Isa 1:10; 2:3; 5:24; 24:5; 30:9; 42:4, 21, 24; 51:4, 7; and especially 8:20)[65] nor any scroll,[66] and the text does not read תורתי or תורתך, which would be necessary to make it "his," but תורה.[67]

There are better arguments, however. Some scholars who argue for a literal understanding have instead claimed that it is not clear what "bind up" (צרר) and "seal" (חתם) would be metaphors for and argued that if these verbs would indeed have been employed in a metaphorical statement, a "less ambiguous preposition than *b*" would have been used, since the idea of "writing on the heart" would have been new and

---

62. Cf. Blenkinsopp 2000, 244, and somewhat similarly Williamson 1994, 111, who emphasizes that the background of these verses would be that the message of the prophet had been rejected and therefore needed to be transmitted in *writing* already in this verse. The latter notion will be questioned below, however.

63. The quote is from Jones 1955, 236, who is among those who proposed this view early on. He even specifies the contents of the scroll as "poetical concentrates of his oracles, together probably with some autobiographical material where necessary."

64. Jones 1955, 236 (emphasis in the original). For the possibility of keeping documents in homes of prophets, see Millard 2010, 110–11.

65. See also Clements 1985, 107.

66. Cf. Wildberger 1991, 366; Watts 2004, 160.

67. Cf. n. 59 above.

strange.[68] Moreover, when taking the use of תעודה and תורה in verse 20 as "unquestionably" referring to written documents, a literal reading is argued to be preferred also in verse 16. Ultimately, then, it is suggested that verse 16 should be taken at "face value" unless there are strong indications to the contrary.[69] That writing is not mentioned is not seen as a problem, since it would have taken place prior to verse 16.[70]

While the critique of the metaphorical interpretation is quite to the point, the suggested solution is not without its problems. As mentioned before, no writing takes place, and verse 20 does not "unquestionably" refer to written documents.[71] In fact, there is a much simpler solution to these issues that requires neither a metaphorical rereading nor any introduction of written elements not present in the text.

If looking first at צרר, which has been translated as "bind" above, it is not a term generally used in relation to documents. Instead, it is regularly found conveying the notion of something "being too narrow," both spatially and figuratively ("distress"), and it is in this sense that the "binding" could be understood: it conveys the notion of keeping something from being scattered, spread out, or diffused.[72] Proverbs 26:8 likens honoring a fool to "binding (צרר) a stone in (ב) a sling," the people wrap up (צרר) their kneading bowls in (ב) their cloaks in Exod 12:34, and YHWH "binds up (צרר) the waters in (ב) his thick clouds" (cf. Prov 30:4), to take a few examples.[73] There is thus ample evidence of the verb being used together with the preposition ב, and given that it would be an unusual term to use in relation to written documents, the most straightforward interpretation is that it conveys that the teaching (in whatever form) is now prevented from being widely disseminated by being transmitted by the disciples only.

The notion of sealing would, then, fit such an interpretation quite well. Certainly used in relation to documents, there are also texts where it conveys a derived (secondary) meaning of something being "securely shut" (see, e.g., Lev 15:3; Deut 32:34; Job 9:7; 24:16; 37:7; Song 4:12),[74] and to be noted is that when used in relation to a document, the document is always explicitly mentioned (1 Kgs 21:8;

---

68. This argument is found in Williamson 1994, 98 (building on Dillmann 1898; cf. Williamson 2018, 302–4), who points to Jer 31, where "unambiguous prepositional phrases" are used. This is also the view of Blenkinsopp 2000, 243, for example.

69. Williamson 1994, 98.

70. See also Williamson 2018, 312.

71. See also more below, n. 93.

72. Cf. Fabry 2003.

73. See similarly Fabry 2003, 457–58.

74. See Otzen 1986.

29:11; Jer 32; Esth 3:12; 8:8, 10; Dan 9:24; 12:4, 9; Neh 9:38; 10:1).[75] This would make the often suggested parallel between Isa 8:16 and Jer 36 unpersuasive,[76] as would the observation that "to seal up," "when used in connection with a document, is suggestive of a formal act of securing the scroll so that its authorship is guaranteed."[77] Instead, it seems reasonable to understand the presence of חתם in Isa 8:16 as conveying the meaning of something "stored up" or "preserved," thus expanding on צרר.

In sum, the occurrence of two verbs not juxtaposed elsewhere in the Hebrew Bible that connote a sense of securely preserving something so that it is not widely disseminated,[78] together with the fact that no writing or writing material is mentioned in the verse and the fact that the preposition ב is used—which often occurs together with צרר to specify *where* something is bound up—provides a straightforward understanding of this verse as conveying the idea of reliable preservation of tradition in a(n unidentified) group of tradents.

A more distant possible support for this conclusion could, then, be found in Isa 29:11–12, a passage often noted to overlap somewhat with Isa 8:16, since both passages mention prophecy and something "sealed." Since Isa 29:11 clearly features a simile (כ + דברי הספר החתום) where the written scroll functions metaphorically as the *vehicle*, it says not "that divine revelation has now been carefully related to the vehicle of a written scroll"[79] but rather that it is understood as being *as unavailable* as words written in a sealed scroll. Worth noting, however, is that the simile is used to explain how a "vision of all (חזות הכל, f.)" has been received. As will be clear later, in the discussion of the paratexts, the entire 'book' called *Isaiah* would eventually be framed as such a "vision" (חזון, m.), and since it would be reasonable to interpret חזות הכל as referring to the totality of a certain prophetic teaching at a certain point,[80] the conceptualizing of it as a sealed scroll would provide

---

75. Cf. Uhlig 2009, 125.

76. See Blenkinsopp 2000, 405.

77. Williamson 1994, 100 (also contra Simian-Yofre and Ringgren 1986 and Gevaryahu 1989, 66).

78. Cf. somewhat similarly Wildberger 1991, 366–68; Eissfeldt 1960, 26; Uhlig 2009, 127.

79. So Childs 2001, 218; cf. Watts 2004, 454; Blenkinsopp 2000, 405, 416. The common view—argued by, for example, Kaiser 1980, 269–70; Wildberger 2002, 81–82—that the two verses are a postexilic comment that implies that prophecies had been collected in a scroll thus similarly misses the point (so also Smith 2007, 499).

80. Possibly but not necessarily transmitted in writing and thus not easily identified with certain chapters in the 'book' called *Isaiah* (cf. Wildberger 2002, 84: "'everything'

the same basic function as Isa 8:16 (this is further strengthened if Isa 29:11–12 is indeed a reinterpretation of Isa 8:16)[81]—that is, that the vision is to be not widely disseminated but transmitted by certain legitimized carriers, only to be revealed (as true) at a later point (29:18).[82] The often suggested parallel between Isa 8:16 and the "tablets of the hearts" in Jer 31:33 is, then, not quite relevant, since Isa 8:16 is not about *writing* but about *preservation.*

This also indicates that the rationale for this preservation is similar to what was observed in relation to Isa 8:1–2. The testimony is to be kept by the disciples so that its contents can be revealed later,[83] while the prophet waits for YHWH (v. 17).[84] Understood in such a way, it can also be noted that the verse does in fact not say anything about that content simply because it is not the purpose.[85] There are thus no grounds for relating this verse to specific parts of the 'book' called *Isaiah,* as is often done.[86] It is not a narrative about how the 'book' called *Isaiah* came into being but a narrative concerned with validating subsequent

---

that God has revealed to his people"), although the literary context would indicate that it relates to the preceding verses or the entire vv. 9–14 (so Exum 1981, 349).

81. For this, see Ackroyd 1978, 28.

82. Cf. Beuken 2010, 121. See somewhat similarly Roberts 2015, 369—"Either hear the word of Yahweh from me (and perhaps from others who agree with me), or you will not hear the word of Yahweh at all"—or Berges 2012b, 34. See also further below, "The Past and the Present," chapter 6.

83. So also Seitz 1993, 83.

84. The suggestion that this is to be interpreted as an indication that "the prophet is turning from public ministry for a while to concentrate on those gathered around him who have accepted his message" (Grogan 2008, 524; cf. Childs 2001, 76) somewhat misses the point. While it is reasonable to conclude that the "first one" is marginalized in the continuing transmission in a way congruent with what was observed in the Mesopotamian tradition, the text says nothing about the possible continuation or cessation of a ministry of a *specific individual* (thus the critique in Ackroyd 1978, 28, also misses the point when arguing that "the fact that we have no historical references in the Isaianic material for the period between the Syro-Ephraimite war in the reign of Ahaz [so vii and viii] and the threat to Ashdod in 713–711 [so xx] is no basis for the supposition that Isaiah did not speak publicly during that period").

85. Contra the redaction critical argument in Roberts 2015, 139; the excursus in Watts 2004, 160; and the arguments of Grogan 2008, 524, and Williamson 2018, 313–15, for example. Since this verse says nothing about any *written* transmission, it says just as little about the relation between תורה and תעודה and chapters in the 'book' called *Isaiah.*

86. This also means that there is no need to suggest, as does Clements 2000, 92, that v. 16 was originally placed after 8:2 and moved to its current location to be part of a conclusion of a written memoir.

ones as tradents of prophecies emanating from an interaction between a deity and a "first one."[87]

Not Really a School

This said, it is necessary to briefly address the fact that this verse has been used as one of the foundational texts for the idea of an Isaianic "school,"[88] since the argument above could be interpreted as providing additional support for such an idea. However, there is a crucial difference between what is suggested here and the hypothesis about a school—namely, that there is nothing in the text that warrants the idea that a group of people *specifically related to a prophet named Isaiah* would have been given the task to further "his" message.[89] What is found here is rather an embodiment of the idea of the transmission of literature across generations so that in light of a Mesopotamian authorship concept, the "disciples" find their closest conceptual counterparts in, for example, the scribes mentioned in the passage from the *Erra Epic* quoted in chapter 3. Consequently, it must be concluded that the attempts to reconstruct a specific school misses the point, which is instead that whoever faithfully transmits the channeled message of the "first one" is included among the "disciples." At the very least, the concept of "subsequent ones" widens the idea of a "school" in a way that entails that these subsequent ones need not have been in any kind of

---

87. It is maybe in this sense that a comparison with Jer 36 becomes relevant. As noted by Davies 2000, 73, that chapter presupposes a sequence that could be understood roughly as YHWH spoke → Jeremiah dictated → Baruch read → the people heard, thus showing with all clarity the distributive Mesopotamian author concept. Davies correctly concludes that this is not, then, a story about *why* there are prophetic scrolls in general, and neither does it account for a shift from oral to written prophecy. If the main argument in this book is correct, it could thus be seen as yet another story reflecting a Mesopotamian author concept.

88. The idea was first presented by Mowinckel 1946, 67–70 (see also the earlier Mowinckel 1926; cf. Mowinckel 2002, 60–64), and further developed by Jones 1955 and Eaton 1959; Eaton 1982; cf. Gevaryahu 1971; Gevaryahu 1989; among others. Clements 1985, 97, notes that "it may be correct, but it does not really explain anything very much."

89. The observation overlaps somewhat with Smith 2007, 229. As observed by Uhlig 2009, 128, למוד is used in the Hebrew Bible to refer to "someone who is taught" or "has learned/got used to something," but it does not always imply a "teacher-pupil-relationship" (Jer 2:24; 13:23). However, his conclusion that למדי would therefore refer to *all* that had been taught by the prophet Isaiah, in particular those who are affected by the commission to harden (131), is doubtful.

personal relation to the "first one" to transmit and reshape literature related to him.[90]

The Dead and the Living

The strength of this interpretation of verse 16 is that it also makes sense of verses 19–20, which have often been deemed by scholars as a kind of appendix[91] that is "only very loosely connected with the preceding verses."[92] In light of what seems to be the main issue here—the preservation of testimony (תעודה) and teaching (תורה) among disciples—the verses can in fact be seen as an appropriate fit, especially since these two terms are mentioned again in verse 20 (לתורה ולתעודה),[93] this time in a slightly ironic condemnation of people who *consult the dead on behalf of the living*. If seeing this as a continuation of the narrative of the transmission of prophecies in verses 16–18, the point seems to be that since the testimony is to be transmitted by the disciples, the people would eventually—when the time comes—be able to return to the testimony of the "first one" without the need for that "first one"

---

90. Thus somewhat contra Williamson 1994, 102, who correctly notes that the disciples are not the same group as the two witnesses in v. 2 (contra, e.g., Clements 1980, 100, although it could be added that they do perform similar functions) but suggests that they were still "closely associated with the prophet." I will return below to a discussion of how subsequent ones have been weaved into the 'book' called *Isaiah* (see "Adding Voices," chapter 6).

91. So Kaiser 1983, 200.

92. Blenkinsopp 2000, 244. The foundational work was laid by Gray 1912, 1:157, and has been followed in general by most. Gray argued that vv. 19–23 could be seen as "three fragments": vv. 19–20; vv. 21–22 (+ last words of v. 20); and v. 23, based on the observation that "vv. 16–18 do not supply any natural explanation of the subject in *they say*, v. 19, or the pronoun *you*; in v. 21 *through it* refers to nothing in vv. 19f., nor does the singular pronoun throughout the last clause of v. 20 and vv. 21f find any satisfactory explanation in vv. 19f." (emphasis in the original). While vv. 21–23 are likely later additions (cf. Williamson 1994, 136–39, who argues that vv. 21–23a were moved here from their original place in the 'book,' see also Høgenhaven 1988, 103–5), I believe that a case can be made for vv. 19–20 being related to vv. 16–18, as will be clear below, although this does not rule out the possibility that vv. 19–20 were added later with such a function in mind (cf. Wildberger 1991, 364–65; Clements 2000, 92; Williamson 2018, 329–31).

93. The use of the two terms here would further underscore the conclusions drawn above, that they need not refer to any written document (contra Wildberger 1991, 370; Williamson 1994, 99). More specifically, the verses indicate that what the people want from the dead is not that they would magically deliver *written* teaching and *written* testimony (that would indeed be an odd outcome of necromancy); they instead want access to the teaching and testimony once revealed to the "first one" (if reading v. 20a in continuation with v. 19).

to be alive.[94] Consequently, the dead (prophet) should not be consulted (cf. 1 Sam 28), and the fact that the people resort to such practices becomes a witness to their depravity, which is placed in sharp contrast to the "first one" himself, who waits faithfully,[95] as implied in the structure of the passage:

> A' Testimony (תעודה) and teaching (תורה) bound up *in the disciples* (v. 16)
>> B' The prophet waits (חכה) and *hopes* (קוה) for YHWH (v. 17)
>>> C The prophet and his children are a sign for the people (v. 18)[96]
> A' Teaching (תורה) and testimony (תעודה) are sought *among the dead* (vv. 19–20a)[97]
>> B' The people act like they have no dawn (שחר, v. 20b, that is, no *hope*)[98]

In sum, even if Isa 8:16 does not contain any explicit indications of writing, it provides an important example of the Mesopotamian author dynamic, and this point is further strengthened by Isa 29:11–12, 18, where a sealed document is found, as discussed above.

---

94. Cf. Carr 2005, 143–44; Roberts 2015, 141; or Williamson 2018, 337: "Far from seeking guidance through necromancy one should turn rather *to the teaching and the testimony*" (emphasis in the original).

95. Similarly, Smith 2007, 230, notes that these verses contrast "the wrong way to inquire about the future with the right way to find out about God's will and his future plans."

96. The notion of the prophet being a "sign" is perhaps also found in one of the Mari letters (see Nissinen 2017, 105). The children could be a designation for the disciples (cf. 2 Kgs 6:1–7, using בן rather than ילד; Budde 1928, 85; Eaton 1959, 148; Gevaryahu 1989, 67). If so, the fact that they are a sign would be a further emphasis on their role as witnesses. Another possibility is that they are the children mentioned earlier (so Wildberger 1991, 369; Williamson 2018, 320; Blenkinsopp 2000, 244).

97. The reverse order of the terms has been noted as significant also by Childs 2001, 76, but given the structural relation between this verse and v. 16, there is no need for the suggestion by Williamson 2018, 338, that תורה has therefore been developed "in a more technical or strictly defined direction."

98. The notion in Grogan 2008, 527, that this would be an introduction of a "divine light" theme seen later (esp. chap. 9) is interesting and would underline the salvific undertones also associated with the time of dawn. For the relation between hope and the morning, see most recently Willgren Davage 2021 (cf. Ziegler 1950). If the above suggestion is to the point, there is no need to seek alternative meanings for שחר (as is done by Wildberger 1991, 364; Watts 2004, 163; Blenkinsopp 2000, 242–43; and Williamson 2018, 328–29, for example).

Writing as a Witness Forever

The last passage to consider is Isa 30:8–11, where, for the second time (cf. Isa 8:1), a(n anonymous) prophet is told to write something down:

Isa 30:8–11

עתה בוא כתבה	8	Go now, write it before/with them
על־לוח אתם		on a tablet,
ועל־ספר חקה		and inscribe it in a document,
ותהי ליום אחרון		so that it may be for the time to come
לעד עדי־עולם		as a witness forever.
כי עם מרי הוא	9	For they are a rebellious people,
בנים כחשים		faithless children,
בנים לא־אבו שמוע		children who will not
תורת יהוה		hear the instruction of YHWH;
אשר אמרו לראים לא תראו	10	who say to the seers, "Do not see";
ולחזים לא תחזו־לנו נכחות		and to the visionaries, "Do not envision to us what is right;
דברו־לנו חלקות		speak to us smooth things,
חזו מהתלות		envision deceptions,
סורו מני־דרך הטו מני־ארח	11	leave the way, turn aside from the path,
השביתו מפנינו		let us hear no more about
את־קדוש ישראל		the Holy One of Israel."

In this passage, writing is clearly taking place, but is it possible to say something more specific about the contents of the tablet mentioned in verse 8? And what about the purpose of writing "it" down?

Starting with the latter, the rationale is described in a way quite similar to Isa 8:1–2 and 16, although expressed more explicitly—prophecy is to be preserved in writing so that in a time to come, people may realize its truth.[100] Why such a preservation is needed is articulated in the verses

---

99. Reading עַד with BHSapp and most commentators.

100. Cf. Clements 1980, 246; Seitz 1993, 218; Watts 2004, 465; Roberts 2015, 388. The notion by Blenkinsopp 2000, 416, that this would be an "emergency measure" is not necessary.

that follow. The basic problem is claimed to be the rebellious attitude of the people (כי עם מרי הוא), more specifically that they want to shut the prophets up, and the vocabulary used to refer to these prophets, ראים and חזים,[101] emphasizes their function as receivers of divine revelation and sheds light upon the specific claims made by the people, that the visionaries stop "seeing" (תראו) and "envisioning" things that are correct about them (לא תחזו־לנו נכחות). In essence, then, they are wishing for a breach in the divine-human interaction so that the prophets can instead speak "smooth things" (הלקות) over them and envision "deceptions" (מהתלות).

Turning to the first question (about contents), the answer is not as straightforward, however. Given that the reference to writing materials includes a ספר, it has been suggested that this passage can best be seen as a kind of *mise en abyme*, a *Spiegeltext*. In this view, this chapter would reflect the formation of the larger 'book.' Several intertwined observations speak against such a conclusion, however.

First, it can be noted that since לוח and ספר are found in a series of parallel statements, they should not be understood as two separate mediums (compare עם and בנים in v. 9, ראים and חזים in v. 10, etc.)[102] but one and the same, and since לוח is mentioned first, it would be reasonable to understand it as the primary referent, thus indicating that ספר is referring to not a lengthy scroll but more reasonably a smaller inscription of some kind (cf. Job 19:23 and more remotely Exod 17:14 and Neh 7:5).[103] The use of חקק ("to inscribe"—i.e., "carving of an inscription into hard material")[104] in relation to ספר supports this view.[105]

Second and proceeding from the observation regarding the size of the tablet, it can be suggested that what is written is not a lengthy collection of prophetic oracles.[106] In fact, this is quite clear from the literary

---

101. On these terms, especially חזה, see below, "Prophetic Words and Nighttime Visions," chapter 7, where I argue that they are in no way "less specific" than נביא, as curiously stated in Blenkinsopp 2000, 416, nor do they imply a critique of the נביא (so Wildberger 1991, 6; 2002, 145); they are instead quite appropriate in a context that deals with written transmission of prophecy.

102. Cf. above, n. 59. So also Blenkinsopp 2000, 415; contra Galling 1971, 209; Gevaryahu 1989, 67; Motyer 1999, 195 (who sees it as a "public record" and a "private one"; cf. Smith 2007, 514).

103. See also Wildberger 2002, 140, who argues that ספר is best translated as "bronze" in this verse; cf. Childs 2001, 226, but against, e.g., Smith 2007, 514, and others who understand ספר as distinct from לוח. See also Blenkinsopp 2000, 415.

104. Kaiser 1980, 293–94; cf. Wildberger 2002, 140, who notes that the verb is never used in relation to writing on scrolls or leather.

105. Cf. Williamson 1994, 104, who notes that one "might have expected 'book' (*sēper*) to be the object of 'write,' and 'tablet' (*lûaḥ*) to be the object of 'inscribe' (*ḥqq*)."

106. Similarly Kaiser 1980, 294; contra Oswalt 1986, 551.

context (both chapter 30 in general and the subsection demarcated by the paratext in v. 6) so that it is only when verse 8 is treated as distinct from verses 6–7 that a referent is missing. More specifically, it can be noted that verse 8 begins by referring to the content of the document by means of two third-person feminine suffixes (חקה ,כתבה) and a verb in the third-person feminine (ותהי). Since the content is not made explicit in verse 8, it would thus be expected that it is found somewhere in the verses immediately preceding it, and this is indeed the case. The oracle beginning in verse 6 ends in verse 7 by referring to Egypt and an unnamed speaker that has called "her" (לזאת, f. sing.) "Rahab who sits still" (רהב הם שבת).[107] There is thus a clear relation between לזאת in verse 7 and כתבה, חקה, and ותהי in verse 8.[108] Understood in such a way, what verse 8 depicts is the writing down of a symbolic summary of the prophetic message concerning Egypt in but a few words, an act with a function similar to the writing down of Maher-shalal-hush-baz in Isa 8:1–2.[109] This would also make sense of the otherwise peculiar notion that the act of writing is taking place "before them" (אתם).[110] If related to the scene in Isa 8:1, אתם would indicate that the prophetic symbolic action is staged in front of the rebellious people (see v. 9).[111]

---

107. See BHSapp.

108. Cf. Wildberger 2002, 133; Williamson 1994, 83–84; Berges 2012a, 191, 195. This identification is thus to be preferred over the view that vv. 9–17 would constitute the content, demarcated by כי in vv. 9 and 15, as mentioned in Motyer 1999, 196 (where the question is left open), and argued in Childs 2001, 226 (see also Galling 1971, 210). In line with the interpretation above, כי is rather understood as having a causal meaning ("for"/"because"). The suggestion that v. 8 refers to תורת יהוה in v. 9, as argued by Roberts 2015, 388, is less persuasive given the clear relation to v. 7. Although some have argued that v. 8 would not be an appropriate conclusion to the section framed with the paratext in v. 6 (e.g., Blenkinsopp 2000, 415) and that it is therefore unlikely that v. 8 relates to v. 7, it is not clear why a connection between vv. 7 and 8 would cast v. 8 as a conclusion, even less so given that the focus of the entire chapter is on the recurring issue of trust, either in God or in human security, here specified as reliance on Egypt (see the overview in Smith 2007, 510; cf. Roberts 2015, 387; and the discussion of the formation of this chapter in Beuken 1997). The argument that v. 9f. "deals with Israel and not with Egypt" (Wildberger 2002, 141) is thus not a problem.

109. Cf. the Near Eastern parallels quoted in that discussion. See also Beuken 2010, 172. This view is thus contra Childs 2001, 226, who claims that so few words would not "fully match the intention of a written testimony that is to confirm an event occurring in the future." As shown above, similar examples are found elsewhere so that the caution raised by Childs seems rather to be the result of a reading into the text a need for historical accuracy and lengthy, detailed descriptions.

110. Cf. Motyer 1999, 196. The suggestion to read אֱתָמוֹ ("come!"; Roberts 2015, 388) is interesting but not necessary.

111. Cf. Wildberger 2002, 143. It is thus not necessary to treat it as a later gloss (as Kaiser 1980, 291). On this, see also Blenkinsopp 2000, 415.

102

Here is also to be noted that similar terminology is used to describe the revelation as was found in Isa 8:16.[112] There, it was referred to as תעודה and תורה; here it is referred to as עד (v. 8) and תורה (v. 9).[113] However, although writing is explicitly mentioned in 30:8, the suggestion that this implicates that the *writing itself* was now a witness is not entirely correct. What the verse rather claims is that the *content* is the witness. As noted above, the verb is found in third-person feminine singular (ותהי ליום אחרון לעד), thus referring back to the message, not to the medium, since לוח and ספר are both masculine nouns. However, it can still be suggested that the tablet, in a derived sense, performs a function similar to the "first one"—it has become a container of divine revelation, a channel through which the witness can now be transmitted. Ultimately, then, what is found in Isa 30:8–11 is a connection between an unnamed prophet and an act of writing that serves to validate the prophetic utterances by means of symbolic action.

To this, an additional observation can be added. The very fact that the symbolic action is to ensure the preservation of the message עד־עולם would presuppose that it was transmitted by people who were "more sympathetic to its contents than the present generation"[114]—that is, inevitably including more agents than the "first one," who would not always be present.[115] What is found in Isa 30:8–11 is, then, quite in line with the Mesopotamian authorship trajectory, including the blurring of agents noted in several passages above. It thus points to the conclusion that what is written is not ultimately emanating from *either* God *or* the prophet but is a result of their interaction.

This is in fact emphasized if reading verses 6–9 in sequence. Throughout verses 6–8, the speaker would be assumed to be YHWH (לכן קראתי, etc.), but in verse 9, someone speaks *of* YHWH (לא־אבו שמוע תורת יהוה, not תורתי). Having the prophet speaking throughout—that is, as both the "I" of verse 7 and the one commanding the writing in verse 8—is not plausible, since it would mean that someone else is doing the symbolic act. Isaiah 30:7–12 thus provides an interesting example of the intertwining of divine and prophetic voices to the point that they are not possible to separate, just as was noted in relation to the *Erra Epic*. Consequently, messages are revealed *to* the prophet—an aspect underlined by the "Do not see!" of the rebellious people, which presumes

---

112. There is no need to argue, as Childs 2001, 226, that Isa 8:16 is closer to this passage than 8:1. Both texts serve as illuminating parallels to what is described here.

113. A notable difference is that תורה is here related explicitly to YHWH.

114. Williamson 1994, 105.

115. Williamson 1994, 105; cf. Oswalt 1986, 551; Wildberger 2002, 142.

that if the prophet closes their eyes to the revelation, they would no longer receive it—while also emanating *from* him. Channeled through speech, symbolic actions, and writings, it is passed on to subsequent ones, and the use of the plural in verse 10 underlines that one need not even understand the "first one" as a single individual.[116] The proclamation of divine visions thus seems to have involved more than one agent.

Between the Old and the New

After Isa 30 (if following the received sequence of chapters), no more texts speak explicitly of any writing activity. As will be seen below, however, the future-orientated function of writing will be picked up (especially in Isa 40–55) and used as a foundation for the proclamation of new revelations. But before moving to these texts, a summary of the main findings so far may be appropriate.

A first and fundamental observation has been that even if some of the texts surveyed above (Isa 8:1–2; 30:8–11) relate a prophet to writing, this prophet is not writing anything "himself" in any of them.[117] Moreover, only a few words are written as a part of symbolic actions. In the other passage, Isa 8:16, writing was not mentioned at all. Ultimately, this is quite in line with what would be expected from the preliminary remarks on written prophecy above (see "Prophets without Books") and shows with all clarity that in these parts of the 'book' called *Isaiah*, a prophet is nowhere explicitly associated with any substantial documents or collections of oracular material.

A second, equally important conclusion is that the acts of writing do not construct the prophet as the *originator* of prophecies. Instead, he is understood as a part of a divine-human interaction, where it is not always possible to distinguish the two and where other agents are ultimately drawn into the transmission. Given that the purpose of writing is recurrently said to be that a later generation will see that they are true—the revelation had been rejected by the contemporary audience—subsequent ones were needed to ensure a reliable transmission. This dynamic is described in Isa 8:16, where the testimony channeled through a "first one" is bound up in subsequent ones, implying that it was in some sense and for some time withheld from a broader

---

116. Cf. Wildberger 1991, 5.
117. Similarly Watts 2004, xliii; cf. Berges 2012a, 42; Seitz 1993, 22; Schniedewind 2004, 10.

audience. Ultimately, then, the explicit indications of writing in the 'book' called *Isaiah* can be understood as fully within what would have been expected in light of the Mesopotamian trajectory, and notable is the often overlooked fact that all voices except the voice of YHWH have so far been anonymous.

Proceeding from these observations, it now needs to be asked how the identified purpose of writing plays out in the remainder of the 'book.' How did later generations deal with the transmitted revelation, and what is said over time about the relation between these prophecies and the prophet Isaiah? In what follows, these issues will be addressed by looking at parts of the 'book' called *Isaiah* that are often judged to be of a later date than the texts surveyed in this chapter. More specifically, it will be shown how the intertwining of divine and human voices continues to permeate prophetic discourses in *Isaiah*—that is, even when more anonymous prophetic voices are introduced.

Chapter 6

THE SUBSEQUENT ONES

If the preceding chapter had a primarily synchronic focus, the current chapter will approach the construction of authorship in *Isaiah* from a more diachronic point of view. Before proceeding to the relevant texts, however, it should first be noted that there has been a lot of puzzlement about why the "authors" of some parts of the 'book' have not identified themselves—neither by name nor by any prose accounts nor by call narratives.[1] To overcome what was often perceived as an embarrassing anonymity, individuals such as "Deutero-Isaiah" and "Trito-Isaiah" have been

---

1. A notable exception is John D. W. Watts, who has argued that the identity of one of the subsequent ones is in fact provided in Isa 42:19. Building on the work of, among others, J. L. Palache (see also Kohn and Propp 1995), Watts takes the difficult משלם to be the proper name Meshullam, and since he is identified as a servant, Watts argues that he is in fact the author of the 'book': "The book of Isaiah depicts its author as Meshullam son of Zerubbabel, born and raised in Babylon, who went back to Jerusalem when Cyrus entered Babylon (48:16b), and was active in Jerusalem after his father's assassination there. He assembled prophetic stories about Isaiah son of Amoz (36:1–39:8; 7:1–14; 20:1–6). Perhaps working with other writers, he created the magnificent Vision of Isaiah. In it, he created a role for himself as a prophet using first-person dialogue . . . [and] made cameo appearances in almost every act" (2004, xliv; the view is not found in the first edition from 1985). Although משלם is enigmatic in its context (Westermann 1969, 108, 110–11, e.g., leaves it untranslated) and therefore often emended (see Baltzer 2001, 150; cf. 259–61), and although it may be a proper name (so, e.g., Blenkinsopp 2002b, 218–19, who sees it as a possible sobriquet for Israel; cf. Paul 2012, 200. Goldingay and Payne 2006a, 260, have, however, argued convincingly against such a view), the idea that the author of the 'book' would be revealed here is quite far-fetched, and the suggestion has not been well received (see, e.g., Berges 2020a, 262, and the critique in Seybold 1999). Notable is also that it is not mentioned in Watt's comment on Isa 42:19 (Watts 1987, 122, 126). This, then, provides a great example of how the desire to get rid of authorless texts is so strong that individual authors are created that never existed, quite like the ancient Greeks may have done with Homer (cf. n. 11 in chapter 4 above).

created,[2] and historical circumstances in which they are assumed to have authored their texts have been reconstructed.[3] In light of what has been argued so far, however, such an endeavor seems to run counter to the dynamics in the texts themselves. In fact, a different picture has started to emerge where anonymity is seen not as an obstacle to be removed but as a resource in uncovering how authorship is constructed. More specifically, it has been seen that anonymous texts are not an exception in *Isaiah*—anonymity permeates all texts dealing with writing, an observation that was quite expected in light of the Mesopotamian trajectory. The possible identities of the tradents are not revealed simply because such information was not considered important. The need for distinction implied in the above-mentioned scholarly constructs is in fact only relevant in contexts where notions like intellectual property or fame related to one's name are valued, but no such notions have so far been identified, and this chapter will further substantiate this conclusion.

It also needs to be said that even if the formation of the 'book' called *Isaiah* is not the focus of this study, for the discussion on the relation between the "first one" and the "subsequent ones" to be successful, it needs to take into consideration that the 'book' has grown over time in ways that are not necessarily linear. As has been persuasively argued, *Isaiah* bears witness to a process where countless small additions have been made throughout and where major blocks of texts have been introduced and reshuffled at various points in time. Recognizing this provides opportunities to inquire into how later voices relate to earlier ones. In other words, the analysis provided below will proceed from (but not argue) the idea that the 'book' called *Isaiah* is not primarily the result of the haphazard (or deliberate) juxtaposition of *originally separate* and *unrelated* works.[4] Although some parts of the 'book' may have circulated independently and written across various scrolls, it will be assumed that the later parts of the 'book' (esp. 40–66) presuppose the former parts,[5] although the exact nature of this dependence or the number of major redactions is still subject to debate.[6]

---

2. For an overview of research on the possible identification of authors of Isa 40–55, including a discussion of reasons behind the creation of "Deutero-Isaiah" and "Trito-Isaiah," see Berges 2010b.

3. See, e.g., Westermann 1969, 6–8.

4. As described in, e.g., Kratz 2015, 69.

5. I am thus persuaded by the arguments initially developed by Williamson 1994 on Isa 40–55 and Stromberg 2011 on Isa 56–66.

6. See also, e.g., the important contributions of Clements 1982; Rendtorff 1984; Sweeney 1996; and Seitz 2002.

As for structure, the discussion below will—after a discussion of how divine and human voices are often intertwined in the 'book' *Isaiah*—provide snapshots and representative examples of how the "first one" has been sidelined, discuss how more voices are added to the mix, and look at a recurring contrast between past and present. Last, a summary will be provided.

Voices Intertwined

Starting with the intertwining of divine and human voices, it is certainly not a new observation that divine speech cannot be easily separated from prophetic speech.[7] On the contrary, this feature—where words are, for example, first framed as divine first-person speech, only to seamlessly transition into talk *about* the deity, or, reversely, as prophetic speech, only to seamlessly turn into divine first-person speech—permeates all prophetic literature, and this is quite expected, given the role and function of prophets.[8] Its relevance may therefore not seem immediately obvious for a discussion of how authorship is constructed. However, a few examples will nevertheless be provided, since the pervasive nature of this feature has as a consequence that it is the voice of not only the "first one" that is intertwined with the voice of the deity but also the "subsequent ones." As the revelation originally channeled through a "first one" is transmitted in writing to new generations, the idea seems not to be that the role of the "subsequent ones" is any different from the "first one"—that they would merely reproduce original content or have access to the revelation only through the "first one." Instead, they proceed as if they had direct access to divine revelation, and a consequence is that the continued transmission is not frozen to a fixed and final product but

---

7. It has been discussed early on by, for example, Westermann 1991, 90–128 (see esp. 94–95; cf. Seitz 2002), and more recently by Quinn-Miscall 2001, see esp. 121–27, who notes that "the frequent difficulty or impossibility of deciding whether the Lord or the prophet is speaking is a significant part of Isaiah's understanding of what a prophet is, of what prophecy is" (126). Speaking of Isa 40–55, Heffelfinger 2011, 144, similarly notes that "there are passages whose speaker is virtually un-decidable. Other passages give the impression of being spoken by either the prophetic poet or 'the servant' only to evince a glimmer of double voicing by the deity." Curiously, though, she nevertheless attempts to calculate the proportions between divine speech and human speech in these chapters and argues that divine speech is dominant (for these calculations, see her appendix 2, 287–89). Building on the research of Heffelfinger, Tull 2017, 158, also notes that "twenty-eight verses [in Isa 40–55] lack semantic or contextual clues for discerning whether the prophet is speaking directly or attributing speech to God."

8. See "Prophets without Books," chapter 5.

continues to overflow.[9] The intertwining of the divine and human voices is thus not restricted to a possible "original" performative setting. Four examples will make this clear.

Consider first Isa 3:16–17. Verse 16 features a divine speech introduced by an unnamed prophetic voice (ויאמר יהוה), but in verse 17, instead of continuing that speech, reading "I will make bald" and "I will lay bare," the text instead states that YHWH will "make bald" (שפח,[10] third-person m. sing.) and "lay bare" (יערה, third-person m. sing.).[11] It would thus seem as if the prophet is speaking again, ultimately intertwining the two voices.

A second example can be found in Isa 8. In verse 11, a message by YHWH, starting in verse 12 (demarcated by לאמר), is introduced as words to a first-person speaker (כי כה אמר יהוה אלי, "for thus did YHWH speak to me"), but the message itself is then addressed to an unidentified plural audience (the verbs are all 2 m. pl.: תאמרון, תיראו, תעריצו)[12] and speaks of YHWH in the third person (את־יהוה צבאות אתו תקדישו, "but YHWH of hosts, him you shall honor as holy," v. 13). The lines between the divine and the human voices are thus blurred.

Third, consider Isa 34, where verse 1 exhorts all nations to listen, "for YHWH is enraged" (v. 2). The prophetic voice then continues to expand on the consequences of this rage but suddenly speaks of "my sword" (חרבי) in first-person speech in verse 5,[13] only to state in verse 6 that the sword belongs to YHWH, as the prophet returns to speak of the deity in the third person.

---

9. For these contrasting models, see figure 1 in "Centralized Authors," chapter 4. This can be seen in the fact that apart from the four examples provided below, similar dynamics are also be found in, e.g., Isa 9:8–10:12ff.; 10:24–27; 13:2ff.; 19:1bff.; 22:15–19ff.; 25:1ff.; 27:2–7ff.; 28:16–21ff.; 29:1–6ff.; 13–15ff.; 30:6–11; 31:4–9; 34:1–5ff.; 38:5–8; 40:27–41:4; 42:10–17; 43:16–21; 44:1–5, 9–20ff., 21–28; 45:14–15ff.; 47:1–4; 48:1ff.; 49:7–13; 52:4–12; 54:1–10; 56:1–8; 60:1–22; 61:1–11; and 66:12–17 (many of these texts are also discussed in Heffelfinger 2011 and Tull 2017; cf. also Quinn-Miscall 2001, 121–27, who also uses Isa 1:1–26 as an example)—that is, in all parts of the 'book' and in all kinds of texts written in a wide range of historical settings.

10. The translation of this term (a *hapax legomenon*) is not straightforward. I here follow Williamson 2014, 276; cf. similarly Wildberger 1991, 149.

11. On the reverse order of אדני and יהוה in 1QIsaᵃ, see Roberts 2015, 59.

12. This change is commonly recognized; cf. Kaiser 1983, 190; Beuken 2003, 228; Roberts 2015, 137.

13. This sudden move has caused some scholars to emend the Hebrew (see, e.g., Kaiser 1980, 351; or Wildberger 2002, 313: "The suffix on חרבי . . . cannot be right . . . , since Yahweh is spoken of in the entire section in the third person"), but as correctly noted by Beuken 2010, 303, such a change lacks text-critical support and rather reflects the need of the scholars in question for identifiable and consistent voices in the text.

The last example is found in Isa 51:1–3, where the voices are often recognized as difficult to identify in any satisfactory way.[14] The passage starts with a call to "listen to me" (שמעו אלי), and the context seems to indicate that this voice is a voice of a prophet,[15] not least since it continues by specifying the addressees as "you who seek YHWH" (מבקשי יהוה). This audience is then exhorted by the prophet to look at Abraham, "your father" (אביכם), and Sarah, "who bore you" (תחוללכם), and the reason given is that "he was but one when I called him, but I blessed him and made him many" (כי־אחד קראתיו ואברכהו וארבהו, v. 2). Since it is unreasonable to believe that the prophet is here described as the one calling Abraham, even though verse 3 returns to speaking about YHWH in the third person, the verse provides a clear example of an intertwining of the voices of the prophet and the deity in a way that, given its pervasive nature throughout the 'book,' seems to have been not only unproblematic but an integral part of how the prophetic speech was transmitted in writing across time.

Sidelining the "First One"

Turning more directly to the issue of the place of the "first one" in *Isaiah*, it would be reasonable to posit that this "first one" is understood to be a prophet called Isaiah, since he is the one mentioned in the 'book.' This said, it can nonetheless be observed that the prophet Isaiah is explicitly named only three times outside of the narrative in Isa 36–39, where he is mentioned by name an additional ten times (Isa 37:2, 5, 6, 21; 38:1, 4, 21; 39:3, 5, 8)—namely, in Isa 7:3 and 20:2, 3. This observation alone indicates that the (name of the) "first one" is not given any central place in the early transmission of the 'book'—that is, prior to the framing of the 'book' by means of the paratexts in Isa 1:1; 2:1; and 13:1.[16] At the very least, then, it seems as if nobody went

---

14. See, e.g., Baltzer 2001, 344. Westermann 1969, 232–37, completely rearranges the verses into the sequence 51:1a → 50:10–11 → 51:4–7a → 51:1b–2 → 51:7b–8, so that the voices are made consistent.

15. Cf. Baltzer 2001, 344; contra, e.g., Smith 2009, 390; Goldingay and Payne 2006b, 221 (understanding v. 1b as "self-referring in the third person"); and Berges 2015, 116, who all identify YHWH as the speaker in v. 1. This is a reasonable possibility and does not detract from the main observation that there is an intertwining of voices throughout the three verses.

16. If Williamson 2018, 103–5, is correct that chapters 7, 20, and 36–39 are related to one another so that they all "started out as (part of?) a composition later than the lifetime of Isaiah that showed particular interest in the person of the prophet and his remarkable

out of their way to specify the identity of the various voices. In fact, the prophet Isaiah is never explicitly said to have spoken anything outside of the narrative in Isa 36–39, although he receives words *from* YHWH in Isa 7:3 and Isa 20:2 (the latter resulting not in prophetic speech but in symbolic action, v. 3). Ultimately, then, the prophet Isaiah ends up sidelined in the 'book' in a way similar to how Enheduanna was sidelined in the *Exaltation of Inanna*. To unpack these observations in more detail, the change of speaker between chapters 6 and 7 will serve as an appropriate starting point.

And He Said

In Isa 7:1, an anonymous voice that is distinct from the "first one" is heard. This voice, which is in clear contrast to the first-person speech in chapters 6 and 8,[17] narrates a series of events in which a prophet called Isaiah was involved. If reading the 'book' synchronically (and without the superscriptions), chapter 7 is in fact the chapter where this prophet is mentioned by name *for the first time* (he is not mentioned in Isa 6 nor in Isa 8), but although it is recounted that he received words from YHWH (v. 3), he is never explicitly introduced as speaking anything,[18] not even in Isa 7:13.[19] Looking at that verse, the *possible implication* that the prophet Isaiah is speaking (i.e., if reading Isa 7:10–17 together with vv. 1–9) is often not deemed enough, and some translations of

---

words and deeds" (104), this observation would be even further underscored, since it is only in these parts that the name Isaiah is found.

17. The voice in Isa 7:1 is recurrently referred to as the voice of an "editor" or "collector" (Clements 1980, 79; Roberts 2015, 109). As has been observed above, the first-person voices in chapters 6 and 8 are anonymous, as also noted by Quinn-Miscall 2001, 127: "Isaiah is named in the titles in 1:1; 2:1; and 13:1 and appears as a named character only in chapters 7, 20, and 37–39. When the prophet speaks in the first person, 'I,' in chapters 6 and 8, he does not name himself."

18. So also Smith 2007, 207. Scholars since Duhm 1892 and Budde 1928 have suggested emendations to relate the words of the 'book' closer to the prophet Isaiah so that it would fit the idea that parts of chapters 6–8 originated as personal memoirs written down by the prophet himself. Clements 1980, 83, for example, states that Isa 7:3 (which reads וַיֹּאמֶר יְהוָה אֶל־יְשַׁעְיָהוּ) "must originally have been recorded in the first person, 'and the Lord said to me,' as a part of the prophet's own memoir," but all these suggestions are without foundation (so also Wildberger 1991, 284; Williamson 2018, 95) and betray anachronistic author concepts. Or with the words of Kaiser 1983, 134, they are "based on a misunderstanding of the literary character of the narrative."

19. Reading through commentaries on the 'book' called *Isaiah*, this is seldom observed. Instead, the commentators proceed as if the text is not anonymous at all, insert the prophet Isaiah continuously, and inquire into the possible intentions of "his" speeches (as but one example, see Roberts 2015, 114).

this verse therefore introduce the prophet by translating וַיֹּאמֶר as "then Isaiah said" (see, e.g., NRSV, NIV, or more expansive translations like the Amplified Bible).[20] This is not necessarily a problematic interpretation in itself,[21] although it assumes a seamless continuity between verses 10–17 and verses 1–9 that has been questioned,[22] but creates an illusion that the text is centered on the prophet Isaiah and his actions rather than acknowledging that the text in fact does not put the prophet in such a pivotal place—what is found here is instead an example of the intertwining of divine and human voices. As made clear in verse 10, YHWH is the named speaker (וַיּוֹסֶף יְהוָה דַּבֵּר אֶל־אָחָז לֵאמֹר, "Again YHWH spoke to Ahaz, saying") so that the most logical referent to the third-person subject in verse 13 (וַיֹּאמֶר) is YHWH as well, indicating that YHWH first spoke and then replied.[23] However, in the quoted divine speech that follows, which probably ends in verse 17, YHWH is then referred to in the third person several times (vv. 14–15, 17), making it clear that the prophet is in fact speaking as well (this is further underlined by the use of אֶת־אֱלֹהַי, "my God," in v. 13), showing once again the intertwining of divine and human voices.

---

20. Such a reading is also suggested by, e.g., Blenkinsopp 2000, 227; Beuken 2003, 184, 203; Roberts 2015, 117; and presumed by Clements 1980, 87; Brueggemann 1998a, 69; Williamson 2018, 149–50. As with Isa 7:3, it has also been suggested that the verb should be emended to the first-person singular (וָאֹמַר), again without foundation (Wildberger 1991, 285; Williamson 2018, 139) but based on the idea of a *Denkschrift*.

21. It should be added that it would not follow from such a reading that the voice is therefore to be understood as the *actual* prophet Isaiah, the idea that lies behind the suggested Isaianic *Denkschrift*. The observation by Foucault about narratives, even ones recounted in the first person, is appropriate here: "It is well known that in a novel narrated in the first person, neither the first person pronoun, the present indicative tense, nor, for that matter, its signs of localization refer directly to the writer, either to the time when he wrote, or to the specific act of writing; rather, they stand for a 'second self' whose similarity to the author is never fixed and undergoes considerable alteration within the course of a single book. It would be as false to seek the author in relation to the actual writer as to the fictional narrator; the 'author-function' arises out of their scission—in the division and distance of the two" (1977, 129). Although the general idea of a *Denkschrift* has been subject to much discussion (for an overview of research, see Uhlig 2009, 122n215), scholars continue to designate parts of chapters 6 and 8 as "authentic," in contrast to additions by later hands. The reason for these conclusions is often that the first-person speech in Isa 6 and 8 "fits well from a traditio-historical point of view with what could be expected of Isaiah" (so Williamson 1994, 30). While this may be true, the fact that the texts are nonetheless anonymous should not be overlooked.

22. See the discussion on the diachronic relationship between the two parts in, e.g., Kaiser 1983, 136–45, or Beuken 2003, 187–91. It can be noted that Beuken argues that the fact that the prophet Isaiah is not mentioned speaks in favor of the seeing vv. 10–17 as having a "Folgecharakter" (201).

23. Cf. similarly Childs 2001, 65.

Agency and Symbolic Action

A similar case is found in Isa 20, where an anonymous narrator introduces a message from YHWH "by the agency"[24] (בְּיַד, v. 2) of a prophet called Isaiah. As in Isa 7, Isaiah is not explicitly speaking anything, but in contrast to Isa 7, he is not even implicitly doing so.[25] Instead, the means by which YHWH speaks "through" the prophet Isaiah is *symbolic action*. He receives a command to remove his sackcloth and his sandals, and it is told that he walked around naked for three years. The explanation for this action is then not provided by the prophet but instead framed by the anonymous narrator as direct speech by YHWH (vv. 3–5).[26] What is found in this passage, then, is a sidelining of the prophet—"the prophet's activity is perceived as if he merely plays the role of being some apparatus that receives instructions sent out by the deity."[27] Needless to say, nothing suggests that these verses are "based upon a first person report from the prophet himself."[28]

A Supporting Character

The picture of a sidelined prophet continues in Isa 36–39. In these chapters, whose place in the 'book' called *Isaiah* and relation to the narratives in 2 Kgs has been subject to much discussion,[29] the prophet

---

24. BDB, s.v. יַד; cf. Roberts 2015, 270: "by means of." The expression thus implies that the words are primarily directed not to the prophet Isaiah (in contrast to the LXX use of πρός) but to the people (cf. Beuken 2007, 210, who translates "durch Vermittlung").

25. This observation has, together with additional considerations, lead scholars like Kaiser 1980, 114, to argue that v. 2 must be an interpolation—that is, since v. 2 opens "oddly with the introduction to a prophetic saying, emphasizing that the action enjoined was a revelation and describing a statement addressed to Isaiah as something Yahweh says through him." This is not necessarily a problem, however, since the conveying of a message from YHWH through human recipients does not always imply that they are to speak. In many cases, it instead implies actions or leads to action, as the current passage makes clear (see also, e.g., the use of דבר־אלהים in Judg 3:20 to allude to action taken by Ehud or the relation between דבר יהוה ביד and actions in, e.g., Num 17:5; 27:23; Judg 6:36; 1 Kgs 8:56; 16:12, 34; 17:16; etc.). On seeing v. 2 as original, see also, e.g., Wildberger 1997, 286–87; Blenkinsopp 2000, 321–22. This is not to say that these verses have not been subject to change. As often argued, there are likely traces of updating, not least because of the chronological difficulties between vv. 1 and 3 (see, e.g., the various views in Clements 1980, 173–74; Seitz 1993, 143–45; Wildberger 1997, 286–91; Childs 2001, 145; Beuken 2007, 209).

26. Cf. the observation by Wildberger 1997, 291, that "chap. 20 is . . . a report from an unknown individual."

27. Wildberger 1997, 292.

28. So Duhm, quoted from Clements 1980, 175.

29. It is beside the point here to enter into any lengthy discussion of the formation of these chapters, the nature of the overlaps with 2 Kgs, or their function in the 'book' called

Isaiah is encountered as an important—not principal but rather supporting—character in a retelling of events surrounding the attack on Judah and Jerusalem by the Assyrians and how the main character, King Hezekiah,[30] handles the crisis. Again, the events are recounted by an anonymous narrator, but in contrast to the narratives in chapters 7 and 20 discussed above and for the first time in the 'book' *Isaiah* (if read synchronically), the prophet Isaiah is explicitly connected to spoken words in Isa 37:6 (ויאמר אליהם ישעיהו, "and Isaiah said to them") and then again in Isa 37:21; 38:1, 21; and 39:3, 5. It is thus as a character in the story that he speaks, and it can be noted that his speech often features כה אמר יהוה, "thus says YHWH" (so Isa 37:6, 21; 38:1), indicating that his words are not his only but always overlap in some way with divine speech (only in Isa 39:3 is no such connection made explicit). Therefore, and as would be expected from the discussion above, some of the passages also intertwine divine and human speech in a way that makes them difficult to distinguish from one another. The case in point would be Isa 38:4–8, where the text is reshuffled, if compared to the version found in 2 Kgs 20:7–8, so that the relation to verses 21–22 (verses that seem dislocated from between vv. 6, 7)[31] is unclear.[32] Keeping the focus on the version in the 'book' called *Isaiah*, it can be observed that in verse 4, it is said that "the word of YHWH came to Isaiah, saying" (ויהי דבר־יהוה אל־ישעיהו לאמר). In verse 5, divine speech indeed follows, as YHWH commands the prophet Isaiah, "Go and say to Hezekiah: 'Thus says YHWH'" (הלוך ואמרת אל חזקיהו כה אמר יהוה). However, arriving at verse 7, the picture is no longer clear, since the third person is suddenly used in relation to YHWH, followed by a return to the first person in verse 8. Who speaks here? Is it the prophet or the deity?[33] Although it

---

Isaiah. For overviews on these issues, I refer the reader to Williamson 1994, 189–211; Childs 2001, 259–66; Beuken 2010, 353–58; and Birdsong 2020.

30. Cf. Blenkinsopp 2000, 483.

31. See, e.g., Clements 1980, 293; Brueggemann 1998a, 308; Smith 2007, 637. Roberts 2015, 478, rather sees them as originally following v. 8; Kaiser 1980, 401, restores v. 21 after v. 1; and Seitz 1993, 259–60, argues that they are quite appropriate as a conclusion to the story (cf. Stromberg 2009; Beuken 2010, 422, 440–42). A common view, based on the idea that this chapter is secondary to the one in 2 Kgs 20, has been to understand vv. 21–22 as an attempt to correct an original omission of these verses when the story was relocated (so, e.g., Clements 1980, 288).

32. For an overview, see Childs 2001, 280–82.

33. Similar observations have been made by Williamson 1994, 205: "God speaks in the first person through Isaiah in verses 5b–6; he is referred to in the third person in verse 7; and the first-person singular in verse 8 is ambiguous, since it could refer either to God or to the prophet." Cf. also the comments in Beuken 2010, 428; Brueggemann

could be tempting to try to sort the voices out, this passage is better seen as yet an example of where no distinction between the voices is upheld.

Anonymous Transmission

In light of the overview of Isa 7 and 20 above, it can thus be concluded that all these chapters—which are the only ones to mention the prophet Isaiah by name—sidelines the prophetic voice in favor of more pressing matters. Although indicating that revelation was originally transmitted through him, Isaiah seems not to have played any significant part in the continued transmission, which was instead carried out by anonymous subsequent ones who shaped and reshaped the narratives in relation to changing needs.

Ultimately, then, it seems as if the 'book'—read without the paratexts—is indeed not a 'book' *of* Isaiah or a 'book' *called* Isaiah but a collection of anonymous prophetic oracles intertwining human and divine voices that sometimes features stories *about* a prophet called Isaiah, where this prophet, when speaking, does so as a supporting character, not as a leading voice.[34]

ADDING VOICES

So far, it has been clear that the revelation flowing through the prophet Isaiah was transmitted in writing by subsequent ones in a way that the "first one" became sidelined. Voices other than the prophet Isaiah are thus present in the 'book' that now bears his name, and this can be developed a bit further by looking at two examples that feature first-person speech by what is reasonably identified as a human voice other than the "first one": Isa 48:16 and 50:4–9.[35]

1998a, 304 (who says that v. 7 "appears to stand alone, almost as an addition"); or Kaiser 1980, 400–403.

34. This is, then, in some contrast to, e.g., Berges 2012b, 48, who claims that starting with Isa 40:1, "the prophet *in* the book (chaps 1–39), now becomes the prophet *of* the book (chaps 40–66)."

35. There are, of course, many more passages that could be relevant to deal with here (some will feature in the discussion below), even if the identification of passages featuring human voices only is not clear-cut. Isa 40, for example, features "a chain of un-named voices" (Heffelfinger 2011, 141). It is often interpreted as some kind of a call narrative (or at least a preface of sorts to chapters 40–55; see Tiemeyer 2011, 333–45) set as a heavenly council scene (Cross 1953) recounting how "Deutero-Isaiah" started "his" ministry (so, e.g., McKenzie 1968, 16–19; Brueggemann 1998b, 19–20). The text itself, however, has always resisted such a categorization (cf. Westermann 1969, 32, observing that the subject is "not the messenger, but the message. . . . The introduction of the messenger is peripheral

A Newcomer Speaks Up

Isa 48:16	קִרְבוּ אֵלַי שִׁמְעוּ־זֹאת	16a	Come near to me, hear this:
	<u>לֹא מֵרֹאשׁ</u> בַּסֵּתֶר דִּבַּרְתִּי	b	I have <u>not</u> spoken in secret <u>from the beginning</u>,
	<u>מֵעֵת הֱיוֹתָהּ</u>	c	[but] since <u>the time</u>[36] of its happening[37]
	<u>שָׁם אָנִי</u>		<u>I have been there</u>,
	<u>וְעַתָּה</u> אֲדֹנָי יְהוִה	d	<u>and now</u>, the lord YHWH <u>has</u>
	<u>שְׁלָחַנִי</u> וְרוּחוֹ		<u>sent me</u> and his spirit.

and forms only a part of the larger whole, a part, moreover, couched in veiled terms";
see also Hanson 1995, 19; Berges 2010a, 563). In fact, it starts with an intertwining
of divine and human voices (the speaking voice in v. 1 is that of an unnamed prophet
who is transmitting words that "your God" [אלהיכם, second-person m. pl.] says [אמר,
third-person m. sing.] to an unidentified people [עמי]; cf. Blenkinsopp 2002b, 178–79;
van Wieringen 2005, 119; Sweeney 2016b, 44; Berges 2020a, 89–91), and then, after the
words of an anonymous speaker in v. 2, the passage continues in v. 3 by introducing an
unidentified (cf. Westermann 1969, 36) "voice" (קול) related to the "mouth of YHWH"
(v. 5) that enters into a dialogue with an unidentified speaker in v. 6. Tull 2017, 163,
captures it well: "The message of comfort travels from voice to voice throughout, but its
sources are as difficult to distinguish as singers echoing in a stone cathedral." Interesting in
this passage is also how these subsequent voices seem to place themselves in continuation
of the task of the "first one," as has been pointed out by Berges 2020a, 83 (connections
have also been made on different grounds by Ackroyd 1982 and Seitz 1990). However,
this chapter does not feature any first-person speech in the MT, although such a speech is
found in v. 6 in the LXX and the Vulgate (although not in the Peshitta). While scholars
have had a tendency to prefer the reading וָאֹמַר (see, e.g., the arguments in Tiemeyer
2011, 14–16), there is nothing in the text itself that precludes the third-person m. sing.
from being original (cf. Childs 2001, 377), and it should thus be kept (Berges 2010a, 562;
Berges 2010b, 590–91). An additional observation to be made is that in contrast to the
relation between prophetic speech in chapters 7–8 discussed above, there is nothing that
indicates that any of the voices in Isa 40 should be identified as the prophet Isaiah's (contra
Berges 2010b, 588–89), since chapter 39 ends with Hezekiah speaking. Apart from Isa
40, other passages that could have illustrated some of the aspects that will be covered
below include, for example, Isa 53, where the first plural is used in a passage that provides
another interesting example of the juxtaposition of a plethora of unidentified voices, some
intertwined with the deity's (see esp. vv. 10–12; cf. also the use of first-person plural in Isa
41:22–23, 26, interpreted as referencing the listening witnesses; Baltzer 2001, 119–20;
Goldingay and Payne 2006a, 191; or as a rhetorical feature, Berges 2020a, 215); 51:19,
which may identify the prophet as one giving comfort (אנחמך; cf. below, n. 1, chapter 10);
the interesting 57:21, where an anonymous voice concludes a series of divine words with
"says *my* God" (אמר אלהי); or 62:1, where a first-person speaker is claiming to not keep
silent until Jerusalem is vindicated. In addition, the 'book' called *Isaiah* also features a lot
of personifications (see the discussion in van der Woude 2011).

36. For the meaning "since" for מעת, see Kronholm 2001, 441.

37. Cf. Berges 2020a, 537: "vom Zeitpunkt seines Werdens/Geschehens."

As an example of the intertwining of subsequent voices in the 'book' called *Isaiah*, this verse provides quite an obscure—albeit potentially important—starting point. Several problems can be identified.

First, it seems to provide yet another unannounced shift of voices—scholars have regularly identified YHWH as the speaker up until אני in verse 16c and argued that he is followed by an unidentified first-person voice in verse 16d that claims to have been sent by YHWH.[38] But who is this second speaker? A prophet?[39] A servant?[40] Cyrus?[41] Suggestions abound, but no consensus is in sight. Needless to say, the speaker seems not to have deemed it important to identify her-/himself.[42]

Second, it is not clear how verse 16b–c is to be translated. It is often suggested that to make sense of the verse, which is taken to overlap with Isa 45:19, לא should be placed after מראש so that the meaning of verse 16b would be something like "from the beginning I did not speak in secret"[43]—that is, a claim by YHWH that he has always spoken in a way that anyone could hear, implying that verse 16c enforces this by saying that YHWH is, moreover, always present.[44] But in such a reading, the infinitive construct in verse 16c is still puzzling, and the notion of presence does not really make sense in relation to secret speech.[45] So even if this is a reasonable suggestion, the consequence is that verse 16d

---

38. So, e.g., Goldingay and Payne 2006b, 142–43; Paul 2012, 316; Blenkinsopp 2002b, 294. The verse has also been called "the first of two crucial transitions within the servant-concept in Isa 40–55" (Poulsen 2014, 216).

39. Cf. Berges 2020a, 537: "die prophetische Gemeinschaft, die als berufener und geläuterter Knecht bereit ist, sich von Babel und ihrem Fremdgötterdienst zu trennen und den Weg in die judäische Heimat anzutreten."

40. So, e.g., Westermann 1969, 203; Childs 2001, 377–78. I will not enter here into any lengthy discussion of the very complex topic of the servant(s) in the 'book' called *Isaiah* but will instead refer to the thorough treatment in Blenkinsopp 1997.

41. So McKenzie 1968, 99; Sweeney 2016b, 141.

42. The idea that Isa 48:16 would be a crafted reflection of Exod 3 (so Baltzer 2001, 293–96) is not convincing (see the critique in Sommer 2004, 151–52). As a note on language, it has been pointed out by Tiemeyer 2011, 26–30, in particular, that the prophetic voices throughout Isa 40–55 are constructed in both masculine and feminine terms (see also the discussion in Goldingay 2006a, 47–49), which suggests that it is wise to avoid too gendered language.

43. See, e.g., Paul 2012, 316.

44. Cf. Smith 2009, 328.

45. On the latter, see also McKenzie 1968, 96.

becomes completely detached. Not surprisingly, it has therefore been regarded as either misplaced[46] or incomplete.[47]

There may not be any satisfactory way to solve these issues, but one possibility not yet considered is that the speaker in this verse, which seems to introduce a new section (vv. 16–19,[48] or even vv. 16–22), is in fact one and the same—a "subsequent one" partaking in the transmission of prophetic tradition and claiming to be sanctioned by YHWH himself. A number of observations could point in such a direction, and even if they are not sufficient in themselves, the cumulative effect is worth considering, especially since this proposal creates interesting overlaps with the dynamics in most other passages that will be dealt with below.

Starting with verse 16d, it has often been noted that its use of the first person, the name used for YHWH,[49] and the reference to his רוח create overlaps with texts like Isa 49:1–6 and 50:4–9, on the one hand (texts that will be dealt with below), and texts like Isa 42:1 and 61:1, on the other.[50] This would indicate that a servant figure is in view, and read in light of the literary context in which verse 16 is found, the task of this servant would primarily be related to speech (vv. 16b, 17–19). If so, how does the message he is supposed to transmit relate to the "first one"? Here, the time references in verse 16b, c, and d are probably indicative. Read in light of one another, they seem to paint a picture where first—from the beginning (מראש)—this individual *did not speak* (in secret). Then, at a new point in time (מעת), also specified with the preposition מן to create a clear parallelism, things began to happen, and at that time, s/he was *present*. Last, in the present time (ועתה), s/he is her-/himself *sent* (to proclaim). In this reading, the speaker is talking about her-/himself in all three lines but claims to have been present only in the two last ones—in the first line, s/he is emphatically *not* (לא) speaking. Read in this way, verse 16b–c reveals a contrast between two times, one where someone spoke in secret and one where things began to happen, and this is well in line with how מראש is used in Isa 40:21;

---

46. Westermann 1969, 203, has famously argued that the verse belongs to chapter 49, where it was originally placed in the margins, only to be inserted in the wrong place by a later scribe.

47. See Blenkinsopp 2002b, 294, who understands ורוחו to be the beginning of a new sentence that is now lost.

48. Cf. Smith 2009, 328.

49. See, e.g., Baltzer 2001, 293.

50. Cf. Blenkinsopp 2002b, 294 (see also Blenkinsopp 1997, 163–64); Berges 2010b, 594; Poulsen 2014, 216. Tiemeyer 2011, 21, relates Isa 48:16d to Isa 40:6ab–7 and argues that רוח is "probably an additional subject alongside YHWH" (325).

41:4; and 41:26, as well as with the contrasting of past and present in these chapters that will be further discussed below ("The Past and the Present"). Anticipating part of that discussion, it could be suggested that the logic of verse 16 is that the unidentified person speaking claims not to have been present at the time when YHWH's words were first spoken and made unavailable (cf. Isa 8:16; 29:11; etc.)[51] but that s/he was indeed present when these words were believed to have shown themselves to be true, and now (cf. the use of ועתה in, e.g., Isa 43:1; 44:1; 47:8; 49:5)[52] s/he is claiming to be legitimized as a tradent of this prophetic tradition, sent by YHWH in a way similar to how the "first one" was sent (cf. שְׁלָחַנִי, *qal* perf. third-person m. sing., in Isa 48:16d with שְׁלָחֵנִי, *qal* imp. m. sing., in Isa 6:8).[53] Put differently, this voice presumes that now is the time to "remove the seal" and continue the proclamation.[54]

Although this is a speculative suggestion that needs to be held only tentatively, it provides a solution to the problems identified above and indicates that the first-person speakers here and in passages that follow are constructed as distinct from the "first one" while at the same time having no less legitimacy as tradents.

The Disciples

Looking next at Isa 50:4–9, the dynamic suggested above is further developed. Verses 4–5a read as follows:[55]

---

51. That is, in contrast to YHWH, who has not spoken in hiding (Isa 45:19) and who has been making things known (נגד; Isa 40:21; 41:26) from the beginning. The use of סתר may thus be either seen as related to the binding of the prophetic tradition discussed above or, if taken together with מראש rather than with דברתי, interpreted as speaking of a time now lost, perhaps reflecting the distance to the receiving of revelation by the "first one" caused by the exile.

52. Schniedewind 2019, 111–16, has demonstrated how ועתה has a background as a transition marker in ancient Hebrew scribal education, an observation that could lend further support to reading v. 16d together with a–c. Cf. also Duperreault 2013, 269.

53. On this, see also Goldingay and Payne 2006a, 47.

54. Needless to say, this does not mean that a prophetic individual must therefore have written these words (see also Berges 2010a, 564).

55. The chiastic structure has been identified by Goldingay and Payne 2006b, 207–8 (who also discusses the Masoretic accents). I have only modified their translation slightly. To be noted with Goldingay and Payne is that "the testimony works in reverse order" (208)—hearing precedes using the tongue.

⁴ The Lord YHWH has given <u>to me</u> *a tongue* (אדני יהוה נתן לי לשון)
  of disciples (למודים),
        to know (how) to sustain the weary. (לדעת לעות את־יעף)
            A word (דבר)⁵⁶
                he wakens in the morning, (יעיר בבקר)
                in the morning he wakens (בבקר יעיר)
            for me an ear (לי אזן)
            to listen (לשמע)
        as one of the disciples, (כלמודים)
⁵ the Lord YHWH opened <u>to me</u> *an ear*. (אדני יהוה פתח־לי אזן)

This passage follows directly after a first-person speech that is best understood as given by a divine voice (at first glance, the two seem to have little to do with each other, although vv. 4–9 could be taken as a response).[57] An anonymous voice speaks of the hardships of being a disciple (and prophet) in a discourse packed with first-person references.[58]

---

56. Goldingay and Payne 2006b, 209, correctly observe that דבר is not likely the subject of the verb יעיר, which is rather the Lord YHWH (this is further emphasized by the chiastic arrangement of the two יעיר, indicating that the referent of both is the same), but the argument that it cannot be the object since "such objects are usually part of the person" is less convincing, and the translation above both avoids the need for an added preposition ("with") and creates a better parallel to לי אזן.

57. Cf. Brueggemann 1998b, 121; Motyer 1999, 316; Heffelfinger 2011, 124. Some have argued that vv. 1–3, or at least parts of them, are to be seen as connected (so, e.g., Baltzer 2001, 335; cf. Goldingay and Payne 2006b, 205; Berges 2015, 98).

58. See also Tull 2017, 167. It is well known that this passage has been known as the third of the *Ebed-Jahve-Lieder* identified by Duhm 1892 ("servant songs"; more specifically Isa 42:1–4 [+5–7]; 49:1–6; 50:4–9 [+10–11]; and 52:13–53:12). The suggested existence of a collection of independent servant songs secondarily inserted in Isa 40–55 wherever there was space left on the manuscript has been convincingly refuted by Mettinger 1983, whose arguments need not be rehearsed here (see also the discussion in Poulsen 2014, 80–83; Berges 2020b). However, seeing a connection between the first-person speech in Isa 48:16; 50:4–6; and 49:1–6 (see, e.g., Blenkinsopp 2002b, 294; 2003, 320) is probably still to the point (although on this see also Tiemeyer 2011, 311–32). Regarding Isa 49:1–6, and as with all passages featuring a servant, there are countless publications attempting to identify "his" identity, a task complicated by the contrast between v. 3 (where the servant is *called* Israel) and vv. 5–6 (where Israel is referred to as a people to be gathered *by* the servant). Keeping the focus on the text itself, however, it is quite clear that the first-person speaker identifies her-/himself as designated by YHWH "to be about the work of healing and emancipation in the world with particular reference to Israel" (Brueggemann 1998b, 110) and so embodies the call of Israel (Childs 2001, 385; Goldingay and Payne 2006a, 46) and that s/he "picks up the voice of the messenger sent in 48:16" (Childs 2001, 382; see, e.g., the use of ועתה in Isa 49:5), being called to use her/his words (v. 2; cf. Isa 50:4). As in Isa 50:4–6 (see below, n. 73), the presentation of this servant also overlaps somewhat with what is found in the 'book' called *Jeremiah* (McKenzie 1968, 104; Westermann 1969, 207; Hanson 1995, 127; Paul 2012, 323; Sweeney 2016b, 167; cf.,

Notable is that the speaker is introduced as one who has received the "tongue of a disciple" (לשון למודים) and who has had his ear opened so that he can listen "as one of the disciples" (כלמודים). As has often been pointed out, למוד is a very rare word. It is used only six times in the Hebrew Bible: two outside of the 'book' called *Isaiah* (Jer 2:24; 13:23) and four times in it (Isa 8:16; 50:4 [2x]; 54:13). As for the occurrences in *Jeremiah*, they are used to convey the meaning of being "accustomed" to something—a wild ass is accustomed to the wilderness in Jer 2:24, and people are accustomed to do evil in Jer 13:23. This seems not to be the case in Isa 50:4–9, however. More relevant, then, are the two passages in *Isaiah*. In fact, since they use this terminology in ways similar to Isa 50:4–9, it seems as if they all relate to one another.[59] This thus needs some further unpacking.

It has already been shown that Isa 8:16 constructed a transmission of prophetic testimony and teaching to "subsequent ones" referred to as disciples. In light of this, it would thus not be far-fetched to see in Isa 50:4 a reference back to this chapter, implying that the speaker in Isa 50:4 is identifying her-/himself as such a "subsequent one."[60] In fact, it has been argued that these verses indicate that this "subsequent one" believed that now was the time "when the sealed document was to be opened and a new message of salvation, to which the earlier prophet had alluded, was to be proclaimed,"[61] a suggestion well in line with what was argued in relation to Isa 48:16.[62] The name by which the prophet refers to God—אדני יהוה—also connects the two passages,[63] and the specific focus of the message

---

e.g., Isa 49:5 with Jer 1:5, although Baltzer 2001, 305–11, points to Moses). Besides noting the possible relation between this text, Isa 48:16, and Isa 50:4–6, I have chosen not to deal with it in any length, since although it is spoken in the first person and thus provides yet an example of the intertwining of subsequent voices, the passage does not address the *relation* to previous voices (apart from v. 5 perhaps "includ[ing] in [its] perspective the work of Isaiah ben Amoz, which Second Isaiah carries on," so Goldingay and Payne 2006b, 161, a point well put, except for the problematic names attached to the voices).

59. In contrast to Berges 2015, 100–101, who only sees a strong connection with Isa 54:13.

60. Cf. Williamson 1994, 108: "It must be regarded as highly probable that all three occurrences in Deutero-Isaiah reflect the influence of 8:16–17" (similarly Goldingay and Payne 2006b, 208; Paul 2012, 350).

61. Williamson 1994, 107. See also similarly Sweeney 2016b, 201; Berges 2020b, 321.

62. According to Childs 2001, 394, the voice in Isa 48:16 is the same as the voice in Isa 50:4–9.

63. Cf. Childs 2001, 394; Berges 2010b, 594. On the possibility that אדני should be read as "my Lord" rather than "the Lord," see Berges 2015, 99.

to be proclaimed—to "sustain the weary" (לעות את־יעף)—is well in line with the message of the chapters in which this speech is found (see also, e.g., Isa 40:27–31).[64] Moreover, the reference to "a word" (דבר) may allude to the prophetic tradition itself,[65] which thus has to be received ("heard," לשמע)[66] as one of the disciples (כלמודים).[67] Put differently, this passage constructs the disciple as a channel for continuous revelation anchored in tradition.

Read in light of Isa 8:16–20, it is also significant that the speaker mentions that YHWH uncovers her/his ear *every morning* and that the result is that s/he can hear as disciples do (לשמע כלמודים). Throughout the 'book' called *Isaiah*, the people are recurrently described as deaf to the message of YHWH, and in Isa 8:20, they were, more specifically, judged to be without dawn (i.e., without hope). In contrast to that situation, where teaching was sealed, this disciple in fact has a dawn.[68] A new hope is presented, ears are uncovered, and there is continuity in the message, as disciples (pl.)—"subsequent ones"—are authorized as new recipients of prophetic revelation.[69] Moving from a single "first one" to a larger group of "disciples," this trajectory will eventually reach its goal in the third and last verse featuring למוד in *Isaiah*: Isa 54:13. Here, in a vision of restoration, a voice intertwining the divine and human proclaims that *all of the children of Israel* (וכל־בניך) will be *disciples of*

---

64. Cf. Blenkinsopp 2003, 319.

65. Cf. Berges 2015, 101. Perhaps contra Childs 2001, 394: "What the servant learned was not information."

66. As noted by van der Toorn 2007, 12, the emphasis on hearing may indicate that the transmission included performative aspects.

67. One argument that has been formulated against seeing the character in this chapter as a disciple modeling himself on Isa 8:16 is that the disciple in Isa 50 does not see her-/himself as the disciple of the prophet Isaiah but as a disciple of YHWH (so, e.g., Smith 2009, 381; similarly Berges 2015, 100–101). Such a critique misses the point, however, both since it is not made clear who the disciples belong to in Isa 8:16, as I argued above—an observation even further strengthened by the constant intertwining of divine-human agency—and since the prophet Isaiah is not central to the transmission of tradition at this point. There is thus no reason to assume that one need to have some kind of relation with this specific individual to be legitimized as a tradent. Instead, it is the revelation that is at the center of attention—not a "first one" nor any "subsequent ones." It therefore makes complete sense that the disciple in Isa 50 is focused primarily on YHWH. Also, contra Childs 2001, 394, it is quite possible to relate this passage to *both* Isa 48:16 and Isa 8:16–20.

68. Williamson 1994, 108–9, has also noted some additional overlaps between the passages: the disciple in chapter 50 describes himself as someone who has not been rebellious (v. 5), and while YHWH is hiding his face in Isa 8:17, the disciple is not hiding his face in Isa 50:6.

69. Cf. somewhat similarly McKenzie 1968, 116–17.

YHWH (לִמּוּדֵי יהוה).[70] A similar vision is also found in Isa 59:21, where a divine word, placed in the mouth of an anonymous recipient upon whom YHWH's רוח rests, is to be transmitted from mouth to mouth across generations.[71]

This reading of Isa 50:4–9 does not mean that the text is therefore to be understood as a window into the mind of an anonymous individual.[72] The portrait is "a *literary* composition in its own right," and it can be observed that "in describing a situation likely to recur, [it] uses familiar and traditional forms of speech."[73] The important conclusion to draw is instead that in Isa 50:4–9, the prophetic voice constructs itself as a new[74] receiver (*his* ear is opened every morning) of divine revelation while at the same time claiming continuity with the message channeled through a "first one" by being one of the למודים.[75] The old

---

70. Cf. Goldingay and Payne 2006b, 208.

71. There is no need to suggest, with Kratz 2015, 77, that the text speaks of "an individual person who can only be identified with the prophet of the book, Isaiah."

72. Cf. Collins 1993, 55: "For the writers and editors of the book, it is the vision rather than the exact words of a particular individual that constitutes the essential 'Isaiah.' . . . Consequently the Isaiah presented to us in the book functions more as a symbolic figure than as a historical personality" (see similarly Quinn-Miscall 2001, 127).

73. Blenkinsopp 2002b, 320 (emphasis in the original); cf. McKenzie 1968, 117; Collins 1993, 55. A good case for the portrait of Jeremiah being influential in Isa 50 has been made by Westermann 1969, 226–28; Baltzer 2001, 340. Among other things, he compares Isa 50:5–6 with Jer 11:19; 15:10; 17:15; 18:18; 20:10; Isa 50:7–8 with Jer 11:20; 17:14; 20:11, 13; Isa 50:8–9 with Jer 11:19; 15:10–11; 17:15–16; 18:18–20; 20:10; and Isa 50:9 with Jer 11:21–23; 15:15; 17:18; 18:21–23; 20:12, but then he points to Moses as a possible identification partner (cf. Isa 50:4 with Deut 1:1–5). Not all of these references are very strong. Other attempts to identify this person have also been made, all attempting to remedy the fact that the transmission of prophetic speeches is in fact anonymous (Whybray 1975, 151–52 [similarly Goldingay and Payne 2006b, 210–11], suggests a prophet arrested by Babylonian authorities; Watts 1987, 201–3, suggests Zerubbabel; etc.). The common identification of these verses with the servant mentioned in v. 10 (see, e.g., McKenzie 1968, 116–17; Westermann 1969, 226; Blenkinsopp 2003, 319; Smith 2009, 378; Paul 2012, 350; Sweeney 2016b, 201) is possible, and if so, it probably indicates that even more "subsequent ones" are heard here (see, e.g., the view by Blenkinsopp 2002b, 323, that vv. 10–11 are to be seen as a comment on vv. 4–9 by a later tradent; Berges 2015, 109–13; cf. Hanson 1995, 141–42; Childs 2001, 395–96: a disciple of the first-person speaker in vv. 4–9).

74. Cf. Goldingay and Payne 2006a, 45, who describe the relation between this voice and the earlier voices as this voice establishing "both a link with and a distinction from" the earlier one (who they identify as the prophet Isaiah). This aspect is further emphasized if reading the passage in light of Isa 48:16.

75. Cf. Berges 2012b, 64; Goldingay and Payne 2006b, 208; and Berges 2020a, 537, on Isa 48:16. This observation is thus not to be taken as a conclusion regarding the composition of the text, as has been done by scholars such as Eaton 1959, 152–53 (see

prophetic tradition is framed as having been picked up and transmitted by a number of anonymous "subsequent ones" who are, like the "first one," quickly sidelined in the continuing transmission—new voices are introduced in verses 10–11 that speak of the voice in verses 4–9 in the third person.

Given that all voices remain anonymous, it is thus not accurate to claim, as is sometimes the case, that "although critical scholarship has correctly identified the prophet in chs. 40–55 as an anonymous prophet of the Babylonian exile known simply as Deutero- or Second Isaiah, within the synchronic literary context of the 'book,' the prophet must be identified as Isaiah ben Amoz."[76] On the contrary! There is nothing in the literary context that necessitates a merging of the different voices under a specific named individual. No name is ever referenced, and the argument of the texts surveyed above is that the voices are indeed *separate*.

The Past and the Present

So far, it has been observed that the voices of "subsequent ones" introduced in the 'book' called *Isaiah* claim to be recipients of divine revelation while at the same time standing in continuity with a tradition channeled through an anonymous "first one." In relation to Isa 48:16, it was also noted that this identification implied a contrast between the past and the present, a contrast that recurs prominently throughout Isa 40–55 and thus provides an important clue when attempting to understand the construction of authorship.[77] In fact, in a few verses prior to Isa 48:16, these dynamics are made explicit in quite a clarifying manner:[78]

---

the critique in Tiemeyer 2011, 24). It only shows that "the notion of a single prophet is unsupported by the text" (Tiemeyer 2011, 50).

76. Sweeney 2016b, 43.

77. It has long been recognized that this aspect distinguishes chapters 40–55 from the rest of the 'book,' perhaps even reflecting the reasons why "subsequent ones" updated the message (so, e.g., Clements 1985, 112n14; Williamson 1994; Blenkinsopp 2000, 88; etc.; cf. Collins 1993, 44; Poulsen 2014, 212–16).

78. For a brief overview of issues often raised in the interpretation of this passage that are not directly relevant to the focus below (most significantly the [speculative; cf. Blenkinsopp 2002b, 286–87; Berges 2020a, 509–10] objection that some of these verses—especially the ones dealing with the failure of the people in vv. 4, 5b, 7b, and 8[b]—are unexpectedly harsh for this context [or for "Deutero-Isaiah"] and therefore must be seen as later insertions), see Childs 2001, 370–72.

Isa 48:3–8

3 הראשנות מֵאָז הגדתי
The former things I declared *long ago,*

ומפי יצאו ואשמיעם
they went out from my mouth and I made them known;

פתאם עשיתי ותבאנה
then suddenly I acted, and they came to pass.

4 מדעתי כי קשה אתה
Because I know that you are obstinate,

וגיד ברזל ערפך
and your neck is an iron sinew

ומצחך נחושה
and your forehead brass,

5 ואגיד לך מאז
I declared them to you from long ago,

בטרם תבוא השמעתיך
before they came to pass I announced them to you,

פן־תאמר עצבי עשם
so that you would not say, "My idol did them,

ופסלי ונסכי צום
my carved image and my cast image commanded them."

6a שָׁמַעְתָּ
You have heard;

b חֲזֵה כֻּלָּהּ
(now) see all this!

c וְאַתֶּם הֲלוֹא תַגִּידוּ
will you not declare it?

d הִשְׁמַעְתִּיךָ חֲדָשׁוֹת מֵעַתָּה
From now on I will let you hear *new things,*

e וּנְצֻרוֹת ולא ידעתם
hidden things that you have not known.

7 עתה נבראו וְלֹא מֵאָז
They are created now, *not long ago;*

ולפני־יום ולא שמעתם
before today you have never heard of them,

פן־תאמר הנה ידעתין
so that you could not say, "I already knew them."

8 גם לא־שמעת
Neither have you heard,

גם לא ידעת
nor have you known,

גם מאז לא־פתחה אזנך
nor has your ear been opened long ago.

כי ידעתי בגוד תבגוד
For I knew that you would deal very treacherously,

ופשע מבטן קרא לך
and that from birth you were called a rebel.

Reading this passage, it becomes quite clear that a contrast between the past and the present is central to the main claim that the words of YHWH spoken in the present should be trusted above the words of idols, since the things he spoke in the past had indeed come true.[79] In brief, the passage reveals a similar dynamic as the one argued in Isa 48:16b–d: Long ago, YHWH spoke (through a "first one") about things to come. Then suddenly, these things happened, and so now, when YHWH is speaking again, proclaiming new things that have not been disclosed (or even existed) before, he should be trusted. In fact, these three steps are rehearsed in verse 6a–c:

שמעת ← חזה כלה[80] ← ואתם הלוא תגידו

"you have heard"[81] → "(now) see all this!" → "will you not declare it?"

What follows is then a stress on the present (עתה), where new things (that have been kept hidden, נצרות; cf. בסתר in v. 16b) will be heard.[82] The answer to the question in verse 6c will, however, not be provided until verse 16.

If reading Isa 48:16 in continuation with this message, it would follow that the message proclaimed by the "subsequent one"—"now . . . , not long ago" (עתה . . . ולא מאז, v. 7)—derives authority from the

---

79. Cf. Westermann 1969, 196; Goldingay and Payne 2006b, 125; Paul 2012, 307; Berges 2020a, 519. This kind of rhetoric is not unique for Isa 40–55. An interesting example is also found in Parpola 1997, 10, in a collection of oracles of encouragement to Esarhaddon: "Could you not rely on the previous utterance which I spoke to you? Now you can rely on this later one too."

80. The use of חזה, which is often connected with prophetic activity and will eventually be used to frame the relation between the 'book' called *Isaiah* and the prophet Isaiah (see below, esp. "Prophetic Words and Nighttime Visions," chapter 7), may indicate that what had been revealed to the prophet was now also revealed to the public—that is, emphasizing the events that are now coming to pass (v. 3) as revelation (cf. Isa 26.11; 33:17). There is thus no need for emendation (so also Blenkinsopp 2002b, 285).

81. Again, asking whether they would have heard the words of a prophet or the words of YHWH (as in Goldingay and Payne 2006b, 128) is hardly relevant.

82. Reading the passage in this way, with a prophet speaking in v. 16, thus eliminates the possible contradiction often observed (so Smith 2009, 312). It may be that the new things and the ones kept hidden refer to the same thing, as context would imply, but they may also be taken as separate. If the latter, the notion of an earlier revelation that has been kept hidden would provide an interesting overlap with Isa 8:16. The verb נצר is also used in relation to the prophet in Isa 42:6; 49:8.

message proclaimed by the "first one" long ago (מאז, v. 3).[83] It is because s/he stands within a tradition that has proven to be true that this tradition can be furthered and reinterpreted in the current situation.[84] Furthermore, just as the "first one" had done, the "subsequent ones" also provide a necessary contrast to the ones the text addresses. The people do not hear, and "long ago" (מאז) their ears were not opened (לא־פתחה אזנך), while the "subsequent ones" are having their ears opened by YHWH every morning (50:4–5a, פתח־לי אזן). While the people have been rebels since birth (ופשע מבטן קרא לך, Isa 48:8), the "subsequent ones," who were called before they were born (Isa 49:1), have not, in fact, rebelled (לא מריתי, Isa 50:5).

If a plausible reading, this text effectively constructs an idea that past revelation provides the foundation for—and lends authority to—fresh proclamation.[85] The point of continuity is, furthermore, YHWH himself (cf. Isa 43:13; 46:3–4; cf. דבר in 45:23; 55:10–11), who states in verse 12 that "I am He, I am the first (ראשון); indeed, I am the last (אחרון)" (cf. Isa 41:4; 44:6).[86]

The effect of this emphasis on YHWH as the point of continuity in the transmission of prophetic tradition and the intertwining of new revelation is not, however, that the role of the prophets is judged as insignificant. Indicative here is Isa 44:26, where new things about to be done by YHWH are explicitly related to both a confirmation (קום, hiphil part.) of a (previous) word of an anonymous servant in the singular (דבר עבדו, sing., the "first one"[?];[87] cf. Isa 20:3)[88] and the counsel

---

83. Sweeney 2016b, 155, is thus to the point when he suggests that the claims made in this chapter "can only be supported by reference to the first portion of the book of Isaiah in chs. 1–33" (cf. Brueggemann 1998b, 102).

84. Cf. Westermann 1969, 157, on Isa 44:26. As correctly pointed out by Duperreault 2013, the veracity of these claims of oracular fulfillment is, of course, not evident for the intended audience but rather constructed and defended throughout these chapters.

85. So also Duperreault 2013, 256. The attempts to determine exactly what has been spoken in the past is not possible (cf. Goldingay and Payne 2006b, 125, contra Baltzer 2001, 282) and beside the point.

86. For a discussion of a possible relation to Isa 8:23b, see Williamson 1993, 98, who suggests that the relevant words in 8:23b have been taken up "as titles for God," implying an understanding of 8:23b as "signifying that it was 'the First' (with a capital 'F') who brought the land into contempt and 'the Last' (with a capital 'L') who would eventually glorify it again" (cf. Williamson 1994, 68–72).

87. Cf. Williamson 1994, 52. Such a close association needs, of course, to be held tentatively but is quite suggestive in this context. Blenkinsopp 2002b, 247 (and many with him) may also be correct in seeing here the voice of a "subsequent one."

88. It is often seen as a curiosity and changed into the plural by recourse to, most significantly, a few LXX manuscripts (including Alexandrinus) and the Targum. But as correctly noted by Baltzer 2001, 215; Smith 2009, 248–49n537; and Berges 2020a, 367;

(עצת) of anonymous messengers in the plural (מלאכיו, pl., "subsequent ones"[?]).[89] Such a double reference is likely not a coincidence. At the very least, the use of the plural shows that more voices than the "first one" have been instrumental in transmitting the prophetic message previously bound up in the disciples,[90] but an even stronger reference to the work of the "first one" may be established. If related to texts like Isa 42:4, 12, the work of the "subsequent ones" may have been constructed in continuity with Isa 8:16 by means of a shared use of תורה. More specifically, in Isa 42:4, 12, תורה "is used in a very unusual fashion, since it can hardly be intended as a reference to Yahweh's 'law' in the later sense. Rather, it appears to refer to Yahweh's 'purpose,' which has shortly to be realized and which has been declared beforehand by the prophets."[91]

If correct, these texts can be taken as yet another indication of the idea that what was sealed in Isa 8:16 was now considered to be out in the open,[92] "magnified" (גדל, *hiphil*, 42:21) and made "glorious" (אדר, *hiphil*), ultimately to be declared to the "coastlands" (איים, v. 4), which are, significantly, explicitly exhorted in by the first-person speaker in the famous passage in Isa 49:1 (שמעו איים אלי).[93]

2010b, 593, the singular is *lectio difficilior* and should be kept (Blenkinsopp 2002b, 244, also notes that the singular is appropriate in relation to 44:2). Such a conclusion is made even more plausible in light of my argument here, where the use of both singular and plural performs an important function.

89. Oswalt 1998, 194, interprets this as referring to "the entire prophetic class." Westermann 1969, 157, who reconstructs עבד in the plural (see n. 88 above), sees a reference in this verse to "both the pre-exilic prophets of doom and Deutero-Isaiah's own proclamation."

90. Smith 2009, 249, suggests that the text "seems to be saying that God's prophetic messengers (including Isaiah) are the authoritative ones people should listen to," but the text speaks not of authoritative prophets as much as of prophets as authorized carriers of authoritative (divine) speech (cf. Hanson 1995, 97).

91. Clements 1985, 107; cf. Poulsen 2014, 106–7.

92. Cf. Goldingay and Payne 2006b, 11, that "each expression [in this part of the verse] has a background earlier in Isaiah," or Sweeney 2016b, 142, that Isa 44:24–48:22 "presumes the announcements . . . in chs. 1–39." See also, in particular, Williamson 1994, 240, who was noted above to argue that the prophet he calls "Deutero-Isaiah" "regarded the earlier work as in some sense a book that had been sealed up until the time when judgement should be passed and the day of salvation had arrived, which day he believed himself to be heralding."

93. This could also indicate that the contrast between the past and the present may be based on the many references in chapters 2–31 to ביום ההוא (Is 2:11, 17, 20; 3:7, 18; 4:1–2; 5:30; 7:18, 20–21, 23; 10:20, 27; 11:10–11; 12:1, 4; 17:4, 7, 9; 19:16, 18–19, 21, 23–24; 20:6; 22:8, 12, 20, 25; 23:15; 24:21; 25:9; 26:1; 27:1–2, 12–13; 28:5; 29:18; 30:23; 31:7), a day that is believed to have happened. Notably, outside of these chapters, the expression is only found in chapter 52. Similarly, Duperreault 2013, 257, suggests

In fact, this view would be well in line with many of the other passages in Isa 40–55 where a contrast between the past and the present is found, passages often using similar vocabulary as in Isa 48:3–8 and often featuring idols in some way.

In 40:21, for example, a series of rhetorical questions are asked to the plural audience,[94] among them the question "Has it not been told you from the beginning?" (הלוא הגד מראש לכם; the answer is supposed to be yes).[95]

Moreover, in Isa 41:21–29, a similar contrast is found in a trial speech (ריב) where gods (later judged to be idols)[96] are first challenged to declare (נגד) the "former things" (הראשנות, v. 22)—"what they are" (מה הנה, v. 22)—that is, their correct interpretation[97]—and the "things to come" (הבאות, v. 22). Then they are judged as having failed to declare (אין־מגיד, v. 26) in advance (מראש, מלפנים, v. 26).[98] In contrast, YHWH both had declared (נגד) it to Zion/Jerusalem (v. 27) and is currently the one declaring new things to come (v. 25).

Similarly, in Isa 43:8–13 (another trial speech), the blind and deaf feature once again (cf. Isa 42:18–20), this time as YHWH's witnesses

---

that for the ones writing these chapters, the יום אחרון mentioned in Isa 30:8 was also considered to be "now."

94. Cf. Berges 2020a, 145.

95. Cf. Smith 2009, 116. It would, of course, be tempting to translate ראש as "first one" in this verse ("has it not been told you from a 'first one'"), but the immediate context as well as the use of מראש in the rest of Isa 40–55 would make such a translation unlikely, although a reference to earlier tradents could still be reasonable (so also Goldingay and Payne 2006a, 118; on possible overlaps with liturgical traditions, see Westermann 1969, 56).

96. That is, not the worshippers of the gods (Goldingay and Payne 2006a, 191).

97. So Westermann 1969, 85: "the *interpretation* of former things" (cf. Gen 21:29; so also Berges 2020a, 216, who translates "Die früheren Dinge, wie war es damit" [207], and Baltzer 2001, 118, who points to Ezek 24:19). It thus overlaps with the way the prophetic task was related to history (on this, see more below, esp. "Kings and Chronicles," chapter 8). The reminder by Duperreault 2013, 255, that "any sort of writing that involves historical reflection necessitates a process of interpretation: past events must first be constituted as such before they can be organized into a coherent whole," is also noteworthy here and captures the dynamic in the contrasting of past and present throughout Isa 40–55 in a good way. BHSapp suggests that the last two final cola in v. 22b should be inverted, an option adopted by many commentators, since it provides a better flow, although it is not entirely necessary to make sense of the verse (Childs 2001, 320).

98. The verse reads, "Who declared it from the beginning so that we might know, and beforehand, so that we might say, 'He is right'? There was *no one* who declared it, none who proclaimed, none who heard your words" (מי־הגיד מראש ונדעה ומלפנים ונאמר צדיק אף אין־מגיד אף אין משמיע אף אין־שמע אמריכם).

130

(cf. Isa 8:16–20; 30:8–11; 44:7–8),[99] and in the passage, YHWH's unmatched ability to foretell is emphasized.

Finally, in Isa 42:9, YHWH says that "the former things have come to pass" (הראשנות הנה־באו), and these things again form the backdrop for YHWH declaring (נגד) "new things" (חדשות) "before they spring forth" (בטרם תצמחנה).[100]

Anonymity and Authority

In this chapter, a number of observations have been made regarding the intertwining of voices in the 'book' called *Isaiah*. First, it was noted that prophetic voices were repeatedly intertwined with the divine voice in a way that made them difficult to distinguish. Second, it was observed that the voice of the "first one" was constantly being sidelined. Almost all prophetic speech was anonymous, and the occasions in the narrative sections of the 'book' in which a prophet called Isaiah was indeed mentioned, he was cast as a supporting character. Put differently, although these stories often transitioned into prophetic speech, sometimes in the first person, so that it could be implied that the prophetic literary tradition related in some way to the prophet Isaiah as a "first one," this prophet not only was nowhere described as writing anything down (see chapter 5) but was explicitly related to speech only in Isa 37:6; 37:21; 38:1, 21; and 39:3, 5—that is, in three chapters that overlap with parts of 2 Kgs 18:13–20:19. It is therefore no stretch to conclude that when transmitted without paratexts, the traditions found in the 'book' that was not yet called *Isaiah* were indeed anonymous and authorship was constructed as distributed to many agents.

This conclusion becomes even more compelling when taking into consideration how the roles of the additional anonymous voices that are intertwined throughout the 'book' were constructed by means of a contrast between past tradition and new revelation.[101] As argued in this chapter, the latter was claimed to be in continuation with the former,

---

99. Williamson 1994, 111.

100. Similar dynamics are found also elsewhere (see, e.g., Isa 45:11–12; 46:8–11).

101. This indicates that there is no dichotomy to be upheld between prophet and poet (see also Duperreault 2013, 259), as has been argued ever since at least Duhm 1916, 285, and his claim that one of the two authors writing at the same time as "dem sogenannten Deuterojesaja" is "mehr Poet als Prophet, der andere ein echter Seher ist." In light of what is known about the Mesopotamian trajectory, a similar critique can evidently be directed to the dichotomy between "author" and "editor." For a discussion of scholarly terminology, see Steck 1997, 237–44.

and it derived its authority from it based on a belief that what had been spoken in the past had now come to pass. Although emphasizing continuity, these new voices (Isa 44:26) were constructed as distinct from the "first one(s)"—they had *not* spoken in the past (Isa 48:16)—and claimed to have been legitimized as carriers and authorized interpreters of that tradition (Isa 50:4) by none other than YHWH himself.[102] This can be seen not least in the way the divine and human voices intertwine in the same way for the "subsequent ones" as they did for the "first one."[103]

To unpack this a bit further, it can be observed that when speaking of "former things" that had come to pass (Isa 48:3), it is nowhere mentioned that they were *written down (or proclaimed) by any named individual*; the recurrent notion is not "As Isaiah said" but "As you have heard" (e.g., Isa 48:6) or "I [i.e., YHWH] declared" (e.g., Isa 48:3).[104] Continuity is not achieved by reference to named human recipients, nor is authority derived in such a way. An inevitable consequence of this is, then, that the subsequent adding of paratexts that features the name Isaiah ben Amoz is not to be interpreted as an attempt to *authorize* previously anonymous texts. They were already authoritative.

In sum, two main points have been made in this chapter. The first is that the prophetic traditions in the 'book' that would eventually be called *Isaiah* were initially transmitted anonymously and that this was the case not only for the work of the subsequent ones but also for the "first one." Second, and as a consequence of the first, it has been argued that the authority of this prophetic tradition is not related to (or derived from) any named individual but constructed along the lines of a contrast between past and present so that the authority of updated prophetic speech was based on the perceived truth of past revelation.

---

102. That is, in contrast to how the names of prophets are commonly understood (see, e.g., Berges 2017, 17).

103. This goes in line with the preliminary observation by Tiemeyer 2011, 11, that all authors, regardless of where in the process they have contributed (she speaks of the ones responsible for "the basic textual layer" and subsequent editors as two groups), "have regarded themselves as inspired by God, hence they can be rightly called prophets, and both groups contributed to the writing of the text, hence they were certainly authors." Schniedewind 1995, 240, is thus missing the point when he argues that the designation "Second Isaiah" is problematic, since it gives that prophet the same prophetic status as the "First Isaiah," a status that he argues cannot be seen in the 'book,' where "the role of this inspired voice is to exhort a new generation of Israel by recontextualizing the prophecies of the eighth-century prophet Isaiah."

104. This observation, combined with the notion of "subsequent ones," renders Berges's 2010b critique of the idea of anonymous prophets unnecessary, although his main point about the improbability of seeing Isa 40–55 as composed by a single individual is certainly correct.

This particular prophetic tradition was thus authoritative long before any name was attached to it, and the work of "subsequent ones" was constructed as taking an active part in the transmission by rewriting, adding, and updating.

One final example provides one of the most explicit indications of this dynamic on a small scale. Placed after a prophecy concerning Moab, Isa 16:13–14 contains an interesting retrospective corrective comment. Verse 13 reads "This was the word that YHWH spoke concerning Moab long ago" (מאז; cf. esp. Isa 48:3 above) and is followed by a claim in verse 14 that while these words are worth preserving (after all, chaps. 15–16 are still part of the 'book'), a new revelation is available, framed as "*but now* (ועתה) YHWH says." An old prophecy was reinterpreted in light of a new historical situation, and in so doing, the creative work of "subsequent ones" was effectively intertwined with that of the "first one."

CHAPTER 7

PARATEXTUAL FRAMINGS

So far, it has been argued that the 'book' called *Isaiah* accommodates a series of anonymous voices that have been intertwined in multiple ways. This said, it is equally clear that these anonymous voices were eventually related to a prophet named Isaiah ben Amoz by means of paratextual framings. To paint the picture of this development further, the current chapter will ask *when* and *to what end* the various paratexts in the 'book' called *Isaiah* were added. The discussion is structured in four main parts.

In the first part, an overview of the paratexts will be given. They will be discussed based on overlapping features, and a relative diachrony will be proposed. The second part will discuss the significance of the fact that words derived from the root חזה are used in the superscriptions naming Isaiah—a fact often understood as somewhat puzzling, if not inappropriate, for a lengthy 'book' such as *Isaiah*. Third, the focus will be on the function of the name Isaiah ben Amoz in Isa 1:1; 2:1; and 13:1, and last, a brief summary will be provided that includes a few additional examples of anonymous circulation.

SURVEYING THE PARATEXTS

In all, there are fourteen superscriptions in the 'book' called *Isaiah* (Isa 1:1; 2:1; 13:1; 14:28; 15:1; 17:1; 19:1; 21:1, 11, 13; 22:1; 23:1; 30:6; 38:9),[1] and to these can also be added four narrative introductions (Isa

---

1. Although included in the count, I will not comment in any length on the psalm superscription in Isa 38:9 (מכתב לחזקיהו מלך־יהודה בחלתו ויחי מחליו). Interesting as it is in and of itself, it contributes little to the question of how prophecy came to be related to the prophet Isaiah.

6:1; 7:1; 20:1–2; 36:1).[2] Many of these superscriptions share features in a way that makes it reasonable to assume that they relate in some way to one another, and so they will be dealt with accordingly.

משא *Superscriptions*

The first set of paratexts that show a high degree of overlap all frame brief prophetic messages:[3]

Isa 15:1	משא מואב	An oracle concerning Moab
Isa 17:1	משא דמשק	An oracle concerning Damascus
Isa 19:1	משא מצרים	An oracle concerning Egypt
Isa 21:1	משא מדבר־ים	An oracle concerning the wilderness of the sea
Isa 21:11	משא דומה	An oracle concerning Dumah
Isa 21:13	משא בערב	An oracle "in the desert"
Isa 22:1	משא גיא חזיון	An oracle concerning the valley of vision
Isa 23:1	משא צר	An oracle concerning Tyre
Isa 30:6	משא בהמות נגב	An oracle concerning the beasts of the Negeb

What all of these superscriptions have in common is that they are very brief. They only include a designation of the text that follows as משא, an "oracle,"[4] together with information about whom or what this message

---

2. Apart from these paratexts, Gevaryahu 1975, 54n44, suggests that Isa 48:22 and 57:21 may be considered superscriptions (cf. Goldingay 1998, 331, who adds Isa 66:24). This is quite unlikely, however (the same can be said about 22:15b, contra Kaiser 1980, 2). Although they may have performed functions that resemble paratextual functions at some point—that is, dividing chapters 40–66 into three parts (cf. Smith 2009, 333)—the fact that they are fully integrated into the text makes it more reasonable to treat them as examples of a repeated stock phrase. There have also been attempts to argue that some of the fourteen superscriptions listed above were originally *colophons* and that they have only subsequently been moved to their present location (so Gevaryahu 1975). Although it does not affect the conclusions in this chapter, I find this to be quite unlikely (see also the critique in, e.g., Tucker 1977; cf. Williamson 2014, 16), not least because colophons have different functions than superscriptions (for a definition, see above, n. 9, chapter 3; cf. Willgren 2016b). Evidently, then, this critique also applies to the argument by Goldingay 1998, 331, that Isa 2:1 is a colophon (see also below, n. 26).

3. To this group also belongs Isa 13:1 and 14:28, but since they differ from the nine paratexts quoted below, I will deal with them later.

4. The meaning and function of משא have been intensely discussed. A common proposal, argued by Floyd 2002 in particular, is that משא designates "a type of prophetic book" (405), thus implying that the literature they frame is to be read in a certain way. Expanding on the unpublished work of Weiss 1986 (cf. briefly Weiss 1992), who argued that משא represented a shift from "dynamic oral" to "fixed literary" transmission (esp. 277–351)—a notion he rightly criticizes (Floyd 2018, 6)—Floyd proposes that משא is best seen as a

concerns.[5] The demarcated units are, as stated above, also quite brief, especially the ones framed by the three paratexts in chapter 21, and noteworthy is that all are anonymous—no prophet is named anywhere, neither in the paratext nor in the oracles proper.[6] At a first glance, they

---

technical designation of a type of *prophetic reinterpretation* or *rerevelation* "that comes into play when the viability of some other prophecy becomes questionable" (Floyd 2018, 14; cf. Floyd 2002, 409–10). Such a conclusion is, however, quite unpersuasive for a number of reasons (in this sense also contra Weyde 2018, 257; for an extensive evaluation and critique of Weiss in particular, see Boda 2006; 2017; Cook 2011, 29–33). Three can be mentioned here. First, the narratives argued to show that משא relates to prophetic reinterpretation of previous revelation do not in fact show this. Looking at 2 Kgs 9:25, for example, משא is not used to define the *reinterpretation* given but refers to the *original prophetic utterance*. The same can be said regarding its use in 2 Chr 24:27. Second, the argument implies that prophecies framed by משא would be qualitatively different from how prophecy and the transmission of prophetic literature work in general, but there is nothing to back up such a claim—the attempt to identify possible "definitive elements of the generic form" is not convincing (Floyd 2018, 7; cf., e.g., the three elements reviewed in Floyd 2002, 409, with the discussion of prophecy and history in 1–2 Chr below, chapter 8, or the way he treats Isa 13–23). Furthermore, if the term משא would have designated attempts to show how previous dubious revelations were being fulfilled, why is, for example, Isa 40–55 not designated as such? Why is it not found in Isa 16:13–14, where it would have been most expected? Third (as with Cook 2011, 30), since many of the משא superscriptions are secondary additions, the relation between the generic composition of a text and its subsequent transmission is not straightforward. Consequently, although attempting to move beyond the dead end of etymological deduction, Floyd creates more problems than he solves. This is also the case with the idea proposed by Willi-Plein 2006, that the basic sense of "carry" or "lift" indicates that משא designates oracles or collections that were not heard by their audience but had to be carried to them by means of being written down on some physical medium. While this could be plausible in some of the cases, it does not work as an overarching definition (see, in particular, 2 Kgs 9:25, where משא relates to spoken words; cf. Floyd 2018, 10–11). I will not enter here into a lengthy discussion of the topic, since it does not affect the relation between these paratexts and other paratexts in the 'book' called *Isaiah*; instead, I conclude this note by referring to the general observations by Weyde 2018, 259, that "in nearly all the occurrences of *maśśā'* in the prophets, the term probably conveys the meaning oracle or message" and that when directed toward "foreign peoples, countries, areas, and cities, *maśśā'* is followed by announcements of judgment." For an overview and discussion of other alternatives, see Cook 2011, 26–39; Weyde 2018; cf. Watts 2004, 235–36.

5. Regularly, these paratexts have been divided into categories based on references to nations and other topics, but such categories are not always helpful, since the suggested categories are often intertwined in the texts themselves (Isa 21:1–10 is, e.g., introduced as a משא מדבר־ים, "an oracle concerning the wilderness of the sea," only to focus on Babylon, while Isa 22 is introduced as a משא גיא חזיון, "an oracle concerning the valley of vision," only to focus on Jerusalem, etc.). The overall designation "oracles *against* the nations" is also somewhat misleading, since it is nowhere assumed that these oracles are delivered *to* the nations. They are rather directed toward the people of God *concerning* the nations.

6. The observation by Weyde 2018, 256, that the superscriptions rarely contain explicit introductions of divine speech is correct, but the conclusions drawn are somewhat

thus seem to demarcate a well-structured section in the 'book' called *Isaiah*, and taken together with either Isa 14:28 or 13:1, they have been seen as reflecting an earlier, independent collection of oracles concerning the nations. A few observations complicate such a conclusion, however.[7]

The first is that the superscription in Isa 30:6 is separated from the other eight if reading the 'book' synchronically, and although it has been argued that it may have been dislocated from its original place in the משא collection,[8] the fact that it fits well in its current location in chapter 30 should not be overlooked.[9] Second, it can be observed that the oracles throughout chapters 13–23 do not all deal with foreign nations (see, e.g., Isa 22) and that these chapters also include oracles that have not, for some reason, been provided with a (משא) superscription (esp. 14:24–27; 17:1; 18:1; 22:15–25; etc.—that is, oracles that cannot easily be understood as additions to the oracles with superscriptions).[10] Third, the chapters include texts that cannot easily be dated to the same period of time but range from pre- to postexilic times. Chapters 13–14 provide a good example of this, since they are often considered to be (late) exilic.[11] Many of the oracles have also been expanded upon,[12] the most explicit example being Isa 16:13–14.[13] Fourth, many of the superscriptions seem to be based on words in the oracles themselves, indicating that they may be later additions, while others do *not* adequately reflect the oracles that follow.[14]

---

overstated given what has been shown about the intertwining of divine and human speech above (an intertwining he also notes).

7. Many of these observations are also made by Cook 2011, 2–22, who provides an overview of recent research on Isa 13–23 that takes the superscriptions into detailed consideration (see also Kim 2020; cf. Seitz 1993, 115–27; Berges 2012a, 123–80).

8. So Duhm 1892, x–xii.

9. See the discussion above in "Writing as a Witness Forever," chapter 5. So also, e.g., Childs 2001, 225; Smith 2007, 513; Roberts 2015, 385; etc. Wildberger 2002, 130–31, however, does not think it is a superscription at all.

10. Cf. Kaiser 1980, 2.

11. For detailed arguments, see Williamson 1994, 157–75; cf. Roberts 2015, 194–200.

12. See, e.g., Blenkinsopp 2000, 273, who argues that the verses introduced by an "on that day" formula are likely such expansions (17:4–6, 7–8, 9; 18:7; 19:16–17, 18, 19–22, 23, 24–25; 22:8b–11, 12–14).

13. Cf. "Anonymity and Authority," chapter 6.

14. As for the first, see, e.g., Blenkinsopp 2000, 303. Arguing in terms of the second is, e.g., Wildberger 1997, 302, 358. It should be noted that the argument that the superscriptions are later additions because they are not *integral parts* of the oracles that follow (so Cook 2011, 37) misunderstands the nature and function of a paratext. There is thus no need to conclude with Blenkinsopp 2000, 271–73, that the original core would constitute a series of unframed sayings that were reconfigured into the משא sequence in

Taken together, these points make it reasonable to assume a messy process of formation for chapters 13–23—at least more complicated than both the suggestion that an originally independent משא collection was inserted into a work including older material[15] and the suggestion that later material was inserted into an older (independent) משא collection.[16] At the same time, there is no reason to assume that these chapters are completely unrelated—the superscriptions rather point to a multilinear development within (as opposed to distinct from) a growing anthology that would eventually be called *Isaiah*.[17]

Narrative Introductions

Turning to the narrative introductions, they are not superscriptions proper but would have functioned as incipits if some of them (Isa 6:1, in particular) stood at the beginning of a collection at some point:

Isa 6:1	בשנת־מות המלך עזיהו . . .	In the year that King Uzziah died . . .
Isa 7:1	ויהי בימי אחז בן־יותם בן־עזיהו מלך יהודה. . .	And it happened in the days of Ahaz, son of Jotham, son of Uzziah, king of Judah . . .
Isa 20:1–2	בשנת בא תרתן אשדודה	In the year that the commander-in-chief came to Ashdod—
	בשלח אתו סרגון מלך אשור	being sent by Sargon, king of Assyria—
	וילחם באשדוד וילכדה	and fought against Ashdod and took it,

(continued)

---

subsequent steps, although his notion of "serial editing" as a way of critiquing the view of Wildberger and Fohrer is well put (cf. also Beuken 2011, 63).

15. So, e.g., Wildberger 1997, 1, 11 (building on, in particular, Fohrer 1960; see also Gray 1912).

16. So, e.g., Cheyne 1895, xxiv–xxv, who argued that the addition of 14:24–26 ("a misplaced conclusion" of 10:5–15 [xxiv]); 17:12–14; 18; and 20 enabled a connection to be made to the prophet Isaiah and that 13:1 was added "to claim the whole collection for Isaiah." The position of Sweeney 1996, 212–17 (cf. Sweeney 1988, 44), who understands the משא superscriptions as defining structural elements, is also problematic, since although some of the superscriptions may have functioned in such a way sometime during its period of formation and transmission, they do not serve as such in the *current* collection.

17. Cf. Cook 2011, 26.

	בעת ההיא דבר יהוה	at that time YHWH spoke
	ביד ישעיהו בן־אמוץ ...	by the agency of <u>Isaiah, son of Amoz</u> ...
Isa 36:1	ויהי בארבע עשרה שנה	In the fourteenth year
	למלך חזקיהו ...	of king <u>Hezekiah</u> ...

All these introductions (except for Isa 6) frame narratives that mention the prophet Isaiah. Moreover, they relate these narratives to the reigns of the kings of Judah. An exception is provided in Isa 20, where Sargon is mentioned, and given its place in the משא sequence, it probably performs a function primarily related to these oracles.[18] The combined effect of the three remaining superscriptions is significant, however, both because they relate prophetic speech to the four kings Uzziah, Jotham, Ahaz, and Hezekiah and because the narratives themselves (again, except for Isa 6) indicate that the prophet Isaiah was in some way instrumental in channeling divine revelation to these kings.

Establishing a Framework

With this in mind, consider Isa 14:28, a superscription that seems to combine parts of the previous superscriptions:

| Isa 14:28 | בשנת־מות המלך <u>אחז</u> | In the year that king <u>Ahaz</u> died |
| | היה <u>המשא</u> הזה | this <u>oracle</u> came: |

The superscription not only features משא, which relates it to the other nine משא superscriptions, but also resembles the narrative introductions, although it distinguishes itself from the latter by being set apart as a paratext by means of the concluding המשא הזה. Moreover, and in contrast to the other משא superscriptions, it does not provide any

---

18. A common view is to understand Isa 20:1–3 as the "center" of Isa 13–23, since it is surrounded by five משא oracles "on each side" (so, e.g., Beuken 2011, 63; cf. Berges 2012b, 37). However, this suggestion does not fit easily with the material, since the superscriptions in both 14:28 and 13:1 differ from the rest. Furthermore, it is often claimed that each part of the twofold structure is introduced by an oracle concerning Babylon, but this is only true if *disregarding* the superscriptions and thus makes little sense as a paratextual structure. Evidently, if disregarding the paratexts, there are not only five oracles on each "side" of Isa 20 but also a series of additional, unframed ones, as noted above. Another view is that of Blenkinsopp 2000, 321, who argues that "several indications suggest that Isa 20:1–6 belongs to the same narrative complex and is in the same historiographical mode" as Isa 36–39 so that it could have been "excerpted from Dtr to complete the Egyptian section of the *maśśā'ôt* series" (322) or could belong to a Deuteronomistic redaction of Isa 1–39.

information about whom or what the oracle concerns,[19] nor does it seem based on any words in the prophecy that follows. It has therefore been argued that it is likely later than the other מַשָּׂא superscriptions,[20] but to understand its function, its overlaps with Isa 6:1 also need to be considered:

Isa 6:1   בִּשְׁנַת־מוֹת הַמֶּלֶךְ עֻזִּיָּהוּ . . .   In the year that King <u>Uzziah</u> died . . .

Isa 14:28   . . . בִּשְׁנַת־מוֹת הַמֶּלֶךְ אָחָז   In the year that king <u>Ahaz</u> died . . .

The similarities are striking—the two superscriptions differ only in terms of the name of the king. Taking all overlaps into consideration, then, Isa 14:28 seems to have been added to introduce a series of מַשָּׂא oracles as the second part of a collection of prophecies by framing them as relating to a historical period distinct from the first, which would then have been introduced by Isa 6:1, thus creating a (somewhat vague) chronological framework.[21]

Adding Isaiah

If the argument so far is reasonable, it can be noted that up to this point, the 'book' called *Isaiah* was still circulating as an anonymous text, since none of the superscriptions included any name. This changes, however, in the next two paratexts that show some degree of overlap:

Isa 13:1   מַשָּׂא בָּבֶל   An oracle concerning Babylon
אֲשֶׁר חָזָה יְשַׁעְיָהוּ בֶּן־אָמוֹץ   <u>that Isaiah, son of Amoz</u>
<u>*envisioned*</u>

---

19. It is thus not likely a superscription to vv. 29–32 only (as suggested by Sweeney 1988, 46).

20. See Kaiser 1980, 2, 51.

21. Contra Floyd 2018, 15, and to a lesser degree Wildberger 1997, 2, 90. The view is similar to the one suggested by Williamson 1994, 163, who regards Isa 14:28 as a "major heading—the heading, in fact, to the section of oracles against the nations as a whole, together with, presumably, the early material now found in chapter 28–32," followed in part by Cook 2011 (cf. also Zapff 1995, 286; Blenkinsopp 2000, 272; Berges 2012a, 131; Mastnjak 2020, 62–63). The overlaps with Isa 6:1 are often noted (see, e.g., Kaiser 1980, 51; Cook 2011, 13). The argument by Berges 2012a, 268, that Isa 36:1 presupposes Isa 14:28 is only true in the sense that it follows it in terms of internal chronology. It is less clear in terms of its wording (Isa 36:1 is instead overlapping extensively with 2 Kgs 18:13). For a thorough and generally convincing discussion of what מַשָּׂא oracles may have been part of the anthology at this stage, see Cook 2011.

Isa 2:1   הדבר   The word
אשר חזה ישעיהו בן־אמוץ <u>that Isaiah, son of Amoz</u>
<u>*envisioned*</u>
על־יהודה וירושלם   concerning Judah and Jerusalem

Looking first at Isa 13:1, it uses משא in a way similar to the first group above, but in contrast to them, it relates this oracle explicitly to a named individual: the prophet Isaiah.[22] Given that this part of the superscription (underlined above) reveals a word-for-word correspondence with Isa 2:1,[23] it could be suggested that the original superscription read משא בבל, that it first related only to chapters 13–14, and that it was later expanded in light of Isa 2:1 to serve as a superscription to a larger section of a prophetic 'book' introduced by Isa 2:1.[24] In light of the scholarly consensus that chapter 1 is likely a late addition to Isaiah (it draws together several parts of the 'book' into an introduction),[25] such a function for Isa 2:1 emanates as quite plausible.[26] If correct, Isa 2:1 would at this point frame the collection as relating somehow to Isaiah ben Amoz while also specifying its general concern as being Judah and Jerusalem. Since this compilation would have included oracles concerning nations outside of Judah and Jerusalem, אשר חזה ישעיהו בן־אמוץ was likely added to Isa 13:1 to demarcate these chapters as a new section, and given the focus of that section, there would have been no reason

---

22. I will avoid calling this an "attribution," since the term is most often used today as something that "has to do with identifying the author (or even the most likely candidates) for a text whose authorship is doubtful, collaborative, or unknown" (so Burrows and Craig 2019, 325). Evidently, it would risk obscuring the dynamics of naming explored here.

23. The similarities are often noted (cf. Childs 2001, 124; Blenkinsopp 2000, 278).

24. Cf. Kaiser 1980, 1.

25. So already Fohrer 1962.

26. Thus contra, e.g., Goldingay 1998. Since it is quite clear that 13:1 is a superscription and not a colophon, there is no reason to assume another function for 2:1 (cf. Williamson 2014, 164). In this sense, then, Isa 2:1 frames not only chapters 2–12* (so Williamson 2014, 164–65) but the whole 'book' at a particular point in time (Childs 2001, 28), including the oracles concerning the nations (which are demarcated by 13:1). The suggestion that it would be a scribal note specifically relating Isa 2:2–4 to the prophet Isaiah (rather than to Micah; see, in particular, Ackroyd 1963; Seitz 1993, 23; Berges 2012a, 42–43; Roberts 2015, 12, 35) is not likely for the same reasons argued against Goldingay 1998 above (see also the suggestion that it frames chapters 2–4; see Watts 2004, 41–42; Sweeney 1988, 31; or that it frames chapters 1–5; see Roberts 2015, 12; cf. Oswalt 1986, 114) but also in light of the observation that there would have been no need to relate a part of a work to a specific individual if the surrounding text was already related to that person by means of Isa 1:1 (contra the function of Isa 13:1; see also n. 53 below).

to change משא into דבר.[27] As for the reference to Isaiah ben Amoz, it is likely depending on the fact that his name featured in both parts of the 'book'—in Isa 7 and, most significantly, Isa 20:1.[28] Notable is also the fact that both superscriptions feature the verb חזה, creating a connection between the prophet Isaiah and visions that may indicate something of the function of the name, as will be explored further below.

Since Isa 13:1 frames a text that is likely no earlier than exilic, these two paratexts also provide a *terminus post quem* for the explicit association of prophetic literature with Isaiah ben Amoz,[29] and this relation would eventually be expanded further as a third superscription mentioning the prophet Isaiah was added.[30]

Framing the Whole

The last superscription to be considered is the one framing the whole 'book:'

Isa 1:1	חזון ישעיהו בן־אמוץ	The *vision* of <u>Isaiah, son of Amoz</u>
	אשר חזה על־יהודה וירושלם	that he *envisioned* concerning <u>Judah and Jerusalem</u>
	בימי עזיהו יותם אחז	in the days of <u>Uzziah</u>, <u>Jotham</u>, <u>Ahaz</u>,
	יחזקיהו מלכי יהודה	and <u>Hezekiah</u>, kings of Judah

---

27. See, similarly, Cook 2011, 42, or Williamson 1994, 164, who notes that the superscriptions in 2:1 and 13:1 are likely the work of the same editor (so also Wildberger 1997, 11). Berges 2012a, 126, speaks of משא בבל as referring "prospectively to the coming chapter," while the rest of the superscription "looks back to 1.1 and 2.1." Although it is sometimes argued that these two superscriptions would have framed independent parts that were subsequently joined (Wildberger 1991, 87), the overlaps rather point in the opposite direction.

28. As captured by Mastnjak 2020, 71, "the most prominent figure within the anthology serves by synecdoche to refer to the whole."

29. Indications of a later date for Isa 2:1 (and 1:1) may be the order in which Judah and Jerusalem are found, although it is somewhat inconclusive. According to Jones 1955, 239–40, it reflects exilic or postexilic use (cf. Wildberger 1991, 3; Blenkinsopp 2000, 175; see also Berges 2012a, 43, who also points to the spelling of Hezekiah's name), and Williamson 2014, 20, has shown that the reverse order is more often found in older sections in the 'book' (e.g., Isa 3:1, 8; 5:3; 22:21). To this can be added that the later order also features in Isa 36:7 (so also Roberts 2015, 11), thus possibly indicating that these chapters were part of the collection when Isa 1:1 was added, as will be suggested below.

30. There is no need to argue with Budde 1920 (cf. Kratz 2015, 42) that Isa 1:1 originally stood at the beginning of 6:1 (i.e., as an introduction to a *Denkschrift*).

Seen in light of the discussion so far, this superscription clearly depends on Isa 2:1 and 13:1.[31] It features Isaiah ben Amoz, frames him as a visionary by means of a אשר חזה formulation and an added חזון, and picks up the focus on Judah and Jerusalem. Moreover, the superscription also presupposes the narrative introductions—the named kings are the ones mentioned in Isa 6:1; 7:1; and 36:1,[32] thus indicating that chapters 36–39 were part of the 'book' at this point.[33] Ultimately, it is shaped into a superscription to the whole 'book' that is based on most of its earlier paratexts.

Activity over Time

In sum, the overview of the paratexts has confirmed the observations in previous chapters that a growing corpus of prophetic oracles was first transmitted (and expanded upon) anonymously. Moreover, it has shown that at some point, this collection was structured into two parts by means of Isa 6:1 and Isa 14:28, where the second part contained (among others) a series of oracles concerning the nations, each framed as משא. Then as more material was added and as the collection grew, two main parts were provided with almost identical superscriptions: Isa 2:1 and 13:1. Both of these superscriptions included the name Isaiah ben Amoz, which was added on the basis of texts like Isa 20:1. They only differed in how they defined the contents of the two parts of the collection. Even later, as the 'book' now called *Isaiah* had grown into a significant collection, Isa 1:1 was added, stitching together the various historical references into a king list and expanding further on the notion of חזה in Isa 2:1 and 13:1. As with all other superscriptions in the 'book,' Isa 2:1 and 13:1 were retained even as the collection grew. Ultimately, it

---

31. So also Williamson 2014, 15; cf. Berges 2012a, 43; Roberts 2015, 11. Contra Jepsen 1980, 287; Freedman 1987.

32. Similarly, Berges 2012a, 43–44, notes that the list of kings is "'strung out' from chaps. 6 to 39" (cf. Blenkinsopp 2000, 175–76), although I would argue that Isa 1:1 is more specifically depending on the superscriptions themselves, since the inclusion of Jotham and Uzziah would otherwise be difficult to account for (Isa 6:1; 7:1, thus solving the possible puzzle; cf. Seitz 1993, 11). This move would, then, also make it possible to read the chapters preceding Isa 6 as relating to the reign of Uzziah (cf. below, "Becoming Literate," chapter 8).

33. In light of the function of Isa 1, most take Isa 1:1 as framing a collection very much overlapping with the current 'book' called *Isaiah* (so Sweeney 1988, 28–32; Wildberger 1991, 3, possibly first only with 1–39 in mind; Blenkinsopp 2000, 175; Childs 2001, 11; Smith 2007, 97; Roberts 2015, 11; etc.).

is in relation to these three superscriptions that a 'book' called *Isaiah* emerges,[34] but what is the function of the name? To answer this question, a closer look at חזה is needed.

Prophetic Words and Nighttime Visions

Turning to the fact that the 'book' called *Isaiah* is framed as חזון, it can first be noted that several scholars have argued that the idea of a "vision" in the singular does not account well for the contents of the 'book' but more likely relates only to a part of it,[35] while others have suggested that חזה, when used in Isa 1:1; 2:1; and 13:1, conveys not the notion of a "vision" but rather a more (collective or) abstract "revelation."[36] Although this latter suggestion has some merit, there is an even more fundamental dynamic to be uncovered here, one that has substantial overlaps with how authorship was constructed in the Mesopotamian trajectory and thus fits well with the observations made so far concerning how the 'book' called *Isaiah* framed explicit acts of writing and the intertwining of voices.

As a way of unpacking this dynamic, it can first be observed that when relating חזה to ראה, the former emanates, to a high extent, as related to prophetic activity (see, e.g., Jer 14:14; 23:16; Ezek 7:26; 12:22–28; 13:6–9; Lam 2:9; Amos 7:12; Hos 12:11; Isa 29:10; Mic 3:5–8; 2 Sam 24:11; 2 Kgs 17:13).[37] Curiously, however, although

---

34. Cf. the early Ackroyd 1978, 32. The notion by van Wieringen 2005, 115, that the paratexts create "one single discursive text" is, however, quite problematic, since the paratexts do not efface the fact that the 'book' is still a multivocal anthology.

35. It is sometimes described as "surprising" (so Blenkinsopp 2000, 175). See also Goldingay 1998, 326; Watts 2004, 6–7.

36. See Blenkinsopp 2000, 175; cf. Duhm 1892, 23; Clements 1980, 29; Sweeney 1988, 29; Wildberger 1991, 5–6; Wildberger 2002, 84. Another alternative would be to interpret it as reflecting a heavenly court setting (so Watts 2004, 7).

37. The vast majority of the occurrences of חזה that do not convey a more literal "seeing," "looking for," etc. (so, e.g., Ex 18:21; 24:11; Isa 26:11; 33:17, 20; 48:6; 57:8; Ezek 7:13; Mic 4:11; Pss 11:4, 7; 17:2, 15; 27:4; 46:9; 58:9, 11; 63:3; Job 19:26–27; 23:9; 24:1; 27:12; 34:32; 36:25; Prov 22:29; 24:32; 29:20; Song 7:1; Dan 2:8, 19, 24, 27; 5:5, 23; Ezra 4:14; excluded from this count are Isa 22:1, 5; 28:18; Job 8:17; passages when the root is used in personal names; etc.) convey the notion of (prophetic) visions. This is true both in the seven instances in narrative texts (Gen 15:1 [Abraham]; Num 24:4, 16 [Balaam]; 1 Sam 3:1 [Samuel]; 2 Sam 7:17 [Nathan]) and in the forty-one occurrences in prophetic literature (Isa 21:2; 29:7, 11; 30:10; Jer 14:14; 23:16; Ezek 7:26; 12:22–28; 13:6–9, 16, 23; 21:34; 22:28; Hos 12:11; Joel 3:1; Mic 3:6; Hab 2:2–3; Zech 10:2; 13:4; Lam 2:9, 14; Ps 89:19; Job 4:13; 7:14; 15:17; 20:8; 33:15; Prov 29:18; 1 Chr 17:15). A notable, later development can also be found in the fifty-two uses in apocalyptic

חזה is best understood as related to some kind of visionary experience, the texts in which it features rarely focus on the transmission of visual images (*Daniel* is the exception here). What is depicted is, instead, the receiving of *words*. This can be seen in Gen 15:1, for example, where it is said that "the *word* of YHWH was to Abram in a vision" (דבר־יהוה אל אברם במחזה); in Ps 89:19, where YHWH is said to have *spoken* (דבר) in a vision (חזון); or in the narrative in 2 Sam 7, where the *word* came (ויהי דבר־יהוה) to Nathan several times during the night (לילה, v. 4), an event referred to as a vision (החזון, v. 17; cf. 1 Chr 17:15).

This is also the case in the interesting narrative in 1 Sam 3, which is framed by a statement that at this time, "visions" (חזון) were not widespread (v. 1). The chapter recounts the appearance of YHWH to Samuel in a vision (vv. 4–14, esp. 10–14), and this vision ultimately confirms Samuel as a prophet (v. 20). More specifically, it is told that YHWH called on Samuel while he was lying down in the temple of YHWH. At first, Samuel does not recognize the one calling, since the word of YHWH "had not been uncovered" (גלה, *niphal*) to him. Eli helps him realize what was going on, and after the encounter, when *morning* came, it is stated clearly by the narrator that Samuel had indeed experienced a vision (המראה, vv. 15, 21). The reference to the morning is likely significant. In fact, when a point in time is specified in texts using חזה in this way, the divine-human interaction is often said to take place during the night.[38] This is thus true not only for 1 Sam 3 but also for Gen 15:1 and 2 Sam 7, which were mentioned above, and more examples could be adduced. In Job 4:12–16 and 33:14–16, for example, the connection is made explicit by a reference to nighttime (חזיון לילה; cf. also Isa 29:7, 10; Job 20:8; 7:14; Zech 10:2; Joel 3:1; Dan 2:19). Furthermore, in Mic 3:5–8, judgment is pronounced over prophets (נביאים) that lead the people astray by promising peace (שלום) in exchange for food, and interestingly, the judgment is that they will

---

dream visions in the 'book' of *Daniel* (Dan 1:17; 2:19, 26, 28, 31, 34, 41, 43, 45; 4:2, 6–8, 10, 15, 17, 20; 7:1–2, 4, 6–7, 9, 11, 13, 15, 20–21; 8:1–2, 5, 8, 13, 15, 17, 26; 9:21, 24; 10:14; 11:14). Of the remaining occurrences, one refers to stargazers (Isa 47:13), while the other twelve are found in paratexts—superscriptions to prophetic literature or epitextual references to written texts (Isa 1:1; 2:1; 13:1; Amos 1:1; Obad 1:1; Mic 1:1; Nah 1:1; Hab 1:1; 2 Chr 9:29; 32:32; 33:19). For an early word study, see Fuhs 1978, who argues that the verb חזה primarily means "Gott schauen."

38. This would later be developed more clearly into a notion of dreams, as can be seen in the many occurrences of חזה in the 'book' called *Daniel* (see above, n. 37). The observation about nighttime visions is also made in Williamson 2014, 18n30, for example, but dismissed as irrelevant in texts where no description is included.

experience nights *without* visions (חזון).[39] Based on these texts, it can therefore be suggested that חזה "refers to a revelation of the divine word, usually at night during a (deep) sleep and sometimes associated with emotional agitation. Visual manifestation, however, plays no role, or at most a minor one."[40]

Understanding חזה in such a way, and if returning again to its occurrence in paratexts (Isa 1:1; 2:1; 13:1; but also Amos 1:1; Obad 1:1; Mic 1:1; Nah 1:1; and Hab 1:1), a striking similarity with the Mesopotamian author concept emanates. Since these paratexts frame not oral performances but written prophecy that was originally transmitted as anonymous literature,[41] the very fact that this literature is conceived of as חזה—that is, as an outcome of a divine-human nighttime interaction—is revealing. Seen in light of the examples provided in the discussion of the Mesopotamian trajectory, especially the *Exaltation of Inanna* and the *Erra Epic*,[42] it in fact makes a lot of sense that this vocabulary is used in relation to a named "first one." More specifically, the use of חזה in all superscriptions featuring Isaiah ben Amoz can be interpreted as constructing his role in relation to the prophecies gathered in the 'book' now called *Isaiah* as the role of a "first one." If reasonable, it also follows that these superscriptions were not intended to streamline the many voices in the 'book'—the Mesopotamian author construction rather implies a continued transmission by "subsequent ones." Nor does the name function as a way of authorizing the 'book.' What the paratexts achieve is instead a classification of a distinct set of prophetic literature that can now be differentiated from other traditions.

---

39. Possibly relevant here is also Isa 29:11, where the "vision of all" is compared to a sealed scroll, since in the preceding verse, the inability to access divine revelation is likened with seers having had their eyes closed and visionaries having their heads covered (v. 10). See also Hab 2:2.

40. Jepsen 1980, 284. The connection is made also by Sweeney 1988, 29.

41. The conclusion is thus in some contrast to Vayntrub 2018, 195, who distinguishes the superscriptions featuring אשר חזה from the ones reading אשר היה and argues that the former is "a narrative of performance" (translating חזה as "prophesized"), while the latter is a "narrative of transmission" (translating היה as "came to"). As my analysis has shown, there is no qualitative difference between the two, and the translation of חזה as "prophesized" places too much emphasis on the prophet, as will be seen below. Ultimately, I cannot see that any of the paratexts depict "moment[s] of speech performance." See also the earlier Freedman 1987, 9–10.

42. See above, chapter 3.

DECENTRALIZING GENITIVES

Proceeding from the observation that the paratexts construct Isaiah ben Amoz as a "first one," a clearer view of the grammar of these paratexts can be obtained. A first observation to be made is that, despite it being often repeated, the paratexts do not emphasize the *prophet* so that "everything that can be found in the following 66 chapters has been connected to this man of God from the Jerusalem of the late 8th century and as such participates in his undisputed prophetic authority."[43] They do not cast the 'book' as the vision of Isaiah, the word of Isaiah, the authority of Isaiah, and so on. A more plausible reading is instead one that gives the center stage to the *visions* and *words*. In Isa 2:1, for example, the phrasing is not דבר ישעיהו, "the word of Isaiah," but only "the word" (i.e., YHWH's), which the prophet Isaiah *envisions* (חזה). Similarly, Isa 13:1 does not say משא ישעיהו, "the oracle of Isaiah," but "an oracle," which the prophet Isaiah *envisions* (חזה).

This picture can be further painted if considering other paratexts framing prophetic discourses in the Hebrew Bible. In Ezek 1:3; Hos 1:1; Joel 1:1; Mic 1:1; and Zeph 1:1, the "word of YHWH" (דבר־יהוה) "was to" the prophet (אשר היה). In *Micah*, this is further specified as something that he "envisioned" (אשר־חזה), while in Hos 1:2, the role of the prophet is made explicit by means of a preposition (בהושע, "through Hosea").[44] The intertwining of divine and human agency noted in the Mesopotamian trajectory is thus visible here too, and emphasis is placed on the word of *YHWH*, as revealed to (אל) or through (ב) the prophet, who has envisioned (חזה) it (cf. Ezek 1:1). This is true also for paratexts that have wording like Jer 1:1 and Amos 1:11 (דברי עמוס; דברי ירמיה; cf. Obad 1:1; Hab 1:1; Nah 1:1), since they also continue with either אשר היה or אשר חזה. What emanates clearly from these examples is, then, that the prophet is conceived of as a person who *channels* visions or words that have overflowed from a divine-human interaction. Consequently, the construct chain in Isa 1:1 (cf. Jer 1:1–2; Amos 1:1; Obad 1:1; Nah 1:1) should not be translated as a *genitive of authorship*[45] nor

---

43. Berges 2012b, 1–2. See also, e.g., Watts 2004, 7: "The idea of Isaianic authorship for the whole was a mistaken product of a tradition that sought to give authority to the work and respect to the prophet by ascribing the whole work to him."

44. The superscriptions in Hagg 1:1 and Mal 1:1 are likely to be interpreted along these lines as well, although they have an increased emphasis on prophetic agency (cf. Isa 20:2, ביד).

45. See Waltke and O'Connor 1990, 143. So also Williamson 2014, 19–20.

as a *possessive genitive*[46] but rather as an *objective genitive*—the vision is shown *to* (ultimately *through*) the prophet Isaiah.[47]

Leaving Anonymity

It has been the main argument of this chapter that originally anonymous prophetic oracles have been paratextually framed and reframed over time and that this activity eventually resulted in the construction of Isaiah ben Amoz as a "first one." Seen in light of what has been argued in chapters 5 and 6, it also emanates clearly that the interest in the prophet Isaiah is of him not as a *writer* but as a *prophet*, and one important consequence of this is that the paratexts are not constructing Isaiah as a lens through which the 'book' is to be read, just as Sîn-lēqi-unninnu was not the lens through which the *Epic of Gilgamesh* was to be read. The 'book' "attempts neither to ground these statements [referring to Isa 44:28; 45:1] in Isaiah son of Amoz's eighth-century milieu nor to hint that these oracles are addressed to a distantly future context."[48] Instead, the act of naming is to be seen in relation to similar developments in the Mesopotamian trajectory, where it related directly to the library interests of Assurbanipal. That such concerns would have affected Hebrew literature as well is not far-fetched.[49]

To conclude this chapter, two final examples that speak to the effect of this transition away from anonymity will be presented. What will be observed is that texts that originally circulated anonymously could be related not only to a single "first one" but to two!

The most well-known example of this dynamic is likely the double transmission in Isa 2:2–5 and Mic 4:1–5. Since the overlaps between the two texts are substantial, it must be concluded that the relation between them reflects a written transmission. Leaving the possible

---

46. Waltke and O'Connor 1990, 145. Contra Oswalt 1986, 82; cf. Watts 2004, 41, on Isa 2:1.

47. See also Williams 2007, 13.

48. Mastnjak 2020, 60. His overall discussion is much to the point, not least that the function of Isa 1:1 is related to specific notions of authorship (72), although it is based partly on the idea that Isa 1:1 would not have been intended to frame the entire 'book' called *Isaiah*. In the view presented above, this issue makes little difference, since the works of subsequent ones are found throughout the whole 'book.'

49. Cf. Gevaryahu 1989, 65. Similar observations can also be made in relation to other prophetic literature in the Hebrew Bible.

issue of dependence aside,[50] it can be noted that the fact that this passage ended up as related to both Isaiah and Micah testifies to an anonymous transmission of prophetic literature.[51] Put differently, the passage would not originally have been related to any name in particular and thus would have been possible to include in several different compilations, a scenario likely further facilitated by the anthological character of most prophetic 'books.'[52] This double transmission also provides support to the conclusion drawn in chapter 6, that the adding of paratexts that included the name Isaiah ben Amoz is not to be interpreted as attempts to *authorize* previously anonymous texts.[53] Evidently, the text found

---

50. For an overview, see Sweeney 1988, 164–74. Of those in favor of the 'book' called *Isaiah* quoting the 'book' called *Micah*, see, e.g., Berges 2012a, 59–60; of those in favor of *Micah* quoting *Isaiah*, see., e.g., Wildberger 1991, 85–87; and of those in favor of the view that both are based on an independent composition, see, in various ways, Gray 1912, 1:42–43; Willis 1997, 311; Oswalt 1986, 115 (cf. the brief overview in Smith 2007, 127–28). See also, e.g., Jones 1955, 240, who suggests, "In neither book can it be understood as part of an original composition. In each it is only intelligible in its setting as we discern the purposes of those who gave it that setting." The cautions voiced by Williamson 2014, 166—in light of the fact that 4QIsa^e sometimes agrees with the MT, sometimes agrees with Mic 4:1–3, and sometimes has its own variation (see details in Williamson 2005)—that a direction of dependence cannot be argued with any sufficient degree of certainty are certainly to the point.

51. In fact, this phenomenon is not unusual (cf., e.g., Obad 1–7 with Jer 49:9–10, 14–16, or the apparent confusion surrounding Micah and Micaiah—see esp. 1 Kgs 22:28, which seems to quote Mic 1:2). Regarding the relation between the prophets Isaiah and Micah, it is not always straightforward. A discussion can be found in, e.g., Ackroyd 1978, 23–25, who argues that it was "to Micah not to Isaiah that later tradition was to attribute a major alleviation of threatened disaster for Jerusalem and its temple" (24) by pointing to texts like Jer 26:17–19; cf. Mic 3:12; 2 Kgs 18:4–5; and 2 Chr 29–31. Although this would somewhat explain the possible overlaps between traditions related to the prophets Micah and Isaiah, it is still the case that the reform of Hezekiah is narrated as somewhat distinct from the activities of the prophet Isaiah in relation to the siege of Jerusalem so that the either/or argument by Ackroyd loses some of its force.

52. See, in particular, Mastnjak 2020. For a discussion of anthologies, see also Willgren 2016a, 21–32.

53. It is sometimes noted as significant that Isa 2:2–4 is placed directly after the superscription in 2:1 (cf. similarly Jepsen 1980, 287). Ackroyd 1963, 320, in particular, has argued that the superscription in Isa 2:1 "belongs to someone who was aware of the problem of the double occurrence, and affirmed his belief that the oracle was of genuine Isaianic origin, thus proclaiming himself as one of the first literary critics." In light of what has been argued in this study, this is not a convincing line of argument. To be noted, however, is that Ackroyd later corrected his suggestion, although he kept a problematic notion of authority: "This insertion may be seen not so much in terms of the activity of a 'first literary critic,' but—since I am less than sure that such questions arise except in relation to concerns with authority—rather as part of a process of claiming a particular kind of status for the prophet and a particular kind of authority for this collection as a whole. It

in Isa 2:2–5 and Mic 4:1–5 was already authoritative, as its inclusion in two sets of demarcated prophetic traditions shows.

The second indication of the anonymous transmission of a prophetic tradition that would eventually be framed as related to the prophet Isaiah is found in 2 Chr 36:22 (= Ezra 1:1):

ובשנת אחת לכורש מלך פרס לכלות דבר־יהוה בפי ירמיהו העיר
יהוה את־רוח כורש מלך־פרס ויעבר־קול בכל־מלכותו וגם־במכתב
לאמר

> In the first year of Cyrus, king of Persia, in fulfillment of the word of YHWH by the mouth of Jeremiah YHWH stirred up the spirit of Cyrus, king of Persia so that he sent a herald throughout all his kingdom and also declared in a written edict . . .

This example is not as straightforward as the previous, since there are no verbatim overlaps with the 'book' called *Isaiah*. However, as is often pointed out, the rebuilding of the temple of Jerusalem under Cyrus is not found anywhere in the 'book' called *Jeremiah* but is prominent in *Isaiah*.[54] As a consequence, many scholars have seen this reference as a misplaced attribution, a kind of pseudepigrapha, so that what belongs to Isaiah has been falsely attributed to Jeremiah. However, such a scenario would be a bit anachronistic. A more straightforward explanation is to see here yet another example of the consequences of the anonymous transmission of texts. Notable is also that the reference to the "mouth" of Jeremiah constructs the transmission as oral, in line with most examples in the Nineveh oracles quoted above (see "Prophets without Books," chapter 5).

In the end, the picture painted in this part of the study has been that of a construction of authorship overlapping extensively with the Mesopotamian trajectory. This author concept permeated not only the way the prophet was related to writing but also the way voices were intertwined and how the 'book' was paratextually framed. So far, then, the prophet Isaiah is best understood as a Mesopotamian author.

---

is, I believe, geared to the presentation of the prophet as authoritative spokesman" (1978, 34).

54. See the discussions in Gray 1912, 1:xxxvii–xxxix; Sommer 1996.

Part IV

NEGOTIATIONS IN THE SECOND TEMPLE PERIOD

CHAPTER 8

TEXTS ATTRACTING NAMES

Having established the prophet Isaiah as a Mesopotamian author in the 'book' called *Isaiah* itself, it is equally clear that the relation between the prophet and the 'book' would eventually be rethought. In light of the negotiations between the Mesopotamian and Greek trajectories observed in the final section of chapter 4, it would be expected that similar processes in the Second Temple period would eventually affect the interpretation of, not least, Isa 1:1; 2:1; and 13:1, and this part of the study will attempt to uncover some initial traces of this transformation. To this end, it is divided into three chapters. In chapter 8, the focus will be on 1–2 Chr. Chapter 9 will then discuss two examples other than the 'book' *Isaiah* of how authorship has been negotiated in this period of time, and chapter 10 will discuss how the relation between the prophet and the 'book' is constructed in the Dead Sea Scrolls.

A CHANGE IS COMING

It was noted in the discussion of the "Catalogue of Texts and Authors" that the first systematically organized library in Mesopotamia coincided with an emerging practice of adding names to compositions, and it was argued that such a practice was developed *within*—not in contrast to—the Mesopotamian distributive author concept, although it also provided a foundation for later reinterpretations such as the ones found in the Uruk tablet.[1] This was also observed in relation to the paratexts of the 'book' called *Isaiah*, and looking for traces of Isaianic authorship outside of the 'book' *Isaiah* but still within the Hebrew Bible, two

---

1. See above, "Hellenistic Negotiations," chapter 4.

passages in 2 Chr seem to provide examples of a similar dynamic.[2] The two texts, which provide two of the three occurrences where the prophet Isaiah is mentioned in the Hebrew Bible outside of the 'book' called *Isaiah* and the narratives in 2 Kgs (the third is 2 Chr 32:20), read as follows:

2 Chr 26:22

ויתר דברי עזיהו הראשנים והאחרנים
כתב ישעיהו בן־אמוץ הנביא

Now the abundance of the acts of Uzziah, <u>the former and the latter</u>, was <u>written by Isaiah, son of Amoz, the prophet</u>.

2 Chr 32:32

ויתר דברי יחזקיהו וחסדיו הנם
כתובים בחזון ישעיהו בן־אמוץ הנביא על־ספר מלכי־יהודה
וישראל

Now the abundance of the acts of Hezekiah, and his good deeds, are <u>written in the vision of the prophet Isaiah son of Amoz in the 'book' of the Kings of Judah and Israel</u>.

A cursory reading of these two passages could suggest that they claim that a prophet named Isaiah ben Amoz penned documents about acts of Uzziah and Hezekiah and, moreover, that the purpose of such references would be to point interested readers to these documents for further reading. There are a number of problems with such a view, however, and to fully unpack the function and implicit claims of these references, a closer look at the way (supposedly) written works are explicitly referred to in the 'books' of Chronicles is needed.[3]

---

2. I will not here discuss a possible date for 1–2 Chr, since it would be beside the point. Assumed here is simply that most of 1–2 Chr is later than most of the 'book' called *Isaiah*. For discussions of dating, see instead, e.g., Blenkinsopp 2011, 89–90.

3. In what follows, I will not refer to these texts as "source citations" (or similarly), since such a designation assumes a relation between *original* works and *later* (distinct) adaptations of those works—a kind of "footnote" interpretation—that is not found in the texts themselves. As will be clear below, the references do not claim that the narrative of 1–2 Chr is extracted from certain sources (this is rather inferred by scholars from the fact that 1–2 Chr depend heavily on Dtr) but rather that there are *more things written elsewhere*. Put differently, they construct an idea of literary overflow not possible to contain within 1–2 Chr itself (similarly Mroczek 2016, 93–96, although unrelated to 1–2 Chr; cf. also n. 10 below).

KINGS AND CHRONICLES

Being a subject that has been intensely discussed, the focus here will not be on locating possible sources used in 1–2 Chr or to argue any particular mode of dependence on 1–2 Sam and 1–2 Kgs.[4] Instead, the notions of literary production embedded in these references will be unpacked, and the common interpretation of them as statements about authorship will be scrutinized.[5] This said, it will be important to compare the references in 1–2 Chr with the ones found in 1–2 Kings, since such a comparison will highlight aspects unique to 1–2 Chr and indicate diachronic developments.[6]

In all, 1–2 Chr includes fifteen references that are part of summative evaluations of acts of various kings.[7] In all cases but one (1 Chr 29:29), these references are found in exactly the same places in the narrative in 1–2 Kgs:[8]

2 Chr 9:29 → 1 Kgs 11:41; 2 Chr 12:15 → 1 Kgs 14:29; 2 Chr 13:22 → 1 Kgs 15:7; 2 Chr 16:11 → 1 Kgs 15:23; 2 Chr 20:34 → 1 Kgs 22:46; 2 Chr 24:27 → 2 Kgs 12:20; 2 Chr 25:26 → 2 Kgs 14:18; 2 Chr 26:22 → 2 Kgs 15:6; 2 Chr 27:7 → 2 Kgs 15:36; 2 Chr 28:26 → 2 Kgs 16:19; 2 Chr 32:32 → 2 Kgs 20:20; 2 Chr 33:18–19 → 2 Kgs 21:17; 2 Chr 35:27 → 2 Kgs 23:28; 2 Chr 36:8 → 2 Kgs 24:5

This indicates that the references have, in some way, been taken over from 1–2 Kgs, but if so, it is also true that their contents have been significantly altered. A cursory glance at the references in 1–2 Kgs will show that the way these are formulated is very schematic. In fact, variation is almost negligible, and this creates a clear contrast to the shape of the references in 1–2 Chr.[9] Consider 2 Chr 12:15 in relation to the *Vorlage* in 1 Kgs 14:29 and 2 Chr 28:26 in relation to 2 Kgs 16:19 as two illustrative examples:

---

4. For such discussions, I refer the reader to Willi 1972; Macy 1975; Japhet 1985; Peltonen 1999; or Klein 2006, 30–44.

5. So, e.g., Williamson 1982, 18.

6. Cf. Glatt-Gilad 2001, 187.

7. Excluded from this count are 1 Chr 9:1 (a passage sharing some of the features, especially והנם and כתובים על־ספר מלכי ישראל ויהודה) and 1 Chr 27:24 (a passage referring to דברי־הימים למלך דויד), since they are not part of any summative evaluations.

8. This observation is often made (see, e.g., Williamson 1982, 17–18; Thompson 1994, 23; Japhet 1993, 19–20; Schweitzer 2011, 39). In only two instances is there no equivalent in 1–2 Chr (2 Kgs 8:23; 21:25).

9. Cf., e.g., Schniedewind 1995, 211. Scholars have attempted to categorize the variation in the references in 1–2 Chr in various ways. According to Williamson 1982, 17–18, a

2 Chr 12:15	ודברי רחבעם	And the acts of Rehoboam
	הראשנים והאחרונים	the former and the latter,
	הלא־הם כתובים	are they not written
	בדברי שמעיה הנביא	in the words of Shemaiah the prophet
	ועדו החזה להתיחש	and Iddo the seer, recorded by genealogy?
1 Kgs 14:29	ויתר דברי רחבעם	Now the abundance of the deeds of Rehoboam,
	וכל־אשר עשה	all that he did,
	הלא־המה כתובים	are they not written
	על־ספר דברי הימים	in the words of the days
	למלכי יהודה	of the kings of Judah?
2 Chr 28:26	ויתר דבריו	Now the abundance of his deeds,
	וכל־דרכיו	all of his ways,
	הראשנים והאחרונים	the former and the latter
	הנם כתובים	are written
	על־ספר מלכי־יהודה	in the 'book' of the kings of Judah
	וישראל	and Israel.
2 Kgs 16:19	ויתר דברי אחז	Now the abundance of the deeds of Ahaz
	אשר עשה	that he did,
	הלא־הם כתובים	are they not written
	על־ספר דברי הימים	in the words of the days
	למלכי יהודה	of the kings of Judah?

---

common suggestion is to divide them into two groups: (1) references to official records and (2) references to prophetic records (see also Japhet 1993, 20, who calls these groups "mutually exclusive," except for in two cases where prophetic works are explicitly stated to be extracts of official records, 2 Chr 20:34; 32:32). Only slightly different is Schweitzer 2011, 39, who argues for three categories: (1) royal records, (2) prophetic writings, and (3) prophetic writings contained within royal records. Despite such categorization, many still argue that the categories do not necessarily reflect different source documents but rather ultimately refer to the same underlying source. Japhet 1993, 645, for example, understands the variation as an indication of a "stylistic inclination" (cf. Klein 2006, 41), something that would explain why the references to a scroll of the kings of Judah and Israel are found in up to five different ways (2 Chr 16:11; 20:34; 24:27; 25:26; 27:7; 28:26; 32:32; 33:18–19; 35:27; 36:8; for an overview, see Klein 2006, 41). Although some see in these references a source distinct from 1–2 Sam and 1–2 Kgs, most agree that such a reconstruction is not necessary.

As seen here, the general structure of the references is the same in both 1–2 Kgs and 1–2 Chr. They begin with referring to "the abundance" (ויתר) of the acts of the king in focus,[10] proceed with an expression of totality, and conclude with the naming of a place where an overflow can be found, introduced by the *qal* passive participle of כתב ("are written"). A general comparative outline could thus look something like the following:[11]

<table>
<tr><td align="center">1–2 KINGS</td><td align="center">1–2 CHRONICLES</td></tr>
<tr><td>the abundance of the deeds of
[king]
all he did
are they not written in
the scroll of the kings of Juda/Israel?</td><td>the abundance of the deeds of
[king]
the former and the latter
they are written in
a wide variety of works explicitly
related to named prophets</td></tr>
</table>

So put, it is also clear that the references in 1–2 Chr differ in a number of ways: (1) a reference to "the former and the latter" (הראשנים והאחרונים) replaces the notion of things the king "did" (אשר עשה), (2) the rhetorical הלא־הם is replaced by an affirmative הנם,[12] (3) the phrase דברי הימים is missing in 1–2 Chr, (4) the name *Israel* is often added, and (5) named individuals are added.

Needless to say, these differences have all been noted before, and not all are relevant to the discussion of author concepts. The addition of the name *Israel* to all references that mention Judah, for example,[13] is

---

10. ויתר is lacking in 2 Chr 12:15; 2 Chr 24:27; and 35:27 (so also 1 Chr 29:29), while it is replaced by the similar ושאר in 2 Chr 9:29 (cf. Klein 2012, 147) and והנה in 2 Chr 16:11. There is probably no significant difference in meaning between the three terms. The root יתר basically means "to be extra, surplus" or "to be left over" (cf. Kronholm 1974, 482), and the noun is therefore often translated as "remainder" in this context. However, in light of the fact that the references refer not to *a specific part* of the acts of a certain king that were *not written* in 1–2 Chr—that is, a reference to a *surplus*, parts that were left out—but in fact to *all* that the king did, *from beginning to end*, taken together with the observation that the meaning of "rest" is often "seen primarily from a negative perspective, implying that what is left is less in number or quantity" (Kronholm 1974, 486), the translation "abundance" could be more suitable here and further emphasizes the notion of literary overflow mentioned in n. 3 above. The presence of ושאר in 2 Chr 9:29 does, however, provide a caution against pressing this view too far.

11. The table is an adaptation of Schniedewind 1995, 212; cf. also Glatt-Gilad 2001, 195–201.

12. Cf. Klein 2012, 242, who notes that the latter "demands acceptance," while the former "could theoretically be answered in the negative."

13. See 2 Chr 16:11; 20:34 (where ישראל replaces יהודה); 25:26; 27:7; 28:26; 32:32; 33:18 (replacing יהודה); 35:27; 36:8.

expected in relation to its importance in the creation of a shared identity for the people in 1–2 Chr and indicates that the reworking of the references in 1–2 Kgs *is not based on any desire to provide accurate names of sources*.[14] The change from הלא־הם to הנם is probably not of any greater significance, since it is not consistently executed,[15] but the reference to "former" and "latter" may be of some significance, despite the fact that it is hardly ever commented upon in any length, apart from pointing out that it is found exclusively in 1–2 Chr.[16] Most significant, however, is the reworking of the anonymous "words of the days" (דברי הימים) into "words" (דברי) of *named individuals*.[17] While such names are found nowhere throughout the references in 1–2 Kgs, they are frequent in 1–2 Chr. Also to be observed is that in 1–2 Chr, these named individuals are always *prophets*. How should this be interpreted?

Prophets and Writing

Consider first the only reference in 1–2 Chr that does not have an equivalent in 1–2 Kgs, the one found in a summary of the acts of David:

1 Chr 29:29	ודברי דויד המלך	Now the acts of David, the king,
	הראשנים והאחרנים	the former and the latter
	הנם כתובים	are written
	על־דברי שמואל הראה	in the words of Samuel, the seer
	ועל־דברי נתן הנביא	and in the words of Nathan, the prophet,
	ועל־דברי גד החזה	and in the words of Gad, the visionary . . .

14. See, e.g., Williamson 1982, 19, 275–76; Selman 1994a, 72; Thompson 1994, 275. Klein 2012, 388, argues that the fact that LXX has the reverse order of Israel and Judah in 2 Chr 27:7 may suggest that some of these additions were first placed in the margins and only subsequently incorporated in the text proper. As to when this would have been made and by whom, Klein says little, and in light of the fact that the additions fit well in 1–2 Chr, the suggestion is somewhat superfluous.

15. הלא־הם is found in 2 Chr 9:29; 12:15; 25:26 (cf. the overview in Glatt-Gilad 2001, 198–99), while an equivalent is entirely lacking in 2 Chr 13:22 and 26:22.

16. So, e.g., Klein 2006, 543 (who notes that the phrase is used in relation to the evaluations of Solomon, Rehoboam, Asa, Jehoshaphat, Amaziah, Uzziah, Ahaz, and Josiah). Williamson 1982, 236, sees no apparent difference in meaning between the two, while Japhet 1993, 644, interprets the latter as a merism, thus expressing totality (so also Klein 2012, 148; cf. similarly Glatt-Gilad 2001, 196n45).

17. Cf. Schniedewind 1995, 218.

As can be seen here, the reference includes all of the characteristics mentioned above as unique for 1–2 Chr,[18] and interestingly, three prophets—Samuel, Nathan, and Gad—are named in relation to acts of writing. Moreover, three different terms are employed that designate them as prophets: Samuel is a "seer" (ראה; cf. 1 Chr 9:22; 26:28; but see 2 Chr 35:18: נביא); Nathan is a "prophet" (נביא; cf. 1 Chr 17:1; 2 Chr 29:25; but see also 1 Chr 17:15, speaking of החזון); and Gad is a "visionary" (חזה; see the survey above; cf. 1 Chr 21:9; 2 Chr 29:25; see also 2 Sam 24:11: חזה + נביא).[19] All of these prophets also feature in the preceding narrative, although playing minor roles:[20] Samuel is mentioned only in passing a couple of times (1 Chr 6:13; 9:22; 11:3; 26:28; 29:29; 2 Chr 35:18), Nathan appears only in relation to the dynastic promise in 1 Chr 17, and Gad plays a role only in relation to the census in 1 Chr 21. Why, then, were they included?

The most likely answer to that question is that their inclusion reflects a specific understanding of how the transmission of traditions inherited from the Deuteronomistic history was carried out.[21] More specifically, 1–2 Chr seems to presume that prophets are responsible for historiography,[22] and in light of the function of prophecy elsewhere in the

---

18. Cf. Williamson 1982, 188.

19. Klein 2006, 544, argues that these three terms are used to stress the "entire range of prophetic activity," while Braun 1986, 291, sees the use of ראה and חזה as prophetic designations as "archaic."

20. Similarly, it is prophets active under the reign of Solomon that are mentioned as transmitting his acts in writing in 2 Chr 9:29: Nathan (נביא; see 1 Kgs 1:1–53), Ahijah (see 1 Kgs 11:29–39; cf. 2 Chr 10:15), and perhaps also Iddo (חזה; see also 2 Chr 12:15; 13:22: נביא), if identified with the unnamed prophet in 1 Kgs 13:1–10. The other prophets mentioned in the references (apart from Isaiah) are Shemaiah (the acts of Rehoboam, 2 Chr 12:15; mentioned also in 2 Chr 11:2; 12:5, 7); Jehu, who is not explicitly referred to as a prophet in 2 Chr 20:35 but can be understood as such in light of 2 Chr 16:7, where his father, Hanani, is described as a ראה, and 19:2, where either Hanani or Jehu is described as a חזה (cf. Schniedewind 1995, 213, 213n16); and Hozai (see below). This use of prophets in 1–2 Chr makes observations such as that the prophet Isaiah is the "only classical prophet" (so Japhet 1993, 887, 997) to whom such a role is ascribed less puzzling, since no other "classical" prophet features in the narratives in the Deuteronomistic history and, more importantly, since the distinction itself is hardly evident in the material. To be noted is that writing is also mentioned in relation to additional individuals, most significantly Moses, David, Solomon, and Jeremiah. Interestingly, the texts supposedly composed by David, Solomon, and Jeremiah are known only by their name.

21. See somewhat similarly the discussion in Klein 2006, 41–42; cf. Willi 1972, 215–44 (*überlieferungsgeschichtliche Konzeption*; so also Schniedewind 1995, 211).

22. Cf. the notion in Japhet 1993, 22, that the texts reflect an idea where the prophets of each generation wrote the history "of their time" (cf. also Braun 1986, 288). However, Japhet also argues that these references indicate that 1–2 Chr used "over ten works." She thus understands the references as possibly indicating that the named prophets

Hebrew Bible, this responsibility is often described as quite surprising, since it is assumed that prophecy and history are essentially different things. Consequently, it is argued as ultimately pointing to a shift in prophetic activity—"the prophets have become historians."[23] But how is the relation between prophecy and "history" understood in the texts themselves? And what is implied in the notion of writing?

Looking at the first prophet that 1 Chr 29:29 relates to written records of the acts of *the king* (המלך) David, a crucial observation can be made. The individual in question, Samuel, died *before* David became king (1 Sam 25:1, while David was still on the run from Saul).[24] Taken together with the fact that 1–2 Chr does not include any narratives set to a time prior to Samuel's death, the reference emanates as quite peculiar. Why would an individual be named as a "source" of a document recounting events in a time after his own death, as the common interpretation of these references would imply?

A solution may be found if the reference is understood not as a footnote but as a narrative of transmission of literary works. More specifically, if understood in line with a Mesopotamian author concept, where a divine-human exchange and the importance of subsequent ones in the transmission are emphasized, and if related to the discussion of the relation between written prophecy and the prophet Isaiah in the 'book' called *Isaiah*, it could be suggested that what is claimed in 1 Chr 29:29 is not that Samuel *wrote a document* about King David but that he performs the function of a "first one" through which events relating to David were channeled into writing.

Further support for this suggestion can be found in the fact that the passage says that acts are written (*qal* passive participle) *in* (על) the words of Samuel—that is, in a piece of literature related to Samuel—similar

---

would have each contributed with a part of a larger literary work so that the references in 1–2 Chr are demarcated segments of such a work (Japhet 1993, 22, 997; cf. Dillard 1987, 74; Thompson 1994, 245). While it is quite clear that the literature of the Hebrew Bible is composite and that it is thus not far-fetched to assume that this is also implicit in 1–2 Chr, such a reading of the references in 1–2 Chr stretches their function too far.

23. Quote from Schweitzer 2011, 40. On this, see especially Schniedewind 1995.

24. This observation is made also by, e.g., Williamson 1982, 188; Japhet 1993, 22; Klein 2006, 39, but often discussed only within a framework of what possible sources may have been referred to. As noted by Japhet 1993, 517, "It is doubtful whether Samuel had recorded David's activities during that period." Such a statement is, of course, almost a truism, not least given the fact that Samuel is nowhere associated with writing in 1–2 Sam or that prophets were regularly not literate, as shown in Nissinen 2017, 57–115. Similarly, it is also often argued that even if literary documents would have been written by these prophets, it is unlikely that they would have survived up until the time of the composition of 1–2 Chr and could thus not have served as "real" sources (see Schniedewind 1995, 227).

to the way the 'book' called *Isaiah* was related to the prophet Isaiah (cf. esp. Isa 2:1). This observation would also indicate that the narratives in 1–2 Chr are constructed as in continuation with this Samuelic tradition.[25] Rather than being seen as a *replacement*, they are framed as a *faithful reimagination* of the past in light of the needs of the present.[26]

Ultimately, this underscores that the reference is not a showcasing of sources used in the composition of 1–2 Chr, nor does it suggest further reading. Instead, it constitutes an appeal to the authority of a tradition by explicitly aligning itself with it.[27] What is new in 1–2 Chr is, then, that the tradition has been paratextually framed in relation to a *named* "first one," but the fact that 1–2 Chr is itself anonymous indicates that a Mesopotamian author concept is still in play.

This said, it still does not explain why 1–2 Chr anchors historically oriented literature in *prophetic* agency. Does it indicate that the "source" was regarded "primarily as prophetic" or that "historiography" was regarded as a "prophetic task"?[28] To paint the picture more fully, two additional elements will have to be considered that are found exclusively in the references in 1–2 Chr—the naming of two prophets that are unknown from 1–2 Kgs and absent from the narrative in 1–2 Chr: Iddo and Hozai.

The Witness and the Visionary

Focusing first on Iddo, it can be noted that he is mentioned three times in the references,[29] where he is related to the narratives of Solomon, Rehoboam, and Abijah, respectively (2 Chr 9:29; 12:15; 13:22). Curiously, and in contrast to all other named prophets (except for Hozai), he is found nowhere else in 1–2 Chr or the Deuteronomistic history. Scholars have therefore attempted to identify him by other means, and a common suggestion, based partly on Josephus (who mentions a certain Ἰάδων in *Ant.* 8.231–35)[30] but also on the fact that 2 Chr 9:29 specifies that he had

---

25. So also Williamson 1982, 188: "in some way in conjunction with, rather than in opposition to, the earlier historical book."

26. Cf. similarly Schniedewind 1995, 221; Leuchter 2011, 192.

27. Cf. the notion of authority in Selman 1994a, 263.

28. See the discussion in Williamson 1982, 236; Thompson 1994, 245. See also Schniedewind 1995, 213: "part of the job description."

29. The variant spellings (יעדו, עדו) are probably to be understood as scribal variants with no apparent significance (following Schniedewind 1995, 222).

30. Cf. Klein 2012, 148; or Japhet 1993, 645, who also discusses Tosefta Sanhedrin 14:4 (14:15), which mentions עידו together with Zedekiah, Hananiah, Jeremiah, Jonah, and Micah in a discussion of false prophets. For a discussion on names in Josephus, see also Thackeray 1929, 91–93.

visions (חזות) relating to Jeroboam, is that he is the unnamed prophet in 1 Kgs 13:1–10.[31] If such an identification is reasonable, it would seem as if 1–2 Chr has supplied a name to a prophet that was previously unnamed. In this sense, then, the name would be a literary creation,[32] and it would not be far-fetched to suggest that the name chosen for the prophet is revealing something about the function of that prophet. Following such a line of inquiry, it can be noted that Iddo is constructed from the root עדד ("to testify") and that he is described as a "visionary" (חזה). Both these aspects would, then, make sense in light of what was observed in relation to the 'book' called *Isaiah*, where the transmission of a tradition designated as a "testimony" (תעודה, Isa 8:16) and a "witness" (עד, Isa 30:8) was understood as carried out by "subsequent ones," who were also witnesses.[33]

So what about Hozai? This prophet is found in the reference in 1–2 Chr that differs the most from 1–2 Kgs. It deals with the reign of Manasseh, a king that is significantly reevaluated in 2 Chr if compared to 2 Kgs:[34]

2 Kgs 21:17

ויתר דברי מנשה

וכל־אשר אשה וחטאתו אשר חטא הלא־הם כתובים

על־ספר דברי הימים למלכי יהודה

Now the abundance of the acts of Manasseh, all that he did, and his sin that he committed, are they not written in the words of the days of the kings of Judah?

2 Chr 33:18–19

18 ויתר דברי מנשה

ותפלתו אל־אלהיו ודברי החזים המדברים אליו

בשם יהוה אלהי ישראל הנם על־דברי מלכי ישראל

19 ותפלתו והעתר־לו וכל־חטאתו ומעלו והמקמות אשר

בנה בהם במות

---

31. See, e.g., Dillard 1987, 74.

32. Cf. Schniedewind 1995, 223: "invented." Possibly lending further support to such an idea is that the name appears to have been secondarily inserted in 2 Chr 13:22. The passage reads הנביא עדו rather than the more common עדו הנביא (Schniedewind 1995, 219n30). This view is thus contra Japhet 1993, 645, who argues that it was "likely that the Chronicler had at his disposal some tradition—written or oral—of a prophet by the name of Iddo who saw the end of Solomon's rule, and was a contemporary of Rehoboam and Abijah."

33. The fact that Iddo is added in 2 Chr 13:22 in relation to מדרש but not in 2 Chr 24:27, which also mentions מדרש, may indicate that the practice of anchoring literature in relation to named individuals was only emerging and thus not implemented consistently (cf. perhaps Leuchter 2011, 184n8).

34. A detailed discussion of this reference is found in Schniedewind 1991.

164

והעמיד האשרים והפסלים לפני הכנעו הנם כתובים על דברי חוזי

[18] Now the abundance of the acts of Manasseh,
his prayer to his God, and the words of the visionaries speaking to him in the name of YHWH, God of Israel, are in the words of the kings of Israel.

[19] His prayer, and how God received his entreaty, all his sin and his faithlessness, the sites on which he built high places and set up the sacred poles and the images, before he humbled himself, are written in the words of Hozai.

The fact that הנם features twice in 2 Chr 33:18–19 and that there seem to be two references, both beginning with ותפלתו but with only the last using the *qal* passive participle of כתב, has led scholars to conclude that parts of this reference (usually v. 19) is a gloss. Since 1–2 Chr departs quite significantly from 1–2 Kgs in all of its references, it is ultimately not possible to reconstruct the composition of this reference in any detail, but the common view that verse 19 expands on and reframes the assessment of Manasseh is probably correct.[35] If so, the relation between חוזי in verse 19 and חזים in verse 18 is probably significant, since it would provide a second example of where a name of a prophet is added to a text where it did not feature originally (cf. Iddo in 2 Chr 13:22).

Possibly problematic for such a conclusion is, however, the fact that many have deemed חוזי an "impossible"[36] reading, unlikely to be original, since no known prophet with that name is mentioned anywhere else in the Hebrew Bible. Consequently, it is believed to be a scribal error, and the text is emended to either חוזיו ("his [i.e., Manasseh's] visionaries"; the ו would then probably have been lost by haplography)[37]

---

35. I refer the reader to earlier work on this subject. Schniedewind 1991, 457–59 (cf. Schniedewind 1995, 225–26), for example, argues that there is a lack of overlap between v. 18 and the narrative, while plenty of overlap is found in v. 19, which suggests that v. 18 may have been taken over from a source *other* than 2 Kgs 21:17 (pointing, among others, to the curious אל־אלהיו), only to be explained and somewhat corrected in v. 19. See also the earlier Williamson 1982, 395; Klein 2012, 486. Japhet 1993, 1012, on the other hand, argues that v. 19 presents a "different spirit from both the story and the preceding v. 18" and was added "to complement or even reverse the 'positive only' statement of v. 18, more in accord with the Deuteronomistic estimate of Manasseh."

36. Williamson 1982, 395, discussing the interpretation of חוזי as "my seer."

37. Preferred by Williamson 1982, 395. Cf. the overview in Schniedewind 1995, 225–26.

or חוזים ("the visionaries"; cf. LXX τῶν ὁρώντων).[38] Both alternatives would create an obvious parallel to the visionaries mentioned in verse 18.

However, in light of the fact that 2 Chr 9:29; 12:15; and 13:22 all mention prophets not found elsewhere in the Hebrew Bible, such a judgment is not necessary, and moreover, the reading found in the LXX is more reasonably understood as a scribal attempt to come to terms with an unknown name. Hozai can thus quite plausibly be seen as yet another example of a literary creation,[39] and in line with the discussion of the name Iddo, the name chosen for this prophet would likely be significant. As has been argued above (see "Prophetic Words and Nighttime Visions," chapter 7), the חזה vocabulary conveys an idea of prophetic activity overlapping extensively with Mesopotamian author concepts, where visionaries are partaking in nighttime divine-human interaction, and interestingly, such an interaction is also made explicit in verse 18, where the visionaries are speaking "in the name of YHWH, God of Israel" (בשם יהוה אלהי ישראל). Such an understanding of חוזי can, then, be further substantiated by the fact that many of the prophets named in the references in 1–2 Chr are related in some way to this vocabulary.[40]

Put differently, the use of this vocabulary indicates that named prophets are introduced in 1–2 Chr as the "first ones" in an anonymous reimagination of Israel's history and that this dynamic is playfully embodied in the construction of two new names: Iddo the "witness" and Hozai the "visionary."

Preservation and Contemporary Significance

It is in relation to this line of argument that the often debated presence of מדרש in 2 Chr 13:22 and 24:27 is best understood. While most would (rightly) agree that its function differs from later rabbinic use,[41] no consensus has emerged as to what it may actually signify in 1–2 Chr.

---

38. Klein 2006, 40; Schweitzer 2011, 65; Blenkinsopp 2011, 99n20.

39. Cf. Japhet 1993, 1012.

40. Schniedewind 1995, 218, interprets the frequent use of חזה as possibly depending on the paratextual framing of prophetic literature. If this is indeed the case, it further underscores the underlying similarities in author concept.

41. Japhet 1993, 700; cf. Selman 1994b, 383; Klein 2012, 349. Support for this conclusion may also be found in the fact that the LXX seems unaware of such a use, instead translating מדרש with βιβλίῳ and γραφὴν in 2 Chr 13:22 and 24:27, respectively.

Some have suggested that it simply means "story,"[42] while others have speculated that it may designate a specific type of source, a literary work containing an embellished version of the Deuteronomistic history.[43] However, a simpler solution may be found. If related to Iddo and Hozai and the observations made in relation to Samuel—that is, if understanding the named prophets as "first ones" who, together with "subsequent ones," constitute a chain of agents responsible for the composition and transmission of written testimonies of past events—the translation "interpretation"[44] would make perfect sense (cf., e.g., the discussion of Isa 41:21–29 above, "The Past and the Present," chapter 6). Put differently, it would indicate that the transmission primarily focused not on preservation but on contemporary significance.[45]

An interesting example of how this can play out in the narratives themselves is found in 2 Chr 16:7–10. Here, the prophet Hanani approaches Asa, king of Judah, and *interprets* the diverging outcomes of two of his actions (relying on Aram and YHWH, respectively) as indicative of events in both the *present* and the *future*. So if (the somewhat problematic term) *historiography* is understood not as a "mere" retelling of past events aiming for accuracy but as *an interpretation of past, present, and future, with a special focus on their contemporary significance and the way they are interconnected*, it is indeed no surprise that prophets are placed at the very center of this activity.[46]

Such a view may also explain the otherwise seemingly unmotivated change from a notion of what the kings "did" (אשר עשה) to a reference to "the former and the latter" (הראשנים והאחרונים). It was noted

---

42. So, e.g., Japhet 1993, 699–700, although she also discusses the possibility that it could be a source relating events in greater detail (854; see n. 43 below). Cf. Williamson 1982, 255, who sees it as little more than a stylistic variant, or Willi 1972, 236–37, who sees here an implicit notion of historical study. Porton 1992, 818, is more pessimistic about knowing the meaning of מדרש in these texts.

43. So, e.g., the early commentary by Edward L. Curtis and Albert Alonzo Madsen (reprinted in Curtis and Madsen 2015): "a reconstructed history of Israel embellished with marvelous tales of divine interposition and prophetic activity" (23; cf. also perhaps Wagner 1978, 306). If understood as specifying a source, the most attractive suggestion is the one by Zeitlin 1953—namely, that it would point to prophetic literature as collections of "prophecies and *interpretations of the inquiries* of the kings and the people" (24). "Midrash" would thus be an appropriate name for a collection "in which were recorded the inquiries of the kings and the answers and explanations of the seers and the prophets" (25).

44. Cf. Schniedewind 1995, 236.

45. Cf. Schniedewind 1991, 461; 1995, 228.

46. Cf. the discussion of 2 Kgs 9:25–26 in Floyd 2002, 410–12, although a problematic connection is made there to the use of משא (see also above, n. 4, chapter 7).

in the discussion of the intertwining of voices in the 'book' called *Isaiah* that a contrast between the past and present was often found and that such a contrast was significant to the way the transmission of this prophetic literature was understood—it provided a framework for the relation between the "first one" and the "subsequent ones" (see above, "The Past and the Present," chapter 6). In fact, the terms are used in Isa 41:22 in a way that betrays a similar understanding of the function of prophets as the one described above. In this verse, YHWH exhorts idols to bring proof of their divinity by displaying a capability to interpret past events:

Isa 41:22	הראשנות מה הנה גידו	Tell us *the former things*, what they are,
	ונשימה לבנו	so that we may consider them,
	ונדעה אחריתן	and that we may know *their outcome*;
	או הבאות השמיענו	or declare to us *the things to come*.

Strikingly, this is exactly what Hanani is doing in 2 Chr 16:7–10, and so it may be suggested that the inclusion in the references of a notion of "former and latter" was not to provide a "merism" indicating that "all" of the acts were transmitted in a specific source but instead to emphasize the continuous nature of historical reimaginations.

If this is a reasonable line of argument, there is, then, no fundamental contradiction between "prophecy" and "history."[47] Neither is there an inherent contrast between *preservation of tradition* and the often noted *creative innovation* in 1–2 Chr,[48] since interpretation in relation to contemporary needs is understood as intrinsic to the transmission of tradition. As an ancient piece of literature reflecting a Mesopotamian author

---

47. On this, see also Schweitzer 2011, 59. Possibly relevant here is also the reference to "many oracles" (ירב המשא) in 2 Chr 24:27 (cf. the משא paratexts in Isa). An indication of this overlap can be found in the fact that there is a lasting interpretative tradition that regards the "historical books" as "former prophets" (this is noted by, e.g., Williamson 1982, 18–19; Thompson 1994, 259; Klein 2006, 544; Blenkinsopp 2011, 101; cf. the notion of the prophet as an "earlier sage" in Rabbinic Judaism in Davies 2000, 71n8).

48. Cf. Blenkinsopp 2011, 100, who also calls it an "emancipation from tradition" (99). Not seldom, this innovation has given rise to the question of *fraud* or *forgery* and claims that sources would be manipulated in 1–2 Chr, perhaps even with an "intention to mislead" (cf. Stott 2008, 67, on *Ezra*), but in line with the argument in this study, such questions are not relevant in relation to the Mesopotamian trajectory but emerge primarily in the Greek one. It thus does not provide an accurate understanding of what is going on in 1–2 Chr. Even Schniedewind 1995, 161, discusses "pious fraud" in light of the observation that "the Chronicler boldly rewrites the word of God" but concludes that he is not, in fact, misleading but "revitalizing the traditions of Samuel–Kings for a new generation."

construct, the 'books' of *Chronicles* are imagined as a continuation of visionary interpretations and claim legitimacy by means of pointing to this continuation.[49] Put differently, the creation of this innovative literary work is framed as faithful to earlier links in the chain of transmission.[50] In the end, it is not that different from what was found in the Sumerian Temple Hymns: "The *compiler* of the tablet (is) Enheduanna. My lord, *that which has been created (here) no one has created (before).*"[51]

Becoming Literate

With this overview in mind, it is time to return to the two references that mention the prophet Isaiah (quoted at the beginning of this chapter). In these two references, Isaiah ben Amoz is described as a prophet (נביא) and is related to the kings Uzziah and Hezekiah.[52] Noteworthy is that

---

49. Cf. Jonker 2011, 161. Fishbane 1989, 17, correctly suggests that "an interpreter may well have often believed that his interpretation was the explicit articulation of the received content of the tradition" (although I would be hesitant to stress the "individual talent" in the way Fishbane does). See also Schweitzer 2011, 59: "Prophecy functions to connect the past with the present by the interpretation of events, whether in the form of historical narrative or oracular material or in a genealogy. Prophecy and prophets function in a very specific way in Chronicles: they are one of the means for promoting innovation in the tradition while at the same time affirming continuity with it."

50. Cf. somewhat similarly Schweitzer 2011, 62: Chronicles is "a composition that creates something new while conveying the notion of consistency with the past," as summarized by Ben Zvi 2011, 4: "Chronicles seeks authoritative status and builds it with references to traditional sources of authority," although I would reframe it as saying that Chronicles works *within* an authoritative stream of tradition, modifying, revitalizing, and updating it.

51. Emphasis added. See the discussion above, "Dying Authors Birthing Texts," chapter 3.

52. It has often been noted that the prophet Isaiah has been somewhat "downplayed" in the narratives in 1–2 Chr. In contrast to 1–2 Kgs and Isa 36–39, where he plays an active role, he is only mentioned in passing in 2 Chr 32:20, where he prays with Hezekiah (cf. Blenkinsopp 2011, 100). This may have something to do with how Hezekiah is portrayed in 1–2 Chr (see, e.g., the idea that he is portrayed as a second Solomon; Williamson 1977, 119–25; cf. Schniedewind 1995, 224–25; Throntveit 2003; Jonker 2008) but also with the construction of prophets as tradents discussed above. Warhurst 2011, however, argues that the narrative is indeed "saturated with literary overtones from material attributed to Isaiah" (169)—more specifically "Isaiah's descriptions of a future restoration after exile"—and that in some aspects, Hezekiah is presented as "a prefigural embodiment of Isaiah's prophetic hopes" (172). In his view, then, "the Chronicler transforms the temporal specificity of the promises and depicts them as realities for Judah throughout their history. As a result, the prophetic vision of restoration assumes a timeless significance with relevance, not only for the future, but also for the past and the present" (181). Reasons for why the prophet Isaiah is not mentioned in the references concluding

2 Chr 26:22 uses כתב in a way that distinguishes this reference from all others, since it is found not in the passive participle but as a direct statement (*qal* third-person m. sing.). According to this reference, then, the prophet Isaiah actively "wrote" the remainder of the acts of Uzziah (ויתר דבר עזיהו). In 2 Chr 32:32, however, the common כתובים is used, and the writing is specified as חזון. How can these features be understood?

It is sometimes noted as odd that the prophet Isaiah is mentioned in relation to Uzziah not only because his "calling" is believed to have taken place in the year that Uzziah died (Isa 6:1)[53] but more importantly because the 'book' called *Isaiah* contains no (explicit) information about any acts of Uzziah[54] and "assigns no prophecies to the time of King Uzziah."[55] This said, it should also be observed that Isaiah does not play any role in relation to Uzziah in 1–2 Kgs or 1–2 Chr either, and so it may be suggested that the reference in 2 Chr 26:22 in fact depends on the paratextual framing of the 'book' called *Isaiah*—it is only here that the connection is made explicit (Isa 1:1; 6:1).[56] Such a relation would also explain the presence of the designation חזון (cf. Isa 1:1),[57] and these references would thus provide an implicit reference to the 'book' called *Isaiah*.

Speaking against such a conclusion is perhaps that the reference itself claims that the vision is part of the "book of the kings of Judah and Israel,"[58] but this is likely explained either as reflecting an awareness that the stories about Hezekiah were transmitted in several works (cf. Isa

---

the stories of Jotham (2 Chr 27:7) and Ahaz (2 Chr 28:26) have also been discussed, but so far, no consensus has emerged. Cf. Japhet 1993, 909: "If we suppose that only kings mentioned in the Book of Isaiah were seen as chronicled by the prophet, then why not Ahaz? And if only righteous rulers, why not Jotham?" (see similarly Dillard 1987, 211). The issue is discussed at some length in Glatt-Gilad 2001, 200–201 (see also Beentjes 2010, 18–21).

53. So Selman 1994b, 472.

54. Thompson 1994, 332; cf. Dillard 1987, 211.

55. Schniedewind 1995, 217. This need not be a problem, however. The fact that there are several chapters of prophetic speech before Isa 6 could easily have been interpreted as related to Uzziah in some way (see, e.g., Milgrom 1964).

56. This is often noted (see Williamson 1982, 340). See also the discussion in Schniedewind 1995, 218, who suggests that generally, the references 1–2 Chr "draw[s] upon a stylistic feature of the editorial superscriptions to the canonical prophets" so that they may even reflect a "similar scribal tradition" (227), while Ackroyd 1978, 34–35, sees the use of חזון as reflecting the whole message and activity of the prophet.

57. Cf. Schniedewind 1995, 216: "This coincidence . . . cannot be fortuitous"; or Williamson 2014, 19.

58. See Klein 2012, 469. Some have also argued that the portrayal of the prophet Isaiah in 1–2 Chr is simply too different (Blenkinsopp 2011, 99; cf. Dillard 1987, 260), but as will be seen below, that is not entirely correct.

1:1; 36:1 [with chapters 36–39]; 2 Kgs 19–20),[59] or—more simply—as being a generic part of the references in 1–2 Chr. If the former is correct, it may be that the "visions" constitute a reference to the 'book' called *Isaiah*, while the "book" (ספר), in turn, refers to the Deuteronomistic history.[60] Evidently, both the 'book' called *Isaiah* and the Deuteronomistic history were known and used in 1–2 Chr.

If reasonable, this indicates not only that the construction in 1–2 Chr of the relation between the prophet and the 'book' has been shaped by the paratexts in the 'book' called *Isaiah* but also that the practice of adding names to texts brought with it some unexpected consequences, especially when combined with the presumed function of prophets in the transmission of past events. While the paratextual framing of the 'book' called *Isaiah* constructed the prophet as a "first one" without relating him to any acts of writing, the two references in 1–2 Chr reimagine this transmission so that the prophet Isaiah *had indeed done some writing*. Since it has been shown that the concept of "first ones" is clearly present in the construction of transmission narratives in 1–2 Chr, there is no need to assume that he was therefore believed to have written the *entire* 'book.' The development is nevertheless significant, and its consequences will start to unfold more clearly in the next few chapters. So far, however, it can be concluded that the negotiations are still taking place *within* the Mesopotamian trajectory and point to a fundamental overlap between the task of a prophet and the task of a scribe:

> If prophets have now become writers, this suggests a perceived relationship between scribalism and prophecy during this period. Thus, scribal activity may be considered prophetic in nature. By association, this link established between scribalism, prophets, and historical writing functions as a means of asserting the authority of the Chronicler's own composition—an account of the past most likely written by a scribe who would claim the same prophetic inspiration for his own work as he assigned to the "prophetic" scribes of the past.[61]

---

59. Japhet 1993, 997; Leuchter 2011, 193; Schniedewind 1995, 216. Cf. also Gerstenberger 2004, esp. 366–67.

60. Cf. Schniedewind 1995, 224–25.

61. Schweitzer 2011, 58. A similar observation is made by Nissinen 2017, 111, but based on a discussion of the inscriptions of Esarhaddon: "The historical narrative of the inscriptions partially depends on prophecies, hence the view of the prophets, ideologically well in line with that of the scribes, is indirectly represented in the work of the scholars."

In sum, then, this confirms in yet another way the major tendencies observed in the discussion of both the Mesopotamian trajectory and the 'book' called *Isaiah* and shows that the significant novelty in 1–2 Chr is not primarily that the role of the prophet has changed to approach that of the scribe but that new conclusions are drawn based on changes in paratextual practices—the explicit naming of "first ones" has made them all literate.

Naming as Fencing

Drawing together the observations made in this chapter, a picture of negotiations within the Mesopotamian trajectory emerges. As seen in the discussions in chapter 7, the name Isaiah ben Amoz was not added to *authorize* a literary transmission of prophetic revelation, and this is also true for the references in 1–2 Chr. They do not "establish" the prophet Isaiah's "authority" behind the 'book' called *Isaiah* but are rather to be seen as a means of classification—a fence around a discourse.[62] The name of this fence could be the name of a "first one" but also the name of a "subsequent one." This was clearly the case when the name Sîn-lēqi-unninnu was related to the *Epic of Gilgamesh* in Neo-Assyrian times, and it is perhaps also reflected in the naming of three prophets in 1 Chr 29:29. Ultimately, this leads to the somewhat unexpected conclusion that there is no need to assume that material contained in a work related to a named individual cannot be either later or earlier than the activity of this individual. Evidently, the *Epic of Gilgamesh* was circulating in various shapes long before it was related to Sîn-lēqi-unninnu.

---

62. So put, it overlaps somewhat with the suggestion by Vayntrub 2018, 186, that "ancient designations of authorship might be in fact closer to ancient designations of genre," in the sense that the superscriptions are attempting not to convey information about the origins of a work by relating it to a named individual but rather to differentiate between various discourses. This is well put, although an important addendum is needed: when understood in terms of Mesopotamian authorship, the designation does not really "provide an interpretive frame for the text it contains" in the sense of "authoriz[ing] and contextualiz[ing] the poem" (Vayntrub 2018, 187).

CHAPTER 9

SETTING THE STAGE

Before looking at how the relation between the prophet Isaiah and the 'book' called *Isaiah* is further developed in the Dead Sea Scrolls and then ultimately transformed as the Greek trajectory becomes more influential, this chapter will set the stage by focusing on two examples of change that are not directly related to the 'book' called *Isaiah* but are nevertheless relevant, since they provide clear examples of negotiations of author concepts in the Second Temple period. The purpose is thus to show that the picture painted so far and the transformation that will be observed in the remainder of this book are not exclusive to *Isaiah* but in fact part of larger processes of cultural change.

The first example picks up on the significance of paratextual activity observed in the previous two chapters by looking at how psalms are increasingly related to David and how this activity is interpreted in significantly different ways in the Mesopotamian and Greek trajectories, respectively. The second example will look at constructions of authorship in the 'book' called *Ben Sira*, a 'book' often claimed to contain the words of the "first Jewish author."[1]

---

1. More examples could evidently be added. I could, for example, point to the superscription to the Song of Songs, which seems to be composite, so that it may first only have read שיר השירים, then related to Solomon by means of אשר לשלמה, only to have that connection interpreted in terms of Greek authorship at a later point. I could also point to the construction of authorship in Ecclesiastes (cf. Bolin 2017), to how LXX modifies the superscriptions in the 'book' of Proverbs to privilege Solomonic authorship (on this, see, in particular, Fox 2000, 56–57; cf. Cook 2012), to the way a Mosaic discourse is developed in the Second Temple period (see Najman 2003), or to ancient discussions of whether or not Mal 1:1 includes the name of a prophet and if that prophet also wrote the 'book' (see below, n. 56, chapter 11). However, too many examples would detract from the focus of this book, so I hope that the ones provided here will be sufficient.

FROM RIVALRY TO BIOGRAPHY

Adding David

Starting with the relation between David and the Psalms, it has long been recognized that the superscriptions featuring his name (most commonly לדוד) are later additions. In fact, the psalms in the Dead Sea Scrolls provide clear evidence that לדוד was added over time and that the process was still ongoing in the late Second Temple period—that is, at a time when psalms were interacted with as authoritative Scripture.[2] Looking at Pss 33, 103, and 104, for example, they are all found both with and without לדוד, and in all cases, the older manuscripts lack לדוד, while the younger ones feature it.[3] That לדוד was added to psalms that were transmitted as authoritative thus underscores the conclusion above that in the Mesopotamian trajectory, attaching names to texts did not *make* them authoritative but rather demarcated them as distinct from other texts.[4] This was not consistently done, however—in neither the Dead Sea Psalms Scrolls nor the MT are there any attempts to supply *every* psalm with a superscription featuring a named individual.

Commenting on Politics

So if the paratext לדוד supports the observations made in relation to the paratexts in the 'book' called *Isaiah*, what about the so-called biographical superscriptions that seem to relate psalms to specific episodes in the life of David (Pss 3:1; 7:1; 18:1–2; 34:1; 51:1–2; 52:1–2; 54:1–2; 56:1; 57:1; 59:1; 60:1–2; 63:1; 142:1)? Are they not added with the purpose to unlock the "inner life" of David by reshaping the psalms as prayers that anyone could pray? Are they not casting psalms fit for personal use and related to various situations in life by making David a model?[5] Could this dynamic not be compared to midrashic exegesis?[6] Claims such as these are often made, and if correct, these superscriptions would provide an interesting example of the influence of a Greek

---

2. I have argued this in length in Willgren Davage 2020b. On the use of psalms in the Dead Sea Scrolls, see also, e.g., Willgren 2017b; Willgren Davage 2019, 2020b; Davage 2021a.

3. Willgren Davage 2020b, 80.

4. I relate this in more detail to the psalms scrolls in Davage 2021a, using the notion of canon ecologies developed by Stordalen 2015. See also Willgren 2016a, 385–93.

5. See, e.g., Wilson 1985, 173; Eissfeldt 1971, 99; Mays 1986, 152; Zenger 1991, 407; Kleer 1996, 126; Rendtorff 2005, 56, 63; etc.

6. The most widely quoted treatment is that of Childs 1971, who relates the superscriptions to "a pietistic circle of Jews whose interest was particularly focused on the nurture of the spiritual life" (149), but an important early contribution is also made by Slomovic 1979.

author trajectory, since these superscriptions would put David at the very center of the interpretive activity by sketching out his biography. The suggested dating of these superscriptions to after 1–2 Chr would also support such a development. However, looking at these superscriptions more closely, a number of problems emerge.[7]

The first observation is that the superscriptions do not seem to relate to events recounted in 1–2 Sam simply because they differ from them in a number of instances: Ps 7:1 features an unknown Cush; Ps 34:1 mentions Abimelech rather than Achish (1 Sam 21:10–15); Ps 56:1 speaks of a seizure (contrast 1 Sam 21:10–22:1); and the events in Ps 60:1–2 differ in detail from 2 Sam 8.[8] Furthermore, many relate not to any specific episode at all but to a more generic series of events so that a connection to 1–2 Samuel is not necessary: Ps 3:1 speaks of David fleeing from Absalom; Pss 57:1 and 142:1 both speak of David being in a cave; and Ps 63:1 speaks generally of David in the wilderness of Judah. Even if overlaps have been suggested for the remaining superscriptions, the simplest conclusion thus seems to be that the 'biographical' notes in fact do *not* depend on 1–2 Sam. The idea of a midrashic exegesis is thus not likely.

Second, the superscriptions in the Masoretic text are concerned not with the life of David *in general* but with a quite *specific sequence of events*: a rivalry between Saul and David prior to the ascension of David to the throne but after his anointing by Samuel.[9] David is set up but escapes (Ps 59), is seized (Ps 56) but plays mad (Ps 34), hides but gets exposed (Pss 52 and 54), and flees again and hides in a cave (Pss 57 and 142) in the desert of Judah (Ps 63[?]). The aim is thus not to fill in the blanks of the stories of David in 1–2 Samuel. It could even be suggested that the superscriptions do not seem interested in David per se, and if seen in light of the fact that psalms were used in a variety of situations long before the superscriptions were added, the function of the paratexts is not to open up the psalms for general use but instead, and in line with how paratexts normally function, to *limit* interpretive options by commenting on a specific rivalry. But at what point in time would a clash between Saul and David be relevant to comment on?

---

7. The following argument can be found in more detail in Willgren 2019b, where I also interact more fully with the research on these superscriptions.

8. For more details, see Willgren 2019b, 420–25.

9. Childs 1971, 148, raises the question of why so few incidents in the life of David are chosen but does not provide any answer apart from the conclusion that "it seems highly likely that there were other factors at work in the formation of the titles which can no longer be determined with certainty."

As has been suggested elsewhere, the best fit is provided by a resurfacing Saulide-Davidic rivalry in the early postexilic period when pro-Davidic groups who returned from exile and settled in Jerusalem clashed with a Benjaminite, pro-Saulide ideology centered at Mizpah.[10] With Mizpah as the capital of the region after Jerusalem was sacked and destroyed,[11] the conflict centered on whether a descendant of the Saulide or Davidide royal houses should now be appointed governor and on where the temple was to be rebuilt.[12] This, then, provides a plausible background to the addition of the biographical superscriptions:

> By infusing the stories of David with well-established psalms, that is, psalms that had been used by the community for a long time, the ones responsible for the notes placed themselves alongside the Davidides but nonetheless provided a critique of both sides of the conflict. Saul is criticized for chasing David, but to those lobbying for a Davidic rule over Yehud, the notes likewise had an urgent message. By not appealing to the Davidide claims to power, and by not painting David in idealistic colours, the notes assert that resistance against power and longing for possession of the land is related to the performing of psalms. It would not have been news for those returning from exile that complaint psalms could sustain hope and resistance in times of distress, but now a bold interpretive move was set in motion, proposing that it was when David turned to YHWH by means of psalmody that he was able to foster a sustained and faithful resistance.[13]

If reasonable, these superscriptions are best seen as an attempt to map a way of continuing resistance in the shadow of a struggle for power in postexilic Yehud. They thus have very little to do with authorship.

This would change, however. When the needs of the specific context were no longer acute—when the Saulide-Davidic rivalry was again to be seen as part of the past (as in 1–2 Chr)—the superscriptions were open to reinterpretation. Although additional superscriptions were eventually added to the MT psalms (e.g., Ps 51), this tendency is seen clearest in the LXX. Rather than focusing on a single episode only, the LXX sketched a fuller portrait of the life of David by adding superscriptions relating to, among others, his anointing (LXX Ps 26:1), the Goliath

---

10. On this, see especially Edelman 2001; Davies 2013; cf. Brettler 1995, 109.

11. For an overview of these events, see Miller and Hayes 2006, 462–63, 482–85.

12. Edelman 2001, 90.

13. Willgren 2019b, 432.

episode (LXX Ps 143:1), the Absalom events (LXX Ps 142:1), and the latter parts of his life when order was in the land (LXX Ps 96:1). Taken together with the translated superscriptions, the LXX now featured most of the major events in David's life (the victory over Goliath, the anointing, the flight from Saul, the Bathsheba episode, the bringing of the ark to Jerusalem, military victories, the flight from Absalom, and the writing of psalms at the end of his life). It would thus be fair to conclude that these superscriptions reveal an interest in reading psalms in light of David. In fact, this can be further confirmed by the observation that the LXX also includes a psalm presented as *written by David himself* (ὁ ψαλμὸς ἰδιόγραφος εἰς Δαυιδ, LXX Ps 151), which also reflects on episodes of his life.[14]

Clarifying Authorship

This renewed interest in the life of David, which is best understood as reflecting an interest in the biographies of authors that overlaps with the Greek trajectory (see above, "Interpreting the Author," chapter 4), parallels the development of the idea that David had written most if not all of the psalms. In contrast to the Davidization of psalmody in the Dead Sea Psalms Scrolls, where not all psalms were provided with לדוד, the LXX adds a superscription to every psalm (except for Pss 1–2) so that the superscriptions now regularly featured a named individual.[15] This consistency indicates that the paratextual activity may have been prompted by a situation where unattributed texts were considered a problem.[16]

It can also be observed that while the Old Greek "consistently rendered *ldwd* by τῷ δαυίδ, in the process of textual transmission the latter was frequently changed to τοῦ δαυίδ, in an apparent effort to clarify Davidic authorship."[17] That the differences between the dative and the genitive were understood in such a way can be seen in Didymus the Blind's comment on Ps 24:1:

εἰς τὸν Δαυὶδ ὁ ψαλμὸς λέγεται· ἄλλο γάρ ἐστιν τοῦ Δαυὶδ εἶναι καὶ ἄλλο τῷ Δαυὶδ. τοῦ Δαυὶδ λέγεται, ὅταν ᾖ αὐτὸς αὐτὸν πεποιηκὼς ἢ ψάλλων. αὐτῷ δὲ λέγεται, ὅταν εἰς αὐτὸν φέρηται

---

14. Note that Ps 151 also features in 11Q5, but without the LXX superscription.

15. For details, see Willgren 2016a, 173–95, with appendix 2 (404–11).

16. Cf. Wyrick 2004, 102, although he fails to acknowledge the difference between the MT and the LXX.

17. Pietersma 1980, 225; cf. Pietersma 2001; 2021.

> The psalm is said to have reference to Dauid. For "of Dauid" and "to Dauid" mean different things; "of Dauid" is used when he himself composed it or played it, whereas "to him" is used when it refers to him.[18]

At the same time, it is clear that both τῷ and τοῦ would also be understood as conveying Davidic authorship. Eusebius, for example, understands τῷ as introducing a psalm as composed "through the Holy Spirit for Dauid."[19]

Paratextual Taming

The discussion of paratextual activity related to the superscriptions of the Psalms has shown that paratexts featuring names of individuals are likely to be interpreted in light of the author concepts of the reader—while the "biographical" superscriptions were originally added to comment on an ongoing political power struggle, when read in light of a Greek trajectory, they were seen as painting a biography of the main author of the psalms, and more superscriptions were added to complete the picture. The paratexts were, so to speak, tamed and reimagined by the Greek interpreter.

It has also been seen how paratexts that look identical may have been added to solve different problems. While לדוד was originally added to provide a fence around authoritative psalms (the authoritativeness of the psalms did hence not derive from the name),[20] similar additions in the LXX were made to solve a *horror vacui*,[21] a problem with unattributed texts. In light of the contrasts between the Mesopotamian and Greek trajectories argued in this study, it comes as no surprise that it is in the Greek LXX that all psalms (except for Pss 1–2) are provided with a superscription, nor is it a surprise that the notion of Davidic authorship is understood in different ways by the early Christian writers and the scribes in Qumran.[22] Ultimately, this points to the conclusion that the late Second Temple period bears witness to complex processes of negotiation between the two trajectories that will inevitably also (re)shape the interpretation of the relation between the prophet Isaiah and the 'book' called *Isaiah*.

---

18. Quoted from Pietersma 2021, 5. For more examples of paratextual variance in LXX superscriptions and their significance for the interpretation of psalms, see Davage 2021b.

19. Pietersma 2021, 5.

20. Contra Wyrick 2004, 89.

21. I borrow the term from Wyrick 2004, 80–110 (although he argues that all acts of adding names to texts were in some way related to this problem).

22. I have overviewed these developments in more length in Willgren 2016a, 289–366.

Reframed Authorship

The second example of ongoing negotiation is the 'book' called *Ben Sira*, a 'book' that is the subject of much scholarly attention, since it is argued that it provides the first example of a self-identifying Jewish author. This "self-presentation as an author of a book" is, moreover, regularly seen as the result of Hellenistic influence,[23] but noteworthy is that such an interpretation is, in fact, mainly "a function of reading the *Greek* version of this work."[24] The Hebrew version tells a slightly different story. The 'book' thus has the potential of providing intriguing snapshots of ongoing author negotiations in the Second Temple period, and so a closer look is needed.

Ben Sira as a Mesopotamian Author

The 'book' called *Ben Sira*, which was probably written in the first quarter of the second century BCE, exists in several versions (Hebrew, Greek, Syriac, and Latin) and bears witness to a long and complicated process of composition and compilation of various traditions.[25] Although primarily known in its Greek version for a long time, parts of the work in Hebrew have been found in Qumran, in Masada, and in the Cairo Genizah,[26] making it possible to compare the constructions of authorship in the Hebrew and Greek texts. Two parts of the 'book' are of particular significance: the praise of the scribe in chapter 39 and the possible self-identification in 50:27. Starting with the Hebrew text of Sir 50:27, it read as the following in MS B:[27]

[27] מוסר שכל ומושל אופנים   לשמעון בן ישוע בן אלעזר בן סירא   Sir 50:27
אשר ניבע בפתור לבן[28]   ואשר הביע בתבונות

[27] Instruction, understanding, and relevant proverbs | of Shime'on ben Yeshua ben Eleazar ben Sira | who poured out with interpretation to a son | and who made utterances with understanding

---

23. See the scholars mentioned in Mroczek 2016, 213n12.

24. Mroczek 2016, 93 (emphasis added).

25. Cf. Newman 2011, 315. Here is not the place to unpack the textual and paratextual variance that can be observed when studying these manuscripts in any detail. For a recent gathering of contributions, see instead Rey et al. 2011.

26. For a detailed discussion of the Hebrew text(s), see Beentjes 1997.

27. Translation from Wright and Mroczek 2021, 218.

28. It has been argued that לבן is "likely a corruption, given the Greek translation of ἀπὸ καρδίας αὐτοῦ" (so, e.g., Wright and Mroczek 2021, 219). However, if I am correct in seeing the various versions of *Ben Sira* as reflecting different ways of negotiating

Seen here is that the verse, in this Hebrew version, speaks of Ben Sira in the third person. Moreover, it contains no notion of Ben Sira actually writing anything in particular,[29] and there is no clear indication that "Ben Sira is attributing his collected wisdom to himself."[30] The wording of this paratext is instead quite in line with what would be expected in a Mesopotamian trajectory,[31] where names (even self-disclosed; cf., e.g., the *Exaltation of Inanna*) are attached to works without implying neither any notion of intellectual property nor any notion of finality or fixation of the text.[32] In fact, there are several parts of the 'book' that overlap extensively with the Mesopotamian trajectory. A clear example is the notion above that the wisdom of *Ben Sira* is conceptualized as *overflowing*, thus implying that others could revive and continue the transmission of wisdom. This image is further elaborated in some of the first-person passages in the 'book.' Consider Sir 24:30–34 (NRSV), where a voice speaks in the first person, describing himself as the following:[33]

---

authorship (see more below on the Greek text of Sir 50:27), it would seem more plausible that a scribe transmitting the work in Greek would mistake the final ן for a ו, simply because it would further strengthen the connection between the work and its author. It is indeed much more difficult to see how καρδίας αὐτοῦ would end up as לבן.

29. Thus contra Wright 2011, 242n44, who argues that since the Greek and Syriac feature a 'book,' it would likely have existed in the original Hebrew of both. While the connection is clearer in the Greek, as will be seen below, the Syriac cannot be taken as relating Ben Sira to 'book' writing simply because the Syriac does not include any name but reads, "All the sayings and riddles of the wise men are written in this book" (see Wright and Mroczek 2021, 218).

30. So Wright and Mroczek 2021, 217; cf. van der Toorn 2007, 25, 31.

31. Indeed, it is not much different from, for example, Prov 1:1–6 or the similar use of ל in the superscriptions to the Psalms (on this use, see also Willgren 2016a, 176–78; on Prov 1:1, see especially Vayntrub 2018).

32. Cf. Newman 2011, 325: "The question of who has the last word is something of a trick question because the book seems to have invited others to add to the collection upon attaining their own wisdom." In this sense, then, the "revelation of Ben Sira's name is, in fact," *not* "outside the norm for his culture" (contra Wright and Mroczek 2021, 214), and there is no need to argue that Ben Sira adds his own name to enable him to become one of the legendary figures of the past (what Wright and Mroczek call "pseudo-pseudepigraphy"), since the Mesopotamian trajectory provides a better framework than pseudepigraphic discourses for understanding the construction of authorship in this text. This said, it is nonetheless clear that the notion of pseudepigraphy may have influenced the Greek translator's choices, indicating that it is the *translator* rather than "Ben Sira himself" that has "grand aspirations" for the work. In fact, as argued by Wright and Mroczek, this is made explicit in the prologue, where "through the grandson's translation, Ben Sira's teaching had become a book of 'education and wisdom' that ranked with the great books of Israel's past" (228).

33. The possibility that chapter 24 is a "later insertion" (not least because it is not preserved in Hebrew; cf. Newman 2011, 316, 316n16) is not necessary to assess here, since metaphors of overflow are not restricted to this chapter.

180

[30] As for me, I was like a canal from a river,
like a water channel into a garden.
[31] I said, "I will water my garden
and drench my flower-beds."
And lo, my canal became a river,
and my river a sea.
[32] I will again make instruction shine forth like the dawn,
and I will make it clear from far away.
[33] I will again pour out teaching like prophecy,
and leave it to all future generations.
[34] Observe that I have not labored for myself alone,
but for all who seek wisdom.

Notably, the text likens the transmission of wisdom to prophecy. It overflows to future generations, and verse 34 makes explicit that this overflow—which in Sir 39:12 is even described as related to the moon, thus possibly overlapping with ideas of nighttime revelations—is not to be considered as the property of the speaker. It is rather shared with "all who seek wisdom."

The idea that the transmission of teaching is rooted in divine revelation[34] in a way similar to how prophets received words from YHWH has been deemed curious in a text belonging to "wisdom literature."[35] Consequently, it has been argued to indicate overlaps with apocalyptic literature.[36] However, it would be more straightforward to see these texts in continuation with the way authorship was constructed in the Mesopotamian trajectory. In fact, Sir 24:28 explicitly mentions a "first one" and "subsequent ones": "The first one (ὁ πρῶτος) did not know wisdom fully, nor will the last one (ὁ ἔσχατος) fathom her." The anonymous first-person speaker then proceeds to describe himself as "the last" (Sir 33:16)—that is, as "the most recent link in the chain of transmission."[37]

This chain of transmission is then painted even further in Sir 39:1–2, 6 (NRSV), where a scribe is described as the following:

---

34. Cf. Wright 2011, 235: "revelatory inspiration"; see also Mroczek 2016, 91.
35. Cf. Wright 2011, 243: "Because his words are written down, like the prophets' words and like the Wisdom embodied in Torah, Ben Sira implies a similar relationship both between himself and the prophets and between his book and the Wisdom-infused Torah. In this way he implicitly establishes his own inspiration and reception of revelation."
36. So, e.g., Wright 2011.
37. Mroczek 2016, 95.

> [1] He seeks out the wisdom of all the ancients,
> and is concerned with prophecies;
> [2] he preserves the sayings of the famous. . . .
> [6] If the great Lord is willing,
> he will be filled with the spirit of understanding;
> he will pour forth words of wisdom of his own
> and give thanks to the Lord in prayer.

As would be expected in the Mesopotamian trajectory, no clear distinction is upheld between authors and scribes or between scribes, sages, and prophets. Ultimately, what is presented is a process of transmission of tradition with a divine-human interaction at the center and where the human is not a mere passive receiver but an active partaker (see, e.g., Sir 6:19–22; 43:31–33)[38] who does not place himself in the center of transmission (cf. Sir 1:30; 24:34).[39] There are thus clear overlaps with what has been observed so far in the 'book' called *Isaiah*.[40]

Ongoing Negotiations

This is not the whole picture, however. Although the first-person speaker is not claiming a prime place for himself, he does so for other figures. Consider, for example, Sir 44:3–9 (NRSV), where a section recounting important figures from the past is introduced by a first-person voice that states that he will now praise famous men:

---

38. Cf. Wright 2011, 237.

39. Thus somewhat contra Wright and Mroczek 2021, 225–26, who read passages like 39:6–11 and 44:7–9 as implicit indications that Ben Sira has revealed his name to "safeguard his own place in the collective memory of Israel and thus assure the memory of his own name and reputation." However, this view demands that ἐχάραξα ἐν is the original reading in Sir 50:27, something that is not certain (see more below), since without this reading, Ben Sira cannot be said to have revealed his own name anywhere in the 'book.' It also cannot be said that the final paratext in MS B praises the name of YHWH (יהי שם ייי מבורך מעתה ועד עולם, MS B 21v 15) while relating to the words of Ben Sira in the third person, as is done in the 'book' called *Jeremiah*: compare עד־הנה דברי ירמיהו (Jer 51:64) with עד הנה דברי שמעון בן ישוע שנקרא בן סירא (MS B 21v 13).

40. So far, then, it does not seem as if Ben Sira "was the first to venture to emerge clearly as a personality (50:27)." It is not "the beginning of a new development, for the stressing of the personality of the individual teacher derived from Greek custom and was probably a sign that the individualism of the Hellenistic period was also gaining significance among the Jewish people," as Hengel 1974, 1:79, has famously stated. Indeed, as correctly observed by Wright and Mroczek 2021, 215, "We do not have to think of the naming of a real author as a phenomenon that is somehow 'foreign,' a new development based on Greek 'influence.' Neither do we have to see it as a phenomenon directly tied to the modern concept of authorship as property, personality, and authentication."

³ There were those who ruled in their kingdoms,
and made *a name for themselves* by their valor;
those who gave counsel because they were intelligent;
those who spoke in (their) prophetic oracles (ἀπηγγελκότες ἐν
     προφητείαις; cf. the MS B 13v וחזי כל בנבואתם, "seers of all
     things, [are praised] for their prophecy");
⁴ those who led the people by *their* counsels
and by their knowledge of the people's lore;
they were wise in *their* words of instruction;
⁵ those who composed musical tunes,
or *put verses in writing*, . . .
⁷ all these were honored in their generations,
and were the pride of their times.
⁸ Some of them have left behind a name,
so that others declare their praise.
⁹ But of others there is no memory;
they have perished as though they had never existed;
they have become as though they had never been born,
they and their children after them. (emphasis added)

The passage clearly emphasizes the centrality of the ancient figures in the written transmission of works and relates their names to their works in a way that was not seen in the 'book' called *Isaiah*. Prophetic oracles are understood as *belonging* to the prophets in some way, and common to all figures in the list is that they are worthy of praise. Moreover, it is notable that this praise is sometimes not possible, since no *name* has been left behind. This may reflect an unease about unattributed texts similar to what was observed in relation to the addition of superscriptions to the Psalms in the LXX and thus may point to Greek influence. Supporting such a suggestion is also the observation that the function of the names is less as a boundary marker and more as a reference to *originators*. This is also what is found in the praise of the scribe in Sir 39:9–11 (NRSV):

⁹ Many will praise his understanding;
it will never be blotted out.
His memory will not disappear,
and *his name will live through all generations.*
¹⁰ Nations will speak of his wisdom,
and the congregation will proclaim his praise.
¹¹ If he lives long, he will leave *a name greater than a thousand*,
and if he goes to rest, it is enough for him. (emphasis added)

In light of what was observed above, there is thus an ambivalence in how the named author functions in *Ben Sira* that points to an ongoing negotiation between Mesopotamian and Greek author concepts. Aspects of both trajectories can be found in the 'book,' and this can also be seen in the way *Ben Sira* interacts with the 'book' called *Isaiah*. In the Greek text of Sir 48:22–25 (NRSV), the prophet is understood to be the principal voice of the *entire 'book,'* and the visions are understood as *his*.[41] As a consequence, many of the prophecies in the 'book' are therefore to be understood as predictions:

> [22] For Hezekiah did what was pleasing to the Lord,
> and he kept firmly to the ways of his ancestor David,
> as he was commanded by the prophet Isaiah,
> who was great and trustworthy *in his visions* [ἐν ὁράσει αὐτοῦ].
> [23] In Isaiah's days the sun went backward,
> and he prolonged the life of the king.
> [24] By his dauntless spirit he *saw the future*,
> and comforted the mourners in Zion.
> [25] He revealed what was to occur to the end of time,
> and the hidden things *before they happened*. (emphasis added)

If the Hebrew version of *Ben Sira* thus shows that the Greek trajectory has started to become influential, this becomes even clearer in the Greek translation.

Ben Sira as a Greek Author

Looking first at the Greek version of Sir 50:27, there is, all of a sudden, a reference to the 'book,' implying that it has been written by Ben Sira himself:

> [27] παιδείαν συνέσεως καὶ ἐπιστήμης ἐχάραξεν ἐν τῷ βιβλίῳ τούτῳ
> ἰησοῦς υἱὸς σιραχ ελεαζαρ ὁ ιεροσολυμίτης ὃς ἀνώμβρησεν σοφίαν ἀπὸ
> καρδίας αὐτοῦ

> [27] Jesus son of Eleazar son of Sirach of Jerusalem, whose heart poured forth wisdom, has written instruction in understanding and knowledge in this 'book.'

---

41. The Hebrew is unfortunately not preserved for vv. 22b–23 (see Beentjes 1997, 87).

As quoted here, the text still refers to Ben Sira in the third person (ἐχάραξεν ἐν), but the Greek transmission is not univocal. In fact, although it is often agreed that the third person is likely original,[42] a view that also makes the most sense of the presence of καρδίας αὐτοῦ (cf. above n. 28), many manuscripts feature the first person (ἐχάραξα ἐν).[43] The agency of Ben Sira is thus made more central in the Greek translation than in the Hebrew, and whether or not the first person is original, it is clear that the Greek version of the text has taken distinct steps away from the Mesopotamian trajectory. This conclusion is further supported by the prologue.

As for the prologue, it presents itself as written by a translator, and in light of the way this translator speaks about his achievements and provides metatextual discourse about the composition (on this, see also below, in "Claiming the Whole Book," chapter 11), it is clear that he works within a Greek author trajectory. When claiming that "my grandfather Jesus . . . was himself also led to write something pertaining to instruction and wisdom," the translator effectively provides a Greek framing of the 'book' that enables the reading of all first-person speeches in the 'book' to be voiced by this named individual.[44] Consequently, it casts words like the ones in 39:32 as Ben Sira's own, so that he now says about himself that "from the beginning I have been convinced of all this, and have thought it out and left it in writing."[45] This transformation also provides a good explanation for the possible change in 50:27 from ἐχάραξεν to ἐχάραξα.

In sum, *Ben Sira* has been seen to provide an interesting example of author negotiations in the late Second Temple period as well as of the impact of paratextual (re)framings. On the one hand, authorship is conceived in ways overlapping with the distributive Mesopotamian trajectory, where a name attached to a 'book' was primarily a witness to a longer chain of transmission, and authorship was conceived of

---

42. As proposed by Ziegler 1980, 362, this reading is to be preferred based on the minuscule manuscripts 336, 358, and 613ᶜ as well as the Vulgate, who he refers to as having *scripsit in* (manuscripts 149, 260, 606 have ἐχάραξε).

43. According to Ziegler 1980, 362, this is true for "the rest," as in all remaining manuscripts, a fact taken by Wright and Mroczek 2021, 218–19—who also point to a variance in the Latin transmission between *scripsit in* (third person) and *scripsi in* (first person)—to indicate that it was probably original (it is also conceived in such a way in both the NRSV and the NETS).

44. Cf. Mroczek 2016, 97. That this need not originally have been the case has been argued persuasively by Wright 2008.

45. As noted by Mroczek 2016, 213n18, this text features כתב but not ספר, and so the Hebrew need not be taken as a reference to the 'book' called *Ben Sira*.

as the result of a divine-human interaction that overflowed from a first one to subsequent ones. On the other hand, the act and significance of attaching names to texts have been reinterpreted in light of a Greek trajectory so that when framed by a Greek preface expanding on the circumstances of both the original composition and the translation, an individual, identifiable authorial voice emerges that inscribes his own name to assure that his memory is celebrated by generations to come.[46]

---

46. Evidently, this perspective has also been the one from which most scholars have read the 'book' in search of the *ipsissima verba* of Ben Sira or to reconstruct "his" life and history. Such an approach has correctly been problematized by Mroczek 2016, 99, and is also discussed in Newman 2011, 314, who calls for a "shift in focus from thinking about Ben Sira as intentional author of a single synchronic whole to considering Ben Sira and his role in the book as a constructed authorial voice, and the book itself as a traveling and shifting accumulation of textual traditions."

CHAPTER 10

DEAD SEA DISCOURSES

Proceeding from what was found in chapter 9, the focus of this chapter will be the earliest preserved manuscripts that include parts of the 'book' called *Isaiah*—namely, the Dead Sea Scrolls. The first section will discuss a single scroll, 4Q176, which quotes extensively from *Isaiah* while also adding new material. The second section will look more broadly at the scrolls and inquire into how the 'book' called *Isaiah* is used in this material. The results will then be summarized in a third and final section.

MORE SUBSEQUENT ONES

Turning first to 4Q176, it is also designated 4QTanḥumim, based on the fact that passages overlapping with the 'book' called *Isaiah* are introduced as תנחומים ("consolations," 1 4).[1] The manuscript consists of fifty-four fragments that vary greatly in size and date to the mid- or early first century BCE.[2] As for its form, it has somewhat defied scholarly

---

1. In 4Q176 is thus found an early example of what later became a synagogue lectionary tradition calling passages from Isa 40–66 "consolation pericopes" (Maier 2000, 915; cf. Lichtenberger 2002, 329; Sawyer 2018, 4). See, e.g., the notion in b. B. Bat. 14b that "Isaiah is full of consolation" (וישעיה כוליה נחמתא); cf. b. Ber. 57b; Gen. Rab. 10:2; 65:12; 100:9; Pesiq. Rab Kah. 17:2; 19:3, 5; 'Abot de Rabbi Nathan 40; Lam. Rab. 56:1; but also Sir 48:14 and 4 Macc 18:14). For a nuancing of the theme of "comfort" as allegedly capturing the essence of Isa 40–55, see Heffelfinger 2011.

2. Høgenhaven 2011, 152. Two scribal hands are found, one in the first column and the second from column two and onward (Høgenhaven 2011, 151–52). Strugnell dates the first hand to 150–30 BCE and the second to mid-Hasmonean, 125–75 BCE (Campbell 2004, 79). Originally, fifty-seven fragments were counted as part of the manuscript, but as successfully argued by Kister 1985, three of these (frags. 19–21) are rather fragments from the 'book' of Jubilees (see also Campbell 2004, 79; Høgenhaven 2011, 151–52). Strugnell 1969, 236, has also raised doubt about the identification of frags.

categorization. The scroll includes not only large excerpts from the 'book' called *Isaiah* but also additional material not found in the 'book.' As with many of the Dead Sea Scrolls, it thus cannot be labeled in relation to a binary "biblical" and "nonbiblical," and it is not strictly speaking an "excerpted" manuscript either.[3] Moreover, both the excerpts and much of the additional material are introduced as "from the 'book' *Isaiah*" (ומן ספר ישעיה, 1 4). It thus provides an interesting opportunity to inquire into how the relation between the prophet Isaiah and the 'book' called *Isaiah* was understood.

Contents

Acknowledging that significant parts of the text are likely missing,[4] what can be said about the contents? The extant text on column 1 starts on some damaged lines and features what seems to be a prayer drawing on Ps 79 (lines 1–4 on frags. 1–2, corresponding to lines 12–15 in the column). It speaks of some kind of trauma, featuring dead priests and contention with kingdoms, alongside God's(?) wondrous work and justice.[5] Then follows a large section that overlaps with passages from the 'book' called *Isaiah*, introduced as ומן ספר ישעיה תנחומים ("and

27, 35, 36, 37, 40, 55, and 57. As for the placement of the fragments, I will follow the reconstruction of the five columns of text as it is presented by Jesper Høgenhaven, who has studied this manuscript in depth (see, most significantly, Høgenhaven 2007, 2011; cf. Høgenhaven 2019). He adjusts the reconstruction suggested by Strugnell 1969, 229–36, who, in turn, corrected the *editio princeps* by Allegro 1968, 60–67, in several significant ways. It should be noted that the reconstruction of cols. 4 and 5 is more hypothetical than the reconstruction of the other columns.

3. For an overview and expanded discussion of excerpted manuscripts, see Strawn 2006, 2007. Høgenhaven 2011, 154, notes that if only cols. 2–3 had survived, it would have been seen as an *Isaiah* manuscript, and if only col. 5 had survived, it would have been treated like a treatise-like text. It is often classified as "exegetical literature"; see, for example, Martínez García 1992; Trebolle-Barrea 2000, 92–93; Lange 2002, 23; VanderKam 2002; Flint 2002, 240; Vermes 2004; Parry and Tov 2004; Campbell 2004; and Wise, Abegg, and Cook 2005, but it differs from texts like 4Q175 or 4Q179 on the one hand and 4QMidrEschat[a.b] and other pesharim on the other hand (cf. Stanley 1992, 576; Lichtenberger 2002, 330). The notion by Vermes 2004, 535, that each citation would have been "accompanied by a sectarian exegesis" that is now lost has no foundation and must be rejected. Stanley 1992, 576, calls 4Q176 the "only document of its kind in the Qumran corpus." Campbell 2004, 78, designates it as an "anthology of scriptural texts on the theme of divine comfort" (cf. Schürer 2014, 448; and earlier Lim 2002, 47, who relates the manuscript to 4Q158, 4Q175, and 4Q177), while Høgenhaven 2019, 352–53, sees it as "a liturgical composition" based on the alternating speakers.

4. See the discussion of column height in Stanley 1992, 576n25; cf. Campbell 2004, 82.

5. Cf. Campbell 2004, 82.

from the 'book' *Isaiah* consolations"). The passages that are extant are Isa 40:1–5a (1 15–20); 41:8–10 (1 20–2 2); 43:1–7 (2 3–11); 44:3 (2 11–13); 49:7 (2 13–15); 49:13–17 (2 15–20); 51:22–23 (2 20–3 1); 52:1–3 (3 2–4); and 54:4–10a (3 5–12). Then follows a section (3 13–17) that does not overlap with *Isaiah*, again featuring תנחומׁם on 3 13, thus creating a frame of sorts around most of the overlaps. Then in column 4, there is more text not overlapping with the 'book' called *Isaiah* in fragment 14, followed by a possible overlap with Zech 13:9 in fragment 15; a repetition of Isa 51:23; 52:1–2a in fragments 42, 12–13, 1–4; and a longer passage not overlapping with *Isaiah* in the fifth column (frags. 16, 17, 18, 22, 23, 33, 51, 53, 1–9).[6]

The core of the surviving parts of this manuscript thus consists of passages overlapping with Isa 40–54, and it has been suggested that the original manuscript did not necessarily include much more than what would have been on these five columns.[7] Proceeding from these preliminary remarks and as the manuscript will now be considered in more detail, the focus will be on how it constructs the relation between the parts from the 'book' called *Isaiah* and the additional material, paying extra attention to how various voices are related to each other.

A Familiar Dialogue

The first stop will be column 1, where passages from the 'book' called *Isaiah* are introduced after a prayer inspired by Ps 79:[8]

  Col 1 frags. 1–2

12 ועשה פלאכה והצדק בעמכה והׁיׁוׁ[ן
13 מקדשכה וריבה עם ממלכות על דמׁ[ן
14 ירושלים וראה נבלת כׁיהניכה[ן

---

6. Apart from this, there are another thirty fragments that have not been placed (frags. 24–32, 34–41, 43–50, 52, 54–57).

7. So Campbell 2004, 79.

8. There are a number of orthographic differences between the text of this manuscript and the MT that will not be noted in full below. The text agrees with 1QIsaᵃ against MT in eight instances; in three instances, it agrees with MT against 1QIsaᵃ; and in nine instances, MT and 1QIsaᵃ agree against 4Q176. Høgenhaven 2007, 110, concludes that the passages were likely copied from a manuscript with a text close to 1QIsaᵃ and 4QIsaᶜ.

15⁹ ואין קובר ומן ספר ישעיה תנחומי֯ם]   *vacat*   נחמו נחמו
עמי[¹⁰

16 יומר אלוהיכם דברו על לב ירושלים וק֯ר[או אליה כ]֯יא מלא[ה]
ה֯ צבא]ה֯ כיא

17 נרצה עוונה כיא לקחה מיד ••••¹¹ כפלים בכול חטו֯תיהא קול
קורה

12 and work your wonder¹² and (give) justice to¹³ your people,
and *hyw*[

13 your sanctuary, and contend¹⁴ with kingdoms over the blood
(of)[

14 Jerusalem, and see the corpses of your priests[

15 *and there is none burying (them)* (cf. Ps 79:3c). And from the
'book' *Isaiah* consolations: [Comfort, comfort my people,]*

16 *says your God. Speak tenderly to Jerusalem and ca[ll to her]*
t[hat]she[has completed] her[service], that

17 *her guilt is acquitted, that she has received from the hand of*
YHWH double for all her transgressions. A voice is calling . . .
(Isa 40:1–3)

As translated above, the verbs in lines 12–14 are understood as imperatives, hence indicating that these lines constitute the last part of a prayer directed to God rather than a pesher.¹⁵ The overlaps with Ps 79 are not extensive enough to be considered a quote. Verbatim overlap is found only between line 15 (ואין קובר) and Ps 79:3b (ואין קובר), but the focus of the first three verses in Ps 79—the nations have defiled the

---

9. To the right of this line is a marginal note. According to Tov 2002, 345, it is probably a paragraph marking (cf. Campbell 2004, 80), and such a view is quite reasonable in light of the contents, as the introduction to the lines overlapping with the 'book' called *Isaiah* is found here.

10. The beginning of Isa 40:1 is reasonably to be reconstructed here, given the contents of the lines that follow 16.

11. יהוה is consistently replaced with four dots, except in col. 2 3.

12. See, for example, Ex 15:11; 34:10; Isa 25:1; Pss 72:18; 77:14; 78:12; 86:10; 88:10; 136:4. Stanley 1992, 569, 573, translates it as "And perform your wonder(s) and righteousness among your people . . ." (cf. Lichtenberger 2002, 333). See also Høgenhaven 2007, 103: "And perform your marvel, and do justice to your people . . ."

13. Alternatively, "do justice among" or perhaps even "justice with" (i.e., using the people as the means by which justice is carried out; cf. 4QMidrEschat^{a.b}; 11Q13; etc.). Cf. the "answer" in col. 2 2 (Isa 41:10).

14. Cf. Lichtenberger 2002, 333: "suit." See the "answer" in 2 20.

15. Thus contra Allegro 1968, 61 (cf. Stanley 1992, 570; Høgenhaven 2007, 112); see also the brief overview in Willgren 2016a, 324–26.

temple, laid Jerusalem in ruins, killed the servants, and poured out their blood—overlaps substantially with lines 12–15, where the prayer seems to be based on a similar series of event: God is to contend with the kingdoms (ממלכות; cf. Ps 79:1: גוים—i.e., the enemies) regarding the blood (דם; cf. Ps 79:3: דמם) of the slain, represented by the bodies of the priests (נבלת כוהניכה; cf. Ps 79:2: את־נבלת עבדיך) as well as the defilement(?) of the sanctuary (מקדשכה; cf. Ps 79:2: את־היכל קדשך) of Jerusalem (line 14; cf. Ps 79:1, 3). Since the lines are spoken by the one(s) oppressed by the kingdoms, the enemies of God, the composition is best described as resembling a complaint psalm.[16] As such, it is inspired by the words of Ps 79:1–3 and possibly also by its protest.[17] Although it is not entirely possible to determine if it would have been a collective or individual psalm, the reference to "your people" (בעמכה) alongside the observation that Ps 79 is also a collective complaint (see, e.g., vv. 8–13) would speak in favor of the former.

If so, it is noteworthy that this psalm is followed by another voice (which is also heard in col. 3 13–17)[18] that provides an introduction of a divine answer in first-person speech that overlaps with passages in Isa 40:1–5a (lines 15–20) and 41:8–9 (lines 20–22). Such a juxtaposition of prayer and divine answer, where a complaint voiced by a collective is put into dialogue with a prophetic retelling of the words of YHWH where the latter provides the response, is, moreover, quite familiar—it is well in line with the way psalms and prophetic speech interact with each other in Isa 40–55 (see, not least, Isa 49:14–15, a passage that is also found in this manuscript, 2 16–20).[19] Notable is also that Isa 41:8 is written on the same line as Isa 40:5a, thus without any indication that they are found in different literary contexts in the 'book' called *Isaiah*.[20]

---

16. Cf. somewhat similarly Høgenhaven 2011, 156 (a "liturgy" or a "prayer") or Maier 2000, 915: "a lament-like poetic genre." Analyses of the manuscript have often noted that there are similarities in the understanding of the situation also in texts such as 4Q179 and 4Q501 (although such similarities should not be seen primarily as literary; cf. Campbell 2004, 86).

17. Although notions of justice or wonders are not found in Ps 79, they are both common in the psalms; cf. n. 12 above.

18. For an interpretation of the different voices as an indication of the function of the manuscript, see Høgenhaven 2007, 2011.

19. For a discussion of passages where Isa 40–55 presupposes psalms or psalmic language in the formulation of answers to the people's complaints, see Willgren 2017a.

20. Cf. Stanley 1992, 570.

Providing Answers

Column 2 then continues with Isa 41:10, followed by Isa 43:1–7; 44:3; 49:7, 13–17; and 51:22–23a, and as above, texts that constitute separate chapters in the 'book' called *Isaiah* are juxtaposed back to back: Isa 44:3 follows on the same line as Isa 43:7, with no interval, and the same goes for Isa 49:7 after Isa 44:3 and Isa 51:22 after Isa 49:17. A divine direct speech ends in line 13 with the passage overlapping with Isa 44:3 and is followed by a new divine speech that ends on line 15, which introduces a contrast between an exhortation to sing for joy and the complaint of Zion (lines 15–16), followed by a quotation of the complaint (line 17) and a divine answer by means of direct speech (lines 16–20). Then follows a new introduction to divine speech on line 20. The actual speech is found on lines 20–22.

The dynamic is thus similar to the one observed for the relation between the psalm and the first extracts in column 1, and it can also be noted that the answers provided here relate quite specifically to the complaints voiced there. In column 1, the people asked God to do justice (והצדק, 1 12). Here, God answers that God will uphold the people with God's just right hand (בימין צדקי, 2 2). There, the people asked God to contend (וריבה, 1 13) with the kingdoms; here God pleads the cause of God's people (יריב אמו, 2 20).

Framing Continuity

Column 3 continues where column 2 left off—with the rest of the divine speech from Isa 51. This is followed by prophetic words of consolation from Isa 52:1–3 on lines 2–4 and Isa 54:4–10a on lines 5–12, intertwining the divine and prophetic voices in the way observed in chapter 6 (see esp. "Voices Intertwined"). Then in 3 13–17, there are a couple of lines that do not overlap with any parts of the 'book' called *Isaiah*:

13 [   ] נ[ואש²¹ עד דברי תנחומי֯ם֯²² וכבוד רב כתוב ב֯]

14 [   ] ב֯אורֿב֯]י [אין עוד מעת]

---

21. So Høgenhaven 2011, 159 (restored on the basis of Isa 57:10). Lichtenberger 2002, 340, reconstructs ואש[. Although Høgenhaven's reconstruction makes sense, a reference to fire cannot be ruled out completely (cf. the mention of fire in relation to a similar overturning of Belial in, e.g., 4Q177 4 6–8 and 11Q13 3 7 or on frags. 25 and 26 to 4Q176). See also below, n. 31.

22. Cf. col. 1 4 above.

[ת ֯י ֯]   בלי]על לענות את עבדיו בו[15 [

]יושבת[אריֿם[ ]וֿ[ ]י ישמֿח[16 [

]תֿמֿע[ ]בֿֿת ֯[17 [

13 desp]airing until the words of consolation and great glory
written in [[23]

14 [ ] among those who love [me] there is no more since the
time of [ ]

15 [Bel]ial to oppress his servants [

16 [ ] will rejoice [ ] I will raise [ ] she that sits

17 [ ] *bt* [ ] *tm'* [

The passage envisages two opposing groups. On one side are the
servants of God—Jerusalem (1 16) and Zion (?), who sit (3 16) in
oppression but whom God will rise (interpreting line 16 as containing
first-person divine speech). On the other side are the enemies—the
kingdoms (1 13) and Belial (3 15)—who oppress but who will be
overturned when God contends against them and establish God's
justice.

So put, both the initial complaint and the answer—the passages
from the 'book' called *Isaiah*—serve as consolations to the oppressed
community. Given that line 13 features תנחמים alongside with
something written (כתוב), and since it follows an extended section
overlapping with the 'book' called *Isaiah*, it would not be far-fetched
to see here some kind of framing,[24] a reference back to the first extant
lines of column 1, which also featured the תנחמים alongside a reference to the 'book' *Isaiah* (1 15). If so, ספר ישעיה could perhaps
be reconstructed where the current line 13 breaks off,[25] indicating
that lines 13–15 provide a summary that relates the consolations just
quoted to an eschatological event (still in the future), when God will

---

23. Høgenhaven 2011, 159, proposes two ways of translating the syntax, either as
a nominal sentence where כבוד רב serves as the subject and כתוב as the predicate
("and great glory is written") or as combining כבוד רב with the preceding דברי
תנחומים so that כתוב begins a new sentence ("words of consolation and great glory.
It is written in . . ."). He deems the first option the more plausible based on the fact
that כבוד does not have a copula. However, it could also be a combination of the two
so that כתוב relates to all of the preceding, implying that despair will be a reality(?)
"until the words of consolation and great glory written in [the 'book' *Isaiah* have
come to pass."

24. Høgenhaven 2007, 114; cf. Stanley 1992, 570.

25. Although it could also be seen as an introduction to a new set of quotations that
would have followed, little in the remainder of the fragments points to such a scenario.

intervene on behalf of the faithful by ending their despair, taking the bowl of wrath away from them, and putting it into the hand of their tormentors (2 20–22).

Seeing these lines as part of a frame does not, however, imply that the manuscript (nor the quotes) ends here.[26] The possible use of divine first-person speech in 3 16 (and perhaps 14, so that the entire 14–16 could be seen as divine speech),[27] taken together with the reference to servants in line 15, points to the interesting possibility that the framing is not necessarily used to distinguish between the contents from the 'book' called *Isaiah* and other, added content but instead is used as a way of creating a continuity of tradition.

Renewing the Call

Moving on to column 4, it is more fragmentary. Fragment 14 has no overlaps with the 'book' called *Isaiah*,[28] although similar characteristics as in 1 12–15 and 3 13–17 are found.[29] There is an explicit first-person plural who addresses God directly and a possible parallel between "there is no one who seeks" (אין לוא דורש, 4 6) and "there is none burying (them)" (אין קובר) in column 1 (1 15). The text is too fragmented, however, to draw any firm conclusions.

Fragment 15,[30] however, includes a text overlapping with a passage from the Hebrew Bible featuring divine speech in the first person, but it is no longer from the 'book' called *Isaiah*; instead, it is similar to Zech 13:9, where it is said that God "will put this third into the fire, refine them as one refines silver, and test them as is tested gold." The events thus seem to relate to what was implied on the last extant lines of column 3—a period of refining in the latter days and the turning of the fortunes of the oppressed righteous community also known from other Dead Sea compositions (see, e.g., 4QMidrEschat[a,b]).[31] Since the extant words are so few (and not fully overlapping with MT Zech), it is not clear if this is in fact a quote or if the Zech text is used as a basis for continued divine

---

26. Thus slightly in contrast to Stanley 1992, 570.

27. Høgenhaven 2011, 159.

28. Allegro 1968, 64, suggested that this fragment may have formed part of the prayer on col. 1, while Campbell 2004, 78, notes that it may be interpreted as an allusion to Jubilees.

29. So Høgenhaven 2011, 160.

30. Stanley 1992, 569, excludes this fragment from his treatment of 4Q176, since "nothing is known about the placement of either of these quotations."

31. For this, see, e.g., Willgren Davage 2019. Possibly strengthening the connection further would be if "fire" (אש) is reconstructed in 3 13, as mentioned above, n. 21.

speech in a way similar to how Ps 79 was used to aid the formulating of a communal complaint.[32]

Then in the last fragments judged to belong to column 4, fragments 42, 12–13,[33] there is a quote from Isa 51:23b followed by Isa 52:1–2a and a *vacat*. The occurrence here of passages already quoted is puzzling. It could perhaps be claimed that they have been dislocated from the main text, but that would be true only as for the actual fragments.[34] A more reasonable way of understanding the verses is instead to see them as taking part in the overall argument of the manuscript. In fact, the *vacat* on line 4 indicates that the overlap with Isa 52:2 ends after the first imperative—that is, excluding the notion of a captive Jerusalem. Consequently, the verses may have been repeated as a renewed call for the people to rise up as a consequence of God taking action. This would, then, be either part of or following the time of refining through fire.

Ultimately, this points to the conclusion that passages from the 'book' called *Isaiah* have been used in different contexts and in slightly different shapes and perform different functions within the same manuscript.

The Creator and the Sanctuary

The last column is reconstructed from a number of fragments (16, 17, 18, 22, 23, 33, 51, 53)[35] that have no obvious overlap with any text from the Hebrew Bible (although דור[ות עולמים on line two has been suggested to relate to Isa 51:9).

Frags. 16, 17, 18, 22, 23, 33, 51, 53

1	ור[̊] [ ]וגם אף ב[̊קדוש]	[ ]̊[ ]	[נחלת ידו בי לוא יצדק[כול איש
2	מ̊ל[פניו]כיא הוא ברא את כול[דור]ות עולמים ו[̊הכין כמש]פטו דרכי כולם ו[האר̊]ץ		

---

32. Cf. Høgenhaven 2007, 107–8.

33. Allegro 1968, 63, suggested that the restatement of Isa 52 could possibly fit at the bottom of column 3. As with frag. 15, Stanley 1992, 569, excludes this fragment from treatment. Strugnell 1969, 233, was the first to place frag. 42 here and reconstruct Isa 51:23 and 52:1. So also Lichtenberger 2002, 342, but not Allegro 1968, 64.

34. The explanation by Allegro 1968, 63, that it would simply be "a restatement of the biblical text at the end of the pesher," is not convincing. Most significantly, this manuscript is not a pesher (see below), but even if it would have been, such a practice is not found in any of the extant pesharim in Qumran.

35. Stanley 1992, 569, excludes these fragments from treatment, since they are deemed as of little interest for his study. The reconstruction was first made by Strugnell 1969, 234, and the main contours are followed by Høgenhaven, although he modifies it slightly in light of the column width, which is deemed too wide in Strugnell's reconstruction.

3   בראֹ[בימי]נו טרם היותם ובעצֹ[ות פק]ד על כול א[יש וכ]רזו הפיל גורל לאיֹשֹ לֹתֹת]

4   ל[ ]ל[ ]ול אמרֹ[ ]במלאך פ ̊ [ ]   ית קודש ולתת פעלת איש ל]

5   [ ] ̊ [ ] [שמונה ש]   ]רֹ על אוהבו ועל שומרי מצ[ותיו

6   ]יֹפע לנו מפֹרֹ[ ]שֹכה את בריתו vacat ול ̊]

7   ע[שוֹ התורה ו]]שֹנאתֹה להיותֹ[ ]ל]

8   [התורה]]כלותם[ל] [̊]

1   and *r*[ ] and even also in the sanctuary [ ]the possession of his hand, for no [man] is justified

2   be[fore him], for he created all of the eternal ge[nerations, and according to] his [just]ice [established] the ways of them all. And the eart[h]

3   he created [with] his r[ight hand] before they came into being. And by his c[ounsel he look]ed after every m[an. And according to] his secret he made the lot fall for men in order to give[

4   *l*[ ]*l*[ ]*wl* said [ ] by the angel of *p*[ ]*yt* holy in order to give the reward of man to[

5   [ ] eight *sh*[ ]*r* regarding those who love him and keep [his] command[ments]

6   [ ]*yp'* to us *mpr*[ ]forgot his covenant. *vacat* And to [ ]

7   they [d]o the law and[ ] you hate. To be[36] [ ]*l*[

8   [ ] the law [ ]to finish them off[ ]*l*[ ]

The text is in continuation with what has been observed for the rest of 4Q176.[37] It, however, is no longer either a prayer or direct speech from God but rather talks *about* God in the third person—at least up until line 7, where speech seems to be directed toward God again (see, e.g., שנאתה),[38] possibly by a collective (cf. לנו, line 6).

The reference to a sanctuary on line 1 (במקדוש) relates to column 1 (1 13; see also 3 16), but what is described here is not a "devastated and defiled city and temple,"[39] as was the case in that column. Rather, the focus seems to be on God's might and power. As creator, God looks after every human (even determines their fate, line 3[?]), and rules

---

36. Cf. Lichtenberger 2002, 345: "you hated to become."

37. Cf. Maier 2000, 915.

38. Cf. Høgenhaven 2011, 163.

39. So Høgenhaven 2011, 163, although he may be right in interpreting וגם אף as an indication "that the enemies have destroyed not only city but 'even also' the sanctuary."

over all of God's creation.[40] The two opposing groups noted in column 3 are also present here. The enemies are likely referenced in lines 7–8, where God(?) is "hating," and in line 8, where some people are to be finished off, while God's servants are described as the ones who love God and keep God's commandments (5 5).

Voices Intertwined

If the fragments are correctly placed and if it is plausible to assume that the manuscript would not have included much more material, this manuscript reveals an overall movement from an initial position of oppression by enemies, voiced as a complaint to God via the consoling answers by God by means of passages from the 'book' called *Isaiah*, to a rich description of how God's answer would come to be realized in the near future. The latter is described as a time when the promised justice of God would finally enable the sitting Zion to rise again and shake off the dust through a period of refining, while the enemies—the haters of God's law and covenant—would get the punishment God had already allotted them.[41]

Looking more closely at the relation between the various voices, it can be seen that large parts of the manuscript consist of direct speech, with some parts introducing such speech and some lines providing comments or summaries of what has been said. At least three voices can be identified: a community, God, and an anonymous voice. Interestingly, these voices are found not only in the extracts from the 'book' called *Isaiah* but also in the passages inspired by Ps 79 and Zech 13 and in the passages that do not overlap with any known text now found in the Hebrew Bible. There thus seems to be no internal distinction made between *Isaiah* and the other material.

This suggestion is further emphasized by the observation that the passages from the 'book' called *Isaiah*—which generally occur in an

---

40. Høgenhaven 2007, 121, has pointed to 4Q418 frag. 81 1–14 as a possible parallel, so that both texts may have been "in a broad sense informed by a common traditional doctrine."

41. See an overlapping description of the contents in Stanley 1992, 576–77; Høgenhaven 2007, 122–23; 2019, 352. I will not discuss issues of provenance at any length here. It is quite clear that the content fits well within the theological framework of the Qumran community, but due to the lack of specific sectarian vocabulary, it might have originated elsewhere and subsequently "taken over" (so Høgenhaven 2007, 123; cf. Høgenhaven 2019, 353).

order overlapping with the 'book'[42]—are juxtaposed to other material in a way that they all work together to provide an answer to the complaint in column 1.[43] Given that only the beginning of the extracted parts is properly demarcated and that the passages from *Isaiah* are followed by a series of direct divine speech and speech about God, it could be argued that someone not familiar with the 'book' called *Isaiah*—or at least not having anything similar to it in front of her/ him—would not necessarily know where the passages from that 'book' ended and "something else" began.[44] The fact that text from Isa 51:23; 52:1–2a is repeated after the second mention of תנחמים in 3 13 shows this with all clarity and somewhat softens the idea that תנחמים would have distinguished passages from the 'book' called *Isaiah* from the surrounding text.[45]

Blurring Boundaries

In light of this analysis, 4Q176 turns out to be an interesting example of how the voices of "subsequent ones" (in the Mesopotamian sense) have been intertwined and joined with the 'book' called *Isaiah* in a way that ultimately blurs the boundaries between the two. The dynamic in 4Q176—a composition structured around a complaint and God's answer to it—is, in this sense, not that different from the dynamic argued for *Isaiah* itself (see chapter 6 above), although it differs from it by means of the explicit reference to the 'book' in 1 15 (and possibly 3 13). 4Q176 thus both depends on the transmission of the 'book' called *Isaiah* and constructs authorship in line with it, not least by being in itself an anonymous composition. Subsequent (anonymous) tradents are drawn into the transmission, and the effect is that *Isaiah* is both preserved and renewed.

---

42. Høgenhaven 2011, 164–66, in particular, has discussed the possible rationale behind the selection of passages and has argued convincingly that they have not been selected on formal grounds but rather based on what they would have to say about the main theme of the manuscript: the end of the oppression of the faithful, which indicates that the enemies will be punished and glory will befall the faithful. Høgenhaven also notes that such an emphasis would explain why otherwise strong themes in Isa 40–55 were not mentioned.

43. The way that these different sections work within the whole makes the statement by Campbell 2004, 85, that what is found are "citation[s] of encouraging passages from Isaiah, Psalms, and Zechariah" a bit too unprecise.

44. As noted by Høgenhaven 2011, 166, in all, Scripture and non-Scripture "exhibit a remarkable thematic and formal similarity."

45. So Høgenhaven 2011, 155.

In fact, such a dynamic, where 'books' are supposed to be kept "up-to-date as new revelations and situations arose,"[46] is made explicit in another composition enjoying popularity in Qumran. In Jubilees 45:16, it is recounted how (written) traditions first received by the "fathers" are handed over to new "subsequent ones." More specifically, Jacob "gave all his books and the books of his fathers to his son Levi so that he could *preserve them* and *renew them* for his sons until today."[47]

In sum, then, it has been argued that 4Q176 constructs authorship in ways that significantly overlap with the Mesopotamian trajectory. The composition itself is anonymous, and although it refers to the extracts as coming from the 'book' *Isaiah*, the prophet himself is nowhere to be found. Turning now to a broader look at the 'book' called *Isaiah* in the Dead Sea Scrolls, these observations will be further substantiated. At the same time, it will be clear that the relation between the prophet Isaiah and writing that was established in 2 Chr 26:22; 32:32 has started to be seen in a new light.

EXPLICIT PENNINGS

There are several indications that the 'book' called *Isaiah* was quite popular in the Qumran community. First, there are as many as twenty-two scrolls that contain parts of the 'book':[48]

---

46. VanderKam 2018, 1115.

47. Translation from VanderKam 2018, 1103 (emphasis added). This distributive notion of authorship (regularly featuring an initial divine-human revelatory interaction) is also present in, for example, the references to writings of Enoch, which are described as received in a nighttime vision and designated as "testimonies" delivered to his sons and their descendants (see esp. Jub. 4:17–19; cf. perhaps 1 En. 91–92), but also in relation to Noah (Jub. 8:11–12; 10:13–14), Abraham (Jub. 12:27; 21:10), etc. (see VanderKam 2018, 1114–15), as well as in the Dead Sea Scrolls (see, e.g., 4Q542 frag. 1 2 9–12).

48. Flint 2002, 229; Tov 2019, 97, also mentions "another copy (X20) derived from an unknown locality." These twenty-two manuscripts should not, however, automatically be taken as "copies" of the 'book' (as does Brooke 1997, 610), since some are very fragmentary and thus preclude any conclusions about its full contents (see similarly Tov 1997, 491n1; Ulrich 2000, 385).

1QIsa[a][49]	Isa 1–66
1QIsa[b] (1Q8)[50]	Isa 7–8; 10; 12–13; 15–16; 19–20; 22–23; 24–26; 28–30; 35; 37–41; 43–66
4QIsa[a] (4Q55)[51]	Isa 1–2; 4–6; 11–13; 17; 19–23; 33(?)
4QIsa[b] (4Q56)	Isa 1–3; 5; 9; 11–13; 17–22; 24; 26; 35–37; 39–46; 48–49; 51–53; 61; 64–66
4QIsa[c] (4Q57)	Isa 9–12; 14; 22–26; 28; 30; 33; 44–46; 48–49; 51–55; 66

49. See Burrows, Trever, and Brownlee 1950; Cross, Freedman, and Sanders 1972; Parry and Qimron 1999. Given its state of preservation, its curious use of *paragraphos*, the many scribal errors and variant readings (Tov 1997, 502; cf. Greenberg 1956, 164), and, most significantly, the fact that the scroll is divided into two parts by a gap at the bottom of col. 27, separating chapters 33 and 34 (cf. Richards 1965; Giese 1988, 61; Evans 1988), two parts written by different scribes (Kahle 1951; Tov 1997, 501; Flint 2002, 230; see also Ulrich 2000, 387, who also notes that "at least four scribes" made revisions; cf. Tov 1997, 502), this manuscript has been subject to considerable scholarly attention (for an overview of the early phases of discovery, see Ulrich 2017, 144–46). This is not the place for an extensive overview (for this, see Tov 1997; cf. Parry 2019), but two aspects—apart from the observation that there is a far-reaching agreement that there is only one literary "edition" of the 'book,' with thousands of variants (see, e.g., Ulrich 2000, 386; Flint 2002, 237)—could be mentioned here that relate to the bisection of the scroll and the use of *paragraphos*. First, it can be observed that although the many variant readings are generally seen as providing an interesting window into the complex composition processes underlying the 'book' (Høgenhaven 1984, 1998; Steck 1998; Ulrich 2001; Stromberg 2009), Drew Longacre has argued the interesting thesis that the variants found in chapters 34–66 are best understood as a result of the scroll being copied from (at least) two exemplars, with the scribe copying chapters 34–66 from a scroll with a damaged bottom edge (Longacre 2013). If seen in light of what will be observed in relation to quotations from the 'book' below, there is thus no reason to take the break between chapters 33 and 34 as reflecting an idea that the 'book' called *Isaiah* was understood as a two-part work (contra Swanson 2009, 200). More likely, it reflects a practice of writing the 'book' called *Isaiah* across two scrolls, as longer scrolls would be quite cumbersome to handle (cf. Brownlee 1962; Brooke 2006, 79; and a similar argument in relation to collections of psalms in Willgren 2016b). This is also confirmed by the fact that most scrolls preserve parts from either half of the 'book' (see the table in Brooke 2020, 431; cf. Swanson 2009, 196, in some contrast to Flint 2002, 234, who argues that "no evidence to indicate that all twenty-two Isaiah scrolls originally contained less than the book in its entirety"). Second, Nathan Mastnjak has suggested that one way of understanding the *paragraphos* is to see them as marking the introduction of new speakers, or at least speaker contexts (Mastnjak 2020; contrast the earlier Bardtke 1953, for example). If correct, it could indicate a Greek influence, although it needs to be put in relation to the picture that will emerge below that indicates that the *whole* of the 'book' called *Isaiah* was understood as spoken by the prophet Isaiah.

50. See Sukenik 1955; Barthélemy and Milik 1955, 66–68; cf. Jain 2002. The contents of the scrolls are generalized to chapters only. Most often, however, only parts of the chapters have been preserved.

51. All cave 4 manuscripts are published in Ulrich et al. 1997.

4QIsa[d] (4Q58)	Isa 45–49; 52–54; 57–58
4QIsa[e] (4Q59)	Isa 2; 7–14; 59
4QIsa[f] (4Q60)	Isa 1–2; 5–8; 20; 22; 24; 27; 28–29(?)
4QIsa[g] (4Q61)	Isa 42–43
4QIsa[h] (4Q62)	Isa 42
4QIsa[i] (4Q62a)	Isa 56–57
4QIsa[j] (4Q63)	Isa 1
4QIsa[k] (4Q64)	Isa 28–29
4QIsa[l] (4Q65)	Isa 7–8
4QIsa[m] (4Q66)	Isa 60–61
4QIsa[n] (4Q67)	Isa 58
4QIsa[o] (4Q68)[52]	Isa 14–15
4QpapIsa[p] (4Q69)[53]	Isa 5
4QIsa[q] (4Q69a)	Isa 54
4QIsa[r] (4Q69b)	Isa 30:23
5QIsa (5Q3)[54]	Isa 40
MurIsa (Mur 3)[55]	Isa 1

Second, there are several pesharim of the 'book' called *Isaiah*. Third, the 'book' is quoted over twenty times in other sectarian texts, which can be compared to, for example, the 'books' called *Jeremiah* and *Ezekiel*, which are explicitly quoted only a few times.[56] Fourth, the 'book' often served as inspiration for new compositions (see, e.g., 1QSb 5 21–26; 4Q521 frag. 2 2 + 4; 11Q5 19 2).[57] Despite this popularity, however, it can also be noted that in contrast to Enoch, Moses, Daniel, and to some extent, David, the prophet Isaiah is *himself* not expanded upon in any greater length—the 'book' seems to have been more important than the person.[58] How is this to be understood, and how is the relation between the prophet and the 'book' conceived of in the Dead Sea Scrolls?

---

52. The scroll perhaps also preserves 16:7–8, although it is deemed unlikely in Flint 2002, 232.

53. It has been argued that this scroll could have been for personal use and thus is not to be counted as a copy of the 'book' called *Isaiah* (Tov 1997, 493n10; cf. Ulrich et al. 1997, 138; Flint 2002, 233).

54. See Baillet, Milik, and de Vaux 1962.

55. See Benoit, Milik, and de Vaux 1962.

56. Tov 2019, 98: "more than the other major prophets"; cf. Brooke 1997, 611–12; Ulrich 2000, 387. According to Brooke 1997, 611–12, a similar pattern can be observed for allusions.

57. See further Brooke 1997, 612–17, who identifies four main uses of the 'book' called *Isaiah*: legal, eschatological, poetic, and exhortatory (but in Brooke 2020, 440–45, he speaks instead of legal, narrative, poetic, and prophetic use).

58. Cf. Ulrich 2000, 387. See also the discussions on the lack of "rewriting" in Davies 1996, 50–51; 2000, 68–69; and Brooke 2006, 81.

By Written Agency

Looking first at texts that provide declared quotations from the 'book' called *Isaiah*—that is, texts that explicitly frame the quotations[59]—the following can be observed:[60]

1. A few texts frame quotes from *Isaiah* as something that the prophet Isaiah "said" (e.g., אמר ישעיה). This can be found in, for example, CD 6 7–8 (Isa 54:16).

2. Some texts introduce passages from *Isaiah* as something "written" (e.g., כתוב) so that it is the text that is doing the "speaking" (e.g., אשר אמר). Several examples are found. In CD 7 10–12, for example, where Isa 7:17 is quoted, it is said that "the word which is written in the words of the prophet Isaiah son of Amoz came (true), which says . . ." (בבוא הדבר אשר כתוב בדברי ישעיה בן אמוץ הנביא אשר אמר . . .). In 4QMidrEschat[a,b] 3 15, Isa 8:11 is introduced as "it is written in the scroll of the prophet Isaiah, regarding the last days" (אשר כתוב בספר ישעיה הנביא לאחרית [ה]ימים). Other examples include 4QMidrEschat[a,b] frag. 15 1–3; 8 2 (both partially reconstructed, introducing Isa 66:22–23 and Isa 37:30, respectively); 4Q265 frag. 1 3–6 (introducing Isa 54:1–2); and 4Q176 1 15 (see above, "More Subsequent Ones").

3. A shorter "as it is written" (כאשר כתוב), which does not necessarily mention the prophet Isaiah, is found in, for example, 1QS 5 17 (Isa 2:22), 8 14 (Isa 40:3; cf. 4Q259 3 5), and 11Q13 2 19–20 (Isa 61:2), 23 (Isa 52:7).

4. To this picture can also be added many (possible) quotes from the 'book' *Isaiah* that are undeclared: CD 5 13–14 (Isa 50:11; 59:5), 16 (Isa 27:11); 6 16–17 (Isa 10:2); 1QpHab 6 12 (Isa 13:18); 1QS 8 7 (Isa 28:16); 9 19–20 (Isa 40:3); 1QSb 5 21–22 (Isa 11:4), 23–26 (Isa 11:4, 2); 4Q185 frag. 1–2 1 10–11 (Isa 40:6–8); 4Q434 frag. 1 1 9 (Isa 42:16); 4Q437 1 8–9 (Isa 49:2); and 11Q13 2 14 (Isa 61:3).[61] Moreover, some are possibly declared but almost entirely reconstructed (if the reconstructions are correct, many

---

59. For a brief introduction to this terminology, see Willgren 2016a, 290–92.

60. Cf. similarly Brooke 1997, 610–11, 611n9.

61. To be added here may also be 4QCryptic text A, which is written in code and features two words that occur together in Isa 11:6–7 (see Pfann and Alexander 2000; Swanson 2009, 208–11).

would relate to one of the three categories above): CD 14 1
(Isa 7:17); 4Q215a frag. 1 2 2 (Isa 48:10); 4Q285 frag. 7
1–3 (Isa 10:34–11:1; cf. 11Q14 frag. 1 1 9–11); 4Q435
frag. 1 8 (Isa 42:16); 4Q471a frag. 1 6 (Isa 19:14), 8 (Isa
5:20); 4Q509 frag. 275 1 (Isa 10:12); 4QMidrEschat[a,b] 8 5
(?), 6 (Isa 32:7), 15 (Isa 22:13); 11Q13 2 4 (Isa 61:1).

Taken together, the combined effect of these quotations is that
the *entire* 'book' called *Isaiah* has now been cast as words related to the
prophet Isaiah in some way. If not including the reconstructions,
he is explicitly related to passages from Isa 2:22; 7:17; 8:11; 10:34–11:1;
37:30; 40:3; 52:7; 54:1–2; 54:16; 61:2; and 66:22–23. This, then, constitutes a new development in the transmission of the 'book' that takes
the connection made between the prophet and the writing in 2 Chr
26:22 and 32:32 a step further, and this is made explicit in CD 4 13–14.

In CD 4 13–14, Isa 24:17 is introduced as words that "God *said by
the agency* of Isaiah the prophet, son of Amoz" (כאשר דבר אל ביד ישעיה
הנביא בן אמוץ לאמר). Notable is that the passage uses ביד in a way that
creates a contrast to what has previously been noted. More specifically,
it was argued in chapters 5 and 6 that in the 'book' called *Isaiah*, this
agency was related primarily to symbolic actions (so Isa 20:2; see above,
"Sidelining the 'First One,'" chapter 6). In CD, however, it has become
related to prophetic *speech* (cf. מפי הנביא in 4Q375 1 1), as preserved
in written form (cf. ספרי הנביאים in CD 7 17).[62] The agency of the
prophet thus seems to have been transformed from symbolic action to
writing, and this is confirmed if looking at another text from the same
document, CD 19 7, where Zech 13:7 is introduced as "the word which
is *written by the agency* of the prophet Zechariah" (הדבר אשר כתוב ביד
זכריה הנביא).[63]

---

62. The use of ביד in Mal 1:1 may be a precursor to this development (דבר־יהוה
אל־ישראל ביד מלאכי; cf. Hag 1:1, 3; 2:1), but it should also be noted that Mesopotamian colophons also regularly mentioned scribes by reference to their hands—"hand
of . . ." etc. (see Hunger 1968; cf. van der Toorn 2007, 32)—while prophetic texts from
the royal archive of Nineveh, for example, regularly have "by the mouth of" (see Nissinen
2003, 97–132).

63. See a similar use of ביד in 1QpHab 2 8–10, where Hab 1:6 is quoted after a passage
mentioning a "priest" (כוהן) that will explain "all the words of his servants the prophets by [whose] agency God recounted all that is to come upon his people" (כול דברי
עבדיו הנביאים [אשר ביד]ם ספר אל את כול הבאות על עמו), or CD 3 21, where ביד is
used in relation to "Ezekiel the prophet," introducing Ezek 44:15 (see also perhaps 1QS
1 3, which refers to "Moses and all his servants the prophets," ביד מושה וביד כול עבדיו
הנביאים; cf. 1QS 8 15–16).

It can thus be concluded that these quotations assume that words from the *whole* of the 'book' of *Isaiah* had been received (from YHWH) and committed to writing by the prophet Isaiah. This is clearly a new development, and a consequence of this is that some of the internal dynamics observed in part 3 above are transformed. One example is that the relation between the "former and the latter" that was observed in Isa 40–55—where words spoken in the past were believed to have come true and thus served to authorize new revelation—is reinterpreted. More specifically, what has happened when all of the words in the 'book' called *Isaiah* are believed to have been spoken by the prophet himself is that the "now" and the "latter" is understood not in relation to the "subsequent ones" in the 'book' itself but in relation to the Qumran community. It was in *their* time that some of the words in the 'book' had come true (see, e.g., the importance of Isa 40),[64] while others were still awaiting fulfillment. The future orientation of the 'book' called *Isaiah* is thus emphasized in a new way.

However, although this is a transformation that departs somewhat from the Mesopotamian trajectory, it can be noted that the fundamental dynamic has nonetheless remained the same. Seen in light of the presupposition in many of the Qumran commentaries that there was a continuing revelation taking place,[65] it could in fact be suggested that the Qumran community is essentially constructing themselves as "subsequent ones," similar to what was argued in relation to 4Q176. Ultimately, these observations all point to an ongoing negotiation between the two trajectories, with additional marks of the Mesopotamian trajectory found not only in the fact that the new compositions are themselves anonymous (as was 4Q176) but also in the fact that the prophet himself had no impact on the *interpretation* of the passages, as the overview of the pesharim will show.

Eschatological Relevance

Turning to the pesharim, six manuscripts comment on the 'book' called *Isaiah*: 3Q4 (3QpIsa); 4Q161 (4QpIsa^a); 4Q162 (4QpIsa^b); 4Q163 (4QpIsa^c); 4Q164 (4QpIsa^d); and 4Q165 (4QpIsa^e).[66] As with the other

---

64. On Isa 40, see, e.g., Brooke 1994; Ulrich 2017, 158.

65. Cf. Lim 2017, 9: "The sectarian interpreter . . . claims that God continued to reveal his mysteries beyond the time of the prophets to the Teacher of Righteousness."

66. Whether or not Stegemann is correct when arguing that only two compositions are reflected in these manuscripts is not relevant here. According to Stegemann 1993, 176–78, 4Q163 and 4Q165 are copies of the same commentary, while 4Q161, 4Q162, and 4Q164 reflect another commentary with a more developed eschatology and

pesharim from Qumran, they consist of a quotation of a base text (from *Isaiah*) followed by a commentary (often introduced by פשר).[67] How, then, is the relation between the prophet and the 'book' conceived of in these compositions?

Surveying the manuscripts, their fragmentary state sometimes precludes any far-reaching conclusions. Starting with 3Q4, it is not necessarily a pesher, since it does not preserve any introductory formulas.[68] Nonetheless, since a verse from the 'book' called *Isaiah* is followed by a text not found elsewhere in the 'book' called *Isaiah*, the latter may have been a comment on the former. The importance of this manuscript is that the passage quoted and commented upon is Isa 1:1 and that the vision that the prophet Isaiah saw (חזון . . . חזה) is interpreted as something "[I]sa[iah] prophesied con[cerning] . . ." (י]שע[יה] [נבא ע]ל, line 3). The observations above that emphasized that the contents of the 'book' called *Isaiah* were seen as spoken by the prophet Isaiah are thus further confirmed, and like the pesharim on other 'books' now found in the Hebrew Bible, the paratext is included and commented on as part of the 'book.'[69] Moreover, the mentioning of Uzziah on line 4 and the day of judgment (י]ום המשפט[י) on line 6 could indicate that Isa 1:2 was quoted at the end of line 4, followed by a comment on line 5, after a *vacat*,[70] but this is only hypothetical.[71] However, given the reference to the day of judgment and how this day is understood elsewhere in the pesharim, it is reasonable to assume that the text is interpreted eschatologically with an eye to contemporary relevance.[72]

Turning to 4Q161,[73] it is much lengthier. Remains of three columns of text have been preserved that comment on parts of Isa 10:22–11:5 (interestingly, some of the verses are repeated and followed by two

---

messianism. The argument has been countered by Brooke on the basis of, among others, observed differences as to structure and introductions of the texts quoted (Brooke 1997, 619).

67. For an introduction, see esp. Horgan 1979 (*Isaiah* on 70–138, 260–61); cf. Lim 2002; Berrin 2005; Tzoref 2019; and the references in Brooke 1997, 618n39.

68. Cf. Horgan 1979, 260. Published in Baillet, Milik, and de Vaux 1962.

69. See, e.g., how superscriptions to Ps 12 are commented upon in 4QMidrEschat[a.b] 8 12–13 (Willgren Davage 2019, 235–36) or the superscription to Ps 45 in 4Q171 (Willgren Davage, forthcoming).

70. See the suggested reconstruction in Horgan 1979, 260–61.

71. Baillet, Milik, and de Vaux 1962, 96, propose that it may have been a commentary on the whole of the 'book' called *Isaiah*. If so, it would have taken up more than one scroll.

72. So also Brooke 1997, 620.

73. See Allegro 1968, 11–15; Strugnell 1969, 183–86; Horgan 1979, 70–86; Brooke 1997, 620–24.

different comments).[74] Most space is taken up by the lengthy quotes, while the comments are brief, except for the comment on Isa 11:1–5, which takes up eight lines (3 22–29). As in 3Q4, the 'book' called *Isaiah* is interpreted as speaking eschatologically about the Qumran community in the latter days (לאחרית הימים, 2 26), where a battle with the "Kittim" will take place (הכתיאים, 3 6–13; cf. 2 27)[75] and a branch of David will take a stand (העומד) and rule over all the nations (3 25–26), supported by God (3 23–24) and advised by (Zadokite?) priests (3 27–28; cf. 11Q19 58 15–21).[76] This is well in line with, for example, 4Q285[77]—where Isa 11:1 is also quoted and said to refer to a Davidic branch that would put the leader of the Kittim to death—and thus points to a shared interpretive approach.[78]

Noteworthy, then, is that—in a way similar to the Mesopotamian commentaries (see above, "Commenting on Texts," chapter 3) and in contrast to contemporary Greek interactions with literary works—the prophet Isaiah is nowhere invoked in the interpretations. Put differently, although believed to be the speaking voice in the text, the possible intentions of the prophet are nowhere taken into consideration, nor is the historical context in which the prophet Isaiah spoke. Ultimately, the 'book' called *Isaiah* is not interacted with as the intellectual property of the prophet Isaiah. It is nowhere assumed that to understand it correctly, one has to understand what the prophet Isaiah may have intended. This picture is confirmed as more pesharim are taken into consideration.

4Q162 quotes Isa 5:5–6, 11–14, 24–25, 29–30 (and possibly 6:9),[79] and each passage is followed by very brief,[80] eschatologically oriented comments that identify parties in the text with people in the latter days (לאחרית הימים, 2 1).[81] Featured in particular are the "scoffers, who are in Jerusalem" (אנשי הלצון אשר בירושלים, 2 6–7, 10; cf. Isa 28:14), and the general outlook is well preserved in 2 1–2:

1   פשר הדבר לאחרית הימים לחובת הארץ מפני החרב והרעב והיה

2   בעת פקדת הארץ

---

74. See Horgan 1979, 82–83; Lim 2002, 28.

75. Horgan 1979, 73, 81; cf. Brooke 1997, 621.

76. As with Brooke 1997, 623, the pesher should be read as a coherent composition.

77. See further references to research on 4Q285 in Brooke 1997, 622n57.

78. So also Brooke 1997, 623.

79. See Allegro 1968, 15–17; Strugnell 1969, 186–88; Horgan 1979, 70–86; Brooke 1997, 624–26.

80. Cf. Lim 2002, 28.

81. Cf. Horgan 1979, 87.

1   The interpretation of the words regarding the latter days
     concerns the condemnation of the land before the sword
     and the famine (cf. Jer 32:24). And it will happen
2   in the time of the visitation of the land.

A similar focus is also found in 4Q164, where (protagonist) parties in the community of the latter days are creatively identified with parts of the rebuilt Jerusalem in Isa 54:11–12,[82] and an eschatological outlook is also likely permeating 4Q165,[83] where commentaries on parts of Isa 11, 14, 15, 21, 32, and 40 are found. Unfortunately, very little of what would likely have been only brief commentaries remain. Notable is that Isa 40:11 is introduced as "written" (אשר כתוב, frag. 1–2 2; cf. Isa 32:5 in frag. 6 2) and that the verses may have been quoted in an order different from the MT.[84]

In 4Q163 (the only of the preserved pesher that is written on papyrus),[85] however, a large number of verses from Isa 8:7 through 31:1 are commented on in sequence,[86] although the pesher skips a number of verses, repeats others, changes the order of some, and refers to passages from other prophetic 'books' as supporting texts.[87] Comments are again mostly very brief and focus on the latter days (אחרית הימים, frag. 6–7 2 14, 13 4, 23 10), a battle (frag. 25 3), and antagonists found in Jerusalem (פשר הדבר לאחרית הימים על עדת ד[ורשי] החלקות אשר בירושלים, frag. 23 10–11; cf. 4QMidrEschat[a.b] 9 12 and 4Q169) who have rejected the law (frag. 23 14a; cf. Isa 5:24).[88]

The consistent picture painted by these pesharim is, then, that although the prophet Isaiah may be understood as the speaking voice, there is very little interest in the prophet himself. Instead, the texts are interpreted as having eschatological relevance by being applied to the contemporary situation.[89] This use indicates that the 'book' called *Isaiah* was invested with prophetic (in the sense that it had foretold events) and ethical (in the sense that it was believed to affirm the identity of the community and promote a certain way of living) authority that was

---

82. Allegro 1968, 27–28; Horgan 1979, 125–31; Brooke 1997, 629.

83. Allegro 1968, 28–30; Horgan 1979, 131–38; Brooke 1997, 630–31.

84. Lim 2002, 29.

85. Allegro 1968, 17–27; Horgan 1979, 94–124; Brooke 1997, 626–28.

86. Cf. Lim 2002, 29.

87. *Jeremiah* is quoted in frag. 1 4; *Zechariah* in frags. 8–10 8 and frag. 21 7; and *Hosea* in frag. 23 2 14[?]. On such a use of supporting texts, see also, e.g., 4QMidrEschat[a.b] and 11Q13.

88. Cf. Horgan 1979, 120–21; Brooke 1997, 628.

89. Cf. Flint 2002, 240; Kratz 2015, 97–101; Ulrich 2017, 162.

ultimately based on the belief that the 'book' called *Isaiah* had been spoken by God *through* the prophet.[90]

SMALL STEPS ONLY

What the survey of the way the 'book' called *Isaiah* was interacted with in the Dead Sea Scrolls has shown is that although the prophet Isaiah is now conceived of as the one speaking in the whole 'book' and even though a greater emphasis was placed on him actually doing the writing (both indications of a Greek emphasis on authors as *originators*), the relation between the 'book' and the prophet still very much bears the marks of the Mesopotamian trajectory. Texts are commented upon without any reference to intentions or notions of intellectual property, and the prophet is not used to provide authority to the text. In fact, the literary activity in Qumran could be conceived of in terms of the work of "subsequent ones." This was quite clear in the way the boundaries between content from *Isaiah* and new revelation was blurred in 4Q176, a composition that was anonymous, like all other texts surveyed here. In the end, although steps have been taken that relate the prophet closer to the 'book,' these steps are still small.

---

90. For these notions of authority, see Davage 2021a.

PART V

THE PROPHET ISAIAH AS A GREEK AUTHOR

CHAPTER II

LEAVING MESOPOTAMIA BEHIND

It has been shown so far that the relation between the prophet Isaiah and the 'book' called *Isaiah* has been conceived of in different ways throughout time. In the 'book' called *Isaiah* itself, no connection is made between the prophet Isaiah and any written text. Instead, the prophetic oracles and other material gathered in this anthology circulated anonymously for quite some time before being paratextually framed with the prophet Isaiah as the "first one," a framing likely inspired by the fact that the prophet Isaiah featured as a character in narratives included in the anthology.

This connection was then picked up in 2 Chr 26:22 and 32:32, where the prophet Isaiah was, for the first time, related to writing (26:22). Seen in light of the other references in 1–2 Chr, it was made clear that no notion of intellectual property was to be found, and neither was any case made for seeing the prophet Isaiah as in some way responsible for the *entire* 'book.' Most plausibly, he was still seen as a "first one," well in line with the Mesopotamian trajectory.

However, since his name had been attached to a clearly demarcated part of the transmission of prophetic literature—the 'book' called *Isaiah*—and since he was now constructed as literate, he would eventually be seen as the one writing the entire 'book' called *Isaiah*. Indications of this transformation were found in the Dead Sea Scrolls. Although the construction of tradents as "subsequent ones" was still found in 4Q176, the scrolls generally presumed that the voice of the prophet Isaiah was heard throughout the *whole 'book.'* Moreover, the notion of YHWH speaking "by the agency" (ביד) of the prophet Isaiah (Isa 20:2) was explicitly linked to writing (so CD 4 13, when read in light of CD 19 7: אשר כתוב ביד), and so the influence of the Greek trajectory could be seen. The inevitable consequence of this new construction was that the prophet was no longer only a *tradent* but also an *originator*.

Nonetheless, the steps taken in the Dead Sea Scrolls were only small. Turning now to a different set of texts, mostly composed in Greek, this image will change considerably, and to inquire into the ways in which the prophet Isaiah eventually emerges more fully as a Greek author, this part of the study is divided into three chapters. Chapter 11 will look at how the relation between the prophet and the 'book' is constructed in the writings of Josephus and in the New Testament, chapter 12 will look at early Christian writings as well as the construction of author biographies, and chapter 13 will focus on rabbinic literature.

Claiming the Whole Book

Turning first to the writings of Josephus, it quickly becomes clear that the distributive, anonymous transmission of literature found in the Mesopotamian trajectory is no longer prominent, although aspects of the author concept of Josephus have some overlaps with it.[1] What is found is instead a recurring emphasis on *intellectual property*, where questions of *intention* are taking center stage. To properly understand his use of the 'book' called *Isaiah*, the following (overlapping) aspects of his way of writing will first have to be surveyed: (1) his recurring habit of clarifying intent, not least through frequent use of metatexts; (2) his way of relating to other sources; and (3) his understanding of prophecy. Again, the focus here is not on the accuracy or historical reliability of Josephus's narrative but on how Josephus understands himself and other characters as authors.

Intent and Metatexts

In his prefaces,[2] Josephus outlines the reasons why he is writing his 'books,' and oftentimes, this is made in dialogue with other, previous writers. In *Jewish War*, for example, he laments that the events he was about to recount had been previously written down in a nonsatisfactory way, giving false accounts of what happened (καταψεύδονται

---

1. Not surprisingly, there has thus been a discussion as to whether Josephus was a "mere copyist" or if he had an "agenda of his own" (with the scholarly consensus now favoring the latter; see briefly in van Henten 2018, 122–23), as if the two would be mutually exclusive.

2. Among the works written by Josephus (*Life*, *Ag. Ap.*, *Ant.*, *J. W.*), all have prefaces except for *Life*, a fact that has contributed to a discussion of whether or not *Life* was originally intended to be read in continuation of *Ant.* (see the discussion in Mason 2001, xiv–xxi; 2016b).

τῶν πραγμάτων, 1.1–2). Since these authors had been failing in relation to *their own goals* (1.7), he himself takes up the task to write an accurate (ἀκριβὲς) portrayal of the events (1.2–3; cf. *Ant.* 1.17 and to some degree *Ag. Ap.* 1.2–3, where he similarly states as an aim of his writing to refute slanders, this time about the Jews).[3] In fact, he judges himself as well suited to do so by claiming "for himself the ideal middle position concerning the assessment of the role of Romans and Jews—, but he also builds on historiographical tropes known from the times of Herodotus and Thucydides onward."[4] There can thus be no doubt that Josephus places himself and his intentions at the very center (see also *J. W.* 1.9; *Ant.* 20.262–68), while at the same time relating to other works as reflecting the intents of their authors. It is also clear that he considers his work to be his property:

> At last *I committed to writing my narrative* of the events. So confident was I of its veracity that I presumed to take as my witnesses, before all others, the commanders-in-chief in the war, Vespasian and Titus. They were the first to whom I presented *my volumes*, copies being afterwards given to many Romans who had taken part in the campaign. *Others I sold* to a large number of my compatriots. (*Ag. Ap.* 1.50–51)[5]

Consider next the preface to *Antiquities*, where Josephus makes his intentions clear:

> I had indeed ere now, when writing the history of the war, already contemplated describing the origin of the Jews, the fortunes that befell them, the great lawgiver under whom they were trained in piety and the exercise of the other virtues, and all those wars waged by them through long ages before this last . . . (*Ant.* 1.6)

> The precise details of our Scripture records will, then, be set forth, each in its place, as my narrative proceeds, that being the

---

3. On the latter, cf. van Henten 2018, 131.

4. van Henten 2018, 139–40. That Josephus was likely influenced by Thucydidean ideals is well established (see, in particular, Thackeray 1929, but also the extensive discussion in Swoboda 2014). On the construction of authority in Greek historiography, see Marincola 1997, 3–12. For the reception of Herodotus in Josephus, see Almagor 2016. See also Schwartz 2016.

5. All translations of Josephus's works are quoted from Thackeray 1926 and Thackeray 1998.

procedure that I have promised to follow throughout this work, neither adding nor omitting anything. (*Ant.* 1.17)

Throughout *Antiquities*, he then guides the reader and comments upon what has been included and excluded, providing the reader with enough information to appreciate his work in a proper way.[6] In the preface, he explains,

> Since well-nigh everything herein related is dependent on the wisdom of our lawgiver Moses, I must first speak briefly of him, lest any of my readers should ask how it is that so much of my work, which professes to treat of laws and historical facts, is devoted to natural philosophy. (*Ant.* 1.18)

He then includes recurring clarifying formulations like "but of this I shall speak hereafter" (*Ant.* 1.142; cf. 2.200); "I shall now speak of . . ." (*Ant.* 1.148; cf. 3.224; 5.341–42); "the cause of its fate I shall indicate in its place"[7] (*Ant.* 1.170; see also 1.192; 3.94; 12.237; or 1.214, "I propose in future to expound this whole subject in detail"; cf. 3.223; 4.198, 302; 20.268);[8] "as we have mentioned in the preceding book" (*Ant.* 4.74; cf. 1.203, where he refers to *J. W.* as his own composition, or *Ag. Ap.* 1.1); and so on. He also sometimes explains *why* he includes a certain narrative (see, e.g., *Ant.* 5.337).

The notion of presenting the narrative and "neither adding nor omitting anything" (*Ant.* 1.17; cf. 10.218),[9] not even adding "for the sake of embellishment" (*Ant.* 4.196) but retold[10] "just as [he] found it in the sacred books" (*Ant.* 2.347),[11] is also interesting, since it is clear that

---

6. Cf. somewhat similarly the discussion of "explicit authorial passages" in Schwartz 2016, 49–50.

7. On this formulation as reflecting the chronological structure of *Ant.*, see Schwartz 2016, 37–38.

8. As to the recurrent reference to a future 'book,' it was likely never written (so Schwartz 2016, 37; cf. Feldman 1990, 389).

9. On this phrase, see the discussion in van Unnik 1978. See also Feldman 1990, 399.

10. Or "translated," so 10.218.

11. This sometimes serves as a disclaimer, especially when recounting "extraordinary" events. See, e.g., "I am constrained to relate them as they are recorded in the sacred books" (*Ant.* 3.81), or the recurring "on this narrative readers are free to think what they please" (*Ant.* 4.158). On this tendency in Greek historiography, see, e.g., Rajak 1982, 469–71; Pitts 2013, 246. This thus somewhat nuances the suggestion by Wyrick 2004, 132, that "while Josephus act as a historian with regard to Greek sources, he does not treat Jewish sources with a similar skepticism."

Josephus indeed adds, omits, and rearranges material if compared to the Hebrew Bible.[12] In the section following *Ant.* 2.293, for example, where he writes about the plagues in Egypt, he states that he shall "recount them all . . . to show that Moses in not one of his predictions to them was mistaken," but nevertheless he omits the fifth plague. Among the more famous examples are also his omissions of the golden calf incident in Exod 32 and David's dealings with Bathsheba in 2 Sam 11.[13] This is not that surprising, however, since it has been noted in relation to both Mesopotamian and Greek trajectories that a faithful transmission did not necessarily entail a word-for-word correspondence (although Josephus uses such a notion to critique Greek historiography; see esp. *Ag. Ap.* 1.23–27, 38–42; cf. 2.182–83)[14] but rather leaves room for a substantial amount of creativity.[15]

Quoting Sources

That Josephus treats 'books' as the intellectual property of named individuals is clear not only by the way he frames his own work but also by the way he refers to other 'books' and how he deals with the origins of

---

12. See, e.g., "I would here record a detail which I omitted . . ." (3.214; cf. 6.350). For a discussion on rearrangements, see Schwartz 2016, 44–49.

13. See similarly El Mansy 2020, 137–38. Cf. also how Josephus himself speaks of things added in *Ant.* 1.129 (cf. 2.176–77) or omitted in *Ant.* 1.68; 3.198.

14. This leads Wyrick 2004 to conclude that for Josephus, there existed a crucial difference between Greek historiography and Jewish transmission (see esp. 111–202). According to Wyrick, "Josephus presents a case in which Greek historiography has no claim to authoritativeness, for the very reason that Greek historians are individualistic, competitive, and rebellious, not to mention that they are more interested in a turn of phrase or a satisfying denouement than in recounting events as they really happened" (113; see, e.g., *Ag. Ap.* 1.19–21). Wyrick also suggests that Josephus's claims that there is no need to edit and correct the Jewish traditions need to be seen in relation to the fact that he is discussing with Apion, "a Homeric philologist who was involved in the creation of such editions" (140). The overall argument is well put (it corrects Cohen 1988 on several points) and needs to be borne in mind below. Nonetheless, it is equally clear that Josephus is criticizing aspects of the Greek trajectory by using the very same framework, although from a Jewish point of view. As observed by Wyrick 2004, 120, Josephus is primarily addressing the relation not between "individual and tradition" but between "truth and fiction," and in his attempt to defend the authenticity of his tradition, he emphasizes both the integrity of its *originator(s)*, who wrote "the events of their own time just as they occurred" (*Ag. Ap.* 1.37), and its faithful and reliable (prophetic) *transmission* (*Ag. Ap.* 1.39–41). Evidently, he thus frames the named individuals in the transmission of this tradition as Greek authors.

15. Cf. somewhat similarly Rajak 1982, 471–74. Possibly relevant in this context is also the discussion of whether or not the so-called *Testimonium Flavianum* is original (see further Whealey 2003; Mason 2016a).

certain ideas. As two examples of the former, consider *Ant.* 1.93–95, where he refers to authors narrating the flood story, and *Ant.* 1.107, where he names even more sources in an attempt to show that the extraordinary ages of the biblical characters are not only narrated in his *Antiquities*:[16]

> This flood and the ark are mentioned by all who have written histories of the barbarians. Among these is Berosus the Chaldaean. . . . These matters are also mentioned by Hieronymus the Egyptian, author of the ancient history of Phoenicia, by Mnaseas and by many others. Nicolas of Damascus in his ninety-sixth book relates to the story as follows: "There is above the country of Minyas in Armenia a great mountain called Baris, where, as the story goes, many refugees found safety at the time of the flood, and one man, transported by an ark, grounded upon the summit, and relics of the timber were for long preserved; this might well be the same man of whom Moses, the Jewish legislator, wrote." (*Ant.* 1.93–95)

> Moreover, my words are attested by all historians of antiquity, whether Greeks or barbarians: Manetho the annalist of the Egyptians, Berosus the compiler of the Chaldaean traditions; Mochus, Hestiaeus, along with the Egyptian Hieronymus, authors of Phoenician histories, concur in my statements, while Hesiod, Hecataeus, Hellanicus, Acusilaus, as well as Ephorus and Nicolas, report that the ancients lived for a thousand years. But on these matters let everyone decide according to his fancy. (*Ant.* 1.107)

In contrast to the function of the references in 1–2 Chr, Josephus uses sources as a way of substantiating his claims and as a way of referring the reader to information that has not been included in his work (see also, e.g., *Ant.* 11.305; 12.390; etc.). Moreover, these sources are referred to by means of their (named) authors (cf. also the long section in *Ag. Ap.* 1.69–218),[17] and Josephus also sometimes discusses

---

16. A list of named sources in *Ant.* not found in the Hebrew Bible is compiled in Schürer et al. 1973, 49n13. For a general discussion, see also Schwartz 2016, 39–41.

17. For a discussion of this passage, see also Barclay 2016, 77–78. A stimulating discussion of how Josephus's way of demarcating sources reflects Greek citation strategies is found in Pitts 2013, who observe a gradual development of the prominence of these strategies in Jewish historiography from Jubilees (where no sources are quoted explicitly but rather weaved seamlessly into the narrative) to Josephus (who uses both declared quotations and mimesis).

their authenticity, as would be expected in light of the developing *Echtheitskritik* (see, not least, *Ag. Ap.* 1.6–18).[18]

The notion of Mosaic authorship found in the reference to Nicolas of Damascus in *Ant.* 1.93–95 above also illustrates how biblical characters have started to be regarded as Greek authors[19]—that is, as the *originators* of 'books.' In fact, Moses is recurrently described as writing things down (cf. 3.213; 3.286; 4.194; 4.196; 4.302; *Ag. Ap.* 1.39–41; etc.) and, by extension, as the authority behind not only certain *parts* of the Torah but the *entire Torah*, including the first chapters of Genesis (1.34) and the verses recounting his own death (4.326), although Josephus also emphasizes that God is the ultimate source (see also 3.85–88):

Furthermore, he [Moses] was committing to writing their constitution and laws . . . all this; however, he drew up under the inspiration of God. (*Ant.* 3.213)

Such was the code of laws which Moses, while keeping his army encamped beneath Mount Sinai, learnt from the mouth of God and transmitted in writing to the Hebrews. (*Ant.* 3.286)

Moses is thus constructed as an inspired author in the Greek sense (cf. figure 1, "Centralized Authors," chapter 4), and in contrast to the Mesopotamian trajectory, which also featured a divine-human interaction, the Torah is understood as in some way the intellectual property of Moses. This is seen clearly when Josephus recounts how Moses has dealt with other sources in his writings. To illustrate this dynamic, consider the following two examples, where the notion of intellectual property is made explicit.[20] In the first, Josephus narrates the interaction between Jethro (Raguel in *Ant.*) and Moses (cf. Exod 18):

---

18. Among others, he argues that the most ancient of all Greek literature, the poetry of Homer, is not that old ("clearly later than the Trojan war") and is initially transmitted not in writing but "by memory," only to be compiled later, creating "numerous inconsistencies" (*Ag. Ap.* 1.12–13; see also below, n. 29). On this, see also Gray 1993, 9–10.

19. Nicolas of Damascus (Herod's court historian) is referred to several times throughout *Ant.*, and it has been suggested that his works were a major source for the latter parts of it (Schwartz 2016, 40, referring to, among others, the references in *Ant.* 14.9, 68, 104; 16.29, 58, 193; etc.).

20. This does not mean, as has been observed before, that Josephus would therefore have been "at the mercy" of his sources. Instead, as noted above, he creatively reworks them for his own purposes, an observation further supported if comparing the way Josephus interacts with the work of Nicolas of Damascus in *Antiquities* and *Jewish Wars*, respectively (on this, see Mason 2016c, 23–24).

Raguel having tendered this advice, Moses gladly accepted it and acted in accordance with his suggestion, *neither concealing the origin of the practice nor claiming it as his own, but openly avowing the inventor to the multitude.* Nay, in the books too he recorded the name of Raguel, as inventor of the aforesaid system, deeming it meet to bear faithful witness to merit, whatever glory might be won by *taking credit for the inventions of others.* Thus even herefrom may one learn the integrity of Moses; but of that we shall have abundant occasion to speak in other parts of this work. (*Ant.* 3.73–74; emphasis added)

What can be seen here is that Josephus praises what he sees as a reluctance toward pseudepigraphy in the sense of false (or fraudulent) attribution (rather than mistaken attribution; see above, "*Echtheitskritik* and Pseudepigraphy," chapter 4)—that is, the claiming of ideas that originated with someone else as one's own. According to Josephus, Moses is therefore a model: he did not present the intellectual property of Jethro as his own. A similar scenario is found in the second example, which concerns the prophecies of Balaam (Num 22–24):[21]

This was the man [i.e., Balaam] to whom Moses did the high honour of recording his prophecies; and though it was open to him to *appropriate and take the credit for them himself,* as there would have been no witness to convict him, he has given Balaam this testimony and *deigned to perpetuate his memory.* (*Ant.* 4.158; emphasis added)

Since Moses is here again credited for not claiming as his own something that originated with somebody else, it is reasonable to suggest that fairly developed notions of intellectual property and pseudepigraphy have affected the way Josephus understood the relation between the 'books' now found in the Hebrew Bible and the names in relation to which they were transmitted.[22] In fact, there are indications that the

---

21. On this passage, see also Feldman 1990, 417, who only notes that Josephus here emphasizes that "the prophecies of Balaam were of such a high order that they could have been claimed by the greatest of all prophets, Moses himself."

22. Notably, his discourse also overlaps with the idea of fame attached to names seen in *Ben Sira* (see above, "Reframed Authorship," chapter 9). To be noted is also the point made by Wyrick 2004, 70, that Josephus here also reflects an "ambivalence toward the appropriation of prophetic traditions from Israel's pagan neighbors" but resolves it by emphasizing that "it is not the identity of the prophet but rather that of the scribe that guarantees the legitimacy of revelation" (71).

paratextual framings of certain texts are explicitly interpreted as author designations in a Greek sense. It is implied in, for example, *Ant.* 4.303, where Josephus refers to Moses as the composer of a poem in "hexameter verse"[23] (cf. Deut 31:30) that has been "preserved in the temple"[24] in a 'book' also containing predictions of future events, or in *Ant.* 7.6, where Josephus claims that "David also composed laments and eulogies for the funeral of Saul and Jonathan, which have survived to [his] own time" (cf. 2 Sam 1:17).

Prophets and Prediction

In line with what was noted in the discussion of 1–2 Chr, Josephus also emphasizes that the history of Israel was written by its prophets (*Ant.* 1.250).[25] However, in contrast to the construction of prophets as *tradents* in 1–2 Chr, Josephus treats them as *originators*. It has already been observed that he believed that Moses (the prophet par excellence) wrote the Pentateuch,[26] and he also mentions other prophets, such as, for example, Samuel, in a similar capacity:[27]

> The prophet [Samuel], *having put in writing* for them all that should come to pass, read it in the hearing of the king and then laid up the book in the tabernacle of God, as a testimony to after generations of what he had foretold. (*Ant.* 6.66–67)

The narrative overlaps with the image conveyed by texts like Isa 8:16 and Isa 30:8–11 but with a Greek twist that becomes apparent in *Against Apion*, where Josephus speaks in more general terms about the writing of history:

---

23. On this expression and its possible allusion to Homeric epic speeches, see Wyrick 2004, 152–53.

24. For a discussion of this notion, see, e.g., Thackeray 1929, 89–91.

25. Cf. Begg 1988, 342, 342n7; Gray 1993, 10–11. The similarities have been noted before (cf., e.g., Blenkinsopp 1974, 241–42; Feldman 1997, 583). On *Ant.* 1.250, see Feldman 1990, 400. A similar idea is expressed also in, e.g., Justin Martyr's *1 Apol.* 31.

26. See also Gray 1993, 11, on the distinction between Moses, who was described as writing "the traditional history," and subsequent prophets, who only wrote of events of their own times. This seems to be a consequence of the paratextual framing of the 'books' (in the case of the Pentateuch, these references would mainly be epitextual), where Moses is connected to the entire Pentateuch (i.e., events long before Moses's time), while prophetic 'books' were presented as relating to more limited periods of time (cf. the discussion of paratexts above, chapter 7).

27. For a general overview of all instances where Josephus mentions "prophet" or "prophesied" where the Hebrew Bible does not, see Feldman 1990, 389–91.

> It is not open to everybody to write the records. . . . The proph-
> ets alone had this privilege, obtaining their knowledge *of the most*
> *remote and ancient history through the inspiration which they owed*
> *to God*, and committing to writing a clear account of the events *of*
> *their own time* just as they occurred. (*Ag. Ap.* 1.37–38, emphasis
> added; cf. *J.W.* 1.17–18)

This activity is, then, related explicitly to the 'books' of the Hebrew
Bible in 1.40,[28] and it thus emanates clearly that named individuals
are believed to be responsible for 'books' in their entirety so that when
events beyond the time of the prophet are described, they are interpreted
as *predictions* by the prophet (cf. *Ant.* 10.35; 10.266–69; 11.337–38).
Put differently, the general statements in the references in 1–2 Chr are
now internalized in named individuals.[29]

The predictive nature of prophecy is certainly not an invention of
Josephus, however, but clearly rooted in the Hebrew Bible. It was seen
above to be an essential component in the construction of authority for
the "subsequent ones" in the 'book' called *Isaiah*, and to be added here
are also passages such as Deut 18:22 or the way this idea is employed
in the Deuteronomistic history. Nonetheless, there is, in the works of
Josephus (as was also seen in the Dead Sea Scrolls), a greater emphasis
on prediction (cf. *Ant.* 8.418–20; 10.142)[30] that transforms it into *an*
essential feature of prophecy. Part of an explanation for this transformation is likely to be found in the scripturalization of prophetic literature,
if understood as a result of the fact that the prophets failed in changing
the ways of their contemporaries (cf. Isa 8:16; 30:8–11). Put differently,

---

28. On this passage, see also Feldman 1990, 397–98. For a discussion of terminology,
see Gray 1993, 23–26.

29. The general background to this view may be that Josephus attempts to show how
his tradition was superior to the transmission of the works of Homer, who "did not
leave his poetry in writing" but only transmitted his works by memory; thus, they were
scattered and united later, with inconsistencies as an inevitable consequence (*Ag. Ap.*
1.12–13; cf. above, n. 18). On this, see esp. Wyrick 2004, 136–202. It was thus of central
importance to emphasize what had previously only been understood as a "first one,"
and the consequence would be that these figures came to take center stage. Moreover,
as argued by Wyrick 2004, 179–80 (who points to the similarities between Josephus's
understanding of prophetic writing activity and "Plato's description of the oracle at Del-
phi," where a "lineage [*genos*] of declarers [*prophêtês* pl.] as judges [*kritês* pl.] over the
inspired [*entheos* pl.] manic utterances [*manteia* pl.]" had been established), the *status* of
this figure became essential for the evaluation of the work. As summarized by Wyrick,
"The classical world's valuation of the writer's signature overpowered the Jewish dislike of
individual agency" (202).

30. So also Blenkinsopp 1974, 242; Feldman 1990, 407–11; Gray 1993, 31.

when transmitted in writing, the prophecies were emphasized as truthful predictions. Consequently, although Josephus's understanding of prophecy clearly stands in a trajectory rooted in the Hebrew Bible, where Israel's history had been written by prophets, and although there is also in Josephus a stress on past, present, and future,[31] he distinguishes himself by recurrently emphasizing predictive truthfulness—that is, that the prophets had *accurately written about future events* (long) before they happened.

This also means that the overlap between prophets and scribes is reconfigured in a similar way. Josephus can, for example, describe "sacred scribes" as "persons with considerable skill in accurately predicting the future" (*Ant.* 2.205; see also 2:209). At the same time, the interpretive feature of prophetic activity is retained. This can be seen in the way Josephus both distinguishes himself from the prophets in the Hebrew Bible and claims continuity and grants himself authority by presenting his writing of history as accomplished by means of exegetical skill and divine inspiration (*J.W.* 3.351–54; cf. the description of the Essenes in *J.W.* 2.159).[32] In other words, he casts himself as a legitimized interpreter of God's will, both as a prophet and in a priestly role (*Life* 2–6; *J.W.* 1.3; 3.351–54),[33] and so confirms a

---

31. Cf. Feldman 1990, 394, who speaks of three major functions of the prophet in Josephus: (1) to declare the utterances of God as mediator between God and man, (2) to interpret the past and create "the Scripture that records this past," and (3) to predict the future.

32. Cf. Blenkinsopp 1974, 247, stating that for Josephus, prophecy had "the primary connotation of the inspired interpretation of biblical texts with reference to present and future fulfilment." On the distinguishing aspect, see Blenkinsopp 1974, 240; Feldman 1990, 404–6; Gray 1993, 15–16, 35–79.

33. *J.W.* 3.353 reads, "He [i.e., Josephus] was an interpreter of dreams and skilled in divining the meaning of ambiguous utterances of the Deity; a priest himself and of priestly descent, he was not ignorant of the prophecies in the sacred books." See the discussion in Blenkinsopp 1974, 240; Grojnowski 2015, 348–50, 349n7; and van Henten 2018, 139–43. To be noted is the emphasis on *dreams* (cf. *Life* 208–10), thus relating somewhat to the discussion of חזון and nighttime visions (see above, "Prophetic Words and Nighttime Visions," chapter 7), although Josephus is more overlapping with the function of dreams in the 'book' called *Daniel,* "one of the greatest prophets" (*Ant.* 10.266; cf. Blenkinsopp 1974, 244–46; see also Feldman 1990, 393–94, 408; Gray 1993, 27–30), and the general idea that divine revelation came through dreams in the Graeco-Roman world (cf. Barton 1986, 125–28). Nonetheless, it is interesting to note that Josephus "supposed that the ancient prophets had received so many of their revelations in dreams" (so Gray 1993, 28) while at the same time believing that prophets were the ones writing their prophecies down. May this indicate yet another transformation of a common imagery as author concepts were negotiated (thus not only an anachronism, as Gray argues)? On the relation between priests and prophets in Josephus, see Feldman 1990, 419–21.

fundamental divine-human interaction while at the same time empha-sizing unbroken succession.[34]

The Prophet Isaiah

Understanding authorship in Josephus as sketched above provides a framework for understanding his references to the prophet Isaiah and the 'book' called *Isaiah*. In *Antiquities*, the prophet Isaiah is first men-tioned in 9.276, where he is introduced as a prophet who "accurately informed" Hezekiah "of future events."[35] He then features primarily in *Ant.* 10.11–35. In this passage, it is clear that Josephus has a high regard for the prophet Isaiah and that he understands him as an author of the entire 'book' called *Isaiah* (written across several scrolls):[36]

> As for the prophet, he was acknowledged to be *a man of God* and marvelously possessed of truth, and, as he was confident of *never having spoken what was false,* he *wrote down in books* [pl.] *all that he had prophesied* and left them to be recognized as true from the event by men of future ages. (*Ant.* 10.35; emphasis added)

The character of the prophet Isaiah is here directly related to him being a man of God (thus underscoring the high regard; cf. *Ant.* 3.180 on Moses)[37] as well as an author writing down all of his prophecies himself. Although passages such as Isa 8:16 and 30:8–11 could be seen behind the idea of preservation of prophetic literature, it is clear that Josephus has merged it with the Greek trajectory so that the prophet Isaiah is understood as the originator of the *whole* of the 'book' called *Isaiah*, a 'book' that he believed contained prophetic predictions.[38] The claim that the prophet Isaiah never spoke falsely is also interesting, especially in light of the fact that Josephus has altered the narrative about

---

34. Cf. Wyrick 2004, 138–39.

35. Cf. Feldman 1997, 587. Josephus combines material from 2 Kgs 18–20 and Isa 36–39 in the composition (Pitts 2013, 247), creating a synthesis of passages featuring the prophet Isaiah that would eventually be commonplace (another example will be seen in chapter 12, n. 91 in relation to traditions surrounding the prophet Isaiah's death).

36. That Josephus includes a reference to the 'book' in this way may have been to indi-cate for the readers that he had access to it (so Pitts 2013, 247). Less clear is the relation between the prophet and the 'book' in, e.g., 2 Esd 2:18 and 4 Macc 18:14.

37. The prophet Isaiah is also often believed to take on a priestly function in *Ant.* 10.12, where he is said to "offer sacrifices for the common safety" (cf. Feldman 1997, 591–92). On the notion of prophets never erring, see, e.g., Feldman 1990, 409–11.

38. Begg 1988, 350.

Hezekiah's illness to avoid such a conclusion.[39] More specifically, in Isa 38:1, the prophet Isaiah tells Hezekiah that he should set his house in order, for he would not recover. In *Ant.* 10.27–28, however, it is the physicians and friends who have no hope, and Isaiah is sent to Hezekiah as an answer to his prayers, telling him that he *will* in fact recover within three days and live another fifteen years.[40]

The predictive writing down of prophecies on the part of the prophet Isaiah also emerges as important in another part of *Antiquities*. Here, it is further underscored that the prophet Isaiah was understood to be the author of the entire 'book'—that is, including chapters 40–66. In narrating how the people were allowed to return to the "land of Judaea" and rebuild "the temple in Jerusalem" (*Ant.* 11.4), Josephus explains that the main reason for this was that the Persian emperor Cyrus had read about this in the 'book' called *Isaiah*:

> These things Cyrus knew from reading the book of prophecy which Isaiah had left behind *two hundred and ten years earlier*. For this prophet had said that God told him in secret, "It is my will that Cyrus, whom I shall have appointed king of many great nations, shall send my people to their own land and build my temple." Isaiah prophesied these things *one hundred and forty years before* the temple was demolished. And so, when Cyrus read them, he wondered at the divine power and was seized by a strong desire and ambition to do what had been written; and, summoning the most distinguished of the Jews in Babylon, he told them that he gave them leave to journey to their native land and to rebuild both the city of Jerusalem and the temple of God. (*Ant.* 11.5–7; emphasis added)

The fact that Josephus dates the prophecies concerning Cyrus to the time of the prophet Isaiah not only indicates that he believed Isaiah wrote the whole 'book' but also reveals a biographical interest in his person so that Josephus relates the authority of the prophecy to the historical circumstances of its composition.[41] Ultimately, this

---

39. Begg 1988, 348–49. See also the discussion in Feldman 1997, 605–6.

40. Feldman 1997, 606; cf. Charlesworth 2019, 2.

41. It may be objected to this observation that Josephus in fact downplays the prophet Isaiah in his work (cf. Feldman 1997, 584–87). This need not be interpreted as contrary to my suggestion above, however, since this curiosity can be quite satisfactorily explained by reference to other factors. For one, it can be noted that Isaiah's relation to the Assyrian empire ran counter to the political stance taken by Josephus (see the overview in Schwartz 2016, 54) and, moreover, that his messianic focus was judged as inappropriate not only

points to the conclusion that by the beginning of the Common Era, the prophet Isaiah was emerging more fully as a Greek author, albeit without losing some of the Mesopotamian characteristics. It could thus be suggested that paratexts such as the one in Isa 1:1 were reinterpreted in a way that had Isaiah colonize all voices in the 'book' and this is indeed what is found in *Ant.* 13.62–71, where a similar scenario as the one in *Ant.* 11.5–7 plays out, this time based on Isa 19:19.[42] More specifically, the high priest Onias wanted to build a temple in Egypt and

> was encouraged chiefly by the words of the prophet Isaiah, who had lived *more than six hundred years before* and had foretold that a temple to the Most High God was surely to be built in Egypt by a Jew. Being, therefore, excited by these words, Onias wrote . . . [a] letter to Ptolemy and Cleopatra . . . "I beg you to permit me . . . to build a temple to the Most High God. . . . For this indeed is what the prophet Isaiah foretold . . . and many other such things did he prophesy concerning this place." This, then, is what Onias wrote to King Ptolemy. . . . [Ptolemy and Cleopatra write in a reply that] "since you say that the prophet Isaiah foretold this long ago, we grant your request if this is to be in accordance with the Law, so that we may not seem to have sinned against God in any way." (*Ant.* 13.64–65, 67–69, 71; emphasis added)

Again, the foretelling aspect of prophecy is stressed (see also *J. W.* 7.432), as is the prophecy related to the historical circumstances of its composition, and the interpretive move in the text seems to be that since the prophecies are preserved in writing, they must be true and hence necessary to fulfill.

ASKING WHY

Turning now to the way the 'book' called *Isaiah* is quoted in the New Testament, the focus will be on declared citations that speak to the

---

because Josephus was himself of Hasmonean descent but also in light of "Christian" claims. For a discussion, see Feldman 1997, who presents possible reasons in more detail; see also further in Begg 1988; Berges 2012b, 91–92. Ultimately, the emphasis placed on the prophet in the *narratives* does not necessarily say much about his role as *author of the 'book.'* Consequently, the observation above is still valid.

42. On the relation between Josephus and Isa 19:19, see, e.g., Feldman 1997, 590–91, 590n18, who also points out that a similar tradition is found in b. Menah 109b.

relation between the 'book' and its author.[43] Framed in such a way, a total of twenty-two verses emanate as significant (Matt 4:14; 8:17; 12:17; 13:14; 15:7; Mark 1:2; 7:6; Luke 3:4; 4:17; John 1:23; 12:38–39, 41; Acts 8:28, 30; 28:25; Rom 9:27, 29; 10:16, 20; 15:12).[44] A few observations can be made.

A 'Book' of Words

An initial observation is that although passages from the 'book' called *Isaiah* are introduced as the words of the prophet Isaiah, it is clear that a divine-human interaction is still imagined that casts Isaiah as a channel of divine revelation. In Matt 3:3, for example, where Isa 40:3 is used as a way of validating the role of John the Baptist, the quote is introduced as "spoken *through* the prophet Isaiah, saying . . ." (ὁ ῥηθεὶς διὰ

43. I am thus not primarily interested in the way the quotes function in the overall argument in the New Testament writings or in textual issues, such as what version of the 'book' called *Isaiah* may have been available at this time. For such questions, I refer the reader to the recent overview by Moyise 2020 or the contributions in Moyise and Menken 2005.

44. Cf. Sawyer 1996, 21. NA²⁸ ("Loci citati vel allegati") lists ninety citations of the 'book' called *Isaiah*, but not all of these mention the prophet. Of the ones not featuring him, some frame the quote as prophetic words: Matt 1:23 (Isa 7:14; 8:8); 21:5 (Isa 62:2); John 6:45 (Isa 54:13); Acts 7:49 (Isa 66:1). Others introduce the quotes as being "written" (γέγραπται)—Matt 21:13 (Isa 56:7); Mark 11:17 (Isa 56:7); Luke 19:46 (Isa 56:7); 22:37 (Isa 53:12); Rom 2:24 (Isa 52:5); 10:11 (Isa 28:16), 15 (Isa 52:7); 11:8 (Isa 29:10), 26 (Isa 59:20), 27 (Isa 27:9); 14:11 (Isa 45:23; 49:18); 15:21 (Isa 52:15); 1 Cor 1:19 (Isa 29:14); 15:54 (Isa 25:5); 2 Cor 9:10 (Isa 55:10); Gal 4:27 (Isa 54:1); 1 Pet 2:6 (Isa 28:16)—occasionally making *scripture* the subject ("scripture says," λέγει γὰρ ἡ γραφή, in Rom 10:11 [Isa 28:16] and, e.g., Rom 9:33 [Isa 28:16]; cf. 1 Cor 15:54 [Isa 25:5]) and once specifying the writing as "law" (νόμος, in 1 Cor 14:21 [Isa 28:11–12]). Many are not declared at all, making the identification of the quote dependent on the methodology used: Matt 24:29 (Isa 13:10; 34:4); Mark 4:12 (Isa 6:9); 9:48 (Isa 66:24); 12:32 (Isa 45:21); 13:24 (Isa 13:10), 25 (Isa 34:4); Luke 7:22 (Isa 29:28); Act 4:24 (Isa 37:16); Rom 9:20 (Isa 29:16); 11:34 (Isa 40:13); 1 Cor 2:16 (Isa 40:13); 14:25 (Isa 45:14); 15:32 (Isa 22:13); 2 Tim 2:19 (Isa 26:13); Heb 10:37 (Isa 26:20); Jas 5:4 (Isa 5:9); 1 Pet 1:24 (Isa 40:6), 25 (Isa 40:8); 2 Pet 2:8 (Isa 8:14), 9 (Isa 43:21), 12 (Isa 10:3), 22 (Isa 53:9), 24 (Isa 53:4, 5, 12), 25 (Isa 53:6); 3:14 (Isa 8:12), 15 (Isa 8:13); 4:14 (Isa 11:2); 2 Pet 3:13 (Isa 65:17; 66:22); Rev 4:8 (Isa 6:1); 7:17 (Isa 25:4); 14:5 (Isa 53:9); 21:4 (Isa 25:8). Apart from these, a few occasions are noteworthy, since they frame the prophetic material not as the words of the prophet Isaiah but as the word of God: Acts 13:34 (Isa 55:3), 47 (Isa 49:6); 2 Cor 6:2 (Isa 49:8), 17 (Isa 52:11); or even as the words of Jesus: Heb 2:13 (Isa 8:17, 18; 12:2). In some places, such as Matt 21:5 (Isa 62:2) or Rom 3:15 (Isa 59:7), texts from the 'book' called *Isaiah* are made part of a string of quotations, framed as either Scripture (so Rom 3:15) or said by a prophet (so Matt 21:5). This brief survey thus corrects the statement by Sawyer 2018, 3, that the "writers of the New Testament often give his name when they quote him."

Ἡσαΐου τοῦ προφήτου λέγοντος),[45] and in Acts 28:25–27, Isa 6:9–10 is introduced as "the Holy Spirit speaking *through* the prophet Isaiah" (τὸ πνεῦμα τὸ ἅγιον ἐλάλησεν διὰ Ἡσαΐου τοῦ προφήτου).[46]

Nevertheless, in most cases, the prophet Isaiah takes an active role in being the one that spoke the prophetic words. This is the case in John 1:23 (Isa 40:3, λέγω); Rom 9:27 (Isa 10:22–23; 28:22[?], κράζω); 10:16 (Isa 53:1, λέγω); 10:20–21 (Isa 65:1, 2, λέγω x2); and 15:12 (Isa 11:10, λέγω), as well as in passages like Matt 15:7–9 (Isa 29:13), where Isaiah is stated to have "prophesied rightly . . . saying" (καλῶς ἐπροφήτευσεν . . . λέγων), and Rom 9:29 (Isa 11:9), where he is said to have "predicted" (προλέγω).

That the notion of speech should not primarily be understood as related to oral tradition is clear from another set of declared citations. In Luke 3:4, Isa 40:3–5 is introduced as "*written* in the 'book' of the *words* of the prophet Isaiah" (γέγραπται ἐν βίβλῳ λόγων Ἡσαΐου τοῦ προφήτου), thus combining λόγος with γράφω, and the notion of written prophecies are also found in Mark 1:2–3 (Isa 40:3, γράφω); 7:6–7 (Isa 29:13, προφητεύω + γράφω); Luke 4:17–19 (Isa 61:1–2, βιβλίον, γράφω); and Acts 8:26–40 (Isa 53:7–8), where an Ethiopian eunuch is reading (ἀναγινώσκω, vv. 28, 30) the "prophet Isaiah."

A number of conclusions can be drawn from this brief survey. First, it is clear that, as in the Dead Sea Scrolls, the voice of the prophet Isaiah has now colonized most voices in *Isaiah*.[47] He is explicitly introduced as the speaker of Isa 6, 10, 11, 29, 40, 53, 61, and 65—that is, passages featuring many different voices, if seen from the perspective of the 'book.' In Isa 40, for example, several human voices are intertwined (see above, chapter 6, n. 35), while in Isa 65, the deity seems to be speaking.[48] Furthermore, it is clear that these voices are written so that

---

45. On the use of the 'book' called *Isaiah* in this passage, see also Beaton 2005, 66–67. Almost identical formulations are also found in Matt 4:14 (framing Isa 8:23b–9:1); 8:17 (Isa 53:4); and 12:17 (Isa 42:1–4).

46. In this context may also be added Matt 13:14–15 (also quoting Isa 6:9–10), where it is the *prophecy* that is speaking (ἡ προφητεία Ἡσαΐου ἡ λέγουσα). Compare also the instances in n. 44 above, where verses from the 'book' called *Isaiah* are framed as either scripture talking or the words of God and Jesus.

47. Similarly Beale 2015, 84. As noted by Berges 2012b, 97, the only chapters not referred to are chaps. 3–4; 15–18; 20; 31; 36; and 39.

48. The tendency to relate all voices to the prophet Isaiah does not mean that he is speaking in every verse, only that all text is believed to originate with him. However, there is an interesting tendency in the Greek translation of the 'book' called *Isaiah* where passages having an unclear speaker in the Hebrew text are clarified. As shown by van der Vorm-Croughs 2014, 58–59, for example, "In order to introduce direct speech, the LXX translator has from time to time added a finite or participle form of λέγω. He can

the 'book' called *Isaiah* is essentially seen as a 'book' constituted by the words of the prophet Isaiah (Luke 3:4), and as in Josephus, these words have a predictive quality (Rom 9:29).

These observations thus point to the influence of the Greek trajectory, and this can be confirmed by another text that frames passages from the 'book' called *Isaiah*—John 12:38–41 (NRSV). This passage, which combines many of the features observed above, reads as follows:

> [38] This was to fulfill [πληρόω] *the word spoken by the prophet Isaiah*: "Lord, who has believed our message, and to whom has the arm of the Lord been revealed?" [Isa 53:1] [39] And so they could not believe, *because Isaiah also said,* [40] "He has blinded their eyes and hardened their heart, so that they might not look with their eyes, and understand with their heart and turn—and I would heal them." [Isa 6:10] [41] Isaiah said this *because* [ὅτι] he saw his glory and spoke about him. (emphasis added)

First, it should be noted that the prophet Isaiah is said to have originally proclaimed both the collective voice in chapter 53 and the intertwined divine and prophetic voices in Isa 6:10.[49] He is thus not primarily speaking *in* the 'book' but actually speaks *the 'book' itself.* In other words, he is the authorial voice behind it—everything in the 'book' called *Isaiah* is his λόγος (sing., v. 38). Second, this 'book' is understood as prophecy in need of fulfillment, and third, it can be observed that John 12:41 provides an *explanation* of the words of the prophet Isaiah (ὅτι).[50] Put differently, the author of the Gospel of *John* not only asks *what* the 'book' called *Isaiah* says but also wants to explain *why* the

---

be assumed to have done this principally because he thought the transition of indirect to direct speech or the change of speaker too abrupt in the Hebrew (see 3:6; 22:15; 30:16; 39:6; 45:14; and 58:3 below). In other places a finite form of λέγω serves to identify the speaker, who would otherwise have remained ambiguous (see 49:1, 15 and 58:6)." Further examples may include Isa 8:2 (cf. Oswalt 1986, 222), where the speaking voices are clarified, as well as Isa 8:16 or Isa 51:1–3 (discussed above, "Voices Intertwined," chapter 6), where the LXX changes v. 3 so that it continues the first-person speech.

49. The version of Isa 6:10 quoted here is distinct from both the MT and the LXX. I understand the third-person m. sing. as referring to YHWH and the first-person sing. as referring to Jesus. For an overview of the extensive scholarly literature on the subject and an argument for this view, see Williams 2005, 108–15. There are many examples of where the text of the 'book' called *Isaiah* quoted in the New Testament differs from both the MT and the LXX (Childs 2004, 17).

50. The manuscript tradition is not univocal regarding ὅτι (Metzger 2005, 238). Although the best manuscripts have this reading (𝔓[66], 𝔓[75], ℵ, A, B, L, Θ, *f*1, 33, cop, etc.), some (D, *f*13, 565, etc.) have ὅτε ("when"), a reading that completely removes the

prophet Isaiah (as the person responsible for its content) said it. Evidently, such a question is only relevant if *intentions* are important, and so it can be argued that the passage provides an implicit indication of the emerging importance of *authorial intent*.[51]

Debated Attribution

In John 12:38–41, a series of quotes were strung together to form a coherent argument. Such a practice can also be found elsewhere, and interestingly, there are examples where one of the passages in such a series is related to the prophet Isaiah despite it not being from the 'book' called *Isaiah*. Although such a double transmission would not be a problem in the Mesopotamian trajectory (see, e.g., "Leaving Anonymity," chapter 7), it would be expected to trouble readers in a Greek trajectory, where mistaken and fraudulent attributions were intensely discussed. Indeed, this is also what is found.

Consider first Mark 1:2–3, which frames a quote that combines Isa 40:3 and Mal 3:1 as "written in the prophet Isaiah" (γέγραπται ἐν τῷ Ἡσαΐᾳ τῷ προφήτῃ). Moving forward a few centuries, this attribution has become subject to some controversy. In his *Comm. Matt.* 3.3, Jerome notes that Porphyry—a Neoplatonic philosopher and historical critic who wrote *Against the Christians*, where he pointed out contradictions in the Christian Scriptures—asks how Christians can think that the citation is "from Isaiah alone"[52] when it is "woven together from Malachi and Isaiah." Jerome's response is simple: the name may have been "added by a mistake of the copyists," a scenario he claimed could be proven also for other passages.[53] In his homily on Mark 1:1–12 (*Hom.* 75), this is expanded even further:

> Now, as far as I recall by going back in my mind and sifting carefully the work of the seventy translators as well as the Hebrew scrolls, I have never been able to locate in Isaia, the prophet, the words: "Behold I send my messenger before thee," but I do find them written near the close of the prophecy of Malachia. If,

---

question of intent (cf. also W: ἐπεί). It may be relevant in this context that *John* is the only gospel whose author is possibly identified (John 21:21–24).

51. This is also how commentators usually interpret the verse; see, e.g., Morris 1995, 538: "To him [i.e., John], it is plain that Isaiah *had in mind* the glory revealed in Christ" (emphasis added).

52. The translation is from Scheck 2008.

53. He refers the reader to "the thirteenth Psalm," probably as quoted in Rom 3:10–18, where a number of texts from the Hebrew Bible are juxtaposed (so Scheck 2008, 68n60).

therefore, this statement is written at the end of Malachia's proph-ecy, on what grounds does Mark, the evangelist, take for granted here: "As it is written in Isaia the prophet"? The utterances of the evangelists are the work of the Holy Spirit. This Mark who writes is not to be esteemed lightly. . . . O Apostle Peter, Mark, your son—son, not by the flesh, but by the Spirit—informed as he is in spiritual matters, is uninformed here, and *credits to one prophet* of Holy Writ *what is written by another*. . . . This is the very passage that the ungodly Porphyry, who has vomited forth his venom in so many volumes written against us, attacks in his fourteenth scroll. "The evangelists," he asserts, "were *such ignorant men*, not only in secular matters, but even in divine Scripture, *that they cited the testimony of one prophet and attributed it to another*." This is what he hurls at us; now, what shall we answer him?[54]

Notable is that Jerome essentially agrees with Porphyry regarding the problem. He is not critiquing Porphyry for misunderstanding the relation between the prophet and the 'book' but rather attempts to solve the issue within the parameters of the Greek trajectory. This time, how-ever, Jerome does not refer to copyists' mistakes but argues that it was intentional by Mark: "The evangelist is really saying: This is John the Baptist, of whom Malachia has also said . . ."[55] The part from *Malachi* was thus understood as added to explain Isa 40:3 so that the extant framing referred only to the latter.

The fact that such a "mistake" is found in *Mark* does show that the negotiations of authorship were quite complex in the late Second Temple period. Put differently, the combination of several sources under an Isaianic frame does not seem to have been a problem at the compo-sition of *Mark*, although it became a problem later on.[56] Consequently,

---

54. Quoted from Liguori Ewald 1966, 121–22 (emphasis added).

55. Liguori Ewald 1966, 122.

56. The fact that it is parts of *Malachi* that are joined with *Isaiah* may also be viewed in light of the probability that Malachi was not unanimously recognized as a prophetic *name*. The 'book' could have been seen by some as anonymous and thus possible to join with other prophetic literary traditions (cf. the discussion of Isa 2:2–4 above, "Leaving Anonymity," chapter 7). In fact, it is quite likely that the gospels themselves were orig-inally transmitted anonymously—that is, before the εὐαγγελιον κατα . . . paratexts were added sometime in the second century CE (on this, see, e.g., Petersen 2006; cf. Gather-cole 2012). If correct, it would provide an interesting example of how author dynamics have changed in a way that unattributed (or misattributed) texts became a problem, especially in a context where works containing what was believed to be false doctrines started to circulate, as is reflected in the Byzantine scholia to Dionysius Thrax. In this example of a Christian use of *Echtheitskritik*, it is emphasized that a scholar "must know

it should not be concluded that the creative usage of texts was instantly coming to an end when Greek notions of authorship were starting to gain influence on the way the 'book' called *Isaiah* was perceived.

In fact, this may be further underscored by the textual history of Matt 13:35.[57] In this text, Ps 78:2 is quoted as "spoken through the prophet, saying . . ." (τὸ ῥηθὲν διὰ τοῦ προφήτου λέγοντος).[58] This is what is often judged as the best reading,[59] but interestingly, some manuscripts (including the first hand in the Codex Sinaiticus) identify this prophet as "Isaiah." This is also noted by Jerome, who suggests, "Because the text is not at all found in Isaiah, I think it was later removed by prudent men."[60] In his view, the text had originally had "through Asaph the prophet" (based on the paratext of Ps 78), but "the first copyist," who did not understand this reference, "changed the name to Isaiah, whose name was more familiar."[61] However, if seeing "Isaiah" as original, it could be suggested that while such a "mistaken attribution" may not have been controversial at the time of the composition of *Matthew*, the growing influence of the Greek trajectory would increasingly cast it as a problem.

---

all the books of the church . . . so that whenever he hears a strange style (*phônê xenê*) and false historical or poetic works, he will not consider [it] as if it were truthful. . . . There are . . . gospels which have the same names as authentic works (= which are *homônumos*) but are false" (quoted from Wyrick 2004, 221). Beale 2015, 99–100, instead argues that the combination of passages in Mark 1:2–3 was not uncommon and that the reference to *Isaiah* only is best seen as a consequence of "Isaiah dominat[ing] Mark throughout the book." As for Malachi, he was occasionally identified as Ezra (see b. Meg. 15a; the Targum to Mal 1:1; and Jerome, who rejects the view in his commentary on *Malachi*; cf. Wyrick 2004, 87).

57. Another example would be Matt 27:9, which relates to Zech 11:12 but is framed as the words of Jeremiah. The reading is well established, but while several witnesses "correct" the verse to Zechariah, two witnesses read "Isaiah" (Metzger 2005, 66–67).

58. For David as psalmist and prophet, see Willgren 2016a; Høgenhaven 2017; Willgren Davage 2019.

59. See, e.g., Metzger 2005, 33.

60. Scheck 2008, 160.

61. Scheck 2008, 160–61.

CHAPTER 12

SEARCHING FOR THE REAL AUTHOR

Having surveyed indications of Greek influence on the construction of Isaianic authorship in the last centuries BCE and the initial centuries CE, this chapter will unpack further the ways in which this influence grows stronger in the centuries that follow, especially among Greek-speaking authors. To paint this picture, three early Christian theologians will be used to illustrate different aspects that became significant in the shaping of the prophet Isaiah as a Greek author: the use of Hellenistic *Echtheitskritik* by Origen of Alexandria (ca. 184–253 CE), the notion of authorial intent in the works of Eusebius of Caesarea (ca. 260–340 CE), and the emphasis on *Hebraica veritas* by Jerome (ca. 342–47 CE).[1] Last, some examples of how the biography of the prophet was expanding will be provided.

ORIGEN AND *ECHTHEITSKRITIK*

That Origen wrote a commentary on the 'book' called *Isaiah* is known from the works of Eusebius, who refers to Origen a lot, but unfortunately,

---

1. Many more examples could evidently be adduced, but I believe these three suffice to make the case. For a more general overview of how the 'book' called *Isaiah* was received and interpreted in early Christian tradition, see Sawyer 1996, esp. 42–64. A detailed overview of quotes is also found in Ngunga 2020, 462–64. Justin, for example, quotes from the 'book' called *Isaiah* several times in *Dial.* in a way similar to what was noted for the New Testament: "Isaiah teaches" (13); "Isaiah preached" (29); "Isaiah thus foretold" (50); "Isaiah records" (63); "the Scripture which Isaiah writes" (65); "predicted by Isaiah" (66); "Isaiah himself said" (70). In *Dial.* 29, Justin also states that the quoted words have not been "embellished by the art of man; but David sung them, Isaiah preached them, Zechariah proclaimed them, and Moses wrote them" (cf. Childs 2004, 34).

it has not survived. There are, however, a number of homilies—twenty-five, to be exact—that have survived in Latin translation (probably translated by Jerome), and they provide an interesting window into the way Origen conceived of the relation between the prophet and the 'book,'[2] a relation that needs to be understood in relation to his detailed work with the text of the Hebrew Bible in his *Hexapla*.

Repairing the Text

Understanding the Hexapla project as aiming toward "seeking to stabilize the fluidity between the Masoretic text and the Greek translations"[3] (in *Comm. Matt.* 15.14, he talks about it as *repairing* the differences)[4] so that a solid foundation could be established on which arguments could be formulated that were to be used in exegetical debates (not least between Christians and their critics),[5] Origen partook in the introduction of a number of critical markers that were originally developed by the Alexandrian grammarians in the early third century BCE. As noted earlier (see "*Echtheitskritik* and Pseudepigraphy," chapter 4), four signs were used in particular: (1) the *obelos*, which was placed in the margins and indicated whether the text was genuine or not; (2) the *asteriskos*, which indicated if a line was also found in another part of the poem; and (3–4) the *sigma* and *antisigma*, both of which indicated if two consecutive lines were interchangeable. Of these, it is known that Origen mentions two in *Ep. Afr.*: "the sign the Greek call" *obelos* is used to mark a passage not found in the Hebrew but extant in the LXX, and the *asteriskos* highlighted passages "which exist in the Hebrew but are not found among us."[6] Used as text-critical markers, they are, then, employed to establish a text "free from forgery," and so it is quite clear that the distributive Mesopotamian author concept, which included the work of "subsequent ones," is no longer dominant.

---

2. An English translation of the first nine can be found in Scheck 2015, 881–928.

3. So Childs 2004, 19.

4. Cf. Martens 2012, 47.

5. Although not necessarily indicating that opponents, such as Jews, would agree on this text (on this, see Martens 2012, 48–49, 48n30).

6. Quoted from Martens 2012, 47. This use is also mentioned by, for example, Jerome in *Ruf.* 2.25: "But I was stimulated to undertake the task by the zeal of Origen, who blended with the old edition Theodotion's translation and used throughout the work as distinguishing marks the asterisk * and the obelus †, that is the star and the spit, the first of which makes what had previously been defective to beam with light, while the other transfixes and slaughters all that was superfluous" (quoted from Schaff 1995). This text is also discussed in Elowsky 2013, 171n6.

Evidently, this entire endeavor betrays a dichotomy between *original* and *copy* that values the former at the expense of the latter.

Origen also uses a wide array of critical methods to ascertain if a text was original or erroneous.[7] As but one example, he uses historical analyses to question if some of the narratives in the Hebrew Bible and the New Testament *actually happened* (Did God *really* "plan[t] a tree in Eden whose literal fruit granted eternal life?"[8] Was there *really* a mountaintop from where Jesus could have seen all the kingdoms of the world?).[9] In fact, he corrects manuscripts and comments on their meaning via a wide range of scholarly fields such as topography, cosmology, geometry, meteorology, mineralogy, zoology, medicine, and so on.[10] Moreover, he conducted literary analyses that proceeded from a presupposed idea that "the authors of Scripture composed their writings with literary precision" (ἀκρίβεια; cf. Josephus's *J.W.* 1.2–3; see "Claiming the Whole Book," chapter 11),[11] hence placing named originators at the center of the interpretive activity.

Establishing Unity

This focus on the (human) author should not, however, be understood as excluding any divine interaction. In fact, the need to create stable texts had as a consequence a notion that the *real* author was not human but the divine spirit. Addressing the multivocality of Scripture—which had not been a problem in the Mesopotamian trajectory but caused trouble in the Greek trajectory—Origen makes the following case:

> Any one who does not understand the peculiar character of the persons in Scripture, both as regards the speakers and the persons addressed, must be much perplexed by what he reads; *he will ask who is speaking, who is spoken to, and when does the speaker cease to speak.* For it often happens that the same person is addressed, though a third person speaks to him; or the person addressed is no longer the same, and a different person takes up what is said, while the same person speaks. And sometimes both the speaker and the person addressed are changed; or, further, though both

---

7. Cf. Wyrick 2004, 335.

8. Quote from Martens 2012, 50.

9. Examples from Martens 2012, 50, who also points to *Hom. 1 Reg.* 5.2–4 and *Comm. Jo.* 10.119–22, 129–30 (50n40).

10. For a discussion, see Martens 2012, 50–53.

11. So Martens 2012, 54. See, e.g., Origen's *Comm. Matt.* 14.13; *Comm. Jo.* 13.360; *Fr. Jo.* 29; *Hom. Luc.* 32.1; 181.11–13; and *Philoc.* 2.3–4.

are unchanged, *it is not clear that they are*. Need I seek an illustration of each of these statements, seeing that *the prophetical writings abound in such changes?* In fact we have here a special, though it may be unrecognised, cause of the obscurity of Scripture. It is also the way of Scripture to jump suddenly from one discourse to another. *The prophets, above all, do this, obscuring their sense and more or less confusing the reader.*

Again, from the 4th Homily on the Acts, "It was needful that the Scripture should be fulfilled which the Holy Spirit spake before by the mouth of David concerning Judas."

In the Psalm wherein the things concerning Judas are written, *one might say that it is not the Holy Spirit Who speaks*, for the words are clearly the Saviour's, "Hold not thy peace, God, at my praise: for the mouth of the wicked and the mouth of the deceitful man is opened upon me," and so on, until we come to "And his office let another take." Now if it is the Saviour Who says this, what does Peter mean by telling us that "It was needful that the Scripture should be fulfilled which the Holy Ghost spake before *by the mouth of David?*" Perhaps the lesson is something like this. The Holy Ghost *employs personification* in the prophets, and if He introduces the person of God, it is not God Who speaks, but the Holy Ghost speaks *as* God. And if He introduces Christ, it is not Christ Who speaks, but the Holy Ghost speaks *as* Christ. *So, then, if He brings in the person of a prophet, or personifies this or that people, or anything whatsoever, it is the Holy Ghost Who devises all these personifications.* (*Philoc.* 7.1–2)[12]

In light of this passage, it can be suggested that the Greek need for an identifiable originator of a work had led to a new kind of marginalization of the named individual in both stories of origin and hermeneutical application. While the latter was still regarded as a (Greek) author, Origen provided a solution to contradictions in the texts by pointing to its divine origins—"the person of the Holy Spirit, by whom Scripture is believed to be written" (*Hom. 1 Reg.* 5.4).[13] In a way, then, Origen works with an author concept similar to the one argued by Foucault:

---

12. Translation from Lewis 1911, 44–45 (emphasis added); cf. Martens 2012, 58.

13. To be sure, it is certainly no innovation on the part of Origen that the Holy Spirit has spoken through biblical characters associated with certain 'books.' This is assumed already in the Hebrew Bible and recurring in the way scripture is quoted in both the Dead Sea Scrolls and the New Testament (cf. the declared quotes surveyed above). What is new is, however, that this notion of inspiration is used as a way of effacing contradictions. The idea that the 'books' of the Bible were in essential agreement can also be found later, not

The author also constitutes a principle of unity in writing where any unevenness of production is ascribed to changes caused by evolution, maturation, or outside influence. In addition, the author serves to neutralize the contradictions that are found in a series of texts.[14]

If correct, it could be suggested that it is thus not until the initial centuries CE that the idea that the "gods" were the "real authors of the works which men just reproduced"[15] (i.e., referring to the idea criticized in the discussion of the Mesopotamian trajectory) has any explanatory value in relation to the 'book' called *Isaiah* and that this notion seems to have come about as a consequence of a negotiation between Mesopotamian and Greek author concepts in relation to a specific set of literature—the 'books' that were transmitted as sacred Scriptures in early Christian tradition. This is, then, the context in which Origen's discussion of various features in the 'book' called *Isaiah* can be understood.

Interpreting Isaiah

Turning to *Isaiah*, in his second homily on the 'book,' Origen discusses differences between Isa 7:14 and the way it is quoted in Matt 1:23:

> The truth of *the original copies of this prophet* says, "*You* shall call." In Matthew, on the other hand, we know that it reads, "And *they* shall call his name Emmanuel." We cannot say that one should *make something less out of the prophet*. How in fact does the Gospel *preserve* this reading of Scripture? Did it come from someone *without understanding* who was rushing on to easier things, just as has been done in many other cases? Or would someone possibly say that the Gospel was published this way from the beginning?[16]

The solution suggested is that the referent in Isa 7:14 is to be identified with the "house of David," and since "David is Christ," the church is now the house of David, which means that the imperative is directed

---

least in Augustine, who claims in *Civ.* 18.41 that "our authors (*auctores*) do not disagree with one another in any way" (quoted from Wyrick 2004, 362). Origen's view on the authorship of Heb, as found in Eusebius's *Hist. eccl.*, is also a good illustration of this dynamic, where Origen argues that "the matter" originates with Paul, although the letter itself may have been composed by somebody else.

14. Foucault 1977, 128.
15. Glassner 2002, 87–88 (see above, "Locating the Author," chapter 3).
16. Scheck 2015, 891 (emphasis added).

to the church in a way that what Matthew is doing is prophesying (in the now established sense of *predicting*) a future where the church will confess Christ as "God with us."[17] A textual discrepancy is thus explained by recourse to authorial intentionality (although first mentioning scribal error as a possibility), and it is clear that the 'book' called *Isaiah* is understood as a stable text ("the truth of the *original* copies") rooted in the prophetic authority of the prophet Isaiah ("one should [not] make something less out of the prophet").

Another example of the idea of a stable text can be found in the fact that Origen mentions the *Ascension of Isaiah* in a discussion of the canonical status of the Susanna narrative. Here, he argues that Jews have sometimes *removed* parts of Scripture that were damning to them, and *Ascen. Isa.* is argued to provide an example of such Jewish tampering—they are accused of *inserting incorrect words* into the text so that it would be discredited and thus not included in their canon (*Ep. Afr.* 9). Evidently, the argument reveals an author concept quite removed from the Mesopotamian "first ones" and "subsequent ones."

Eusebius and Authorial Intent

Moving on to Eusebius, who is sometimes called "the first real historian of early Christianity"[18] and whose extensive commentary on the 'book' called *Isaiah* has survived,[19] it can be noted that several aspects already observed in Josephus, the New Testament, and Origen are found here as well.[20] First, as with his predecessors, Eusebius regards *prediction* as an essential component of prophecy. This is seen clearly in his comments on Isa 44:24–45:13, where he builds explicitly on Josephus's *Ant.* 11.5–7:[21]

> Josephus testifies to this word in his *Jewish Antiquities*, writing in his characteristic style. Thus says King Cyrus "Since God almighty appointed me to be king over the earth, I believe that he is the

---

17. On this, see also Childs 2004, 70.

18. Childs 2004, 75.

19. Elowsky 2013, xxvi. According to Jerome, two commentaries of the 'book' called *Isaiah* had been written prior to Eusebius (in *Vir. Ill.* 61, 74, he mentions that commentaries had been written by Hippolytus of Rome and Victorinus of Pettau), but none of them have been preserved.

20. I will not enter here into any lengthy discussion about Eusebius's use of *Echtheitskritik*. I refer the reader to the survey in Wyrick 2004, 292–315.

21. See also Elowsky 2013, xxix, xxixn35.

236

one that the nation of the Israelites worships, for he foretold my name through the prophets and that I should build him a temple at Jerusalem in the country of Judea." Cyrus knew these things because he had read the book in which Isaiah had written down his prophecy two hundred and ten years prior. And these things have been recorded in the eleventh book of the *Antiquities*.[22]

Furthermore, it is recurrently emphasized that this predictive quality is enabled by divine inspiration through the Spirit so that the authorial voice is often implied to be the Spirit.[23] The recurring "he says" thus refers in various degrees to either "the prophetic Spirit," "God," "Isaiah," or sometimes even "the Savior" (on Isa 49:8) but in a way that never effaces the authorial role of the prophet Isaiah.[24] For example, in the comment on Isa 30:1–5, Eusebius talks about how "the prophet Isaiah mentions events approximately *fifty years before* the time of Jeremiah. And *therefore* he writes concerning those very people who did not obey the voice of God through Jeremiah, forbidding them to go to the Egyptians."[25]

Furthermore, Eusebius relates how the prophet Isaiah structures the prophetic 'book' and how he can refer to things said earlier in the 'book,' and he also sometimes provides reasons *why* Isaiah said certain things. A good example of the latter is found in the comment on Isa 1:1. First, Eusebius discusses how the vision that the prophet Isaiah saw should be understood, arguing that it was not received "while asleep but awake, as the divine Spirit shone on his soul."[26] He then discusses the reasons *why* the prophet Isaiah prophesized in the first place:

Isaiah set to prophesying neither as a pastime nor in order to give lessons for profit, but after leaving his field and livelihood (and very life, at least as it is known to many), he devoted himself to

---

22. Translation from Elowsky 2013, 226–27.

23. See, e.g., his comments on 7:20 ("Through Isaiah, the prophetic Spirit provided a prediction of what would occur"); 43:14–18 ("He [i.e., God] spoke prophetically through Isaiah about events that had not yet happened and were yet about to be as though they were already fulfilled"). Translation from Elowsky 2013, 40, 219.

24. The passage reads, "The following verses are prophesied from the mouth of the Savior. The prophetic Spirit says to him from the mouth of the Savior: . . ." (Elowsky 2013, 243).

25. Elowsky 2013, 150. Cf. also the contrasting of the words of the prophet Isaiah with the words of Jesus in the commentary on Isa 55:1.

26. Elowsky 2013, 1.

the quiet contemplation of the inspiration and wisdom he had received.[27]

After having spent some time explaining that in doing so, the prophet Isaiah could be considered a great evangelist, Eusebius asks,

> Why then did he begin to speak first against Judea, as it would seem, and then later on "against Babylon" and "Egypt"? He began with those who thought themselves to be dedicated to God, according to what has been said elsewhere: "Begin at my sanctuary" and the "mighty men will be mightily tested." After the period of these four kings had been sealed, a new state of affairs for the Jewish people arrived, and it seems that neither the truths in the literal sense nor those in the underlying sense concerning these affairs failed to happen later, in times then still distant. The reader should notice that *the book as a whole appears to have been joined together into a unity and that the message was delivered by the prophet in parts over several lengthy intervals of time, so that the book contains a great deal of precise information about future events.* Isaiah wrote in this way *in order that* the interpretation of the prophecies recorded in it could be determined after a while and so that the prophecy would also be applicable to the events that occurred in each reign. After fifty years, the time of the appointed kings was completed, according to what was said and proclaimed throughout the whole book.[28]

Although Eusebius speaks of a complex material gathered over some period of time, it is clear that the prophet Isaiah is himself the one both speaking and gathering "his" prophecies for the benefit of future generations—he constructs Isaiah as a Greek author, an author whose work is to be interpreted in line with his intent.

Second, as with Origen, Eusebius constantly compares the Greek of the LXX with the translations of Symmachus, Aquila, and Theodotion, often in search for theological significance in "even the minutest exchange of synonyms."[29] Consider his comment on Isa 40:1–2 as an example:

---

27. Elowsky 2013, 1.
28. Elowsky 2013, 2 (emphasis added).
29. Elowsky 2013, xxxi.

We do not find the phrase *O priests, comfort the people* either in the Hebrew text or in the other Greek translations, and therefore this phrase is marked with obeli in the Septuagint. And therefore, according to Symmachus, the text reads: *Console, O console my people, says your God. Encourage the heart of Jerusalem.* The other Greek translations are equivalent to this. And there are certain individuals whom the Word does find worthy to appoint *to comfort the people* . . . that is, the apostles and disciples of our Savior, and the evangelists and others such as these . . . all those who have received the comforting Spirit are appointed *to comfort the people* of God but neither Israel nor Jacob nor Judah.[30]

Siding with the Hebrew text evidently enables Eusebius to identify the referent of the imperatives as the church,[31] and taken together with the other examples above, there can be little doubt that Eusebius works within a Greek author tradition, recurrently inquiring into the prophet Isaiah's authorial intent and constantly seeking to interpret the *original* text (sing.).

Jerome and *Hebraica Veritas*

A final example of the influence of the Greek trajectory on the way the prophet Isaiah is constructed as an author can be found in the discussion surrounding the role and place of the Hebrew text in relation to the LXX, a discussion that reveals a fundamental distinction between originators and imitators.

Prophets and Mere Interpreters

Prior to Jerome, it had been commonplace among Christian theologians to see the LXX not only as a translation, conveying an authoritative Hebrew text in a different language, but as an *inspired writing*—that is, in no way lesser in terms of authority than the Hebrew text.[32] This view was supported by various retellings of a legendary story of how the LXX came into being that are found in the Letter of Aristeas, Philo, and

---

30. Elowsky 2013, 191–92 (emphasis in the original).

31. Noteworthy is that Justin Martyr quotes the reading featuring priests in his *Dial.* 50, where he quotes from Isa 39:8–40:17 (consecutively) as the words of the prophet Isaiah foretelling "the office of forerunner discharged by John the Baptist."

32. Jewish tradition would grow more negative over time; see, e.g., Decock 2008, 208–10, 212.

Josephus, all with different emphases.[33] While Josephus speaks of it as a "single agreed-upon text" approved by the people (*Ant.* 12.104–9),[34] both Let. Aris. and Philo (and numerous other writers) emphasized the process as divinely inspired and prophetic.[35]

In *Moses* 2.37, 40, for example, Philo recounts how the translators

> *became as it were possessed, and, under inspiration, wrote,* not each several scribe something different, but the same word for word, as though dictated to each by an invisible prompter (37). . . . If Chaldeans have learned Greek, or Greek Chaldean, and read both versions, the Chaldean and the translation, they regard them with awe and reverence as sisters, or rather *one and the same,* both in matter and words, and speak of *the authors not as translators but as prophets* and priests of the mysteries, whose sincerity and singleness of thought has enabled them to go hand in hand with the purest of spirits, *the spirit of Moses.* (40)[36]

A distinction between prophets and "mere interpreters" can be seen here, where the latter are considered (unoriginal) imitators—ultimately likely to be tainting the text with unwarranted alterations (cf. the severity in which this is described in Let. Aris. 308–16).[37] According to Philo, the LXX is the work of the former, and this is seen by the fact that despite the translators being separated from one another (some would even talk about them being put in separate rooms or cells; see, e.g., b. Meg. 9a or Augustine's *Doctr. chr.* 2.15.22), they produced identical translations. Notable is also the reference to the *spirit of Moses* as authentically conveyed by the translation, which bears clear marks of the Greek trajectory and its emphasis not only on texts but on poets. It was noted above that since these poets were seen as inspired, it required inspiration to interpret them,[38] and this idea also recurs in Origen's

---

33. On the relation between the LXX and the Peisistratus Legend, see Wyrick 2004, 260–72, who discusses the LXX legend at length.

34. Wyrick 2004, 264.

35. As stated in Let. Aris., the translation was necessary due to the state of preservation of the Hebrew, which was seen as "both incomprehensible (due to language), and false (due to poor transmission of the Hebrew)" (so Borchardt 2017, 16, who discusses these aspects in more length).

36. Translation from Colson 1935 (emphasis added).

37. Cf. Decock 2008, 207.

38. See chapter 4 above, with figure 1 in "Centralized Authors." This is also made clear in Irenaeus's retelling: "For the one and the same Spirit of God, who proclaimed by the

240

comment on Num 11:16–25, a passage that was often seen as related to the activity of the translators. According to Origen, it was as if

> *Moses, and the Spirit who was in Moses,* were the lamp of some very brilliant light from which God kindled seventy other lamps. The principal splendor of that light came to the others in such a manner that the very origin of the light suffered no loss from the sharing of its source. (*Hom. Num.* 6.2.1)[39]

It was against this legend that Jerome argued. Proceeding from the distinction between prophet-as-originator and translator-as-imitator, he writes in his prologue to Genesis that the LXX is indeed no revelation but a translation:[40]

> I do not know whose false imagination led him to invent the story of the seventy cells at Alexandria, in which, though separated from each other, the translators were said to have written the same words. Aristeas, the champion of that same Ptolemy, and Josephus, long after, relate nothing of the kind; their account is that the Seventy assembled in one basilica consulted together, and did not prophesy. *For it is one thing to be a prophet, another to be a translator.* The former through the Spirit, foretells things to come; the latter must use his learning and facility in speech to translate what he understands. It can hardly be that we must suppose Tully was inspired with oratorical spirit when he translated Xenophon's Œconomics, Plato's Protagoras, and the oration of Demosthenes in defense of Ctesiphon. *Otherwise the Holy Spirit must have quoted the same books in one sense through the Seventy Translators, in another through the Apostles, so that, whereas they said nothing of a given matter, these falsely affirm that it was so written.*[41]

For Jerome, then, the issue was closely related to the use of the Hebrew Bible in the New Testament, and in his understanding, it was clear that the NT used a Hebrew text, not the Greek LXX.[42] His argument for the primacy of the Hebrew text was thus not primarily

---

prophets what and of what sort the advent of the Lord should be, did by these elders give a just interpretation of what had been truly prophesied" (*Haer.* 3.21.2–4).

39. Translation from Hall 2009, 21 (emphasis added).

40. Cf. Decock 2008, 216.

41. Quoted from Schaff 1995 (emphasis added).

42. Decock 2008, 215–16.

philological; rather, he asserted that the authority of Christ and the apostles should be the primary guide in these matters. He also noted that many of the LXX texts needed revision, since they were filled with mistakes (observations likely made possible in part by Origen's Hexapla) that were the consequence of the translation processes, and so he wanted to "make clear and correct the texts, which [were] ambiguous, deleted, or distorted."[43] For this revision to be possible, the Hebrew Bible needed to be viewed from a post-Christ perspective. Put differently, according to Jerome, the apostles were in a better position to translate than the seventy interpreters (cf. *Ruf.* 25.65–67) simply because the seventy lived before Christ and thus did not know him ("what we understand better, we translate better," as he writes in *Praef. In Pent.* 38–39).[44] The dynamic is explained as the following in his preface to the translation of 1–2 Chr:

> Recently I have written a book *On the Best Method of Translating*, demonstrating that these verses from the Gospels: *From Egypt I called my son* (Matt 2:15), *Since he will be called a Nazarene* (Matt 2:23), *They will look to him whom they pricked* (John 19:37), and this verse of the Apostle: *Those which the eye did not see, the ear did not hear, and did not go up to the heart of human, those which God prepared for those who love him* (1 Cor 2:9), and the other similar verses are found in the books of the Hebrews. Certainly the Apostles and the Evangelists knew the seventy interpreters, but from where was it for them to say those things which are not in the Seventy? Christ, our God, and the founder of each Testament, says in the Gospel according to John: *The one believing in me, as the Scripture said, rivers of living water flow out of his belly* (John 7:38). That which the Savior attests that it is written is certainly written. Where is it written? The Seventy does not have it, and the Church does not know Apocrypha. Accordingly one should return to the Hebrew books, from which even the Lord speaks and the disciples draw their examples. (*Praef. in Par. [IH]* 19–31)[45]

Revelation and Intent

Arguing against Jerome were, however, no other than (most notably) Augustine and Hilary of Poitiers, who both defended the LXX.[46] Hilary,

---

43. Kato 2019, 422n6.
44. Kato 2019, 432.
45. Quoted from Kato 2019, 424–25 (emphasis in the original).
46. Kato 2019, 421; cf. Rebenich 1993, 53.

for example, argued in his *Tract. Ps.* 2:2–3 that the seventy elders had received a *separate revelation* from Moses—a teaching that was transmitted orally that gave them control over "the polysemous aspect of the [Hebrew] words"[47] (Matt 23:2–3 was taken as proof that the teaching was preserved). Then he argued in contrast to Jerome that

> the authority *of the seventy translators* remains absolute. This is because in the first place, they translated *before* the bodily advent of the Lord, and an adulatory bias in translation, as applied to the circumstance, cannot be attributed to them, since the time of the translation was so much earlier.[48]

Hilary thus emphasizes revelation, but in contrast to its construction in Qumran, for example, where *new* and *continuous* revelation was provided to correctly interpret texts (see, e.g., 1QpHab 7 1–5),[49] he sees it *not as new* but as possible to trace back all the way to Moses. Similarly, Augustine emphasizes that since the same spirit was at work in both the LXX and the Hebrew text, the same meaning could be expressed by different formulations. Interestingly, the activity of the spirit also meant that new meanings could be generated that did not contradict the original sense of the text but complemented it:[50]

> For the same Spirit who was in the prophets when they spoke these things was also in the seventy men when they translated them, so that assuredly they could also say something else, just as if the prophet himself had said both, because it would be the same Spirit who said both; and could say the same thing differently, so that, although the words were not the same, yet the same meaning should shine forth to those of good understanding; and could omit or add something, so that even by this it might be shown that there was in that work not human bondage, which the translator owed to the words, but rather divine power, which filled and ruled the mind of the translator. . . . For in that manner He spoke as He chose, some things through Isaiah, some through Jeremiah, some through several prophets, or else the same thing through this prophet and through that. Further, whatever is found in both editions, that one and the same Spirit willed to say through

---

47. Translation from Kamesar 2005, 271.
48. Translation from Kamesar 2005, 272 (emphasis added).
49. See also above, "Explicit Pennings," chapter 10.
50. See Childs 2004, 19.

both, but so as that the former preceded in prophesying, and the latter followed in prophetically interpreting them; because, as the one Spirit of peace was in the former when they spoke true and concordant words, so the selfsame one Spirit has appeared in the latter, when, without mutual conference they yet interpreted all things as if with one mouth. (*Civ.* 18.43)[51]

He goes on to provide an example: although the MT is historically correct in speaking of "forty days" until Nineveh is overthrown in Jonah 3:4, the LXX makes explicit a hidden significance by translating "three days"—namely, that it prophetically related to Christ, with Nineveh as the (penitent) church of the Gentiles. According to Augustine, in such a reading, both the forty days and the three days made sense: Christ rose on the third day and then spent forty days with his disciples before ascending to heaven.

That Augustine was also occupied with authorial intent and *Echtheitskritik* is very clear. In a discussion of the 'book' called *Enoch*, for example, he states that he believes that Enoch prophesied, since he is quoted in Jude 14, but nonetheless doubts the reliability of the 'book' *Enoch*:

Because of [its] remoteness in time it seemed advisable to hold them suspect, for fear of advancing false claims to authenticity. . . . The purity of the canon has not admitted these works, not because the authority of these men, whom God approved, is rejected, but because these documents are not believed to belong to them. (*Civ.* 18.38; cf. Tertullian *Cult. Fem.* 1.3)[52]

He also emphasized the importance of authorial intention in the interpretive work while at the same time recognizing that such intentions are never singular—texts can always have more meanings, since they bear witness to the truth:

Let no one go on to annoy me by saying: "Moses did not mean what you say; he meant what I say." Of course, if he said to me: "How do you know that Moses' thought corresponds to the interpretation you give of these words of his?"—that I ought to endure without getting disturbed; and I might give the same answer,

---

51. Translation from Dods 2017.
52. Translation from Dods 2017.

perhaps, that I did above, or a somewhat fuller one, if he were a more difficult opponent. But, when one says: "He did not mean what you say but what I say," yet does not deny that both our statements may be true, O Life of the poor, O my God, in whose bosom there is no contradiction, send down a rain of soothing waters into my heart, so that I may tolerate such people with patience! These people do not tell me this because they are godlike men who have seen what they say in the heart of Thy servant, but because they are proud and did not know Moses' meaning; rather, they love their own opinion, not because it is true, but because it is their own. Otherwise, they would love another true one equally, just as I love what they say, when they tell the truth—not because it is theirs, but because it is true, and, precisely because it is true, not theirs either. (*Conf.* 12.25)[53]

By the fourth century, then, it is quite clear that an author was conceived of as an individual penning a text with specific intentions in mind and that this view is transferred back to the biblical authors, who were understood as having written "their" works in similar ways. Anachronistically, Augustine assumes that authenticity "had always been foremost in the minds of the Jews who had created the canon of the Old Testament."[54]

Situating the Prophet

Returning to Jerome, it is thus no surprise that a Greek construction of authorship, albeit informed by the Mesopotamian trajectory, shines forth in the way he handles the 'book' called *Isaiah* in his commentary. Here, the prophet Isaiah is the one speaking throughout the whole 'book,' and it is *his* message that is to be interpreted.[55] In the eighth 'book,' for example, Jerome states, "My purpose is that [the prophet] Isaiah be understood through my instrumentality, and not that my words be lauded under the pretext of writing on Isaiah."[56] Therefore, Jerome not only recurrently returns to his *persona* in commenting on various parts of the 'book' but also spends time situating the prophet *historically*. In commenting on Isa 1:1, he explains that the prophet Isaiah is speaking chiefly about two tribes (Judah and Benjamin); that he lived at the same time as Hosea, Joel, and

---

53. Quoted from Bourke 1953.
54. Wyrick 2004, 357.
55. Cf. Scheck 2015, 51.
56. Scheck 2015, 386.

Amos (referring to kings named in the paratexts to these 'books'); and that his father was not the prophet Amos but another Amoz (since they are spelled differently). Moreover, he explains that the reference to "seeing" in Isa 1:1 should be understood as referring to "the things that are *said*"[57] and that all that is in the 'book' relates to prophecies by the prophet Isaiah under Uzziah (Isa 1–5), Jotham (Isa 6), Ahaz (Isa 7–14:28), and Hezekiah (Isa 14:28–66) so that

> until the end of the book, he [i.e., the prophet Isaiah] reports and writes down what the Lord revealed to him separately under Uzziah, Joatham, Ahaz, and Hezekiah. We should know too that Hezekiah began to reign in Jerusalem in the twelfth year of Romulus. . . . Hence it is shown clearly how much older our histories are than those of the other nations.[58]

Ultimately, then, Jerome attempts to interpret *the prophet Isaiah*, who is believed to have expressed words received from God in writing:

> I shall expound Isaiah in such a way that I will show him *not only as a prophet, but as an evangelist and apostle*. For he himself says of himself and other evangelists, "How beautiful are the feet of those who evangelize, (announcing) good things, who preach peace" (Isa 52:7; cf. Rom 10:15), and God speaks to him as if to an apostle: "Whom shall I send and who will go to this people," and he replied, "Here I am, send me" (Isa 6:8).[59]

He also argues against the idea that the prophets would have spoken in ecstasy, not knowing what they were saying, claiming,

> (The prophets) indeed knew what they were saying. For if the prophets were wise, which we cannot deny . . . (then) how were these wise prophets ignorant of what they were saying, in the manner of brute beasts? . . . It was not air struck by the voice that reached their ears, but God was speaking in the mind of the prophets.[60]

---

57. Scheck 2015, 71 (emphasis in the original).

58. Scheck 2015, 72.

59. Scheck 2015, 67 (emphasis added).

60. Scheck 2015, 68–69.

Combined with the notion of *Hebraica veritas*, this meant that the words in the Hebrew version of the 'book' could be related to the hand of the prophet himself. Consider, for example, the comment on Isa 5:7, where he states that he wants to "introduce Latin ears to what we have learned from the Hebrews" and then explains a wordplay that can only be seen in the Hebrew text and ascribes this to the skill of the prophet Isaiah: "By changing or adding one letter he has fittingly created a similarity between the words. . . . Indeed in the Hebrew language he [i.e., the prophet Isaiah] has produced an elegant construction and sound of the words."[61] The words of the prophet Isaiah are, consequently, primarily heard in the Hebrew text, which he himself composed, and so one may suggest that the "search for the *Hebraica veritas* reflected his [Jerome's] concern to recover the original documents of the inspired prophet,"[62] as it was only the Hebrew that provided an "unfiltered and direct avenue to divine speech."[63]

At the same time, he affirms that the 'book' called *Isaiah* should also be understood spiritually,[64] and many of the readings clearly go in such a direction, like his interpretation of the prophetess in Isa 8:3 as the Spirit (Jerome refers to the fact that רוח is a feminine noun) so that the child is in fact Christ. Another example is his interpretation of Isa 8:16 as referring to a binding of the Old Testament that is then given to the apostles, and as with all of his other interpretations, they are related to authorial intent: "*This is why* the prophet responded: because the law was closed and sealed among the Jews when the gospel succeeded it, and you are commanding it to be unsealed not for the Jews but for the Gentiles, therefore *I will wait* for Emmanuel whom you promise will come."[65] The children waiting with him are "preacher[s] of the new gospel."[66]

Throughout his commentary, Jerome also compares different translations and interpretations—while constantly identifying the voice of the prophet Isaiah as the one guiding the reader through the 'book' (although others are sometimes also heard; see, e.g., Hezekiah in the psalm in Isa 38)—and argues that some narratives had been damaged. A good example is Isa 38, which Jerome sees as being "in a confused

---

61. Scheck 2015, 134.
62. Childs 2004, 95.
63. Childs 2004, 100.
64. See similarly Gemeinhardt 2016, 322–23; the discussion in Scheck 2015, 21–23; and more generally Berges 2012b, 111–18.
65. Scheck 2015, 183 (emphasis added).
66. Scheck 2015, 184.

order, as it were in a prophecy. It reads more coherently in the Book of Kings."[67] Verse 21 thus needed "to be read before the 'prayer' or writing of Hezekiah."[68]

Ultimately, then, the prophet Isaiah has taken center stage as a Greek author of the 'book' called *Isaiah*, and investigations into his life and death were needed as a way of gaining more knowledge about the text.

FILLING BIOGRAPHICAL BLANKS

A final aspect of the construction of the prophet Isaiah as a Greek author that needs to be addressed is the emergence of author biographies. It was noted in the overview of the Greek trajectory (see above, "Interpreting the Author," chapter 4) that when authors were placed at the center of the interpretive activity, information about an author's life could both inform the reading of a text and be extracted from it. This indeed can be seen in the way early Christian authors commented on the 'book' *Isaiah*.

Moreover, in the Greek trajectory, authors were also made the subject of new poems and were honored with statues. Since the authorship of the prophet Isaiah was being reshaped in light of the Greek trajectory, it would thus be expected that similar tendencies would be found. More specifically, once it was presumed that the entire 'book' called *Isaiah* was penned by the prophet Isaiah, one consequence was that the events and prophecies in the 'book' could be understood as relating to various periods of his life, and when read together with other passages in Scripture where he also featured (the prophet Isaiah is mentioned by name also in 2 Kgs 19:2, 5–6, 20; 20:1, 4, 7–9, 11, 14, 16, 19; 2 Chr 26:22; 32:20, 32), it was possible to place the prophet in both time and space and to map out the main contours of his life. However, as this was done, some parts of this portrait would still be missing, most notably information about his *lineage* (who was Amoz?) and the circumstances under which he *died*. Interestingly, both of these gaps are filled by traditions emerging in the late Second Temple period.

Sawed in Two

Starting with circumstances under which the prophet Isaiah died, there is a well-known martyrdom tradition that probably originated sometime

---

67. Scheck 2015, 522.
68. Scheck 2015, 528.

during the last centuries BCE that recounts how the prophet Isaiah was sawed in two. It is alluded to in Heb 11:37, which refers to those "sawn in two" (ἐπρίσθησαν) in a list of fates that had come upon heroes from the past.[69] It is also mentioned in Justin's *Dial.* 120,[70] by Tertullian (*Pat.* 14; *Scorp.* 8), and in the *Apocalypse of Paul* 49, and is picked up and renarrated in b. Yebam. 49b and y. Sanh. 10:2 (cf. b. Sanh. 103b, where the death of the prophet Isaiah is related to 2 Kgs 21:16 and the shedding of innocent blood by Manasseh).[71] In all of these references—except for some of the rabbinic texts—only a very brief mention of the fate of the prophet Isaiah is made, but a more expanded narrative has been preserved in the early Christian apocalypse *Ascension of Isaiah*, which is commonly dated to 70–120 CE.[72] This work, whose composition history has been subject to much debate,[73] probably originated in Jesus-believing communities in Syria (notable is the recurring references to the "Beloved"—i.e., Christ).[74] The entire composition is preserved only

---

69. Cf. Schneemelcher 1992, 605.

70. Interestingly, Justin accuses Jews of having deleted that passage (cf. "Origen and *Echtheitskritik*" above) and says that they would have done the same with passages from the 'book' called *Jeremiah* and the Psalms had they only understood them. Regarding the Psalms, he likely refers to Ps 96:10 (for a discussion, see Anni Maria Laato 2020; Antti Laato 2020), and as for *Jeremiah*, the passage is quoted in *Dial.* 72 and referred to several times by Irenaeus, with various attributions. It is related to the prophet Isaiah(!) once, in *Haer.* 3.20.4; to Jeremiah twice, in *Haer.* 4.22.1 and *Epid.* 78; to an unidentified "prophet" once, in *Haer.* 5.31.1; to "others" once, in *Haer.* 4.33.12 (possibly both the prophets Isaiah and Jeremiah?); and quoted without introduction once, in *Haer.* 4.33.1.

71. See also Charlesworth 2019, 6.

72. Knight 2020, 250.

73. An early theory, now abandoned by most scholars (see Hall 2004, 18; Knight 2013, 358), is presented in, e.g., Knibb 1985. According to this view, the work is a combination of two (or even three) independent works, one Jewish and one Christian (cf. Berges 2012b, 110; Graves 2015, 117; and to a lesser degree Wyrick 2004, 102–3). The Jewish work was identified as chapters 1–5* and designated the *Martyrdom of Isaiah* (see also the idea by Charles 1900 that this work was also composite, with 3:13–4:22 as an independent *Testament of Hezekiah*), while chapters 6–11 were seen as a Christian *Ascension of Isaiah*. When the two were joined, some additions were also made to chapters 1–5 (see, e.g., Knibb 1985, 156–64, who regards 1:2b–6a; 3:13–4:22; and 5:15–16 as expansions). Much work has been done to try to distinguish Jewish parts from Christian, but needless to say, when speaking of second-century CE literature, such dichotomies are too simplistic. Hall 1994, 466, calls the terms "slippery" and later states that the work is "as Jewish as it is Christian" (Hall 2016, 345; cf. Gemeinhardt 2016, 320–21). Since parts of chapters 1–5 presuppose 6–11 (Knight 2013, 359, points esp. to 1:3–4 as setting the scene for the entire composition), a combination of two separate works seems unlikely, and as concluded by Hall 1994, 483, "The Vision of Isaiah contains no break in logic or narrative for a source theory to explain" (cf. also Verheyden 2021, 72).

74. For a discussion, see esp. Hall 1990 (cf. Knight 2013, 358; 2020, 250).

in Ethiopic, although probably composed in Greek,[75] and is made up of two intertwined parts.[76] Chapters 6–11, which may have been written first,[77] recount a vision of the prophet Isaiah who ascends through the heavens, and chapters 1–5, which seem to presuppose chapters 6–11 (see n. 73), "present an eschatological prophecy that predicts the return of Christ"[78] by recounting how the prophet Isaiah was martyred under Manasseh by being sawed in two. So put, the subject matter is not the prophet Isaiah per se. He is used to address other, more pressing issues, but by giving him a central role in the narrative, he is made into a model,[79] and his biography is developed in some significant ways. A brief walk-through will make this clear.

Starting with chapters 1–5, the main plot can be summarized as follows. The story begins with Hezekiah summoning Manasseh in the presence of "Isaiah, the son of Amoz, the prophet,"[80] and Isaiah's son "Josab" (*Ascen. Isa.* 1:1–2; cf. Isa 7:3) to give him, among others, "the words of righteousness which the king himself had seen" (*Ascen. Isa.* 1:2–3)[81] as well as "the written words . . . which Isaiah the son of Amoz had given to him, and to the prophets also, that they might write out and store up with him what he himself had seen" (1:5). The text then specifies these written words as seen "in the twentieth year of the reign of Hezekiah" and "handed to Josab his son," which is a reference to the vision in chapters 6–11 (see 6:1).[82] The prophet Isaiah is thus understood as a visionary, and although not explicitly writing himself, his visions were nonetheless written down while he lived and transmitted by others. The passage also presumes that there are visions originating with the prophet

---

75. Cf. Knight 2020, 250. Knibb 1985, 144, and other older works would see some of the parts (esp. the ones identified as "Jewish") as originally composed in Hebrew. The work is also extant in Latin and Slavonic versions—which only feature chapters 6–11 and do not completely overlap—and there are some smaller fragments in Greek, Coptic, and Provençal (see Verheyden 2021, 70, 70n1).

76. Regardless of the classification of the two parts, a two-stage composition is generally accepted (see, e.g., Norelli 1995; cf. Knight 2013), although there are opposing voices (most notably Bauckham 1998).

77. But nonetheless suggested to work as "une sorte d'appendice" when read as a part of the final composition (Norelli 1993, 9).

78. Knight 2020, 250.

79. Cf. Hall 2004, 26: "The author of the *Ascension of Isaiah* wants us all to be like Isaiah." Similarly Verheyden 2021, 79–80.

80. It is unclear if the designation "prophet" refers to Isaiah or Amoz. On the latter, see also below, in the subsection "Legacy and Ancestry."

81. All translations are from Knibb 1985.

82. Cf. Knibb 1985, 156.

Isaiah that are *not* recorded in the 'book' called *Isaiah*. Before unpacking this a bit further, the rest of the story must be discussed.

Understanding why Hezekiah had summoned Manasseh, Isaiah responds that it is pointless to continue giving commands and words to Manasseh, since they will have no effect on him (1:7). In fact, Manasseh will become a follower of Beliar,[83] and the prophet himself "will be sawed in half . . . by his hands" (1:9–10). When he hears this, Hezekiah wants to kill Manasseh, but Isaiah intervenes (1:12–13).

The story then moves to narrate how Isaiah's prediction was fulfilled. As Manasseh becomes king after the death of Hezekiah, he turns away from YHWH and serves Beliar (2:1–6). This causes Isaiah to withdraw, first from Jerusalem to Bethlehem and then from Bethlehem to a "mountain in a desert place" together with some other individuals, all prophets (Micah, Ananias, Joel, Habakkuk, his son Josab, and the "faithful who believed in the ascension into heaven";[84] 2:7–10). They took nothing with them (2:7–11).[85] After two years, they are found by a man named Belkira—a false prophet and follower of Manasseh (3:1)—and Isaiah is accused of prophesying against Jerusalem, Judah, Benjamin, and the king (3:6–7); contradicting Moses by claiming to have seen YHWH (thus identifying the prophet Isaiah with the speaker in Isa 6:1);[86] and calling Jerusalem Sodom and the princes of Judah and Jerusalem Gomorrah (3:8–10, thus identifying Isa 1:11 as spoken by the prophet Isaiah). Hearing these accusations, Manasseh seized Isaiah (3:12).

Then follows a longer section where Beliar is angry with Isaiah "because of the vision" he had seen, a vision dividing history into four periods:

(1) A golden age of Jesus and apostles (3:13–20); (2) a period of decline and strife within the church during which the Holy

---

83. On Beliar/Belial as a name for Satan, see Stokes 2019, e.g., 85–86, 142–94. On possible traditions behind the narrative, see briefly Knight 2020, 251.

84. On the relation between ascension stories and mountains, see the discussion in Gieschen 1998, 229–44, who argues that *Ascen. Isa.* is "rooted in a Jewish Christian community that revered mystical ascent and ascetic practices in deference to what the author(s) sees happening in the wider Christian church" (230).

85. As accurately described by Hall 2004, 20, by this narrative, the reader is urged "to eschew Beliar, vainglory, wealth, and worldly power and to cleave to the prophets, to the Spirit, to worldly poverty, and to heavenly glory."

86. This is repeated in 4 Bar 9:22, where the people want to kill Jeremiah by stoning him because he had spoken words similar to "Isaiah the son of Amos, saying, 'I saw God and the son of God.'"

Spirit withdraws from many (3:26) and the prophets are actively repressed (3:31); (3) a time of reign for "the great angel" Beliar (4:1–13), who will incarnate himself in a future Roman emperor (Nero *redivivus*)[87] and persecute Christians on earth who await the Beloved's return (4:14); and (4) the return of the Beloved One (4:14–22), who will establish his earthly rule and destroy Belial before the righteous ascend to heaven (4:17).[88]

Because of Beliar's anger over these visions and because he "dwelt in the heart of Manasseh," Manasseh sawed Isaiah "in half with a wood saw" (5:2). As this happens, Belkira and other false prophets stand by laughing, urging Isaiah to take back his words and speak favorably over Manasseh (and Belkira), but Isaiah refuses, and while he "was being sawed in half, he did not cry out, or weep, but his mouth spoke with the Holy Spirit until he was sawed in two" (5:14–15; cf. Isa 53:7 and, e.g., Matt 26:62–63).[89]

After chapter 5, the story returns to the twentieth year of the reign of Hezekiah (cf. 1:6, above) and recounts a vision where Isaiah ascends through the seven heavens (chaps. 6–11), and when reaching the seventh heaven, he sees Christ's incarnation, infancy, crucifixion, resurrection, and ascension (chap. 11).[90] The story then ends with stating that "because of these visions and prophecies Sammael Satan sawed Isaiah the son of Amoz, the prophet, in half by the hand of Manasseh" (11:41).

In brief, the story blames Manasseh for the murder of Isaiah, who was sawed in two with a wooden saw. These components—the wickedness of Manasseh, wood, and sawed in two—seem to be the main ones in the traditions surrounding Isaiah's death; they also recur in b. Yebam. 49b and y. Sanh. 10:2, albeit with some variations.

In b. Yebam. 49b, it is recounted how Rabbi Shimon ben Azzai found a scroll of lineages (מגלת יוחסין) in Jerusalem, and among the things written in it is that Manasseh killed Isaiah (מנשה הרג את ישעיה). The text then continues by describing the circumstances in more detail. In this version, Manasseh judged Isaiah for having made statements that contradicted Moses: Isaiah 6:1 (the prophet Isaiah's claim to have seen God, thus overlapping with *Ascen. Isa.*) is contrasted with Exod 33:20; Isa 55:6 (God is not always near) is contrasted with Deut 4:7; and

---

87. On the allusions to this myth, see also Knight 2013, 365.

88. Knight 2020, 250.

89. On the contrast between the forces of good (here the Holy Spirit in the prophet Isaiah) and evil (Beliar in Manasseh), see also Verheyden 2021, 76–77.

90. On the contrasting timelines in these chapters as compared to chapters 1–5, see Hall 2004.

2 Kgs 20:6 (Hezekiah's life was prolonged; cf. Isa 38:6)[91] is contrasted with Exod 23:26. Faced with the charges, Isaiah realized that Manasseh would not accept any explanation, and since he would not want to make Manasseh intentionally transgress (since he would kill Isaiah anyway), he tried to escape. He uttered a (divine) name (אמר שם) and was swallowed by a cedar tree (איבלע בארזא). The escape was unsuccessful, however, since the cedar was brought to Manasseh and sawed in two. As the saw reached the mouth of Isaiah, he died.[92]

In sum, although the narrative about the death of Isaiah features a wicked Manasseh, a claim of false prophecy, a sawing in two, and wood, it differs from *Ascen. Isa.* in a number of ways. One interesting aspect is that Isaiah views Manasseh more favorably, since he attempts to clear him from intentional transgression, while the text at the same time puts some blame on Isaiah for his death: it is described as a punishment for his words in Isa 6:5.[93]

A third version is found in the briefer narrative in y. Sanh. 10:2:

> When Manasseh arose, he pursued Isaiah, wanting to kill him. Isaiah fled from him. He escaped to a cedar, which swallowed him up, except for the show fringes of his cloak, which revealed where he was. They came and told him. He said to them, "Go and cut the cedar down." They cut the cedar down, and blood showed [indicating that Isaiah had been sawed also]. "And also for the innocent blood that he had shed; for he filled Jerusalem with innocent blood, and the Lord would not pardon" (2 Kgs 24:4).[94]

The narrative overlaps with b. Yebam. 49b, except for the added part on the showing of the cloak, which gives Isaiah away, and in contrast to *Ascen. Isa.*, it is not a wooden saw but a cedar tree. Moreover, the death of Isaiah is explicitly related to the shedding of innocent blood on the part of Manasseh (so also b. Sanh. 103b).

---

91. That b. Yebam. 49b quotes from 2 Kgs and not Isa 38 can be seen in the fact that it reads הוספתי rather than יוסף (as in Isa 38). Consequently, a synthesis has been made of passages in the Hebrew Bible that relate to the prophet Isaiah.

92. The text then moves on to discuss whether the contradictions pointed out by Manasseh can be resolved.

93. That Moses's authority trumps Isaiah's can be noted in some contrast to *Ascen. Isa.*, where the reverse scenario can be observed (on this, see Knight 2013, 365–67, who argues that three groups of opponents are addressed in the apocalypse: fellow Christians, Romans, and Jews), although Verheyden 2021, 75, is correct in observing that in the vision in *Ascen. Isa.* 6–11, the prophet Isaiah never sees the face of YHWH.

94. Translation from Neusner 2010.

Returning to *Ascen. Isa.*, it was noted above that apart from the death of the prophet Isaiah, the narrative included some interesting references to *written* texts that need to be further unpacked. Although the prophet Isaiah is primarily a visionary in *Ascen. Isa.* and although the primary referent of the written prophecy in 1:6 is likely not the 'book' called *Isaiah* but chapters 6–11 of *Ascen. Isa.*, it is nevertheless clear that strict boundaries between the two are not upheld.[95] Looking at 3:13–4:22, where Beliar was said to be angry with the prophet Isaiah because of his vision about events surrounding "the Beloved," it can be noted that when dealing with the second coming of "the Beloved," it is said that

> the rest of the words of the vision are written in the vision of Babylon (cf. LXX Isa 13:1). And the rest of the vision about the Lord, behold it is written in parables in the words of mine that are written *in the book which I prophesied openly*. And the descent of the Beloved into Sheol, behold it is written in the section where the Lords says, 'Behold, my son shall understand.' (cf. LXX Isa 52:13)

The new, expanded vision is thus seen as a (hidden; see below) continuation of earlier (public) prophecies written in the 'book' called *Isaiah* so that *Ascen. Isa.* in fact borrows authority from the latter by claiming to align itself with it.[96] It also follows, then, that the prophet Isaiah is understood as responsible for all of the words of the 'book' called *Isaiah*, words passed on to his son Josab and Hezekiah (1:6; 2:9; 6:1, 16). This 'book' is, moreover, in agreement with several other books:[97]

> And all these things, behold they are written in the Psalms, in the parables of David the son of Jesse, and in the Proverbs of Solomon

---

95. This observation overlaps with the argument by Knight 2013, 363, that chapters 6–11 and 1–5 understand prophecy in different ways. While authoritative revelation is received by means of ascension through the heavens in *Ascen. Isa.* 6–11, prophecy is understood as "exegesis of the sacred writings with a distinct Christological emphasis" in *Ascen. Isa.* 1–5 (most notably in 4:21–22). Put differently, the composition combines old texts and new revelation so that the authority of the latter is derived from the former.

96. As noted by Sawyer 1996, 45, "For the author of this work, the Book of Isaiah contains details of the birth, life, death and resurrection of *Christ*" (emphasis added). At the same time, one could also understand *Ascen. Isa.* as providing an explanation to why the 'book' called *Isaiah* was so often cited in Christian works: the prophet had indeed really seen Jesus from his birth to his death and ascension (so Verheyden 2021, 84–85).

97. On the notable exclusion of Moses in this passage, see Knight 2013, 366; and n. 93 above.

his son, and in the words of Korah and of Ethan the Israelite, and in the words of Asaph, and in the rest of the psalms which the angel of the spirit has inspired, (namely) in those which have no name written,[98] and in the words of Amos my father and of Hosea the prophet, and of Micah, and of Joel, and of Nahum, and of Jonah, and of Obadiah, and of Habakkuk, and of Haggai, and of Zephaniah, and of Zechariah, and of Malachi, and in the words of the righteous Joseph, and in the words of Daniel. (4:21–22)

The new vision of the prophet Isaiah is thus claiming authority by means of aligning itself with earlier traditions, and overlaps with the Greek trajectory can be seen in that the end of the composition addresses a possible problem—namely, that someone could claim that the words of this vision were in fact not genuine (i.e., not the prophet Isaiah's). Chapter 11:39–40 reads, "Isaiah made him [Hezekiah] swear that he would not tell this to the people of Israel, and that he would not allow any man to copy these words."[99] The vision is thus cast as originating with the prophet Isaiah but is sealed up and hidden from the public. Put differently, the authority of the work was not primarily that it was a faithful (but anonymous) continuation of the 'book' called *Isaiah* but rather that the vision *originated with the prophet Isaiah himself*, that it had been kept secret and was now revealed.[100] Presented in such a way, this idea is likely indebted to the way the transmission of tradition is presented in the 'book' of *Isaiah* itself (see esp. Isa 8:16; 30:8–11), albeit transformed in light of the apocalyptic worldview of *Ascen. Isa.* The secrecy involved in the transmission also indicates that not everyone would understand the vision or be fit to read it (evidently, it ends up killing the prophet Isaiah).[101]

---

98. The references to David, Solomon, Korah, Ethan, Asaph, and nameless psalms are probably all to be taken as references to psalms in the 'book' of Psalms. This would explain the notion of Davidic "parables," for example, or the mention of Solomon in this context (cf. Pss 71; 127).

99. The dynamic is thus somewhat similar to what was observed in Hilary of Poitiers's defense of the LXX (see above, "Jerome and *Hebraica Veritas*"). The observation may be further supported by the suggestion by Hall 2004, 18, that chapters 1–5 were written "in order to win a hearing for the pre-existing report of Isaiah's heavenly trip."

100. Cf. Wyrick 2004, 105.

101. On this, see Verheyden 2021, 73: "The author really wants to communicate that this message was not meant to be divulged without further ado." It can also be noted that in the vision in chaps. 6–11, there are some additional references to 'books.' When the prophet Isaiah reaches the seventh heaven, for example, he is shown 'books' where all the deeds of the children of Israel were written, 'books' unlike anything in this world. For 'books' in apocalyptic imagination, see further Mroczek 2016.

Ultimately, *Ascen. Isa.* provides an interesting expansion of the biography of Isaiah as a prophet and visionary that implicitly paints him in the colors of a Greek author. Nonetheless, it is also to be noted that the work itself is anonymous and that the narrative framing of the vision speaks of the prophet Isaiah in the third person so that the author "acts as the prophet's interpreter, or rather as the one who steers the prophet and the reader alike in getting a sense of the whole process."[102]

Legacy and Ancestry

That the author ideals of the Greek trajectory had created a need for author biographies can be seen not only in the fact that the blanks surrounding the death of the prophet Isaiah were filled but also by the fact that attempts were made to make sure that his legacy would endure, which included expanding on the sparse notions of ancestry found in the 'book' called *Isaiah*.

An example of the former is found in *Lives of the Prophets*, a composition probably originally written in Greek and possibly dated to around the first century CE.[103] It provides honoring information surrounding the lives and deaths of prophets, and one of them is the prophet Isaiah, which is featured in the first chapter.[104]

In this chapter, it is first said that Isaiah was from Jerusalem and "died under Manasseh by being sawn in two." Then some additional information is supplied. The first is that the prophet was buried under "the Oak of Rogel," which according to the narrative was close to Siloam.[105] Second, God is said to have "worked the miracle of Siloam for the prophet's sake." The prophet had asked for water before he died, and water had been sent to him. He had also prayed for water at the time of the Jerusalem siege under Hezekiah, and a little water had come out. So "as a memorial" of this, the prophet Isaiah was buried nearby "with care and in great honor, so that through his prayers even after his death they might enjoy the benefit of the water" (1:8).[106] The notion of "care" and "great honor" may indicate that a monument was erected (cf. Matt

---

102. Verheyden 2021, 82.

103. For an introduction and isagogic discussions, see Hare 1985, 380–84.

104. van der Toorn 2007, 29–30, is indeed correct when he states that this text is quite different from what he calls "spiritual biographies" written by scholars in the nineteenth and twentieth centuries, but overlooks the significance of the text as an example of a more general biographical interest.

105. There is no need here to decide exactly *where* this may have been, since the point of the analysis above is to overview the story, not assess its historicity.

106. Berges 2012b, 90, suggests that the water story is a reference to Isa 12:3.

23:29; Luke 11:47),[107] which would further underscore that the "dead prophet's lively existence is to be experienced at his grave."[108] Although such a possibility cannot be satisfactorily assessed, it is well known that Isaiah would be commemorated in artworks in both Jewish and Christian traditions.[109] The earliest known possible depiction of the prophet Isaiah is from about 150 CE and is found in the catacomb of Priscilla in Rome, where he, if correctly identified,[110] stands next to Mary (who has the infant Jesus on her lap) and points to a star (cf. Isa 11:1, 10; Num 24:17; and Justin Martyr's *1 Apol.* 32).[111] Notably, a scroll would eventually become the prophet's most common attribute.[112]

The location of the tomb also speaks to his ancestry. It is described as located "near the tomb of the kings,"[113] thus probably conveying the idea that the prophet Isaiah descended from the kings of Judah. A similar idea is found in b. Meg. 10b, for example, where it is said that Amoz, the father of Isaiah, was a brother of Amaziah, king of Judah, ultimately descending from Judah and Tamar (cf. b. Soṭah 10b). The picture is not consistent, however, since Isaiah is elsewhere described as a son of a prophet. Lev. Rab. 6:6, for example, states that "wherever a prophet's own name is specified and his father's name also, he is a prophet the son of a prophet," and so Amoz is understood as a prophet.[114] Rabbinic tradition seems to agree, however, that the children mentioned in Isa 8:16–18 are not "real" children but rather disciples so precious that they were regarded as his children (Gen. Rab. 42:3 = Esth. Rab. 1, 8:2.1; cf. Lev. Rab. 11:7).[115]

Ultimately, both information about Isaiah's *lineage* and the circumstances under which he *died* had been supplied.

---

107. Cf. Hare 1985, 386n1.

108. Hare 1985, 383.

109. For a discussion of artistic depictions of the death of the prophet Isaiah, see, e.g., Bernheimer 1952. A general overview of Isaiah (both 'book' and prophet) in art is found in Sawyer 1996, 2020; cf. Berges 2012b, 118–46. As noted by Sawyer 1996, 42, the beginnings of Christian iconography are to be found already in the second century CE.

110. For a discussion, see Parlby 2008, 47–48.

111. A picture is found in Sawyer 1996, plate 3. He is also possibly one of the four figures flanking the central panel in the Dura synagogue (see Levine 2012, 103–5, with figure 53), although the identification is uncertain (on the art in this synagogue, see also Fine 2010, 174–85).

112. Cf. Berges 2012b, 118. A clear example, from the sixth century, is found in San Vitale in Ravenna, where he stands holding a closed scroll (see image 4 in Berges 2012b, 131).

113. See also the discussion in Gevaryahu 1989, 64.

114. See also Berges 2012b, 4. In Christian tradition, Amoz is sometimes confused with the prophet Amos from the 'book' called *Amos.* Translations of Lev. Rab. are from Freedman and Simon 1939b, unless stated otherwise.

115. In these texts, the binding and sealing are interpreted as Ahaz seizing synagogues and schools—i.e., not in relation to transmission and tradition of prophetic messages.

CHAPTER 13

NOT LEAVING AFTER ALL

In the last two chapters, the negotiation between the Mesopotamian and Greek trajectories has been sketched primarily in Greek-speaking contexts. Not surprisingly, a substantial influence from the Greek trajectory has been found, but what can be said about the way the relation between the prophet Isaiah and the 'book' called *Isaiah* is constructed in Jewish discussions? Turning now to this issue, it is to be noted that the 'book' *Isaiah* is frequently quoted. Before turning to an overview of how these quotations are framed, however, something must be said about author concepts implied in the literature itself, since the way the rabbis understood their own literary activity will likely have affected the way they interpreted the literary activity of the prophet Isaiah. The ensuing discussion will therefore be structured into three parts followed by a brief summary.

The first part will consider the implications of the curious tension between the fact that rabbis are often mentioned by name *in* the compositions and the fact that the compositions *themselves* are, as in the Mesopotamian trajectory, anonymous and unattributed (although with some notable exceptions).[1] Moreover, it is clear that interpretive glosses

---

1. See the overview in Stern 1995, 193–94, who notes some inconsistencies (see also Bregman 1999, 35), and Stern 1994, 49, who speaks of a contrast to "contemporary Graeco-Roman and Christian works, which were nearly all ascribed to specific authors." See also Wyrick 2004, 135; Ben-Eliyahu, Cohn, and Millar 2012, 10–11. As for the exceptions, the redaction of the Mishnah is, for example, attributed in b. Yebam. 43a, 64b, and individual tractates are also sometimes attributed (see, e.g., Pesiq. Rab Kah.; b. Yoma 14b, 16a–17a; b. Nid. 46b). Notable, however, is that in most of these cases, the attributions are epitextual, not peritextual. Put differently, they are made part of discussions, often introduced by, for example, "who is the tanna [who taught] . . . ?" (מאן תנא), rather than being an integral part of the framing of the texts themselves. Hence a similar development from anonymous to named texts as was seen in the late Second Temple period could be postulated here. To be noted is, however, that most rabbis are not strictly speaking referred to as *authors*. Cf. Ben-Eliyahu, Cohn, and Millar 2012, 12 (cf. 16): "Individual

and additional layers of text have been incorporated into, for example, the Talmudic text without any external indications—that is, in a way that would have been deemed quite problematic if working within the constraints of Hellenistic *Echtheitskritik*.[2] The second part will make observations regarding how biblical authors are conceived of, focusing especially on texts discussing the authorship of the Pentateuch. Finally, in the third part, texts explicitly focusing on the prophet Isaiah and the 'book' called *Isaiah* will be discussed.

Ascription and Authority

Since much of the rabbinic literature is related to named rabbis, scholars have spent much time attempting to reconstruct developing traditions by means of aligning sayings diachronically and creating biographies (and genealogies) of rabbis.[3] However, the recurrent claims that a certain rabbi said something does not necessarily mean that the named rabbi *actually said it*. In fact, it is oftentimes the case that the expressed saying is related to the rabbi in a more loose sense, to be understood as "Rabbi x *thought*, or 'Rabbi x *was of the opinion*'"[4] or even as a later *interpretation* of his opinions—not primarily as a verbatim quote.[5] Put differently, these references are not primarily expressing historical facts about the origins of sayings and thus do not provide reliable sources for diachronic reconstructions.[6] Their function is rather to be sought elsewhere, and it will be seen below that it bears the marks of both Mesopotamian and Greek trajectories. Put briefly, on the one hand, the interactions with "sources" are often both distributive and anonymous and hence in line with the Mesopotamian trajectory.[7] On

---

rabbis are almost always quoted in our literary texts not as the authors of written works, but as the source of opinions delivered orally; and it is sometimes argued that the entire body of material itself circulated orally, and was recorded in writing only after the end of antiquity." Since many of the examples below deal with issues that could be understood in terms of intellectual property, it will nonetheless be illuminating to study the above-mentioned tension, since it potentially casts light on the way the relation between the prophet Isaiah and the 'book' called *Isaiah* is conceived.

2. Cf. Stern 1994, 50.

3. Stern 1994, 28.

4. Stern 1994, 37.

5. Cf. Bregman 1999, 37.

6. Cf. Stern 1994, 38.

7. Cf. the notion in Bregman 1999, 32, that anonymous references to "the sages" were generally seen as more authoritative than ascriptions to named individuals.

the other hand, there is a tendency to provide (named)[8] older links in the chain of transmission with a higher degree of authority than subsequent ones and see sayings as in some sense the "property" of these named individuals, thus creating overlaps with the Greek trajectory.

Giving Appropriate Credit

In the rabbinic texts, when a teacher-student dynamic is envisaged, authority is often located with the rabbi, not his students. As it is put in b. Pesaḥ 112a, "If you want to hang yourself, do it in a big tree" (אם בקשת ליחנק היתלה באילן גדול)[9]—that is, "If you want your words to be accepted, attribute it to a great sage."[10] This also meant that it was important that the students appropriately credited the rabbi. An illustrative example can be found in b. Yebam. 96b–97a:[11]

> R. Eleazar came and reported this statement at the schoolhouse *but did not report it in the name of R. Johanan.* When R. Johanan heard this he was annoyed. . . . Thereupon R. Jacob b. Idi came in and said to him: "'As the Lord commanded Moses his servant, so did Moses command Joshua, and so did Joshua; he left nothing undone of all that the Lord commanded Moses' (Josh 11:15); did Joshua, then, concerning every word which he said, tell them,

---

8. It can be noted, however, that even if names of rabbis are provided, there is seldom any biographical information provided. This is observed by Ben-Eliyahu, Cohn, and Millar 2012, 18: "What is most distinctive about the Jewish literature of the period is the almost complete absence of biography and history, both of which play a large part in Christian literature in all the relevant languages. The absence of biography is particularly striking, because, as indicated repeatedly above, many of these works are built on quotations of the spoken opinions or rulings of named rabbis. But, as noted before, almost none of these rabbis is credited with any written work; and in no case do the references to any particular rabbi go beyond individual incidents, anecdotes or sayings, or offer more than brief accounts of his origins, life, teaching, pupils and death. The contrast with the mass of Christian biographical writing, whether relatively historical or just improving fiction, could hardly be stronger."

9. Unless otherwise stated, the Hebrew and Aramaic rabbinic texts are all quoted from https://www.sefaria.org.

10. The passage continues with "and when you teach your son, teach him from a corrected scroll" (וכשאתה מלמד את בנך—למדהו בספר מוגה); cf. b. Ketub. 19b, 106a), indicating that as for the actual biblical *text*, great care was taken to ascertain that it was reliable. For a discussion of ספר מוגה, see Tov 2012, 32–33.

11. The English translation of the parts of Babylonian Talmud quoted in this chapter is from Epstein 1935 (sometimes slightly modified), unless otherwise noted. The translation is available online at https://www.halakhah.com. For a survey of editions and translations of Jewish literature from the late antiquity, see esp. Ben-Eliyahu, Cohn, and Millar 2012.

'Thus did Moses tell me'? But, the fact is that Joshua was sitting and delivering his discourse without mentioning names, and all knew that it was the Torah of Moses. So did your disciple R. Eleazar sit and deliver his discourse *without mentioning names and all knew that it was yours.*" . . . Why was R. Johanan so annoyed? . . . R. Johanan stated in the name of R. Simeon b. Yohai: "The lips of a [deceased] scholar, in whose name a traditional statement is reported in this world, move gently in the grave."

Apparently, R. Johanan was annoyed because his student did not credit him with the teaching he provided, and the reason why he would have considered this important is said to be that he wanted to earn eternal fame (cf. the discussion of *Ben Sira* above, "Reframed Authorship," chapter 9, or the quote from Theognis, "Interpreting the Author," chapter 4).[12] His anger was thus kindled only when it was made clear that his authority was assumed *even if he was not named*, and so the student had not acted in deceit.[13] B. Moʿed Qaṭ 24b makes a similar point:[14]

R. ʿAnani b. Sason gave a discourse at the door of the Prince [and said]: "One day [of mourning] before ʿAzereth [the Feast of Weeks] with [one day of] ʿAzereth count as fourteen days [out of the thirty]." R. Ammi heard of this and was indignant saying: "Is that his own view? It is what R. Eleazar [b. Pedath] said as citing R. Oshaia!" R. Isaac the smith gave a discourse at the marquee of the Exilarch [and said]: "One day [of mourning] before ʿAzereth with the [one day of] ʿAzereth, count as fourteen days [out of the thirty]." R. Shesheth heard of this and was indignant, saying, "Is that his own view? It is what R. Eleazar said, as citing R. Oshaia!"

Knowing One's Place

The texts quoted above could perhaps be interpreted as stressing the importance of the correct attribution of a saying to the individual with which it *originated*, but such a conclusion would not be entirely accurate, since it is not always clear that the originator is the one being named:

---

12. Cf. the discussion in Stern 1994, 32.

13. Stern 1994, 47.

14. See also the notion of false attributions in b. Yebam. 17b–18a (on this passage, see the discussion in Stern 1994, 45).

רבי חזקיה רבי ירמיה רבי חייא בשם רבי יוחנן אם יכול את לשלשל
את השמועה עד משה שלשלה ואם לאו תפוש או ראשון ראשון או
אחרון אחרון

R. Hezekiah, R. Jeremiah, R. Hiyya in the name of R. Yohanan:
"If you can chain the saying until Moses, chain it; and if not, take
either the very first or very last ones." (y. Qidd. 1:7)[15]

Consequently, they are better understood in light of the suggested
teacher-student dynamic. The use of a chain as a metaphor for the transmission of tradition in the y. Šabb 6b passage is notable, not least in the
way it relates to "first" and "last" ones. Put differently, the passage states
that if a point of origin cannot be located, a saying can just as well be
attributed to a later tradent—perhaps the one who brought it to the
study house—or to an earlier authority.[16] So put, it is in line with what
was seen in relation to the concept of "subsequent ones" in the Mesopotamian trajectory. It thus indicates that these texts do not necessarily
construct "the individual as a highly autonomous, creative force" but
rather emphasize the transmission of traditions in a *distributive* way.
The stress on correct attribution is thus not so much rooted in a pre-
occupation with *origins* as it is concerned with *knowing one's place in the
chain*, an idea shining through also in b. Ber. 27b:

R. Zera said in the name of R. Assi reporting R. Eleazar who had
it from R. Hanina in the name of Rab: At the side of this pillar
R. Ishmael son of R. Jose said the Sabbath Tefillah on the eve
of Sabbath. When Ulla came he reported that it was at the side of
a palm tree and not at the side of a pillar, and that it was not
R. Ishmael son of R. Jose but R. Eleazar son of R. Jose, and that it
was not the Sabbath Tefillah on the eve of Sabbath but the end-of-
Sabbath Tefillah on Sabbath.

At the same time, *origins* are not insignificant. On the contrary,
the chains of rabbis indicated that the real point of origin was Sinai:
"Whatever the sages [of any generation] will agree upon is what Moses
was commanded by God, provides legal warrant for attributing to God

---

15. Translation from Neusner 2010 modified.
16. Cf. Stern 1994, 44.

what has been arrived at by human reason."[17] Contemporary traditions were thus constantly derived from earlier, often anonymous traditions in a way that Mosaic authority was distributed across generations:[18]

> Nahum the scribe said: "I have a tradition from R. Me'asha, who received it from Abba, who received it from the Zugoth, who received it from the prophets as an *halachah* of Moses from Sinai." (m. Pe'ah 2:6; cf. m. 'Ed. 8:7)

Fencing Discourses

Understanding the attributions not as referring to the creations of individual geniuses but as reflecting a distributive notion similar to the Mesopotamian trajectory thus makes a lot of sense, and this is confirmed not only by the use of the chain metaphor but also by the notion of boundaries or fences around discourses:

> Whence do we learn that if one substitutes R. Joshua's view for that of R. Eliezer, or vice versa, or says that the unclean is clean or that the clean is unclean, he transgresses a negative commandment? From the same verse, *Thou shalt not remove thy neighbor's landmark* (Deut 19:14). (Sifre Deut. 188)[19]

A similar notion is also present in the long passage in Pirkei Av. 6:6, where the virtues of a student of the Torah are listed. Among other things, it is told that a student is to make a "fence" around words without taking credit for oneself (והעושה סיג לדבריו ואינו מחזיק טובה לעצמו) while at the same time listening and adding (שומע ומוסיף), making his teacher wiser (המחכים את רבו), and saying a thing in the name of him who said it (והאומר דבר בשם אומרו). Why? Because saying something in the name of him who said it "brings deliverance forever" (מביא גאלה לעולם).

---

17. Bregman 1999, 38. This means that sayings could be placed in the mouth of God, despite it having "little or no scriptural basis" (cf. Bregman 1999, 28–29). Cf. the argument in Stern 1995, 189, that attributions in the Babylonian Talmud "works in two complementary directions: on the one hand, the Bavli's redactors claim that attributed sayings were actually earlier, anonymous traditions; whilst on the other hand, they claim that collective, anonymous traditions were actually authored by identifiable individual figures."

18. Cf. Bregman 1999, 36n45.

19. All translations of Sifre Deut. are from Hammer 1986.

Quite in contrast to the Mesopotamian trajectory but in line with the author function of Foucault, however, the view that names provide "fences" around discourses sometimes had as a consequence that these discourses were expected to be coherent. Possibly a result of the influence of Greek notions of intellectual property, there was thus sometimes a need to resolve contradictions within the sayings of a single rabbi (see, e.g., b. 'Abod. Zar. 48b; b. Qidd. 25b). However, it can also be observed that in occasions where a teaching of one rabbi overlapped extensively with another so that no substantial difference was observed between them, a switch of attribution could sometimes occur (see, e.g., b. Šebu. 19a; in contrast to b. Mo'ed Qaṭ 24b above).[20] This underscores, then, that the primary focus is nonetheless still the *tradition*, not the *name*, and innovations that moved "outside the fences" could therefore have severe consequences: "Whoever says something which he has not heard from his master causes the divine presence to depart from Israel" (b. Ber. 27b).

Distribution and Tradition

In sum, if seeing rabbis as authors in some sense, the act of naming shows clear overlaps more with the Mesopotamian, distributive author concept and less with the Greek concept, although influence from the latter can also be found. More specifically, attributions did not primarily specify individual originators of sayings but placed rabbis in a longer chain of transmission so that the name could refer to a disciple or a teacher, to an earlier authority or a later tradent. Seen in light of the fence and chain metaphors, most attributions are thus best seen as indicating that new sayings were to be understood as extensions of earlier traditions, which, in turn, could very well be anonymous (see, e.g., the notion of having heard from teachers or not heard from teachers in b. Yebam. 67a; b. Sukkah 27b–28a; m. Neg. 9:3),[21] although ultimately stretching back through the biblical authors to Moses at Sinai (cf. b. Bek. 58a; b. Ḥul. 137b; or b. Ḥul. 137a). Sometimes, it is argued that authorship in the rabbinic literature is therefore to be understood as "collective," but the notion of a "distributive" author concept captures the dynamic in a better way. Ultimately, what is found is an author concept with variously related agents that interact with a *tradition* (not primarily with each other) in a transmission process across both space and time.

---

20. See also the brief discussion in Ben-Eliyahu, Cohn, and Millar 2012, 15.

21. A similar dynamic is probably also found in, e.g., 1 Cor 7:10, 25.

On Who Wrote the Bible

If the author concept implicit in rabbinic literature is best understood as distributive, what implications does this have for how the authors of biblical texts were described? Are there, for example, any signs of the *Echtheitskritik* that was recurrently employed in early Christian tradition?

Anchored in Moses

The first observation to be made is the one already mentioned above—namely, that the entire tradition, both written and oral, is believed to go back to Moses:

> R. Levi b. Hama says further in the name of R. Simeon b. Lakish: "What is the meaning of the verse: 'And I will give thee the tables of stone, and the Torah and the commandment, which I have written that thou mayest teach them?' (Exod 24:12) 'Tables of stone': these are the ten commandments (לחת אלו עשרת הדברות); 'Torah': this is the Mikra (תורה זה מקרא); 'the commandment': this is the Mishnah (והמצוה זו משנה); 'which I have written': these are the Prophets and the Writings (אשר כתבתי אלו נביאים וכתובים); 'that thou mayest teach them': this is the Talmud (להורותם זה תלמוד). It teaches [us] that *all these things were given to Moses on Sinai* (מלמד שכולם נתנו למשה מסיני)." (b. Ber. 5a)[22]

This statement aligns well with what has already been observed and provides a framework in relation to which rabbinic discussions of biblical authorship can be understood.[23] Relating it all to Moses does not mean, however, that discussions about who penned the Torah or other passages of Scripture are therefore nonexistent, only that they need to be seen within this dynamic, unless there are good reasons not to.

Consider, for example, Sifre Deut. 1, where the paratextual framing of parts of the Torah and the prophetic writings is discussed and claims are made that the paratexts should not be interpreted as if the named individual wrote only the sections framed by them:

> "These are the words which Moses spoke" (Deut 1:1): Did Moses prophesy nothing but these words? Did he not write (כתב) the

---

22. Slight modification of the Epstein 1935 translation (emphasis added).
23. Stern 1995, 188.

266

entire Torah, as it is said, "And Moses wrote this Torah" (Deut 31:19)? Why then does the verse state, "These are the words which Moses spoke?" Hence we learn that they were words of rebuke, as it is said . . . (Sifre Deut. 1; cf. also Sifre Deut. 2)

The passage then continues with similar discussions about the prophet Amos in Amos 3:1 (contrasted with Amos 1:1 and words of rebuke in Amos 4:1), the prophet Jeremiah in Jer 40:4 (contrasted with 51:64 and a rebuke in Jer 30:5–7), David in 2 Sam 23:1 (contrasted with 2 Sam 23:2 and the rebuke in v. 6), and Solomon in Eccl 1:1 (contrasted with the notion of him writing "three books" and the rebuke in Eccl 1:4–7).[24]

The Divine-Human Interaction

Even if Sifre Deut. 1 argues that Moses wrote the entire Torah, the way the divine-human interaction—the foundation for the writing—worked was not always agreed on. Consider b. Sanh. 99a in contrast to b. Meg. 31b:

> Another [*baraita*] taught: "Because he hath despised the word of the Lord"—this refers to him who maintains that the Torah is not from Heaven. And even if he asserts that the whole Torah is from Heaven, excepting a particular verse, which [he maintains] was not uttered by God *but by Moses himself,* he is included in "because he hath despised the word of the Lord." (b. Sanh. 99a)

> Abaye said: "This rule was laid down only for the curses in Leviticus, but in the curses in Deuteronomy a break may be made. What is the reason?—In the former Israel are addressed in the plural number and Moses uttered them *on behalf of the Almighty* [lit. 'from the mouth of,' מפי]; in the latter Israel are addressed in the singular, and Moses uttered them *in his own name* [מפי עצמו]." (b. Meg. 31b)

---

24. Given the notion of writing in these examples, the claim by Jacobs 1991, 40, based on a discussion of b. B. Bat. 14b–15a, that a distinction is made in rabbinic literature between "authorship" and "recording in writing" is not accurate. On this passage, see further below.

Evidently, the agency of Moses could be variously interpreted,[25] although it would likely miss the point to interpret b. Meg. 31b as arguing that the whole Torah had not been given by God. Both passages would likely agree that Moses did not go outside of the received tradition when preserving it, although they construct his creative space in contrasting ways.

In fact, this dynamic was discussed already by Philo. In his work on the decalogue, for example, he states that

> some of them [the laws] God judged fit to deliver in His own person alone without employing any other, and some through His prophet Moses whom He chose as all of men the best suited to be the revealer of verities [cf. 1.175: "selected for his merits and having filled him with the divine spirit, chose him to be the interpreter of His sacred utterances"]. Now we find that those which He gave in His own person and by His own mouth alone include both laws and heads summarizing the particular laws, but those in which He spoke through the prophet all belong to the former class. (*Decalogue* 1.18–19)[26]

The Ten Commandments are thus seen as "summaries of the special laws" (*Decalogue* 1.154), proclaimed by God through a miraculous voice and without any intermediary (1.32–35, 44–49; cf. Josephus *Ant.* 3.89, who nevertheless stresses that Moses was the one responsible for these laws; 3.273).

Non-Mosaic Verses

This said, there were also occasionally discussions about whether or not Moses wrote about his own death.[27] In b. Makk. 11a, for example, R. Judah claims that Joshua would have written the final eight verses in the Pentateuch, while R. Nehemiah disagrees and thinks that Joshua wrote the passages on the cities of refuge. Notable, however, is that this discussion is not based on any methodological *Echtheitskritik* but

---

25. Cf. Bregman 1999, 27–29, 27n4.

26. Translation from Colson 1937. On the relation between divine and human agency in this passage, see especially Bingham 2016. See also the discussion in Wyrick 2004, 82–83, who notes that "no matter how much Philo wishes to equate Moses with Greek philosophers, he always avoids granting him an unqualified role in composition" (83).

27. Cf. also Ibn Ezra's comments on Deut 34:1.

focuses on the proper interpretation of Josh 24:26, which is understood to claim that Joshua wrote words in the Torah.

Another example of where authorship issues are raised based on internal observations is the discussions surrounding ולא יסף ("he added no more") in Deut 5:22, which seems to have been interpreted by some as indicating that only the Ten Commandments were authored by God:

> Rabbi Matna and Rabbi Samuel bar Nahman said, "By rights they should recite the verses of the Ten Commandments every day. And why do they not do so? On account of the claims of the heretics (מינים). So that people should not have any cause to say that only these [Ten Commandments] were given to Moses on Mount Sinai." (y. Ber. 1:5; cf. b. Ber. 12a)[28]

The idea of these heretics, or "Minim," is thus that God only spoke the Ten Commandments in direct communication, a view somewhat overlapping with Philo above,[29] and it has been argued that the Minim may have been Hellenistic Jews acquainted with Greek philosophical thought.[30]

There is thus some contrast between how issues of composition are discussed in the rabbinic literature and what was seen in the Greek trajectory, and this can be seen clearly if contrasting the passage in b. Makk. with the way the issue was debated in a Christian context, where the claim of Porphyry that the "law" was a forgery of Ezra the

---

28. Translation from Zahavy 1989.

29. The issue is not straightforward, however, since Philo also states in *Spec. Laws* 1.64–65 that a prophet is "possessed by God" and "will suddenly appear and give prophetic oracles," and when this is done, "nothing of what he says will be his own, for he that is truly under the control of divine inspiration has no power of apprehension when he speaks but serves as the channel for the insistent words of Another's prompting." Philo then comments on the special laws by recurrently referring to Moses as the one responsible for the writing (see, e.g., "according to Moses," κατὰ Μωυσέα, in 4.176; cf. 4.180). This is also the case in the recurrent asking "why" Moses says something in *QG*, which "in its form resembles Hellenistic commentaries on the Homeric poems" (Marcus 1953, ix). See, e.g., *QG* 1.1: "Why, when he (Moses) considers and reflects on the creation of the world, does he say, 'This is the book of the coming into being of heaven and earth when they came into being'? . . . the expression, 'this is the book of coming into being' is meant to indicate a supposed book which contains the creation of the world and an intimation of the truth about the creation of the world."

30. See Vermes 1968, who also provides a more detailed discussion. Relevant here may be that the "problem" is solved in a different way in, for example, Codex Neofiti 1, Targum Pseudo-Jonathan, and Targum Onkelos, who all have "he ceased not" (ולא סוף/אסף) instead of "he added no more" (ולא יסף).

scribe (quoted in length by Macarius Magnes, writing in the fifth century CE) needed to be countered:[31]

> [3.1] "But it seems to me that the statement 'If you believed in Moses, you would believe in me, for he spoke concerning me' (John 5:46) is a great load of stupidity. After all, nothing written by Moses is extant. For all his writings are said to have been burned in the temple, while whatever is written under the name of Moses was written *1,180 years after Moses's death*, by Esdras and those of his circle (2 Esd 14:21–48). But even if one grants that the writing is by Moses, it is not possible to show that the Christ is anywhere called 'God,' or 'God-*Logos*,' or 'Creator.' For that matter, who said Christ would be crucified?" . . . [10.2] But while you say that the writings of Moses suffered during the Captivity and were rewritten inaccurately by Esdras, it will be found that they were rewritten with complete accuracy. For it was not that one person spoke to Esdras and another to Moses, but the same Spirit taught both and dictated the same things clearly to both. (Macarius Magnes, *Apocriticus* 3:3.1, 10.2)[32]

Another example would be the Pseudo-Clementine Homilies (see esp. 2.38 and 3.47–52), where it is claimed that parts of the Torah of Moses had been falsified by others:

> [2.38] The prophet Moses having by the order of God handed over the law with the elucidations to seventy chosen (men) that they might prepare those who were willing among the people, after a short time the law was committed to writing. At the same time some false pericopes intruded into it. . . .

---

31. A similar discussion concerned parts of the 'book' called *Daniel*, where Porphyry argues that the 'book' cannot have been written by the prophet, since it was clearly written in Greek (it has wordplays only appropriate in the Greek), and Jerome answers (by referring to Eusebius, Apollinaris, and other Christian writers) that there are indeed parts of the 'book' written in Greek (Sus and Bel) but that these should not be included in the Hebrew text—thus marked with a critical symbol and not seen as having Scriptural status (on this, see also Speyer 1971, 152–55). A discussion is also found in, e.g., Origen's *Ep. Afr.*, where he arrives at an opposite conclusion.

32. Translation from Schott and Edwards 2015 (emphasis added). On the story that recounts how Ezra copied Mosaic works after their destruction at the time of the Babylonian captivity and the potential problems this story may have caused in relation to Mosaic authorship, see Wyrick 2004, 281–343, esp. 337–43.

3.47 Moses delivered the law of God orally to seventy wise men that it might be handed down and administered in continuous sequence. After the death of Moses, however, it was written not by Moses himself, but by an unknown person; for in the law it is said: *And Moses died and was buried. . . .* But how, after his death, could Moses write: *And Moses died . . . ?* And as in the time after Moses—about five hundred or more years later—it was found in the temple that had lately been built, after a further five hundred years it was carried away, and in the reign of Nebuchadnezzar it was consumed by fire. And since it was written in the time after Moses and was repeatedly destroyed, the wisdom of Moses is shown in this; *for he did not commit it to writing,* foreseeing its disappearance. But those who wrote the law, since they did not foresee its destruction, *are convicted of ignorance and were not prophets.* [48] In the providence of God a pericope was handed down intact in the written law so that it might indicate with certainty which of the things written are true and which false. . . . [49] In the conclusion of the first book of the law it stands written: *A ruler shall not fail from Judah nor a leader from his loins, until he come whose it is, and him will the Gentiles expect. . . .* If he accepts this doctrine, then will he learn which portions of the Scriptures answer to the truth and which are false. [50] And Peter said: "That what is true is mixed with what is false."[33]

Clearly, nothing of this kind is found in the rabbinic sources, thus pointing to the dominance of the Mesopotamian rather than the Greek trajectory. However, there are some exceptions, and notably, these exceptions feature Greek vocabulary. More specifically, when occasionally discussing possible "forgery," it is noteworthy that the Greek πλαστόν is used

---

33. Translation from Schneemelcher 1992, 533–34. Peter then points to passages describing God as grieving, repenting, being jealous, hardening hearts, making blind, and so on that are claimed to be opposite to the truth about God. On possible datings of the Pseudo-Clementine Homilies, see Shuve 2008. Interestingly, in *Contestatio*, it is recounted how to properly handle the 'books' containing the preachings of Peter. They are to be transmitted unaltered and with great care by a trustworthy, believing Christian who had passed a six-year-long evaluation before being trusted with more than one 'book.' No copies were allowed, and if any falsehoods were detected, the 'books' were to be returned. This, then, provides the foundation to an exhortation by James in *Cont.* 5:1–2: "Hear me, brethren and fellow-servants. If we pass on the books to all without discrimination and if they are falsified by audacious men and are spoiled by interpretations—as indeed you have heard that some have already done—then it will come to pass that even those who earnestly seek the truth will always be led into error" (Schneemelcher 1992, 496).

(פלסטיר, פלסטון).[34] In Yal. Shim. on Jer. 321, for example, the claim of a Roman judge—"As far as I can see, your Law is a forgery" (מה שאני רואה את תורתכם פלסטרין הוא; cf. also Num. Rab. 8:4)—is met with the statement that not a word in the Torah is a forgery or a lie, but it is all truth (אין דבר בתורה פלסטרין ולא דבר של שקר אלא כל התורה היא אמת).

Writing without Distinction

Before turning to the 'book' called *Isaiah*, a final passage needs to be considered that relates to the idea that later tradents could be named as "fences" around written tradition—the section on authors in b. B. Bat. 14b–15a, where it is said that David incorporated the work of ten earlier elders in the 'book' of Psalms and, interestingly, that Moses incorporated the prophecies of Balaam, which are, as in Josephus, singled out as a distinct section of the Torah in both b. B. Bat. 14b–15a and y. Sot. 5:6, the latter saying that "Moses wrote five books of the Torah and then he went back and wrote the pericope of Balak and Balaam (פרשת בלק ובלעם), and [at the end], he wrote the book of Job."[35] Notably, although b. B. Bat. 14b–15a is among the most often quoted passages when discussing the authorship of biblical literature,[36] it is quite an exception if seen in the rabbinic literature as a whole.[37] Although biblical 'books' are here related to authors, these authors do not play a large role in the interpretation of the texts, and even in light of what has been noted about Moses above, it needs to be concluded that in general, the rabbis show very little interest in who wrote their Scriptures.[38]

Further underscoring this observation is also that the context in which this passage occurs in b. B. Bat. is an odd one—it is found in an

---

34. So Bregman 1999, 28, 28n6. This is not always the case, however. In Sifre Deut. 26, for example, Moses and David are recounted to have asked that their transgressions be recorded, and in the case of Moses, it is "so that people will not say, 'Moses seems to have falsified the Torah,' or 'said something he had not been commanded to say'" (cf. Lev. Rab. 31:4, where the transgressions are specified in relation to why Moses did not enter the land, with God saying, "By your life! I shall write down that it was only because of the water," חייך שאני כותב שלא היתה אלא על המים). For the plausibility that Jewish communities in late antiquity Palestine were bilingual, see Ben-Eliyahu, Cohn, and Millar 2012, 7.

35. All translations of the Jerusalem Talmud are from Neusner 2010 unless stated otherwise. Cf. Jacobs 1991, 38. Ultimately, then, even when discussing divine-human interaction, the basic view is still that Moses wrote the Pentateuch; the issue was simply if he made anything up on his own (cf. Jacobs 1991, 35).

36. On the possible dating of this text to around 200 CE, see Graves 2015, 118, 118n9.

37. So also Graves 2015, 120.

38. Cf. Jacobs 1991, 32.

272

"off-hand manner"[39] following a discussion of the division of property (see b. B. Bat. 12b), which then led to a section on whether or not it was possible to divide a scroll containing sacred writings (כתבי הקודש) if two people had inherited it (b. B. Bat. 13b). The rabbis answered the question in the negative and continued to discuss what to do if there were two scrolls. This then led to a discussion about the proper way of combining biblical 'books' (Should the Torah, the prophets, and the writings be on separate scrolls, or should they be juxtaposed? Should each 'book' have its own scroll? How much space should be between the 'books'? Should the scrolls be wound around one or two poles?) and a discussion about their size and storage followed by the often quoted passage.

Turning, then, to this passage, it is structured as the following. First, the order of the 'books' is discussed, providing rationales for the somewhat peculiar placing of the 'book' called *Isaiah after* the 'books' called *Jeremiah* and *Ezekiel*, despite the fact that "Isaiah preceded Jeremiah and Ezekiel"—that is, the *prophet* Isaiah (b. B. Bat. 14b). The sequence is explained as the result of an overarching movement from destruction to desolation: *Jeremiah* is entirely destruction, *Ezekiel* begins with destruction but ends with consolation, and *Isaiah* is entirely consolation.[40] Similar explanations are given for the order of the writings, and then comes the section about who wrote the 'books':

> Who wrote the Scriptures?—Moses wrote his book (כתב ספרו), the portion of Balaam, and (the book of) Job. Joshua wrote his book (כתב ספרו) and [the last] eight verses of the Torah. Samuel wrote his book (כתב ספרו), the book of Judges, and (the book of) Ruth. David wrote the book of Psalms (כתב ספר תהלים), by means of (על ידי) ten elders, namely, Adam—the first—Melchizedek, Abraham, Moses, Heman, Yeduthun, Asaph, and the three sons of Korah. Jeremiah wrote his book (כתב ספרו), the book of Kings, and Lamentations. Hezekiah and his colleagues wrote (כתבו) (mnemonic: ימשק) Isaiah, Proverbs, the Song of Songs, and Ecclesiastes. The men of the Great Assembly wrote (כתבו) (mnemonic: קנדג) Ezekiel, the Twelve Prophets, Daniel, and the scroll of Esther.

---

39. Jacobs 1991, 32.

40. Krochmal 1851 (cf. Jacobs 1991, 35; Blenkinsopp 2002a, 61) made the interesting suggestion that *Isaiah* was placed after *Jeremiah* and *Ezekiel* because the early rabbis recognized that in the 'book' called *Isaiah*, there is material belonging to the period of the Twelve and later even than Ezekiel, but since there is not much to further substantiate this, the issue cannot be properly settled (on this, see also, e.g., Pesiq. Rab Kah. 16:10 below, "On Isaianic Authorship").

Ezra wrote his book (כתב ספרו) and the genealogies of the book of Chronicles up to his own time. (b. B. Bat. 14b–15a)[41]

Given what has been said about rabbinic conceptions of authorship, it should come as no surprise that this text does not distinguish between originators and later tradents.[42] It sometimes includes both "first ones" and "subsequent ones" and sometimes only "subsequent ones." As an example of the first, consider that David is described as the one "writing" the 'book' of Psalms, but he does so by the agency (על ידי)[43] of several other named and unnamed individuals. As an example of the second, see how the authors of *Ezekiel*, the twelve, *Daniel*, and *Esther* are described to be anonymous members of a collective. Moreover, as the passage continues, more authors are mentioned. Not only did Joshua finish the Torah, but Eleazar and Pinehas completed the 'book' called *Joshua*, while Gad and Nathan completed the 'books' called *Samuel*. Similarly, Ethan the Ezrahite is suggested to be added to the authors of the Psalms, and Mosaic authorship is discussed in relation to the 'book' called *Job* based on lexical links.[44] Evidently, then, "individualism in

---

41. Epstein 1935, slightly modified.

42. This is often considered a problem. See, e.g., van der Toorn 2007, 45, who first notes that there is an "absence of a clear distinction between author and editor" but then goes on to say that when it is said that Hezekiah wrote the 'book' called *Isaiah*, it is "clearly not implying authorship." Thus van der Toorn concludes that the sages "were not concerned with authorship at all." Wyrick 2004 also discusses this issue, similarly noting that "*katav* as used in Baba Bathra does not appear to distinguish between authorship and scribal activity" (41), and argues that כתב is best understood as "copied out"—neither "to author" nor "to edit" (51–58)—but then still curiously argues that David, for example, is *not* seen as a composer in this text, thus assuming an implicit upholding of the distinction anyway. This is also the case when he concludes that the passage "is concerned with the written transmission of biblical books *rather* than with composition" (73; emphasis added). Graves 2015, 124n36, is, then, more to the point when simply translating it as "to put into writing."

43. For a discussion of this usage, see Wyrick 2004, 29–30, who observes that the common interpretation as "including in it," which probably derives from Rashi—who states that "he wrote in it the words which the ten elders composed"—is unlikely, since it is not a translation as much as an explanation. Based on its usage in m. Šeqal. 6–7, he instead suggests the translation "on behalf of": "David does for the ten elders what they could not do for themselves" (30). The issue need not be settled here—there are also plenty of examples of the meaning of "by means of" (as translated above)—since the main point that the agency of David is explicitly intertwined with the agency of several other named and unnamed individuals still stands.

44. However, it is also to be noted that a case is also made for them to be contemporaries. The need for the "first one" to be contemporary with the events recorded is thus underlined (cf. Wyrick 2004, 26) and points to a similar negotiation of trajectories as was found in the Uruk tablet from the second century BCE discussed above (see "Hellenistic Negotiations," chapter 4).

composition"[45] is not in focus here, and it can also be seen that a divine-human interaction is placed at the center ("the Holy One, blessed be He, dictated, Moses repeated, and Moses wrote," b. B. Bat. 15a).

Interesting is also that this tradition would later be modified in a way that clarified possible confusion about the authorship of the 'book' called *Isaiah*.[46] In the Masoretic Masorah, there are three instances where alternate versions of this passage are found, and these three also overlap with the Genizah fragment T-S D1.37. Following the statement that Jeremiah wrote "his own book, Kings, and Lamentations" and preceding the writings of the members of the Great Assembly, these three texts relate the penning of the 'books' called *Isaiah*, Proverbs, Song of Songs, and Ecclesiastes not to Hezekiah and his men but to the prophet Isaiah himself:

B. B. BAT. 14B	T-S D1.37[47]	GINSBURG 175/177/180[48]
חזקיה וסיעתו כתבו ישעיה משלי שיר השירים וקהלת	ישעיה כתב ספרו וספר משלי ושיר השירים וקהלת	ישעיה(ו) כתב ספרו ומשלי ושיר השירים וקהלת
Hezekiah and his colleagues wrote *Isaiah*, Proverbs, the Song of Songs, and Ecclesiastes.	*Isaiah wrote his 'book,'* the 'book' of Proverbs, the Song of Songs, and Ecclesiastes.	*Isaiah wrote his 'book,'* Proverbs, the Song of Songs, and Ecclesiastes.

Rather than concluding that while b. B. Bat. 14b primarily features scribal activity and T-S D1.37 and the Masorah speak of authorship,[49] it could be suggested that the altered tradition may have been the result of a more rigid author concept, where it was not as acceptable to relate to Hezekiah as an author in the same sense as Moses, David, and others.

---

45. Wyrick 2004, 79.

46. About relative dating, see provisionally Phillips 2016. As described by Graves 2015, 124, there is also an even later tradition in Rashi and the Tosafot that claim that since the prophet Isaiah died so unexpectedly (see the martyr tradition above, "Filling Biographical Blanks," chapter 12), he did not have time to write down his 'book' (prophets were believed to write down their 'books' just before they died), and since Hezekiah was also dead at this point, it was the generation after Hezekiah—i.e., the "colleagues" referred to in b. B. Bat. 14b—that wrote the 'book.'

47. The manuscript can be seen online here: https://dlmenetwork.org/library/catalog/cambridge_genizah-16400.

48. Quoted from Ginsburg 1880, 338, 339, 340.

49. So Phillips 2016.

The interesting combination of both traditions in *Sifte Yeshenim* may provide further support for such a conclusion.[50] This would thus mean that while b. B. Bat. 14b operates more within a Mesopotamian distributive author concept where all agents were seen as tradents, the Geniza fragment and the Masorah proceed from a distinction between author and editor and change the text accordingly.

On Isaianic Authorship

Turning now more directly to how the relation between the prophet Isaiah and the 'book' called *Isaiah* is conceived of, a survey of the way quotes from the 'book' called *Isaiah* are introduced will be provided as a basis for the discussion.[51]

Framing Quotations

It was noted above that although rabbis are frequently mentioned in rabbinic literature, the literature is itself anonymous and thus possible to understand as overlapping with the Mesopotamian trajectory, although also influenced by the Greek one. In fact, this anonymity is also reflected in the way quotations from the 'book' called *Isaiah* are introduced: the overwhelming majority of quotes do not mention the prophet Isaiah at all. More specifically, about 44 percent of the occurrences do not have any particular demarcation.[52] These quotes are simply either part of a teaching of a rabbi, as in y. Taʻan 2:1 ("It has been taught in the name of R. Meir [תני בשם רבי מאיר]: 'For behold, the Lord is coming forth out of his place . . .' [Isa 26:21]"; cf. y. Taʻan. 4:1; y. Yebam. 16:3; y. Ketub. 11:3; y. Soṭah 7:5; 9:3),[53] or part of a series of quotes (see, e.g., Mek. Rab Ish. 75:1).[54] Only slightly more frequent are the instances where a quotation from the 'book' called *Isaiah* is declared as part of "scripture." This is regularly spelled out with either אמר ("it is said"; e.g., שנאמר) or

---

50. See Phillips 2016, n12.

51. The following overview and calculations are based on the anthology of quotations from the 'book' called *Isaiah* in Neusner 2007a and Neusner 2007b.

52. Around 1,100 quotations out of 2,500 (the figures have been rounded off).

53. Such formulations need not always be including a commentary on the passage, hence seemingly attributing the biblical passage as a saying of the named rabbi (cf. also Stern 1994, 45n37, on y. ʼAbot 4:19).

54. There are also some examples of more lengthy expositions and commentaries, such as Lev. Rab. 34:11–16 on Isa 58:7–14; Pesiq. Rab Kah. 15:7–11 on Isa 1:21–27; or Pesiq. Rab Kah. 19:1–6 on Isa 51:12–16.

כתב ("it is written"; e.g., כתיב) and frames 50 percent of all quotes from *Isaiah*.[55] It can thus be concluded that in the overwhelming majority of instances, the prophet Isaiah is nowhere to be found. He is completely marginalized in the interpretive process. This is an important observation that provides a framework for the discussion of the remaining cases, which will take up more space below.

Of the remaining 6 percent of occurrences, parts of the 'book' *Isaiah* are associated with God (around twenty times), the Holy Spirit (see, e.g., b. Pesaḥ 117a), Zion (see Lam. Rab. 91:1; b. Ber. 32b), Hezekiah (e.g., y. Sanh. 10:1), Isaac (Gen. Rab. 67:5), Sanherib (Lev. Rab. 7:6), the prophet Beeri (Lev. Rab. 6:6; 15:2), Israel (Pesiq. Rab Kah. 6:2; Cant. Rab. 4:5), Jacob (Pesiq. Rab Kah. 17:3; Cant. Rab. 4:1), Jerusalem (Pesiq. Rab Kah. 20:7), the Messiah (Cant. Rab. 30:4), or even unspecified prophets in the age to come (Cant. Rab. 4:5). There is thus ample examples of where voices other than the prophet Isaiah's are identified in the 'book' called *Isaiah*,[56] although this does not detract from the general view that the prophet Isaiah is nevertheless speaking in the (whole) 'book,'[57] and to underscore this conclusion is the fact that about a hundred quotes are introduced by explicitly naming the prophet.

The Prophet Said

Turning to these explicit frames, the first set of texts introduce a quote simply as "Isaiah said," "called," or "spoke" (see, e.g., Sifre Deut. 28; y. Ber. 5:1; Gen. Rab. 41:3; 42:3; Pesiq. Rab Kah. 12:21; 16:4; Cant. Rab. 52:1; Lam. Rab. 1:1; 36:2; 124:1; 131:1; b. Mak. 24a). Sometimes, it is mentioned that Isaiah was a prophet (Esth. Rab. 1:23.2; cf. b. Mak. 10b, where the 'book' is counted as "from the prophets," מן הנביאים), and other times, reference is made only to the "prophet" (Lev. Rab. 5:5; b. Sanh. 94a–94b; 105a; Lam. Rab. 47:1; cf. b. Ketub. 8b).[58] That references to "Isaiah" most often imply the prophet and not always the 'book' can be seen in relation to three texts: the first is b. Ta'an 29a, where the prophet Isaiah is mentioned as lamenting (ועליהן קונן ישעיהו הנביא; cf. b. Ḥag 14a); the second is an extended demarcation speaking about "the prophet Isaiah, peace be upon him" (Mek.

---

55. Around 1,200 quotations out of 2,500.

56. On this, see also Mastnjak 2020, 63, who mentions the passage dealing with the authorship of Isa 8:19–20 in relation to the prophet Beeri, which will be expanded on further below.

57. Cf. Graves 2015, 133.

58. Cf. the discussion in Tov 2019.

Rab Ish. 25:1, ‏ישעיהו הנביא עליו השלום‎);[59] and the third gives the prophet Isaiah agency (not seldom by means of the expression ‏על ידי‎ ; see Lam. Rab. 142:1). An additional example is found in Sifre Deut. 27:3, where Isa 49:5 is understood as spoken by the prophet Isaiah: "Isaiah called himself a servant, as it is said . . . [quoting Isa 49:5], and the Holy One, blessed be He, called him a servant, as it is said . . . [quoting Isa 20:3]." That it is ultimately God who speaks *through* the prophet is only occasionally made explicit, however. Apart from the just mentioned quotation, the clearest occurrence may be Cant. Rab. 12:2: "R. Isaac said, this is why he criticized them *by the agency of* Isaiah, as it is said" (‏אמר רבי יצחק זה הוא שמקנתרן על ידי ישעיהו שנאמר‎).

More extended introductions are also sometimes found, such as the one in Pesiq. Rab Kah. 13:2: "Two men, Solomon and Isaiah—said Rabbi Yudan—prophesied against scorn of God. Solomon said . . . (Prov 1:22). Isaiah said . . . (Isa 28:22)."[60] Another example, which overlaps with more expansive narratives about the prophet Isaiah (see "Filling Biographical Blanks," chapter 12), is from Cant. Rab. 6:1, where it is said that

> none among my sons rejoiced more than Isaiah, but because he said: "And I dwell in the midst of a people of unclean lips" (Isa 6:5). God said to him: "Isaiah, you can say of yourself 'Because I am a man of unclean lips' (6:5), but can you say 'And in the midst of a people of unclean lips I dwell?' (6:6)." Note what is written there: "Then flew to me one of the seraphim with a glowing stone in his hand." (Isa 6:6)[61]

Rabbi Isaiah

Next is a set of texts where the relation between the 'book' called *Isaiah* and the prophet is understood along the lines of the rabbinic understanding of tradition sketched above. A couple of examples will paint the picture.

---

59. All texts and translations of Mekhilta de-Rabbi Ishmael are from Lauterbach 2004.

60. All translations from Pesiq. Rab Kah. are from Braude 2002. The work was likely composed in the fifth century CE (along with Genesis Rabba and Leviticus Rabba) following the redaction of the Jerusalem Talmud (Braude 2002, xiii). On the attribution of the work to Rabbi Kahana, see lxxxviii–lxxxix.

61. Cf. Sawyer 2018, 4, who speaks of a "legend that Isaiah was rebuked by God for calling his people 'unclean.'"

First are texts like b. Sanh. 99b that frame quotes from the 'book' called *Isaiah* as belonging to the "tradition" (ועליו מפורש בקבלה, "concerning him it is spelled out in tradition") or introducing the prophet Isaiah as someone who explains or interprets (פרש) tradition (Sifre Num. 112:2, בא ישעיה ופירש בקבלה; cf. Gen. Rab. 69:5, בא ישעיה ופרש). Sometimes, this is portrayed as in line with earlier tradition, such as Sifre Deut. 306, where the prophet Isaiah follows Moses and provides further support (בא ישעיה וסמך לדבר); other times, it is stated that the prophet Isaiah revokes the decrees of Moses (see b. Mak. 24a, where Isa 27:13 is said to revoke Lev 26:38).[62]

Second, it can be observed that in several instances, a prophet living chronologically later is placed in continuity with the 'book' called *Isaiah*. In Lam. Rab. 36:2, it is said, "And so you find that all the severe prophecies which Jeremiah prophesied against Israel Isaiah anticipated healed" (וכן את מוצא שכל נבואות קשות שנתנבא ירמיה על ישראל הקדים ישעיה ורפאן),[63] and the passage then continues by putting quotes from the 'books' called *Jeremiah* and Lamentations in dialogue with quotes from the 'book' called *Isaiah*. The passage thus indicates that the 'book' called *Isaiah* was seen as related to the prophet Isaiah in its entirety and completed before the time of Jeremiah, who is seen as the author of both the 'books' called *Jeremiah* and Lamentations. This relation between the prophets Isaiah and Jeremiah is also found in Lam. Rab. 52:1, where 2 Chr 34:22 is interpreted as speaking of Jeremiah, "who said to Josiah: 'I have this tradition from my teacher, Isaiah'" (שאמר ליאשיהו כך מקבלני מישעיה רבי), and then quotes from Isa 19:2.

Traditions are also in play in a rabbinic attempt to find an interpretation (פשרה) of a perceived disagreement between Hezekiah and the prophet Isaiah, "two righteous men" (שני צדיקים), about whom should visit the other (b. Ber. 10a). As the narrative unfolds, a solution is found in the recounting of how suffering is brought upon Hezekiah (הביא יסורים על חזקיהו), and so the prophet Isaiah is commanded to go to him. A dialogue ensues in which the impending death of Hezekiah (which has consequences for his share in the world-to-come) is explained as a punishment for not being fruitful and multiplying. Hezekiah then

---

62. The passage in b. Mak. 24a states, "Our Rabbi Moses pronounced four [adverse] sentences on Israel, but four prophets came and revoked them (וביטלום)," and then places the word of Moses (משה אמר) against the word of the prophet Isaiah (בא ישעיהו ואמר). The three other prophets annulling Mosaic decrees are Amos, Jeremiah, and Ezekiel.

63. Translations of Lam. Rab. are from Freedman and Simon 1939a, unless stated otherwise.

attempts to solve this error by asking for Isaiah's daughter's hand in marriage, but Isaiah declines and makes clear that judgment is already passed. The door being closed, Hezekiah first asks for Isaiah to leave ("son of Amoz, finish your prophecy and go," בן אמוץ כלה נבואתך וצא) and then chooses to rely on a different tradition, one received from the house of his father's father (כך מקובלני מבית אבי אבא), saying that even if a sharp sword rests upon someone's neck, one can always pray for mercy.

The notion of an Isaianic tradition found in the 'book' called *Isaiah*, where the prophet Isaiah plays the role of its rabbi, is also found in two texts recounting events surrounding the prophet Daniel. In the first, Cant. Rab. 38:2, the Israelites have gathered around Daniel complaining that all of the bad prophecies of Jeremiah had been fulfilled but not the good ones. Daniel's response is interesting. He asks them to bring the *scroll of Isaiah* and starts reading from it up until Isa 21:1. The passage then continues with a rabbinic discussion of Isa 21:1–5, which is, in turn, followed by a discussion of Isa 47:1–4, where the prophet Isaiah returns by means of a reference to a "prophet," and Ps 75:9 is given as a reason for why he spites Babylon (הוא שהנביא מקנתר ואומר).

The second text, from Cant. Rab. 96:1, reads as follows:

Hananiah, Mishael, and Azariah, who were the three from Israel, went and determined to resist and did not worship the idol. They went to Daniel and said to him: "Our rabbi Daniel, Nebuchadnezzar has set up an idol and chosen three from each nation, and we are the three chosen from the whole of Israel. What have you got to say to us? Shall we bow down to it or not?" He said to them: "Lo, there is a prophet available to you, go to him!" They went their way forthwith to Ezekiel. They spoke to him as they had spoken to Daniel: "Shall we bow down to it or not?" He said to them: "I have indeed received the tradition from Isaiah, my rabbi: 'Hide yourself for a little moment, until the indignation is past' (Isa 26:20)."[64]

Evidently, these texts cast the prophet Isaiah as a link in a longer chain in transmission, indicating that the author concept of the rabbis writing these stories has been retrojected onto the 'book' called *Isaiah*.

---

64. Translation from Neusner 2007b, 451.

Non-Isaianic Verses

As seen above in the discussion of b. B. Bat. 14b–15a, the rabbinic literature did not identify only one person as the "author" of the 'book' called *Isaiah*. Nonetheless, the passages surveyed above show that they saw the prophet as the dominant voice in the 'book,' with his name providing the fence around it, prohibiting other texts from being attached to it. There is one notable exception to this, however. In Lev. Rab. 6:6 and a parallel passage in Lev. Rab. 15:2, the voice of Isa 8:19–20 is claimed to be a prophet named Beeri (father of the prophet Hosea; cf. Hos 1:1):

> R. Simon said: "Beeri spoke prophetically only two verses, and since they were not sufficient to constitute a [separate] book, they were attached to [the Book of] Isaiah. The verses are these: '*When they shall say,*' etc., and its companion verse." (Lev. Rab. 6:6; emphasis in the original)

> R. Aḥa said: "Even the Holy Spirit resting on the prophets does so by weight, one prophet speaking one book of prophecy and another speaking two books." R. Simon said: "Two things [i.e., verses] did Beeri speak as a prophet, and because they were not sufficient to form a book they were included in the Book of Isaiah, namely, '*And whey they shall say unto you: Seek unto the ghosts and the familiar spirits,*' etc., and its companion verse." (Lev. Rab. 15:2; emphasis in the original)

Evidently, Isa 8:19–20 is viewed as added to the 'book' called *Isaiah* despite not belonging to it, but notable is that the discussion does not focus on intellectual property, as in Josephus's discussion of the words of Jethro and Balaam, for example (see above, "Claiming the Whole Book," chapter 11). This can be further seen in a passage discussing the main recipients of Isa 40:

> *Your God will keep saying* (Isa 40:1) [that He will comfort all succeeding generations]. Rabbi Ḥanina bar Papa and Rabbi Simon gave different reasons for the phrasing of this verse. According to Rabbi Ḥanina bar Papa, Israel said to Isaiah: "Our teacher Isaiah, are we to suppose that you came to comfort only the generation in whose days the Temple was destroyed?" He replied: "I came to comfort all generations. Hence Scripture does not say, 'God said,'

but *Your God will keep saying.*" On the other hand, according to Rabbi Simon, Israel said to Isaiah: "Our teacher Isaiah, perhaps all the things you say *you make up out of your own head?*" Isaiah replied: "Scripture does not say 'Your God [spoke to me alone],' but says *Your God will keep saying* [so that all the world will hear. Concurring with Rabbi Simon], Rabbi Ḥanina bar Rabbi Abba pointed out that *Your God will keep saying* occurs eight times in Scripture [i.e., in the 'book' *Isaiah*] to prefigure the coming of eight Prophets, namely, Joel, Amos, Zephaniah, Haggai, Zechariah, Malachi, Ezekiel, and Jeremiah, each of whom would prophesy [concerning what was to happen] after the destruction of the Temple." (Pesiq. Rab Kah. 16:10)

The idea that the 'book' called *Isaiah* would be the work of the prophet Isaiah's imagination is refuted by referring to subsequent named tradents of tradition anchored in the prophet Isaiah (cf. Lam. Rab. 24:2). There are, however, occasions where a passage from the 'book' called *Isaiah* is explained by referring to circumstances in which the prophet Isaiah would have uttered the words or to who the prophet Isaiah was. In Pesiq. Rab Kah. 14:3, for example, the sharp words in Isa 1:10 is explained as voiced in that way *because* the prophet Isaiah was a "city man" (בן מדינה) from Jerusalem, in contrast to Jeremiah, who was a "countryman" (עירוני) from Anathoth and therefore reprimanded Israel in a kindly way. Another example, also from Pesiq. Rab Kah., explains Isa 1:21 as voiced by the prophet Isaiah *because* he saw Israel in their prosperity (15:6, ישעיה ראה אותן בפחזן; cf. Lam. Rab. 35:1, ישעיה ראה אותם בפחזזותם). These examples are not very numerous, however. Nor are they as developed as they were in Jerome, for example (see "Jerome and *Hebraica Veritas*," chapter 12).

Rewriting Stories

A final way in which the rabbinic literature interacts with the 'book' called *Isaiah* is by means of rewritten stories. It has already been noted above that the interaction between the prophet Isaiah and Hezekiah was subject to rabbinic commentary and that the biography of the prophet Isaiah had been expanded on, especially in relation to his death (see "Filling Biographical Blanks," chapter 12). Apart from those examples, there are several instances where other stories found in the 'book' called *Isaiah* are expanded upon. Two examples will be given here.

Consider first the way Isa 6 is treated in Lev. Rab. 10:2 (cf. Pesiq. Rab Kah. 16:4). Here, Ps 45:7 is interpreted as speaking of the prophet Isaiah and expanded on as the following:

> Isaiah said: "I was strolling in my study house and I heard the voice of the Holy One [blessed be He] saying: *'Whom shall I send? And who will go for us'* (Isa 6:8) . . . *And I said, 'Here I am! Send me!'* (Isa 6:8)." [God] said to him: "Isaiah, my children are depraved, they are troublesome. If you agree to be humiliated and beaten up by my children, you may go on my mission, but if not, you may not go on my mission." He said to him: "[I agree] on that condition: *I gave my back to the smiters, and my cheeks to them who pulled out the hair* (Isa 50:6). Am I not worthy of going on a mission to your children?" He said to him: "Isaiah, *'You love righteousness.'* You love to show my children to be righteous. *'You hate wickedness.'* You hate declaring them to be guilty. *'Therefore, God, your God has anointed you with the oil of gladness above your fellows'* (Ps 45:7)." What is the meaning of "above your fellows"? He said to him: "By your life! In the case of all other prophets, they each received the power of prophecy from another prophet. . . . But you (received the gift of prophecy) directly from the mouth of the Holy One, blessed be He: *'The spirit of the Lord God is upon me, because the Lord has anointed me'* (Isa 61:1). By your life! All the other prophets prophecy prophecies without repetition, but you (will prophecy) words of consolation that are (even) repeated." (Lev. Rab. 10:2)[65]

Several aspects are noteworthy. First is that the prophet Isaiah is strolling in a study house (בית תלמודי) when he hears the divine voice, underscoring the notion of him being learned and literate. Second is that he is depicted as the one speaking in the first-person narratives in Isa 50:6 and 61:1—that is, implicating his presence throughout the whole 'book' called *Isaiah*. Third, he is elevated above all other prophets (including Moses?) by means of having received the power of prophecy directly from the deity.

A second example is from a discussion concerning a habit of writing מרבה ("abundance") with a *mem sofit* (מרבה) in Isa 9:6. More specifically, Ruth Rab. 64:1 applies Isa 9:5–6 to Hezekiah, and the explanation given to the *mem sofit* is that Hezekiah had been intended to be the

---

65. Translation from Neusner 2007a, 286–87, slightly modified. The passage then quotes from Isa 51:9; 51:17; 61:10; 51:12; and 40:1, where words are repeated.

Messiah but was "shut up from that honor because he had not sung God's praises."[66] The thread is picked up in Cant. Rab. 52:3, where 2 Chr 32:25 is explained as indicating that Hezekiah was too proud to sing a song (אלא גבה לבו מלומר שירה):

> Isaiah came to Hezekiah and his court and said to them: *"Sing to the Lord"* (Is 12:5–6). . . . They said to him: "Why should we?" "For he has done gloriously." They said: "This already has been 'made known in all the world.'" Said R. Abba b. Kahana: "Said Hezekiah: 'The Torah with which I am occupied makes atonement for the song [that I have not sung].'" Said R. Levi: "Said Hezekiah: 'Why are we supposed to recite the miracles and mighty acts of the Holy One, blessed be He? This is already known from one end of the world to the other!" (Cant. Rab. 52:3)[67]

Throughout the rabbinic literature, the interactions between the prophet Isaiah and Hezekiah take up much of the narrative space given to Isaiah, as was also the case in the Hebrew Bible. It is thus not necessary to conclude from these examples that there is a clear interest in painting an author portrait in any Greek sense. The underlying dynamic is instead related to the interpretation and explanation of curiosities in the biblical text. Moreover, when seen in light of the overall interaction with the 'book' called *Isaiah* in the rabbinic material noted above, these biographical sketches cannot be judged as more than marginal features.

THE ANONYMOUS TRADENT

In the end, this chapter has shown that in the rabbinic literature, the pervasive picture is a far-reaching lack of interest in the *prophet* while quoting recurrently from the 'book.' Put differently, the 'book' is most often quoted anonymously, as part of a larger tradition (this was the case in 94 percent of all surveyed quotes), and when Isaiah is named, it is primarily as the main *voice* of the 'book' called *Isaiah*—not as someone whose intentions needed to be taken into consideration in the interpretive activity.

If related to the Mesopotamian and Greek trajectories, it can be suggested that the relation between the prophet and the 'book' has been

---

66. Translation from Neusner 2007b, 413.
67. Translation from Neusner 2007b, 451.

constructed in a way that the distributive Mesopotamian author concept emanates as the dominant one, although somewhat transformed in light of the Greek emphasis on *origins* and *authority*. Few instances of questions of intent and intellectual property were found. Instead, the prophet Isaiah was constructed as a fixed point in the stream of tradition flowing first through Moses. Although he was seen as a "first one" in the composition of the 'book,' more agents were mentioned as intertwined in its subsequent transmission.

PART VI

THE BOOK "OF" ISAIAH

Chapter 14

THE STORY ONCE AGAIN

How did Isaiah become an author? Throughout this book, it has been shown that the answer to such a question depends, to a high degree, on what one means with "author." As a historically contingent concept, it not only changes over time but also takes different shapes in different contexts at any given time. Authorship is and has always been under constant negotiation.

At the outset of this study, this was exemplified by how Barthes, despite formulating an appealing theory that attempted to decentralize the author in the interpretive work, did not succeed in taming the public interest in a Romantic author. On the contrary, both views continue to coexist, and the naming of authors in relation to "their" works remains a widely established paratextual practice. Designated as such, one of the main functions of these paratexts is to tame the text by suggesting interpretive ways through it. At the same time, an act of taming is also performed by the reader—s/he interprets the paratext in line with her/his own author constructs. A reading of paratexts without historical awareness, then, leads to inevitable anachronisms.

In relation to the 'book' called *Isaiah*, it has been seen that such anachronisms have since long marked the interpretation of paratexts like Isa 1:1. When read in light of modern ideas of authorship, it is often understood as added by scribes as an attempt to either use the great, ancient prophet Isaiah to create legitimacy for the text by rooting it in his authority or claim that the prophet was in some way responsible for the contents of the 'book.' Throughout this study, both approaches have been shown to somewhat miss the point. At the very least, it has hopefully become clear that the very common claim—most often stated as a fact—that "up until the development of the historical-critical method . . . [t]he 8th century Isaiah was considered *unisono* to be the author who had received from God the ability to foresee the future of

Jerusalem, Judah, and the nations" (with the only "exception" being Abraham ibn Ezra)[1] is far too generalized, since it supposes that prior to the eighth century CE, there was only *one* author concept that *everyone* adhered to. This book has painted quite a different picture.

Rehearsing Native Concepts

In the search for native author concepts to understand the anonymous origins of the 'book' called *Isaiah* and its subsequent transmission as the "vision" that the prophet Isaiah "saw," two contrasting trajectories were identified.

The first, called a "Mesopotamian" trajectory, was shown to be in some contrast to current-day concepts. It was almost as if looking at a situation where Barthes had succeeded in killing off the author—authors were not named at all in most of the transmission and were never considered important in the interpretive task. The few texts that spoke on the origins of works—such as the *Exaltation of Inanna*, the *Erra Epic*, the *Epic of Gilgamesh*, or *Enuma Elish*—showed that these texts emanated from an interaction between a divine agent and a human agent, with the human—the "first one" in a chain of transmission—quickly sidelined. Being but one link in a longer chain, for the text to survive, it had to attract new tradents—"subsequent ones"—who kept the text relevant throughout time. Although texts were eventually starting to attract names in the context of Ashurbanipal's libraries, this change in paratextual practice did not fundamentally alter the author concept, as was seen in the analysis of the "Catalogue of Texts and Authors." As in the earlier examples, texts were claimed to be not composed by a single originator but channeled through numerous agents over time. Put differently, authorship was not understood as a process of writing that resulted in a product that was the property of the creative genius who had penned it so that it needed to be transmitted in a way faithful to the intentions of that genius. Instead, subsequent agents were as legitimate as tradents as the "first one." Consequently, when names were added, these names could belong to either the "first one" or one of the "subsequent ones." Name tags served as fences around discourses. They did not point to their origin.

---

1. Berges 2010b, 576. This is agreed on by both mainstream scholars and scholars who hold more conservative views of the origins of the 'book' called *Isaiah* (see, e.g., Schultz 2015, 7; Dillard and Longman 1994, 272).

The situation was quite different in the Greek trajectory, however. Sharing with the Mesopotamian trajectory the idea that a divine-human interaction was often found at the very core of the composition of texts, an interest in origins together with a competitive focus of the individual poets created a dynamic in which a slightly different author concept was constructed. In contrast to the Mesopotamian trajectory, texts were rarely anonymous, and the name attached to a composition was treated as significant to the interpretive activity. More specifically, to understand a work, one needed to read it in relation to its originator, which lead to a clear hierarchy between the one penning the work and the ones transmitting it. The name tag identified the founder of specific discourses as individuals, and there was a clear interest in author biographies.

A consequence of this dynamic that placed specific individuals in authoritative positions in relation to the texts was also that texts were seen as the intellectual property of their authors—using parts of someone's work without giving proper credit was considered literary theft. To ensure a truthful relation between the author and her/his text, early grammarians therefore started to develop methods to assess attributions—*Echtheitskritik*—and as they did so, they recognized that there were both unintentional and intentional errors. Pseudepigraphy was born, and a lot of different explanations were given as to the reasons why.

Although presented as distinct, it was then shown that the two trajectories would have interacted with each other in numerous ways across time. Focusing especially on Hellenistic times, clear traces of negotiation were found.

How Isaiah Became an Author

Turning to the 'book' called *Isaiah* proper, it was argued that its construction of authorship could be understood as completely within the Mesopotamian trajectory. The transmission of the 'book' was described as having a divine-human interaction at its center, where an unnamed "first one" was marginalized in favor of new, authorized (still anonymous) "subsequent ones" who were to faithfully transmit the revelation (Isa 8:16–20). Moreover, texts that featured writing never explicitly said that a "first one" wrote down anything of substantial length, only that he performed symbolic actions (Isa 8:1–2; 30:8–11). In fact, as far as the prophet Isaiah goes, he was only named in the 'book' as a *character* in three different narrative sections (Isa 7; 20; 36–39) and only explicitly related to prophetic speech as such a character in chapters 36–39. Indeed, such a dynamic was expected in light of what was known about prophets and prophecy in the ancient Near East.

It could also be observed that the 'book' continuously intertwined more voices with a "first one" and that these voices were constructed as legitimized tradents—"subsequent ones"—not by means of deriving prophetic authority from a "first one" but by means of divine sanction and by being tradents of authoritative revelation (Isa 48:16; 50:4–9). This was seen in particular in a recurrent contrast between past and present. In the past, YHWH had spoken through the (anonymous) "first one," and since these words had now come true (Isa 48:3–8), the people should listen to YHWH's new revelation through "subsequent ones." Ultimately, this all pointed to a centralization of revelation at the expense of the tradents, who were sidelined in the transmission. Remaining anonymous, they did not lend authority *to* the text but derived authority *from* it.

Throughout this process of transmission, paratexts were added, and some would eventually include the name of the "first one." As in the Mesopotamian trajectory, where a similar development was noted, this did not change the author dynamic. In fact, it was observed that the very vocabulary used in Isa 1:1 (חזון, חזה) had clear overlaps with the stories about authorship in the Mesopotamian trajectory, thus constructing the prophet Isaiah as a first recipient and tradent rather than indicating that the visions would in some sense be "his." An effect of the paratexts' addition was, though, that the prophet Isaiah became more intrinsically related to *written* transmission of prophecy, and thus it would not take long until the first explicit notion of the prophet as a writer would show up. More specifically, in 2 Chr 26:22; 32:32, he was claimed to be the writer of history—that is, of interpretations of past, present, and future with special focus on contemporary significance and the way they are interconnected.

Following the construction of the prophet Isaiah as literate in 2 Chr, indications of both the Mesopotamian and Greek trajectories were seen when turning to the Dead Sea Scrolls. On the one hand, "subsequent voices" could still be seamlessly intertwined into the text of the 'book' now called *Isaiah* (4Q176), and the prophet Isaiah was still not considered important in the interpretive activity. This thus pointed to a continuing influence of the Mesopotamian trajectory. On the other hand, the voice of the prophet Isaiah had now colonized all parts of the 'book,' a 'book' that he was, moreover, understood as having written down (CD 4 13–14; cf. CD 19 7). This pointed to Greek influence.

Leaving Qumran and turning to Josephus, the first unambiguous signs of Greek readings of the 'book' called *Isaiah* were found. To Josephus, everything in the 'book' was the words of an eighth-century prophet named Isaiah, who had foretold events that would occur many years after the prophet himself was dead (*Ant.* 10.35; 11.5–7; 13.64–71). One reason why Josephus assumed this to be the case was found in the way he constructed himself as a Greek author. In his works, he consciously and recurrently reflected on his choices and uncovered his intentions through metatexts. He gave credit to sources where needed and praised Moses for not claiming prophecies for himself that belonged to somebody else (*Ant.* 3.73–74; 4.158). Without closer consideration, he thus assumed that the biblical "authors" were authors in the same sense that he was, and so he shaped the author role of Isaiah in his own image.

More traces of negotiation were then found in the New Testament, where the prophet Isaiah was also seen as the main voice in the 'book' and where an early attestation was found of somebody asking not only *what* the prophet said but *why* he said it (John 12:38–41). This thus pointed to Greek influence, but marks of the Mesopotamian trajectory were also found. The gospels were all originally anonymous writings, and they did not always seem to bother about "correct attribution"— texts from both Isa 40:3 and Mal 3:1 were quoted as written in *Isaiah* in Mark 1:2–3, for example. As the Greek trajectory grew to become more dominant, however, both these aspects would be reframed: names were added to the gospels, and problematic attributions were dealt with.

The last steps toward a more thoroughly Greek understanding of the relation between the prophet and the 'book' were taken by early Christian writers such as Origen, Eusebius, and Jerome. Their use of *Echtheitskritik*, combined with changing notions of authorial intent and a stress on coming as close to the original wording of the prophet as possible, resulted in a conviction that to properly interpret *the 'book,'* one now needed to properly understand *the prophet*. As Isaiah emerged more fully as a Greek author, the biographical blanks of his story were also filled.

That the story told in this book is not one where a Mesopotamian trajectory would eventually be marginalized in favor of a Greek one but rather one where the two would be continuously negotiated over time was seen in the discussion of rabbinic literature. While many Christian authors leaned toward the Greek trajectory, albeit without ever making the prophet Isaiah the sole center of interpretation—authorship had instead ascended so that God was the "true" author, the one guaranteeing consistency—Jewish authors would tend to lean more toward the Mesopotamian trajectory, constructing the prophet Isaiah as a link in a long chain that was ultimately anchored in the divine-human encounter between YHWH and Moses. Further indications of this influence were seen in the fact that several individuals could be associated with the transmission of a specific 'book' (b. B. Bat. 14b–15a), thus overlapping with the idea of a "first one" and "subsequent ones." A distinction between originator and imitator was thus not upheld in any consistent way, although it was also seen that when named, the prophet Isaiah was generally considered to be the main voice in the 'book.' Since this 'book' was conceived of in terms of a discourse related to its "founder," Greek influence could be identified. Ultimately, this underscored that aspects of both trajectories are likely to coexist over time, with the center of gravity constructed in different ways by different communities.

CHAPTER 15

LOOKING AHEAD

The story I have tried to tell in this book, a story whose main contours have been rehearsed in the previous chapter, has some possible implications for how biblical scholars think about biblical texts and their authors that I would like to briefly consider in this final chapter.

The first aspect relates to my goals outlined in the preface: I wanted to show that biblical scholars have had anachronistic tendencies when reconstructing ancient authors and that the ancient world did not have only one author concept. Indeed, it has been one of the main contentions of this book that it is not possible to speak of a monolithic, cross-cultural "ancient" conception of authorship that contrasts with the "modern one." Instead, a lot of variation and negotiation has been found, both through time and across contemporaneous contexts. Hopefully, my outlining of the Mesopotamian and Greek trajectories has been both precise enough and sufficiently generalized to inspire a renewed discussion on biblical "authors."

The second aspect relates to my argument that when understood in light of the Mesopotamian trajectory, names added to compositions were not to indicate *origins*, nor to provide texts with *authority*, despite the latter being often repeated in biblical studies. Both these aspects rather belong to the Greek trajectory, while in the Mesopotamian trajectory, the named individual is conceptualized as *one (of many) in a chain of transmission*—not necessarily even the "first one" in that chain. Material both older and younger than that named individual could therefore be found in the transmitted tradition. If I am correct, there is thus a need to somewhat rethink matters of textual and authorial authority. It is also important to unpack further the specifics of the negotiations in the Second Temple period by, for example, asking questions about how different *kinds* of authority are constructed (e.g., scriptural, ethical, prophetic, etc.) and in what ways authority is distributed across the agents that are involved with the transmission of written tradition.

Another consequence of this line of inquiry is that the addition of names did not emanate as a practice in the Mesopotamian trajectory because of any *horror vacui* but as a way of demarcating discourses from one another. I have argued that these paratexts are best seen as fences that separate neighboring gardens—not as signs that display the names of their owners. If I am correct, the notion of Greek pseudepigraphy is thus rarely appropriate as a framework for understanding Hebrew Bible paratexts, since it imports author constructs foreign to the work and risks misconstruing its claims. Ultimately, not all who tag a text do so because they want to write "in someone else's name." This said, it was nonetheless clear that when the Mesopotamian and Greek trajectories met, anonymous texts would eventually become a problem—some of the paratexts found in the Hebrew Bible are thus likely to be seen as the result of attempts to solve this problem.

All this points to what I see as one of the biggest challenges facing scholars dealing with authorship in antiquity: to start treating the anonymity of "originators" in textual production and transmission not as a problem to be solved but as something to cherish and explore more fully. Indeed, there have been a lot of important steps taken in this direction long before I wrote this book, and we have indeed come a long way from the genesis of critical research, where names like "Deutero-Isaiah" were created to "preserve a prestigious and important text like Isa 40–55 from the fate of redactional anonymity, which would have condemned it exegetically to meaninglessness,"[1] as one scholar put it. But how can native author constructs be taken into fuller consideration? My thesis is that if we would take seriously the fact that no conceptual distinction is made between the "first one" and the "subsequent ones" in terms of authority and legitimacy so that the modern-day categories of "original author" and "subsequent editor" are not relevant, the very notion of the Mesopotamian texts being "anonymous" would be reframed, since the names of tradents—scribes—are found everywhere. But while our paratextual practices are aimed at creating a fixed relationship between names and texts, the Mesopotamian transmission constantly sidelined the names. Since originals were not more valued than copies, the names of scribes were only indications of temporary channels of a vast and ever-flowing stream of tradition.

---

1. Joachim Becker, quoted in Berges 2010a, 558.

In the end, I have only scratched the surface of this fascinating dynamic by focusing on the relation between the prophet Isaiah and the 'book' that is called *Isaiah*. If considered successful, there are many more stories to write.

The argument I have made in this book also points to the need for a paratextual sensitivity that has often been lacking in critical research. More specifically, I have suggested that there is a double act of taming related to paratexts. On the one hand, paratexts have been added to tame the *text*, to suggest certain ways in which it is supposed to be read. Prefaces, superscriptions, epilogues, marginal notes, and even the layout of the text all serve this purpose. On the other hand, it is clear that when a paratext has become a part of the transmission of the text, it is also (often unintentionally) tamed by the reader—it is interpreted in light of paratextual practices that are sometimes anachronistic. A fence becomes a property sign, a psalm becomes a preface, and so on. It is therefore essential for any study of the composition and transmission of biblical texts to take paratextual activity into consideration, and as manuscripts are becoming increasingly available, we are indeed presented with a rich source for inquiries about reading habits and the transmission of texts that can help us contextualize author concepts and paratextual functions.

In the end, I hope that this study has been successful in showing that to speak of Proto-, Deutero-, and/or Trito-Isaiah—despite the fact that most would agree that far more agents were involved—is to introduce anachronistic stories about textual composition and transmission that should be seen as very problematic in a field of study that aims for historical sensitivity. More specifically, it imports Romantic and Greek notions of authorship into a text formed within a Mesopotamian trajectory and so potentially confuses the understanding of crucial passages in the 'book' itself. Despite aiming for the opposite, the 'book' ultimately becomes detached from the context in which it was composed, used, and interpreted. Because as it turns out, the prophet Isaiah has always been an author. Just not in the way we thought.

BIBLIOGRAPHY

Ackroyd, Peter R. 1963. "A Note on Isaiah 2:1." *ZAW* 134/3, 320–321.

———. 1978. "Isaiah I–XII: Presentation of a Prophet," pages 16–48 in John Emerton (ed.), *Congress Volume Göttingen 1977*. VTSup 29. Leiden: Brill.

———. 1982. "Isaiah 36–39: Structure and Function," pages 3–21 in W. C. Delsman et al. (eds.), *Von Kanaan bis Kerala: Festschrift L. P. M. van der Ploeg*. AOAT 211. Neukirchen-Vluyn: Neukirchener Verlag.

Allegro, John M. (ed.). 1968. *Qumran Cave 4.I*. DJD V. Oxford: Clarendon.

Almagor, Eran. 2016. "'This Is What Herodotus Relates': The Presence of Herodotus' Histories in Josephus' Writings," pages 81–100 in Jessica Priestley and Vasiliki Zali (eds.), *Brill's Companion to the Reception of Herodotus in Antiquity and Beyond*. Brill's Companions to Classical Reception 6. Leiden: Brill.

Anderson, R. T. 1960. "Was Isaiah a Scribe?" *JBL* 79, 57–58.

Attinger, Pascal. 2019. "Innana B (Ninmešara) (4.7.2)." *Zenodo*, 1–12. https://doi.org/10.5281/zenodo.2667767.

Aurelius, Erik. 2014. "Bundestheologie im Alten Testament: Ein Buch von Lothar Perlitt und seine Folgen." *ZTK* 111/4, 357–373.

Badura, Christian, and Melanie Möller. 2019. "Authorship in Classical Rome," pages 64–80 in Ingo Berensmeyer, Gert Buelens, and Barysa Demoor (eds.), *The Cambridge Handbook of Literary Authorship*. Cambridge: Cambridge University Press.

Baillet, Maurice, Jozef T. Milik, and Roland de Vaux (eds.). 1962. *Les "Petites Grottes" de Qumran: Textes*. DJD III. Oxford: Clarendon.

Baltzer, Klaus. 2001. *Deutero-Isaiah*. Translated by Margaret Kohl. Hermeneia. Minneapolis, MN: Fortress.

Barclay, John. 2016. "Against Apion," pages 69–74 in Honora Howell Chapman and Zuleika Rodgers (eds.), *A Companion to Josephus*. Oxford: Wiley-Blackwell.

Bardtke, Hans. 1953. "Die Parascheneinteilung der Jesajarolle I," pages 33–75 in Horst Kusch (ed.), *Festschrift Franz Dornseiff zum 65. Geburtstag*. Leipzig: VEB Bibliographisches Institut.

Baron, Sabrina Alcorn, Eric N. Lindquist, and Eleanor F. Shevlin (eds.). 2007. *Agent of Change: Print Culture Studies after Elizabeth L. Eisenstein*. Massachusetts: University of Massachusetts Press.

Barthélemy, Dominique, and Jozef T. Milik (eds.). 1955. *Qumran Cave 1.* DJD I. Oxford: Clarendon.

Barthes, Roland. 1967. "The Death of the Author." *Aspen* 5–6. https://www.ubu.com/aspen/aspen5and6/.

———. 1968. "La mort de l'auteur." *Manteia* 5, 1–10.

———. 1974. *S/Z: An Essay.* Translated by Richard Miller. New York: Farrar, Straus and Giroux.

———. 1977. "The Death of the Author," pages 142–148 in Stephen Heath (trans.), *Image–Music–Text.* London: Fontana.

Barton, John. 1986. *Oracles of God: Perceptions of Ancient Prophecy in Israel after the Exile.* Oxford: Oxford University Press.

Bauckham, R. J. 1998. *The Fate of the Dead.* NovTSup 93. Leiden: Brill.

Beale, G. K. 2015. "'Isaiah the Prophet Said': The Authorship of Isaiah Reexamined in the Light of Early Jewish and Christian Writings," pages 81–113 in Daniel I. Block and Richard L. Schultz (eds.), *Bind Up the Testimony: Explorations in the Genesis of the Book of Isaiah.* Peabody, MA: Hendrickson.

Beaton, Richard. 2005. "Isaiah in Matthew's Gospel," pages 63–78 in Steve Moyise and Maarten J. J. Menken (eds.), *Isaiah in the New Testament: The New Testament and the Scriptures of Israel.* London: T&T Clark.

Becker, Joachim. 1968. *Isaias: Der Prophet und sein Buch.* Stuttgarter Bibelstudien 30. Stuttgart: Katholisches Bibelwerk.

Becker, Uwe. 2020. "The Book of Isaiah: Its Composition History," pages 37–56 in Lena-Sofia Tiemeyer (ed.), *The Oxford Handbook of Isaiah.* Oxford: Oxford University Press.

Beecroft, Alexander. 2010. *Authorship and Cultural Identity in Early Greece and China: Patterns of Literary Circulation.* Cambridge: Cambridge University Press.

Beentjes, Pancratius C. 1997. *The Book of Ben Sira in Hebrew: A Text Edition of All Extant Hebrew Manuscripts and a Synopsis of All Parallel Hebrew Ben Sira Texts.* Brill: Leiden.

———. 2010. "Isaiah in the Book of Chronicles," pages 15–24 in Michaël N. van der Meer et al. (eds.), *Isaiah in Context: Studies in Honour of Arie van der Kooij on the Occasion of His Sixty-Fifth Birthday.* VTSup 138. Leiden: Brill.

Begg, C. T. 1988. "The 'Classical Prophets' in Josephus' Antiquities." *LS* 13, 341–357.

Ben-Eliyahu, Eyal, Yehudah Cohn, and Fergus Millar. 2012. *Handbook of Jewish Literature from Late Antiquity, 135–700 CE.* Oxford: Oxford University Press.

Bennett, Andrew. 2005. *The Author.* New York: Routledge.

Benoit, P., J. T. Milik, and Roland de Vaux (eds.). 1961. *Les Grottes de Murabba'ât*. DJD II. Oxford: Clarendon.

Ben Zvi, Ehud. 2011. "Introduction," pages 1–12 in Ehud Ben Zvi and Diana V. Edelman (eds.), *What Was Authoritative for Chronicles?* Winona Lake, IN: Eisenbrauns.

Berensmeyer, Ingo, Gert Buelens, and Barysa Demoor. 2019. "Introduction," pages 1–10 in Ingo Berensmeyer, Gert Buelens, and Barysa Demoor (eds.), *The Cambridge Handbook of Literary Authorship*. Cambridge: Cambridge University Press.

Berges, Ulrich F. 2010a. "The Book of Isaiah as Isaiah's Book: The Latest Development in the Research of the Prophets." *OTE* 23/3, 549–573.

———. 2010b. "Farewell to Deutero-Isaiah or Prophecy without a Prophet," pages 575–595 in André Lemaire (ed.), *Congress Volume Ljubljana 2007*. VTSup 133. Leiden: Brill.

———. 2011. "Kollektive Autorschaft im Alten Testament," pages 29–39 in C. Meier and M. Wagner-Egelhaaf (eds.), *Autorschaft. Ikonen-Stile-Institutionen*. Berlin: de Gruyter.

———. 2012a. *The Book of Isaiah: Its Composition and Final Form*. HBM 46. Sheffield, UK: Sheffield Phoenix.

———. 2012b. *Isaiah: The Prophet and His Book*. Sheffield, UK: Sheffield Phoenix.

———. 2015. *Jesaja 49–54*. HThKAT. Freiburg: Herder.

———. 2017. "'Singt dem Herrn ein neues Lied': Zu der Trägerkreisen von Jesajabuch und Psalter," pages 11–33 in Frank-Lothar Hossfeld, Johannes Bremer, and Till Magnus Steiner (eds.), *Trägerkreise in den Psalmen*. BBB 178. Bonn: Bonn University Press.

———. 2020a. *Jesaja 40–48*. HThKAT. Freiburg: Herder.

———. 2020b. "The Servant(s) in Isaiah," pages 318–333 in Lena-Sofia Tiemeyer (ed.), *The Oxford Handbook of Isaiah*. Oxford: Oxford University Press.

Bernhardt, Inez, and Samuel N. Kramer. 1956. "Götter-Hymnen und Kult-Gesänge der Sumererauf zwei Keilschrift- 'Katalogen' in der Hilprecht-Sammlung." *WZJ* 6, 389–395.

Bernheimer, Richard. 1952. "The Martyrdom of Isaiah." *Art Bulletin* 34/1, 19–34.

Bernstein, Moshe J. 1999. "Pseudepigraphy in the Qumran Scrolls: Categories and Functions," pages 1–26 in Esther G. Chazon and Michael E. Stone (eds.), *Pseudepigraphic Perspectives: The Apocrypha and Pseudepigrapha in Light of the Dead Sea Scrolls*. STDJ 31. Leiden: Brill.

Berrin, Shani. 2005. "Qumran Pesharim," pages 110–133 in Matthias Henze (ed.), *Biblical Interpretation at Qumran*. Studies in the Dead Sea Scrolls and Related Literature. Grand Rapids, MI: Eerdmans.

Bertens, Hans. 2019. "Postmodernist Authorship," pages 183–200 in Ingo Berensmeyer, Gert Buelens, and Barysa Demoor (eds.), *The Cambridge Handbook of Literary Authorship*. Cambridge: Cambridge University Press.

Beuken, Willem A. M. 1997. "Isaiah 30: A Prophetic Oracle Transmitted in Two Successive Paradigms," pages 369–397 in Craig C. Broyles and Craig A. Evans (eds.), *Writing & Reading the Scroll of Isaiah: Studies of an Interpretive Tradition*. Vol. 1. VTSup 70/1. Leiden: Brill.

———. 2003. *Jesaja 1–12*. HThKAT. Freiburg: Herder.

———. 2007. *Jesaja 13–27*. HThKAT. Freiburg: Herder.

———. 2010. *Jesaja 28–39*. HThKAT. Freiburg: Herder.

———. 2011. "From Damascus to Mount Zion: A Journey through the Land of the Harvester (Isaiah 17–18)," pages 63–80 in Archibald L. H. M. van Wieringen and Annemarieke van der Woude (eds.), *"Enlarge the Site of Your Tent": The City as Unifying Theme in Isaiah*. OtSt 58. Leiden: Brill.

Biagioli, Mario. 2011. "Genius against Copyright: Revisiting Fichte's *Proof of the Illegality of Reprinting*." *Notre Dame Law Review* 86/5, 1847–1868.

Bingham, D. Jeffrey. 2016. "'We Have the Prophets': Inspiration and the Prophets in Athenagoras of Athens." *ZAC* 20/2, 211–242.

Birdsong, Shelley L. 2020. "The Narratives about Isaiah and Their Relationship with 2 Kings and 2 Chronicles," pages 95–110 in Lena-Sofia Tiemeyer (ed.), *The Oxford Handbook of Isaiah*. Oxford: Oxford University Press.

Black, Jeremy A. 1998. *Reading Sumerian Poetry*. EANES. London: Athlone.

———. 2002. "En-hedu-ana Not the Composer of *The Temple Hymns*." *NABU* 4, 2–4.

Black, Jeremy A., Graham Cunningham, Eleanor Robson, and Gábor Zólyomi. 2004. *The Literature of Ancient Sumer*. Oxford: Oxford University Press.

Blenkinsopp, Joseph. 1974. "Prophecy and Priesthood in Josephus." *JJS* 25, 239–262.

———. 1997. "The Servant and the Servants in Isaiah and the Formation of the Book," pages 155–175 in Craig C. Broyles and Craig A. Evans (eds.), *Writing & Reading the Scroll of Isaiah: Studies of an Interpretive Tradition*. Vol. 1. VTSup 70/1. Leiden: Brill.

———. 2000. *Isaiah 1–39*. AB 19. New York: Doubleday.

———. 2002a. "The Formation of the Hebrew Bible Canon: Isaiah as a Test Case," pages 53–67 in Eugene Ulrich, Lee Martin McDonald, and James A. Sanders (eds.), *The Canon Debate*. Peabody, MA: Hendrickson.

————. 2002b. *Isaiah 40–55*. AB 19A. New York: Doubleday.

————. 2003. *Isaiah 56–66*. AB 19B. New York: Doubleday.

————. 2011. "Ideology and Utopia in 1–2 Chronicles," pages 89–103 in Ehud Ben Zvi and Diana V. Edelman (eds.), *What Was Authoritative for Chronicles?* Winona Lake, IN: Eisenbrauns.

Block, Daniel I., and Richard L. Schultz (eds.). 2015. *Bind Up the Testimony: Explorations in the Genesis of the Book of Isaiah*. Peabody, MA: Hendrickson.

Blum, Rudolf. 1991. *Kallimachos: The Alexandrian Library and the Origins of Bibliography*. Translated by Hans H. Wellisch. Wisconsin: University of Wisconsin Press.

Boda, Mark J. 2006. "Freeing the Burden of Prophecy: *Maśśā'* and the Legitimacy of Prophecy in Zech 9–14." *Biblica* 87/3, 338–357.

————. 2017. "Freeing the Burden of Prophecy: משא and the Legitimacy of Prophecy in Zechariah 9–14," pages 135–152 in *Exploring Zechariah*. Vol. 2: *The Development and Role of Biblical Traditions in Zechariah*. ANEM 17. Atlanta, GA: SBL.

Boehmer, J. 1936. "'Jahwes Lehrlinge' im Buch Jesaja." *AR* 33, 171–175.

Bolin, Thomas M. 2017. *Ecclesiastes and the Riddle of Authorship*. Bible World. New York: Routledge.

Borchardt, Francis. 2017. "What Do You Do When a Text Is Failing? The Letter of Aristeas and the Need for a New Pentateuch." *JSJ* 48, 1–21.

Bourke, Vernon J. 1953. *Saint Augustine: Confessions*. The Fathers of the Church: A New Translation 21. Washington, DC: Catholic University of America Press.

Braude, William G., and Israel J. Kapstein (eds.). 2002. *Pesikta de-Rab Kahana: R. Kahana's Compilation of Discourses for Sabbaths and Festal Days*. JPS Classic Reissues. Philadelphia: Jewish Publication Society of America.

Braun, Roddy. 1986. *1 Chronicles*. WBC 14. Waco, TX: Word.

Bregman, Marc. 1999. "Pseudepigraphy in Rabbinic Literature," pages 27–41 in Esther G. Chazon and Michael E. Stone (eds.), *Pseudepigraphic Perspectives: The Apocrypha and Pseudepigrapha in Light of the Dead Sea Scrolls*. STDJ 31. Leiden: Brill.

Brettler, Marc Zvi. 1995. *The Creation of History in Ancient Israel*. London: Routledge.

Brisch, Nicole. 2010. "A Sumerian Divan: Hymns as a Literary Genre," pages 153–169 in Regine Pruzsinszky and Dahlia Shehata (eds.), *Musiker und Tradierung: Studien zur Rolle von Musikern bei der Verschriftlichung und Tradierung von literarischen Werken*. WOO 8. Berlin: LIT.

Brooke, George J. 1994. "Isaiah 40:3 and the Wilderness Community," pages 117–132 in George J. Brooke and Florentino García Martínez (eds.), *New Qumran Texts and Studies: Proceedings of the First Meeting of the International Organization for Qumran Studies, Paris 1992.* STDJ 15. Leiden: Brill.

———. 1997. "Isaiah in the Pesharim and Other Qumran Texts," pages 609–632 in Craig C. Broyles and Craig A. Evans (eds.), *Writing & Reading the Scroll of Isaiah: Studies of an Interpretive Tradition.* Vol. 2. VTSup 70/2. Leiden: Brill.

———. 2006. "On Isaiah at Qumran," pages 69–85 in Claire Mathews McGinnis and Patricia K. Tull (eds.), *"As Those Who Are Taught": The Interpretation of Isaiah from the LXX to the SBL.* SBLSymp 27. Leiden: Brill.

———. 2020. "Isaiah in the Qumran Scrolls," pages 429–450 in Lena-Sofia Tiemeyer (ed.), *The Oxford Handbook of Isaiah.* Oxford: Oxford University Press.

Brown-deVost, Bronson. 2019. *Commentary and Authority in Mesopotamia and Qumran.* Göttingen: Vandenhoeck & Ruprecht.

Brownlee, W. H. 1962. "The Literary Significance of the Bisection of Isaiah in the Ancient Scroll of Isaiah from Qumran," pages 431–437 in *Proceedings of the 25th Congress of Orientalists.* 2 vols. Moscow: Tzolatel'stvo Vostochnoi Literatary.

Brueggemann, Walter. 1998a. *Isaiah 1–39.* Westminster Bible Companion. Louisville, KY: Westminster John Knox.

———. 1998b. *Isaiah 40–66.* Westminster Bible Companion. Louisville, KY: Westminster John Knox.

Budde, Karl. 1920. "Zwei Beobachtungen zum alten Eingang des Buches Jesaja." *ZAW* 38, 58.

———. 1923. "Über die Schranken, die Jesajas prophetischer Botschaft zu setzen sind." *ZAW* 41, 154–203.

———. 1928. *Jesajas Erleben: Ein gemeinverständliche Auslegung der Denkschrift des Propheten (Kap. 6,1–9,6).* Gotha: Klotz.

Burrows, John, and Hugh Craig. 2019. "Attribution," pages 325–340 in Ingo Berensmeyer, Gert Buelens, and Marysa Demoor (eds.), *The Cambridge Handbook of Literary Authorship.* Cambridge: Cambridge University Press.

Burrows, Millar, John C. Trever, and William H. Brownlee. 1950. *The Dead Sea Scrolls of St. Mark's Monastery.* Vol. 1: *The Isaiah Manuscript and the Habakkuk Commentary.* New Haven: ASOR.

Bury, R. G. (trans.). 1929. *Plato: Timaeus, Critias, Cleitophon, Menexenus, Epistles.* LCL 234. Cambridge, MA: Harvard University Press.

Campbell, Jonathan G. 2004. *The Exegetical Texts.* Companion to the Qumran Scrolls 4. London: T&T Clark.

Cancik-Kirschbaum, Eva, and Klaus Wagensonner. 2017. "Abschrift, Offenbarung, Sukzession: Autoritätsnarrative in der Textkultur

Mesopotamiens," pages 33–53 in Almut-Barbara Renger and Markus Witte (eds.), *Sukzession in Religionen*. Berlin: de Gruyter.

Carr, David M. 2005. *Writing on the Tablet of the Heart: Origins of Scripture and Literature*. Oxford: Oxford University Press.

Cerquiglini, Bernard. 1989. *Éloge de la Variante: Histoire Critique de la Philologie*. Paris: Seuil.

———. 1999. *In Praise of the Variant: A Critical History of Philology*. Translated by Betsy Wing. Re-visions of Culture and Society. Baltimore: John Hopkins University Press.

Charles, R. H. 1900. *The Ascension of Isaiah Translated from the Ethiopic Version*. London: Black.

Charlesworth, James H. 2019. "The Unperceived Continuity of Isaiah," pages 2–33 in James H. Charlesworth (ed.), *The Unperceived Continuity of Isaiah*. London: Bloomsbury T&T Clark.

Cheyne, T. K. 1895. *Introduction to the Book of Isaiah*. London: Adam and Charles Black.

Childs, Brevard S. 1971. "Psalm Titles and Midrashic Exegesis." *JSS* 16/2, 137–150.

———. 2001. *Isaiah: A Commentary*. OTL. Louisville, KY: Westminster John Knox.

———. 2004. *The Struggle to Understand Isaiah as Christian Scripture*. Grand Rapids, MI: Eerdmans.

Civil, Miguel. 1975. "Lexicography," pages 123–158 in Stephen J. Lieberman (ed.), *Sumerological Studies in Honor of Thorkild Jacobsen on His Seventieth Birthday June 7, 1974*. AS 20. Chicago: Oriental Institute of the University of Chicago.

———. 1980. "Les limites de l'information textuelle," pages 225–232 in M.-T. Barrelet (ed.), *L'archéologie de l'Iraq du début de l'époque néolithique à 333 avant notre ère: Perspectives et limites de l'information anthropologique des documents*. Paris: Centre Nationale de la Recherche Scientifique.

Clements, Ronald E. 1980. *Isaiah 1–39*. NCBC. Grand Rapids, MI: Eerdmans.

———. 1982. "The Unity of the Book of Isaiah." *Int* 36/2, 117–129.

———. 1985. "Beyond Tradition History: Deutero-Isaianic Development of First Isaiah's Themes." *JSOT* 31, 95–113.

———. 2000. "The Prophet as an Author: The Case of the Isaiah Memoir," pages 89–103 in Ehud Ben Zvi and Michael H. Floyd (eds.), *Writings and Speech in Israelite and Ancient Near Eastern Prophecy*. SBL SymS 10. Atlanta, GA: SBL.

Cohen, Shaye J. D. 1988. "History and Historiography in the *Against Apion* of Josephus." *History and Theory* 27/4, 1–11.

Collins, Terence. 1993. *The Mantle of Elijah: The Redaction Criticism of the Prophetical Books*. Sheffield, UK: Sheffield Academic.

Colson, F. H. (trans.). 1935. *Philo: On Abraham, on Joseph, on Moses*. LCL 289. Cambridge, MA: Harvard University Press.

Colson, F. H., and G. H. Whitaker (eds.). 1937. *Philo: On the Decalogue and on the Special Laws*. LCL 320. Cambridge, MA: Harvard University Press.

Cook, Johann. 2012. "The Septuagint of Proverbs," pages 87–174 in Johann Cook and Arie van der Kooij (eds.), *Law, Prophets, and Wisdom*. Leuven: Peeters.

Cook, Paul M. 2011. *A Sign and Wonder: The Redactional Formation of Isaiah 18–20*. VTSup 147. Leiden: Brill.

Cross, Frank M. 1953. "The Council of Yahweh in Second Isaiah." *JNES* 12/4, 274–277.

Cross, Frank Moore, David Noel Freedman, and James A. Sanders. 1972. *Scrolls from Qumran Cave I: The Great Isaiah Scroll, the Order of the Community, the Pesher to Habakkuk*. Jerusalem: Albright Institute of Archaeological Research.

Curtis, Edward L., and Albert Alonzo Madsen. 2015. *Chronicles I and II*. Bloomsbury Academic Collections, Biblical Studies: The Hebrew Bible. London: Bloomsbury.

Davage [formerly Willgren], David. 2021a. "A Canon of Psalms in the Dead Sea Scrolls? Revisiting the Qumran Psalms Hypothesis." *BTB* 51/4, 35–44.

———. 2021b. "Paratextual Framings of Psalm 72 and the Shaping of Interpretive Possibilities." *Acta Theologica Supplementum* 32, Transforming Theology and Religion, 345–367.

Davies, Philip R. 1996. "The Audiences of Prophetic Scrolls: Some Suggestions," pages 48–62 in Philip R. Davies and Stephen Breck Reid (eds.), *Prophets and Paradigms: Essays in Honor of Gene M. Tucker*. JSOTSup 229. Sheffield, UK: Sheffield Academic.

———. 2000. "'Pen of Iron, Point of Diamond' (Jer 17:1): Prophecy as Writing," pages 65–81 in Ehud Ben Zvi and Michael H. Floyd (eds.), *Writings and Speech in Israelite and Ancient Near Eastern Prophecy*. SBL SymSer 10. Atlanta, GA: SBL.

———. 2013. "Saul, Hero and Villain," pages 131–140 in Diana V. Edelman and Ehud Ben Zvi (eds.), *Remembering Biblical Figures in the Late Persian and Early Hellenistic Periods: Social Memory and Imagination*. Oxford: Oxford University Press.

Deazley, Ronan. 2004. *On the Origin of the Right to Copy: Charting the Movement of Copyright Law in Eighteenth-Century Britain (1695–1775)*. Oxford: Oxford and Portland Oregon.

Decock, Paul B. 2008. "Jerome's Turn to the Hebraica Veritas and His Rejection of the Traditional View of the Septuagint." *Neot* 42/2, 205–222.

de Grenouillac, Henri. 1930. *Textes Religieux Sumériens du Louvre*. TCL 15, 28. Paris: Geuthner.

Delnero, Paul. 2006. *Variation in Sumerian Literary Compositions: A Case Study Based on the Decad*. PhD diss.: University of Pennsylvania.

———. 2010. "Sumerian Literary Catalogues and the Scribal Curriculum." *ZA* 100, 32–55.

Dillard, Raymond B. 1987. *2 Chronicles*. WBC 15. Waco, TX: Word.

Dillard, Raymond B., and Tremper Longman III. 1994. *An Introduction to the Old Testament*. Grand Rapids, MI: Zondervan.

Dillmann, August. 1898. *Der Prophet Jesaja*. 6th ed. Kurzgefasstes exegetisches Handbuch zum Alten Testament 5. Leipzig: S. Hirzel.

Dods, Marcus. 2017. *The City of God by Saint Augustine*. Overland Park, KS: Digireads.com Publishing.

Duhm, Bernhard. 1892. *Das Buch Jesaja*. HKAT. Göttingen: Vandenhoeck & Ruprecht.

———. 1916. *Israels Propheten*. Tübingen: J. C. B. Mohr.

Duperreault, Danielle. 2013. "The Poetics of History and the Prophecy of Deutero-Isaiah," pages 255–274 in Mark J. Boda and Lissa M. Wray Beal (eds.), *Prophets, Prophecy, and Ancient Israelite Historiography*. Winona Lake, IN: Eisenbrauns.

Durand, J.-M. 1988. *Archives épistolaires de Mari I/1*. Paris: Éditions Recherche sur les civilisations.

Easley, Alexis. 2019. "The Nineteenth Century: Intellectual Property Rights and 'Literary Larceny,'" pages 147–164 in Ingo Berensmeyer, Gert Buelens, and Barysa Demoor (eds.), *The Cambridge Handbook of Literary Authorship*. Cambridge: Cambridge University Press.

Eaton, John H. 1959. "The Origin of the Book of Isaiah." *VT* 9, 138–157.

———. 1982. "The Isaiah Tradition," pages 58–76 in R. Coggins, A. Phillips, and M. Knibb (eds.), *Israel's Prophetic Tradition: Essays in Honour of Peter R. Ackroyd*. Cambridge: Cambridge University Press.

Edelman, Diana V. 2001. "Did Saulide-Davidic Rivalry Resurface in Early Persian Yehud?," pages 69–91 in J. Andrew Dearman and M. Patrick Graham (eds.), *The Land That I Will Show You: Essays on the History and Archaeology of the Ancient Near East in Honor of J. Maxwell Miller*. JSOTSup 343. Sheffield, UK: Sheffield Academic.

Eisenstein, Elizabeth L. 1980. *The Printing Press as an Agent of Change: Communications and Cultural Transformations in Early-Modern Europe*. Cambridge: Cambridge University Press.

————. 2011. *Divine Art, Infernal Machine: The Reception of Printing in the West from First Impressions to the Sens of an Ending*. Philadelphia: University of Pennsylvania Press.

Eissfeldt, Otto. 1960. *Der Beutel der Lebendigen*. Berlin: Akademie-Verlag.

————. 1971. "Die Psalmen als Geschichtsquelle," pages 97–112 in Hans Goedicke (ed.), *Near Eastern Studies in Honor of William Foxwell Albright*. Baltimore: John Hopkins University Press.

Eliot, T. S. 1982. "Tradition and the Individual Talent." *Perspecta: The Yale Architectural Journal* 19, 36–42.

El Mansy, Aliyah. 2020. "Ambi-gui(l)ty: The 'Sin of David' in Post-biblical Tradition and Josephus," pages 120–146 in Erkki Koskenniemi and David Willgren Davage (eds.), *David, Messianism, and Eschatology: Ambiguity in the Reception History of the Book of Psalms in Judaism and Christianity*. Studies in the Reception History of the Bible 9. Åbo: Åbo Akademi University.

Elowsky, Joel C. (ed.). 2013. *Eusebius of Caesarea: Commentary on Isaiah*. Translated by Jonathan Armstrong. Ancient Christian Texts. Downers Grove, IL: IVP Academic.

Epstein, Isadore (trans.). 1935–1952. *The Talmud*. 35 vols. London: Soncino.

Evans, Craig A. 1988. "On the Unity and Parallel Structure of Isaiah." *VT* 38/2, 129–147.

Exum, J. Cheryl. 1981. "Of Broken Pots, Fluttering Birds and Visions in the Night: Extended Simile and Poetic Technique in Isaiah." *CBQ* 43/3, 331–352.

Ezell, Margaret J. M. 2019. "Manuscript and Print Cultures 1500–1700," pages 115–132 in Ingo Berensmeyer, Gert Buelens, and Barysa Demoor (eds.), *The Cambridge Handbook of Literary Authorship*. Cambridge: Cambridge University Press.

Fabry, Heinz-Josef. 2003. "צַר," pages 455–464 in G. Johannes Botterweck, Helmer Ringgren, and Heinz-Josef Fabry (eds.), *TDOT* 12. Translated by Douglas W. Stott. Grand Rapids, MI: Eerdmans.

Feldman, Louis H. 1990. "Prophets and Prophecy in Josephus." *JTS* 41/2, 386–422.

————. 1997. "Josephus' Portrait of Isaiah," pages 583–608 in Craig C. Broyles and Craig A. Evans (eds.), *Writing & Reading the Scroll of Isaiah: Studies of an Interpretive Tradition*. Vol. 2. VTSup 70/2. Leiden: Brill.

Fichte, Johann Gottlieb. 1793. "Beweis der Unrechtmässigkeit des Büchernachdrucks: Ein Räsonnement und eine Parabel." *Berliner Monatsschrift* 21, 443–483.

————. 1846. "Beweis der Unrechtmässigkeit des Büchernachdrucks: Ein Räsonnement und eine Parabel," pages 223–244 in Johann

Gottlieb Fichte (ed.), *Johann Gottlieb Fichte's sämmtliche Werke 3. Populärphilosophische Schriften*. Berlin: Verlag von Veit und Comp.

Fincke, Jeanette C. 2003. "The Babylonian Texts of Nineveh: Report on the British Museum's Ashurbanipal Library Project." *AfO* 50, 111–149.

Fine, Steven. 2010. *Art and Judaism in the Greco-Roman World: Toward a New Jewish Archaeology*. Rev. ed. Cambridge: Cambridge University Press.

Finkel, Irving L. 1988. "Adad-apla-iddina, Esagil-kīn-apli, and the series SA.GIG," pages 143–159 in Erle Leichty, Maria deJ. Ellis, and Pamela Gerardi (eds.), *A Scientific Humanist: Studies in Memory of Abraham Sachs*. Philadelphia: University Museum.

Fishbane, Michael. 1989. *The Garments of Torah: Essays in Biblical Hermeneutics*. Bloomington: Indiana University Press.

Flint, Peter W. 2002. "The Book of Isaiah and the Dead Sea Scrolls," pages 229–251 in Edward D. Herbert and Emanuel Tov (eds.), *The Bible as Book: The Hebrew Bible and the Judaean Desert Discoveries*. London: British Library & Oak Knoll.

Floyd, Michael H. 2002. "The מַשָּׂא (*Maśśā'*) as a Type of Prophetic Book." *JBL* 121/3, 401–422.

———. 2018. "The Meaning of *Maśśā'* as a Prophetic Term in Isaiah." *JHebS* 18/9, 1–31.

Flückiger-Hawker, Esther. 1996. "Der 'Louvre-Katalog' *TCL* 15 28 und sumerische *na-ru$_2$-a*-Kompositionen." *NABU* 4, 105–106.

Fohrer, Georg. 1960. *Das Buch Jesaja*. Züricher Bibelkommentare. Zürich: Zwingli Verlag.

———. 1962. "Jesaja 1 als Zusammenfassung der Verkündigung Jesajas." *ZAW* 74, 251–268.

Foster, Benjamin R. 1991. "On Authorship in Akkadian Literature." *AION* 51, 17–32.

———. 1996. *Before the Muses: An Anthology of Akkadian Literature*. 2nd ed. 2 vols. Bethesda, MD: CDL.

———. 2003. "Epic of Creation (1.111) (*Enūma Elish*)," pages 390–402 in William W. Hallo (ed.), *The Context of Scripture*. Vol. 1: *Canonical Compositions from the Biblical World*. Leiden: Brill.

———. 2016. *The Age of Agade: Inventing Empire in Ancient Mesopotamia*. London: Routledge.

———. 2019. "Authorship in Cuneiform Literature," pages 13–26 in Ingo Berensmeyer, Gert Buelens, and Barysa Demoor (eds.), *The Cambridge Handbook of Literary Authorship*. Cambridge: Cambridge University Press.

Foucault, Michel. 1969. "Qu'est-ce qu'un auteur?" *Bulletin de la Societé française de philosophie* 63/3, 73–104.

———. 1977. "What Is an Author?," pages 113–138 in Donald F. Bouchard (ed.), *Language, Counter-memory, Practice: Selected Essays and Interviews*. Translated by Donald F. Bouchard and Sherry Simon. New York: Cornell University Press.

Fowler, Harold North, and W. R. M. Lamb (trans.). 1925. *Plato: Statesman, Philebus, Ion*. LCL 164. Cambridge, MA: Harvard University Press.

Fox, Michael V. 2000. *Proverbs 1–9*. AB 18a. New York: Doubleday.

Frahm, Eckart. 2011. *Babylonian and Assyrian Text Commentaries: Origins of Interpretation*. Münster: Ugarit-Verlag.

Freedman, David N. 1987. "Headings in the Books of the Eighth-Century Prophets." *AUSS* 25/1, 9–26.

Freedman, H., and Maurice Simon. 1939a. *Midrash Rabbah: Deuteronomy and Lamentations*. London: Soncino.

———. 1939b. *Midrash Rabbah: Leviticus*. London: Soncino.

Fuhs, Hans F. 1978. *Sehen und Schauen: Die Wurzel ḥzh im Alten Orient und im Alten Testament; Ein Beitrag zum prophetischen Offenbarungsempfang*. FB 32. Würzburg: Echter Verlag.

Gadd, Cyril J., and Samuel N. Kramer. 1963. *Ur Excavations, Texts VI: Literary and Religious Texts, First Part*. London: British Museum Publications.

Gadotti, Alhena, and Alexandra Kleinerman. 2011. "'Here Is What I Have, Send Me What I Am Missing': Exchange of Syllabi in Ancient Mesopotamia." *ZA* 101, 72–77.

Galling, Kurt. 1971. "Tafel, Buch und Blatt," pages 207–224 in Hans Goedicke (ed.), *Near Eastern Studies in Honor of William Foxwell Albright*. Baltimore: John Hopkins.

Gathercole, Simon. 2012. "The Earliest Manuscript Title of Matthew's Gospel (BnF Suppl. gr. 1120 ii 3/P4)." *NovT* 54, 209–235.

Geller, M. J. 1990. "Astronomy and Authorship." *BSOAS* 53/2, 209–213.

———. 2000 "Incipits and Rubrics," pages 225–258 in Andrew R. George and Irving L. Finkel (eds.), *Wisdom, Gods and Literature: Studies in Assyriology in Honour of W. G. Lambert*. Winona Lake, IN: Eisenbrauns.

Gemeinhardt, Peter. 2016. "Isaiah (Book and Person): IV. Christianity, A. Greek and Latin Patristics," pages 320–325 in *Encyclopedia of the Bible and Its Reception*. Vol. 13: *Integrity—Jesuit Order*. Berlin: de Gruyter.

Genette, Gérard. 1997. *Paratexts: Thresholds of Interpretation*. Translated by Jane E. Lewin. Cambridge: Cambridge University Press.

George, A. R. 2013. "The Poem of Erra and Ishum: A Babylonian Poet's View of War," pages 39–72 in Hugh Kennedy (ed.), *Warfare and Poetry in the Middle East*. London: I. B. Tauris.

Gerstenberger, Erhard S. 2004. "Prophetie in den Chronikbüchern: Jahwes Wort in zweierlei Gestalt?," pages 351–367 in F. Hartenstein (ed.), *Schriftprophetie: FS für Jörg Jeremias zum 65. Geburtstag.* Neukirchen-Vluyn: Neukirchener Verlag.

Gevaryahu, Hayim M. I. 1971. "Limmudim (Scribal Disciples) in the Book of Isaiah (in Hebrew)." *Beth Mikra* 47, 438–456.

———. 1975. "Biblical Colophons: A Source for the 'Biography' of Authors, Texts and Books," pages 42–59 in G. W. Anderson et al. (eds.), *Congress Volume: Edinburgh 1974.* VTSup 28. Leiden: Brill.

———. 1989. "The School of Isaiah: Biography and Transmission of the Book of Isaiah." *JBQ* 18/2, 62–68.

Gieschen, Charles A. 1998. *Angelomorphic Christology: Antecedents and Early Evidence.* AGJU 42. Leiden: Brill.

Giese, Ronald L., Jr. 1988. "Further Evidence for the Bisection of 1QIs^a." *Text* 14/1, 61–70.

Ginsburg, Christian D. 1880. *The Massorah: Compiled from Manuscripts, Alphabetically and Lexically Arranged.* Vol. 2: *Caph–Tav.* London: Brög.

Glassner, Jean-Jacques. 2001. "Être auteur avant Homère en Mésopotamie?" *Diogène* 196/4, 111–118.

———. 2002. "Who Were the Authors before Homer in Mesopotamia?" *Diogenes* 196/49, 86–92.

———. 2004. *Mesopotamian Chronicles.* Edited by Benjamin R. Foster. WAW 19. Atlanta, GA: SBL.

Glatt-Gilad, David A. 2001. "Regnal Formulae as a Historiographic Device in the Book of Chronicles." *RB* 108/2, 184–209.

Godley, A. D. (trans.). 1920. *Herodotus: The Persian Wars.* Vol. 1: *Books 1–2.* LCL 117. Cambridge, MA: Harvard University Press.

Goldingay, John. 1998. "Isaiah I 1 and II 1." *VT* 48/3, 326–332.

———. 2014. *The Theology of the Book of Isaiah.* Downers Grove, IL: IVP Academic.

Goldingay, John, and David Payne. 2006a. *Isaiah 40–55.* Vol. 1. ICC. London: T&T Clark.

———. 2006b. *Isaiah 40–55.* Vol. 2. ICC. London: T&T Clark.

Graves, Michael W. 2015. "The Composition of the Book of Isaiah in Jewish Tradition," pages 115–134 in Daniel I. Block and Richard L. Schultz (eds.), *Bind Up the Testimony: Explorations in the Genesis of the Book of Isaiah.* Peabody, MA: Hendrickson.

Gray, George Buchanan. 1912. *A Critical and Exegetical Commentary on the Book of Isaiah I–XXXIX.* 2 vols. The International Critical Commentary on the Holy Scriptures of the Old and New Testaments. New York: Charles Scribner's Sons.

Gray, Rebecca. 1993. *Prophetic Figures in Late Second Temple Jewish Palestine: The Evidence from Josephus*. Oxford: Oxford University Press.

Graziosi, Barbara. 2002. *Inventing Homer: The Early Reception of Epic*. Cambridge Classical Studies. Cambridge: Cambridge University Press.

Green, Stefan. 2020. *Toward Apocalypticism: A Thematic Analysis of Isaiah 65–66*. Åbo: Åbo Akademi University Press.

Greenberg, Moshe. 1956. "The Stabilization of the Text of the Hebrew Bible, Reviewed in the Light of Biblical Materials from the Judean Desert." *JAOS* 76/3, 157–167.

Grogan, Geoffrey W. 2008. "Isaiah," pages 433–863 in Tremper Longman III and David E. Garland (eds.), *Proverbs–Isaiah*. The Expositor's Bible Commentary 6. Grand Rapids, MI: Zondervan.

Grojnowski, Davina. 2015. "Flavius Josephus, Nehemiah, and a Study in Self-Presentation." *JSJ* 46/3, 345–365.

Hall, Christopher A. (ed.). 2009. *Origen: Homilies on Numbers*. Translated by Thomas P. Scheck. Ancient Christian Texts. Downers Grove, IL: IVP Academic.

Hall, Robert G. 1990. "The *Ascension of Isaiah*: Community Situation, Date, and Place in Early Christianity." *JBL* 109/2, 289–306.

———. 1994. "Isaiah's Ascent to See the Beloved: An Ancient Jewish Source for the Ascension of Isaiah." *JBL* 113/3, 463–484.

———. 2004. "Disjunction of Heavenly and Earthly Times in the *Ascension of Isaiah*." *JSJ* 35/1, 17–26.

———. 2016. "Isaiah, Martyrdom and Ascension Of," pages 344–345 in *Encyclopedia of the Bible and Its Reception*. Vol. 13: *Integrity—Jesuit Order*. Berlin: de Gruyter.

Halliwell, Stephen (trans.). 1995. *Aristotle: Poetics*. 2nd ed. LCL 199. Cambridge, MA: Harvard University Press.

Hallo, William W. 1962. "New Viewpoints on Cuneiform Literature." *IEJ* 12/1, 13–26.

———. 1963. "On the Antiquity of Sumerian Literature." *JAOS* 83/2, 167–176.

———. 1966. Review of C. J. Gadd and Samuel N. Kramer, *UET 6/1*. *JCS* 20/2, 89–93.

———. 1975. "Another Sumerian Literary Catalogue?" *StOr* 46, 77–80.

———. 1976. "Toward a History of Sumerian Literature," pages 181–203 in S. J. Lieberman (ed.), *Sumerological Studies in Honor of Thorkild Jacobsen on His Seventieth Birthday June 7, 1974*. AS 20. Chicago: University of Chicago Press.

———. 1996. *Origins: The Ancient Near Eastern Background of Some Modern Western Institutions*. SHANE 6. Leiden: Brill.

Hallo, William W., and Johannes J. A. van Dijk. 1968. *The Exaltation of Inanna*. YNER 3. New Haven: Yale University Press.

Hammer, Reuven. 1986. *Sifre: A Tannaitic Commentary on the Book of Deuteronomy*. YJS 24. New Haven: Yale University Press.

Hanson, Paul D. 1995. *Isaiah 40–66*. Interpretation. Louisville, KY: Westminster John Knox.

Hare, D. R. A. 1985. "The Lives of the Prophets," pages 379–399 in James H. Charlesworth (ed.), *The Old Testament Pseudepigrapha: Expansions of the "Old Testament" and Legends, Wisdom and Philosophical Literature, Prayers, Psalms and Odes, Fragments of Lost Judeo-Hellenistic Works*. Vol. 2. Peabody, MA: Hendricksons.

Heeßel, Nils P. 2010. "Neues von Esagil-kīn-apli: Die ältere Version der physiognomischen Omenserie *alamdimmû*," pages 139–188 in Stefan M. Maul and Nils P. Heeßel (eds.), *Assur-Forschungen: Arbeiten aus der Forschungsstelle "Edition literarischer Keilschrifttexte aus Assur" der Heidelberger Akademie der Wissenschaften*. Weisbaden: Harrassowitz Verlag.

Heffelfinger, Katie M. 2011. *I Am Large, I Contain Multitudes: Lyric Cohesion and Conflict in Second Isaiah*. BibInt 105. Leiden: Brill.

Heinen, Sandra. 2019. "Exegesis without Authorial Intention? On the Role of the 'Author Construct' in Text Interpretation," pages 7–23 in Clarissa Breu (ed.), *Biblical Exegesis without Authorial Intention? Interdisciplinary Approaches to Authorship and Meaning*. BibInt 172. Leiden: Brill.

Helle, Sophus. 2018. "The Role of Authors in the 'Uruk List of Kings and Sages': Canonization and Cultural Contact." *JNES* 77/2, 219–234.

———. 2019a. "Enheduanna and the Invention of Authorship." *Authorship* 8/1, 1–20.

———. 2019b. "What Is an Author? Old Answers to a New Question." *Modern Language Quarterly* 80/2, 113–139.

———. 2020a. "The Birth of the Author." *Orbis Litterarum* 75, 55–72.

———. 2020b. *The First Authors: Narratives of Authorship in Ancient Iraq*. PhD diss.: Aarhus University.

Hengel, Martin. 1974. *Judaism and Hellenism: Studies in Their Encounter in Palestine during the Early Hellenistic Period*. Translated by John Bowden. 2 vols. London: SCM.

Hicks, R. D. (trans.). 1925a. *Diogenes Laertius: Lives of Eminent Philosophers*. Vol. 1: *Books 1–5*. LCL 184. Cambridge, MA: Harvard University Press.

——— (trans.). 1925b. *Diogenes Laertius: Lives of Eminent Philosophers*. Vol. 2: *Books 6–10*. LCL 185. Cambridge, MA: Harvard University Press.

Hilber, John W. 2015. "Isaiah as Prophet and Isaiah as Book in Their Ancient Near Eastern Context," pages 151–174 in Daniel I. Block and Richard L. Schultz (eds.), *Bind Up the Testimony: Explorations in the Genesis of the Book of Isaiah*. Peabody, MA: Hendrickson.

Høgenhaven, Jesper. 1984. "The First Isaiah Scroll from Qumran (1QIsᵃ) and the Massoretic Text: Some Reflections with Special Regard to Isaiah 1–12." *JSOT* 8/28, 17–35.

———. 1988. *Gott und Volk bei Jesaja: Eine Untersuchung zur biblischen Theologie*. ATDan 24. Leiden: Brill.

———. 1998. "The Isaiah Scroll and the Composition of the Book of Isaiah," pages 151–158 in F. H. Cryer and T. L. Thompson (eds.), *Qumran between the Old and New Testaments*. JSOTSup 290. Sheffield, UK: Sheffield Academic.

———. 2007. "The Literary Character of 4QTanhumim." *DSD* 14/1, 99–123.

———. 2011. "4QTanḥumim (4Q176): Between Exegesis and Treatise?," pages 151–167 in George J. Brooke and Jesper Høgenhaven (eds.), *The Mermaid and the Partridge: Essays from the Copenhagen Conference on Revising Texts from Cave Four*. STDJ 96. Leiden: Brill.

———. 2017. "Psalms as Prophecy: Qumran Evidence for the Reading of Psalms as Prophetic Text and the Formation of Canon," pages 231–251 in Mika S. Pajunen and Jeremy Penner (eds.), *Functions of Psalms and Prayers in the Late Second Temple Period*. BZAW 486. Berlin: de Gruyter.

———. 2019. "Tanḥumim," pages 352–353 in George J. Brooke and Charlotte Hempel (eds.), *T&T Clark Companion to the Dead Sea Scrolls*. London: Bloomsbury.

Horgan, M. 1979. *Pesharim: Qumran Interpretations of Biblical Books*. CBQMS 8. Washington, DC: Catholic Biblical Association of America.

Hunger, Hermann. 1968. *Babylonische und Assyrische Kolophone*. AOAT 2. Neukirchen-Vluyn: Neukirchener Verlag.

Ingold, Tim. 2010. "The Textility of Making." *Cambridge Journal of Economics* 24, 91–102.

Jacobs, Louis. 1991. *Structure and Form in the Babylonian Talmud*. Cambridge: Cambridge University Press.

Jain, Eva I. 2002. "Die materielle Rekonstruktion von 1QJesᵇ (1Q8) und einige bisher nicht edierte Fragmente dieser Handschrift." *RevQ* 20/79, 389–409.

Japhet, Sarah. 1985. "The Historical Reliability of Chronicles: The History of the Problem and Its Place in Biblical Research." *JSOT* 33, 83–107.

———. 1993. *I & II Chronicles*. OTL. Louisville, KY: Westminster John Knox.

Jepsen, A. 1980. "חָזָה," pages 280–290 in G. Johannes Botterweck and Helmer Ringgren (eds.), *TDOT* 4. Translated by Douglas W. Stott. Grand Rapids, MI: Eerdmans.

Johns, Adrian. 1998. *The Nature of the Book: Print and Knowledge in the Making*. Chicago: University of Chicago Press.

Johnson, J. Cale. 2013. "The Origins of Scholastic Commentary in Mesopotamia: Second-Order Schemata in the Early Dynastic Exegetical Imagination," pages 11–55 in Shai Gordin (ed.), *Visualizing Knowledge and Creating Meaning in Ancient Writing Systems*. BBVO 23. Berlin: PeWe.

Jones, Douglas. 1955. "The Traditio of the Oracles of Isaiah of Jerusalem." *ZAW* 67, 226–246.

Jonker, Louis. 2008. "Who Constitutes Society? Yehud's Self-Understanding in the Late Persian Era as Reflected in the Books of Chronicles." *JBL* 127/4, 703–724.

———. 2011. "The Chronicler and the Prophets: Who Were His Authoritative Sources?," pages 145–164 in Ehud Ben Zvi and Diana V. Edelman (eds.), *What Was Authoritative for Chronicles?* Winona Lake, IN: Eisenbrauns.

Kahle, Paul. 1951. *Die hebräischen Handschriften, aus der Höhle*. Stuttgart: Kohlhammer.

Kaiser, Otto. 1980. *Isaiah 13–39*. Translated by John Bowden. OTL. London: SCM.

———. 1983. *Isaiah 1–12*. Translated by John Bowden. OTL. Philadelphia: Westminster.

Kamesar, Adam. 2005. "Hilary of Poitiers, Judeo-Christianity, and the Origins of the LXX: A Translation of *Tractatus Super Psalmos* 2.2–3 with Introduction and Commentary." *VC* 59/3, 264–285.

Kato, Teppei. 2019. "Hebrews, Apostles, and Christ: Three Authorities of Jerome's *Hebraica Veritas*." *VC* 73, 420–439.

Katz, Peter. 1946. "Notes on the Septuagint." *JTS* 47/187, 166–169.

Kim, Hyun Chul Paul. 2020. "The Oracles against the Nations," pages 59–78 in Lena-Sofia Tiemeyer (ed.), *The Oxford Handbook of Isaiah*. Oxford: Oxford University Press.

Kister, Menahem. 1985. "Newly-Identified Fragments of the Book of Jubilees: Jub. 23:21–23, 30–31." *RevQ* 12, 529–536.

Kleer, Martin. 1996. *"Der liebliche Sänger der Psalmen Israels": Untersuchungen zu David als Dichter und Beter der Psalmen*. BBB 108. Bodenheim: Philo.

Klein, Ralph W. 2006. *1 Chronicles: A Commentary*. Hermeneia. Minneapolis, MN: Fortress.

————. 2012. *2 Chronicles: A Commentary*. Hermeneia. Minneapolis, MN: Fortress.

Knibb, M. A. 1985. "Martyrdom and Ascension of Isaiah: A New Translation and Introduction," pages 143–176 in James H. Charlesworth (ed.), *The Old Testament Pseudepigrapha: Expansions of the "Old Testament" and Legends, Wisdom and Philosophical Literature, Prayers, Psalms and Odes, Fragments of Lost Judeo-Hellenistic Works*. Vol. 2. Peabody, MA: Hendricksons.

Knight, Jonathan M. 2013. "The Political Issue of the *Ascension of Isaiah*: A Response to Enrico Norelli." *JSNT* 35/4, 355–379.

————. 2020. "Isaiah, Ascension Of," pages 250–252 in Daniel M. Gurtner and Loren T. Stuckenbruck (eds.), *T&T Clark Encyclopedia of Second Temple Judaism*. Vol. 1. London: T&T Clark.

Koch-Westenholz, Ulla. 2000. *Babylonian Liver Omens: The Chapters Manzāzu, Padānu and Pān Tākalti of the Babylonian Extispicy Series, Mainly from Aššurbanipal's Library*. Copenhagen: Carsten Niebuhr Institute Publications.

Kohn, R. Levitt, and W. H. C. Propp. 1995. "The Name of 'Second Isaiah': The Forgotten Theory of Nehemiah Rabban," pages 223–235 in Astrid B. Beck et al. (eds.), *Fortunate the Eyes That See: Essays in Honor of David Noel Freedman in Celebration of His Seventieth Birthday*. Grand Rapids, MI: Eerdmans.

Kraebel, Andrew. 2019. "Authorship in Medieval English Literature," pages 98–114 in Ingo Berensmeyer, Gert Buelens, and Barysa Demoor (eds.), *The Cambridge Handbook of Literary Authorship*. Cambridge: Cambridge University Press.

Kramer, Samuel N. 1942. "The Oldest Literary Catalogue: A Sumerian List of Literary Compositions Compiled about 2000 B.C." *BASOR* 88, 10–19.

————. 1961. "New Literary Catalogue from Ur." *RA* 55/4, 169–176.

Kratz, Reinhard G. 2015. *The Prophets of Israel*. Translated by Anselm C. Hagedorn and Nathan MacDonald. Critical Studies in the Hebrew Bible 2. Winona Lake, IN: Eisenbrauns.

Krause, Christian Sigmund. 1783. "Ueber den Büchernachdruck." *Deutsches Museum* 1, 400–430, 487–514.

Krochmal, Nachmann. 1851. מורה נבוכי הזמן. Leopoli: Joseph Schnayder.

Kronholm, Tryggve. 1974. "יָתַר," pages 482–491 in G. Johannes Botterweck and Helmer Ringgren (eds.), *TDOT* 6. Translated by David E. Green. Grand Rapids, MI: Eerdmans.

————. 2001. "עֵת," pages 434–451 in G. Johannes Botterweck, Helmer Ringgren, and Heinz-Josef Fabry (eds.), *TDOT* 11. Translated by David E. Green. Grand Rapids, MI: Eerdmans.

Laato, Anni Maria. 2020. "'The Lord Reigns from the Tree': Psalm 96:10 in Early Christian Writings," pages 269–281 in Erkki Koskenniemi and David Willgren Davage (eds.), *David, Messianism, and Eschatology: Ambiguity in the Reception History of the Book of Psalms in Judaism and Christianity*. Studies in the Reception History of the Bible 9. Åbo: Åbo Akademi University.

Laato, Antti. 2020. "The Origin of the Christian Interpolation in Psalm 96:10," pages 258–268 in Erkki Koskenniemi and David Willgren Davage (eds.), *David, Messianism, and Eschatology: Ambiguity in the Reception History of the Book of Psalms in Judaism and Christianity*. Studies in the Reception History of the Bible 9. Åbo: Åbo Akademi University.

Lamb, W. R. M. (trans.). 1967. *Plato in Twelve Volumes: II Laches Protagoras Meno Euthydemus*. LCL 165. Cambridge, MA: Harvard University Press.

Lambert, W. G. 1957. "Ancestors, Authors, and Canonicity." *JCS* 11/1, 1–14.

———. 1962. "A Catalogue of Texts and Authors." *JCS* 16/3, 59–77.

Lange, Armin. 2002. "The Status of the Biblical Texts in the Qumran Corpus and the Canonical Process," pages 21–30 in Edward D. Herbert and Emanuel Tov (eds.), *The Bible as Book: The Hebrew Bible and the Judaean Desert Discoveries*. London: British Library & Oak Knoll.

Latham, Sean. 2019. "Industrialized Print: Modernism and Authorship," pages 165–182 in Ingo Berensmeyer, Gert Buelens, and Barysa Demoor (eds.), *The Cambridge Handbook of Literary Authorship*. Cambridge: Cambridge University Press.

Lauterbach, Jakob Z. 2004. *Mekhilta De-Rabbi Ishmael*. 2 vols. Philadelphia: JPS.

Leuchter, Mark. 2011. "The 'Jeremiah' Doublet in Ezra-Nehemiah and Chronicles," pages 183–200 in Ehud Ben Zvi and Diana V. Edelman (eds.), *What Was Authoritative for Chronicles?* Winona Lake, IN: Eisenbrauns.

Levine, Lee I. 2012. *Visual Judaism in Late Antiquity: Historical Contexts of Jewish Art*. New Haven: Yale University Press.

Lewis, George. 1911. *The Philocalia of Origen: A Compilation of Selected Passages from Origen's Works Made by St. Gregory of Nazianzus and St. Basil of Cæsarea*. Edinburgh: T&T Clark.

Lichtenberger, Hermann. 2002. "Consolations (4Q176 = 4QTanḥ)," pages 329–349 in James H. Charlesworth and Henry W. M. Rietz (eds.), *The Dead Sea Scrolls: Hebrew, Aramaic, and Greek Texts with English Translations, 6B: Pesharim, Other Commentaries, and Related Documents*. Tübingen: Mohr Siebeck.

Lied, Liv Ingeborg, and Hugo Lundhaug. 2017. "Studying Snapshots: On Manuscript Culture, Textual Fluidity, and New Philology," pages 1–19 in *Snapshots of Evolving Traditions: Jewish and Christian Manuscript Culture, Textual Fluidity, and New Philology*. TUGAL 175. Berlin: de Gruyter.

Liguori Ewald, Sister Marie (ed.). 1966. *The Homilies of St. Jerome*. The Fathers of the Church: A New Translation 2 (Homilies 60–96). Washington, DC: Catholic University of America Press.

Lim, Timothy H. 2002. *Pesharim*. Companion to the Qumran Scrolls 3. London: Sheffield Academic.

———. 2017. "An Indicative Definition of the Canon," pages 1–24 in Timothy H. Lim (ed.), *When Texts Are Canonized*. BJS 359. Providence, RI: Brown Judaic Studies.

Liverani, Mario. 2010. "'Untruthful Steles': Propaganda and Reliability in Ancient Mesopotamia," pages 229–244 in Sarah C. Melville and Alice L. Slotsky (eds.), *Opening the Tablet Box: Near Eastern Studies in Honor of Benjamin R. Foster*. CHANE 42. Leiden: Brill.

Longacre, Drew. 2013. "Developmental Stage, Scribal Lapse, or Physical Defect? 1QIsaᵃ's Damaged Exemplar for Isaiah Chapters 34–66." *DSD* 20, 17–50.

Loprieno, Antonio. 2019. "Authorship in Ancient Egypt," pages 27–45 in Ingo Berensmeyer, Gert Buelens, and Barysa Demoor (eds.), *The Cambridge Handbook of Literary Authorship*. Cambridge: Cambridge University Press.

Macy, Howard Ray. 1975. *The Sources of the Books of Chronicles: A Reassessment*. PhD diss.: Harvard University.

Maier, Johann. 2000. "Tanḥumin and Apocryphal Lamentations," page 915 in Lawrence H. Schiffman and James C. VanderKam (eds.), *EDSS* 2. New York: Oxford University Press.

Malamat, Abraham. 1998. *Mari and the Bible*. Studies in the History and Culture of the Ancient Near East 12. Leiden: Brill.

Marchant, E. C., and O. J. Todd (trans.). 2013. *Xenophon: Memorabilia, Oeconomicus, Symposium, Apology*. 2nd ed. LCL 168. Cambridge, MA: Harvard University Press.

Marcus, Ralph (trans.). 1953. *Philo: Questions on Genesis*. LCL 380. Cambridge, MA: Harvard University Press.

Marincola, John. 1997. *Authority and Tradition in Ancient Historiography*. Cambridge: Cambridge University Press.

Martens, Peter W. 2012. *Origen and Scripture: The Contours of the Exegetical Life*. Oxford: Oxford University Press.

Martínez García, Florentino. 1992. *The Dead Sea Scrolls Translated: The Qumran Texts in English; The Most Comprehensive One-Volume Edition of the Dead Sea Scrolls Available.* 2nd ed. Leiden: Brill.

Mason, Steve. 2001. *Life of Josephus: Translation and Commentary.* Flavius Josephus: Translation and Commentary 9. Leiden: Brill.

———. 2016a. "Josephus as a Roman Historian," pages 89–107 in H. H. Chapman and Z. Rodgers (eds.), *A Companion to Josephus.* Blackwell Companions to the Ancient World 110. Chichester: Wiley-Blackwell.

———. 2016b. "Josephus's *Autobiography* (*Life of Josephus*)," pages 69–74 in Honora Howell Chapman and Zuleika Rodgers (eds.), *A Companion to Josephus.* Oxford: Wiley-Blackwell.

———. 2016c. "Josephus's Judean War," pages 13–35 in Honora Howell Chapman and Zuleika Rodgers (eds.), *A Companion to Josephus.* Oxford: Wiley-Blackwell.

Mastnjak, Nathan. 2020. "The Book of Isaiah and the Anthological Genre." *HS* 61, 49–72.

Mays, James L. 1986. "The David of the Psalms." *Int* 40/2, 143–155.

McKenzie, John L. 1968. *Second Isaiah.* AB. New York: Doubleday.

Meade, David G. 1986. *Pseudonymity and Canon: An Investigation into the Relationship of Authorship and Authority in Jewish and Earliest Christian Tradition.* WUNT 39. Tübingen: Mohr Siebeck.

Mettinger, Tryggve N. D. 1983. *A Farewell to the Servant Songs: A Critical Examination of and Exegetical Axiom.* Lund: CWK Gleerup.

———. 1987. *Namnet och närvaron: Gudsnamn och Gudsbild i böckernas bok.* Örebro: Libris.

———. 1988. *In Search of God: The Meaning and Message of the Everlasting Names.* Minneapolis, MN: Fortress.

Metzger, Bruce M. 2005. *A Textual Commentary on the Greek New Testament.* 2nd ed. Peabody, MA: Hendrickson.

Michalowski, Piotr. 1996. "Sailing to Babylon: Reading the Dark Side of the Moon," pages 177–193 in Jerrold S. Cooper and Glenn M. Schwartz (eds.), *The Study of the Ancient Near East in the 21st Century: The William Foxwell Albright Centennial Conference.* Winona Lake, IN: Eisenbrauns.

Milgrom, Jacob. 1964. "Did Isaiah Prophesy during the Reign of Uzziah?" *VT* 14/2, 164–182.

Millard, Alan. 2010. "'Take a Large Writing Tablet and Write on It': Isaiah—a Writing Prophet?," pages 105–117 in Katharine J. Dell, Graham Davies, and Yee Von Koh (eds.), *Genesis, Isaiah and Psalms: A Festschrift to Honour Professor John Emerton for His Eightieth Birthday.* Leiden: Brill.

Miller, J. Maxwell, and John H. Hayes. 2006. *A History of Israel and Judah*. 2nd ed. London: Westminster John Knox.

Morris, Leon. 1995. *The Gospel according to John*. Rev. ed. NICNT. Grand Rapids, MI: Eerdmans.

Moser, Christian. 2012. *Umstrittene Prophetie: Die exegetisch-theologische Diskussion um die Inhomogenität des Jesajabuches von 1780 bis 1900*. Biblisch-Theologische Studien 128. Neukirchen-Vluyn: Neukirchener Verlagsgesellschaft.

Motyer, J. Alec. 1999. *Isaiah: An Introduction and Commentary*. TOTC. Downers Grove, IL: InterVarsity.

Mowinckel, Sigmund. 1926. *Jesaja-Disiplene: Profetien fra Jesaja til Jeremia*. Oslo: Aschehoug.

———. 1946. *Prophecy and Tradition: The Prophetic Books in Light of the Study of the Growth and History of the Tradition*. Oslo: Dybwad.

———. 2002. *The Spirit and the Word: Prophecy and Tradition in Ancient Israel*. Edited by K. C. Hanson. Minneapolis, MN: Fortress.

Moyise, Steve. 2020. "Isaiah in the New Testament," pages 531–541 in Lena-Sofia Tiemeyer (ed.), *The Oxford Handbook of Isaiah*. Oxford: Oxford University Press.

Moyise, Steve, and Maarten J. J. Menken (eds.). 2005. *Isaiah in the New Testament: The New Testament and the Scriptures of Israel*. London: T&T Clark.

Mroczek, Eva. 2016. *The Literary Imagination in Jewish Antiquity*. Oxford: Oxford University Press.

Mualem, Shlomy. 2012. *Borges and Plato: A Game with Shifting Mirrors*. Ediciones de Iberoamericana 54. Iberoameriacana and Vervuert: Madrid and Frankfurt am Main.

Najman, Hindy. 2003. *Seconding Sinai: The Development of Mosaic Discourse in Second Temple Judaism*. Supplements to the Journal of the Study of Judaism 77. Leiden: Brill.

———. 2014. *Losing the Temple and Recovering the Future: An Analysis of 4 Ezra*. Cambridge: Cambridge University Press.

Najman, Hindy, and Irene Peirano. 2019. "Pseudepigraphy as an Interpretative Construct," pages 331–356 in Matthias Henze and Liv Ingeborg Lied (eds.), *The Old Testament Pseudepigrapha: Fifty Years of the Pseudepigrapha Section at the SBL*. Atlanta, GA: SBL.

Neusner, Jacob. 2007a. *Isaiah in Talmud and Midrash, Part A: Mishnah, Tosefta, Tannaite Midrash-Compilations, Yerushalmi and Associated Midrash-Compilations*. Studies in Judaism. Lanham: University Press of America.

———. 2007b. *Isaiah in Talmud and Midrash, Part B: The Later Midrash-Compilations and the Bavli*. Studies in Judaism. Lanham: University Press of America.

———. 2010. *The Jerusalem Talmud: A Translation and Commentary on CD*. Translated by Jacob Neusner and Tzvee Zahavy. Peabody, MA: Hendrickson.

Newman, Judith H. 2011. "Liturgical Imagination in the Composition of Ben Sira," pages 311–326 in J. Penner, K. M. Penner, and C. Wassén (eds.), *Giving Thanks to the Lord: Essays on Prayer and Poetry in the Dead Sea Scrolls and Related Literature: Essays in Honor of Eileen Schuller on the Occasion of Her 65th Birthday*. Leiden: Brill.

Ngunga, Abi T. 2020. "Isaiah in Greek," pages 451–468 in Lena-Sofia Tiemeyer (ed.), *The Oxford Handbook of Isaiah*. Oxford: Oxford University Press.

Nichols, Stephen G. 1990. "Introduction: Philology in a Manuscript Culture." *Spec* 65/1, 1–10.

Nissinen, Martti. 2000. "Spoken, Written, Quoted, and Invented: Orality and Writtenness in Ancient Near Eastern Prophecy," pages 235–271 in Ehud Ben Zvi and Michael H. Floyd (eds.), *Writings and Speech in Israelite and Ancient Near Eastern Prophecy*. SBL SymSer 10. Atlanta, GA: SBL.

———. 2003. *Prophets and Prophecy in the Ancient Near East*. Atlanta, GA: SBL.

———. 2017. *Ancient Prophecy: Near Eastern, Biblical, and Greek Perspectives*. Oxford: Oxford University Press.

———. 2019. *Prophets and Prophecy in the Ancient Near East*. 2nd ed. Atlanta, GA: SBL.

Norelli, Enrico. 1993. *L'Ascension du prophète Isaïe*. Turnhout: Brepols.

———. 1995. *Ascensio Isaiae: Commentarius*. CCSA 8. Turnhout: Brepols.

Oswalt, John N. 1986. *The Book of Isaiah: Chapters 1–39*. NICOT. Grand Rapids, MI: Eerdmans.

———. 1998. *The Book of Isaiah: Chapters 40–66*. NICOT. Grand Rapids, MI: Eerdmans.

Otzen, B. 1986. "חתם," pages 263–269 in G. Johannes Botterweck and Helmer Ringgren (eds.), *TDOT* 5. Translated by Douglas W. Stott. Grand Rapids, MI: Eerdmans.

Parkinson, R. B. 1997. *The Tale of Sinuhe and Other Ancient Egyptian Poems 1940–1640 BC*. Oxford World's Classics. Oxford: Oxford University Press.

Parlby, Geri. 2008. "The Origins of Marian Art in the Catacombs and the Problems of Identification," pages 41–56 in Chris Maunder (ed.), *The Origins of the Cult of the Virgin Mary*. London: Burns & Oates.

Parpola, Simo. 1997. *Assyrian Prophecies*. Helsinki: Helsinki University Press.

Parry, Donald W. 2019. *Exploring the Isaiah Scrolls and Their Textual Variants*. Supplements to the Textual History of the Bible 3. Leiden: Brill.

Parry, Donald W., and Elisha Qimron. 1999. *The Great Isaiah Scroll (1QIsaᵃ)*. STDJ. Leiden: Brill.

Parry, Donald W., and Emanuel Tov (eds.). 2004. *Exegetical Texts*. DSSR 2. Leiden: Brill.

Paul, Shalom M. 1973. "Heavenly Tablets and the Book of Life." *JANES* 5, 345–354.

———. 2012. *Isaiah 40–66*. ECC. Grand Rapids, MI: Eerdmans.

Peirano, Irene. 2012. *The Rhetoric of the Roman Fake: Latin Pseudepigrapha in Context*. Cambridge: Cambridge University Press.

Peltonen, K. 1999. "Function, Explanation, and Literary Phenomena: Aspects of Source Criticism as Theory and Method in the History of Chronicles Research," pages 18–69 in M. Patrick Graham and Steven L. McKenzie (eds.), *The Chronicler as Author: Studies in Text and Texture*. JSOTSup 263. Sheffield, UK: Sheffield Academic.

Petersen, Silke. 2006. "Die Evangelienüberschriften und die Entstehung des neutestamentlichen Kanons." *ZAW* 97, 250–274.

Pfann, Stephen J., and Philip S. Alexander (eds.). 2000. *Qumran Cave 4: Cryptic Text and Miscellanea, Part 1*. DJD XXXVI. Oxford: Clarendon.

Pfeiffer, Rudolf. 1968. *The History of Classical Scholarship from the Beginnings to the End of the Hellenistic Age*. Oxford: Clarendon.

Phillips, Kim. 2016. "Who Wrote the Bible?" Fragment of the Month: August 2016. University of Cambridge. https://www.lib.cam.ac.uk/collections/departments/taylor-schechter-genizah-research-unit/fragment-month/fragment-month-4.

Pietersma, Albert. 1980. "David in the Greek Psalms." *VT* 30, 213–226.

———. 2001. "Exegesis and Liturgy in the Superscriptions of the Greek Psalter," pages 99–138 in Bernard A. Taylor (ed.), *X Congress of the International Organization for Septuagint and Cognate Studies, Oslo, 1998*. SBLSCS 51. Atlanta, GA: SBL.

———. 2021. "From the Exodus to the Exile: A Commentary on the Greek Text-as-Produced Psalm 80." Academia. https://www.academia.edu/42681731/Psalm_80.

Pitts, Andrew W. 2013. "The Use and Non-use of Prophetic Literature in Hellenistic Jewish Historiography," pages 229–252 in Mark J. Boda and Lissa M. Wray Beal (eds.), *Prophets, Prophecy, and Ancient Israelite Historiography*. Winona Lake, IN: Eisenbrauns.

Pongratz-Leisten, Beate. 2002. "'Lying King' and 'False Prophet': The Intercultural Transfer of a Rhetorical Device within Ancient Near Eastern Ideologies," pages 215–243 in A. Panaino and G. Pettinato (eds.), *Ideologies as Intercultural Phenomena: Proceedings of the Third Annual Symposium of the Assyrian and Babylonian Intellectual Heritage Project*. Milano: Università di Bologna & IsIAO.

Porton, Gary. 1992. "Midrash," pages 818–822 in David N. Freedman (ed.), *ABD* 4. New York: Doubleday.

Poulsen, Fredrik. 2014. *God, His Servant, and the Nations in Isaiah 42:1–9*. FAT II 73. Tübingen: Mohr Siebeck.

Quinn-Miscall, Peter D. 2001. *Reading Isaiah: Poetry and Vision*. Louisville, KY: Westminster John Knox.

Rajak, Tessa. 1982. "Josephus and the 'Archaeology' of the Jews." *JJS* 33/1–2, 465–477.

Rebenich, Stefan. 1993. "Jerome: The 'Vir Trilinguis' and the 'Hebraica Veritas.'" *VG* 47, 50–77.

Rendtorff, Rolf. 1984. "Zur Komposition Des Buches Jesaja." *VT* 34, 295–320.

———. 2005. "The Psalms of David: David in the Psalms," pages 53–64 in Peter W. Flint and Patrick D. Miller (eds.), *The Book of Psalms: Composition and Reception*. VTSup 99. Leiden: Brill.

Rey, Jean-Sébastien, et al. (eds.). 2011. *The Texts and Versions of the Book of Ben Sira: Transmission and Interpretation*. Leiden: Brill.

Richards, K. H. 1965. "A Note on the Bisection of Isaiah." *RevQ* 5, 257–258.

Roberts, Alexander, and James Donaldson (eds.). 1965. *Church Fathers: Ante-Nicene Fathers*. Vol. 3: *Tertullian*. Altamonte Springs, FL: Accordance.

Roberts, J. J. M. 2015. *First Isaiah*. Hermeneia. Minneapolis, MN: Fortress.

Robson, Eleanor. 2001. "The Tablet House: A Scribal School in Old Babylonian Nippur." *RA* 93, 39–66.

———. 2003. "Bird and Fish in the OB Sumerian Literary Catalogues." *NABU* 3, 76–78.

Rogers, Pat (ed.). 2006. *Alexander Pope: The Major Works, including* The Rape of the Lock *and* The Dunciad. Oxford World's Classics. Oxford: Oxford University Press.

Rubio, Gonzalo. 2009. "Sumerian Literature," pages 11–76 in Carl S. Ehrlich (ed.), *From an Antique Land: An Introduction to Ancient Near Eastern Literature*. Lanham, MD: Rowman & Littlefield.

Sawyer, John F. A. 1996. *The Fifth Gospel: Isaiah in the History of Christianity*. Cambridge: Cambridge University Press.

———. 2018. *Isaiah through the Centuries*. Wiley-Blackwell Bible Commentaries. Hoboken, NJ: Wiley-Blackwell.

————. 2020. "Isaiah in Art and Music," pages 574–597 in Lena-Sofia Tiemeyer (ed.), *The Oxford Handbook of Isaiah*. Oxford: Oxford University Press.

Schaff, Philip (ed.). 1995. *Church Fathers: The Nicene and Post-Nicene Fathers, Second Series*. Vol. 3: *Theodoret, Jerome, Gennadius, Rufinus: Historical Writings, Etc.* Edinburgh: T&T Clark.

Scheck, Thomas P. (ed.). 2008. *St. Jerome: Commentary on Matthew*. The Fathers of the Church: A New Translation 117. Washington, DC: Catholic University of America Press.

————. 2015. *St. Jerome: Commentary on Isaiah, including St. Jerome's Translation of Origen's Homilies 1–9 on Isaiah*. Ancient Christian Writers 68. New York: Newman.

Schellenberg, Betty A. 2019. "The Eighteenth Century: Print, Professionalization, and Defining the Author," pages 133–146 in Ingo Berensmeyer, Gert Buelens, and Barysa Demoor (eds.), *The Cambridge Handbook of Literary Authorship*. Cambridge: Cambridge University Press.

Scherbenske, Eric W. 2013. *Canonizing Paul: Ancient Editorial Practice and the Corpus Paulinum*. Oxford: Oxford University Press.

Schneemelcher, Wilhelm (ed.). 1992. *New Testament Apocrypha*. Vol. 2: *Writings Relating to the Apostles: Apocalypses and Related Subjects*. Translated by R. McL. Wilson. Louisville, KY: Westminster John Knox.

Schniedewind, William M. 1991. "The Source Citation of Manasseh: King Manasseh in History and Homily." *VT* 41/4, 450–461.

————. 1995. *The Word of God in Transition: From Prophet to Exegete in the Second Temple Period*. JSOTSup 197. Sheffield, UK: Sheffield Academic.

————. 1999. "The Chronicler as Interpreter of Scripture," pages 158–180 in M. Patrick Graham and Steven L. McKenzie (eds.), *The Chronicler as Author: Studies in Text and Texture*. JSOTSup 263. Sheffield, UK: Sheffield Academic.

————. 2004. *How the Bible Became a Book: The Textualization of Ancient Israel*. Cambridge: Cambridge University Press.

————. 2019. *The Finger of the Scribe: How Scribes Learned to Write the Bible*. Oxford: Oxford University Press.

Schott, Jeremy M., and Mark J. Edwards (eds.). 2015. *Macarius, Apocriticus: Translated with Introduction and Commentary*. Translated Texts for Historians 62. Liverpool: Liverpool University Press.

Schultz, Richard L. 2015. "The Origins and Basic Arguments of the Multi-author View of the Composition of Isaiah: Where Are We Now and How Did We Get Here?," pages 7–31 in Daniel I. Block and

Richard L. Schultz (eds.), *Bind Up the Testimony: Explorations in the Genesis of the Book of Isaiah*. Peabody, MA: Hendrickson.

Schürer, Emil, et al. 1973. *The History of the Jewish People in the Age of Jesus Christ (175 B.C.–A.D. 135)*. Vol. 1. London: Bloomsbury.

———. 2014. *The History of the Jewish People in the Age of Jesus Christ (175 B.C.–A.D. 135)*. Vol. 3.1. London: Bloomsbury.

Schwartz, Daniel R. 2016. "Many Sources but a Single Author: Josephus's Jewish Antiquities," pages 36–58 in Honora Howell Chapman and Zuleika Rodgers (eds.), *A Companion to Josephus*. Oxford: Wiley-Blackwell.

Schweitzer, Steven J. 2011. "Judging a Book by Its Citations: Sources and Authority in Chronicles," pages 37–65 in Ehud Ben Zvi and Diana V. Edelman (eds.), *What Was Authoritative for Chronicles?* Winona Lake, IN: Eisenbrauns.

Scodel, Ruth. 2019. "Authorship in Archaic and Classical Greece," pages 46–63 in Ingo Berensmeyer, Gert Buelens, and Barysa Demoor (eds.), *The Cambridge Handbook of Literary Authorship*. Cambridge: Cambridge University Press.

Seitz, Christopher R. 1990. "The Divine Council: Temporal Transition and New Prophecy in the Book of Isaiah." *JBL* 109/2, 229–247.

———. 1993. *Isaiah 1–39*. Louisville, KY: Westminster John Knox.

———. 2002. "Isaiah 1–66: Making Sense of the Whole," pages 105–126 in Christopher R. Seitz (ed.), *Reading and Preaching the Book of Isaiah*. Eugene, OR: Wipf & Stock.

Selle, Hendrik. 2008. *Theognis und die Theognidea*. Berlin: de Gruyter.

Selman, Martin J. 1994a. *1 Chronicles: An Introduction and Commentary*. TOTC. Downers Grove, IL: InterVarsity.

———. 1994b. *2 Chronicles: An Introduction and Commentary*. TOTC. Downers Grove, IL: InterVarsity.

Seybold, Klaus. 1999. "Der Name Deuterojesajas," pages 211–215 in Klaus Seybold (ed.), *Die Sprache der Propheten: Studien zur Literaturgeschichte der Prophetie*. Zürich: Pano.

Shuve, Karl Evan. 2008. "The Doctrine of the False Pericopes and Other Late Antique Approaches to the Problem of Scripture's Unity," pages 437–445 in Albert Frey Amsler, Charlotte Touati, and Renée Girardet (eds.), *Nouvelles Intrigues de pseudo-clémentines / Plots in the Pseudo-Clementine Romance*. Prahins, Switzerland: Éditions du Zébre.

Siker, Jeffrey S. 2017. *Liquid Scripture: The Bible in a Digital World*. Minneapolis, MN: Fortress.

Simian-Yofre, H., and Helmer Ringgren. 1986. "עוד," pages 495–516 in G. Johannes Botterweck, Helmer Ringgren, and Heinz-Josef Fabry (eds.), *TDOT* 10. Translated by Douglas W. Stott. Grand Rapids, MI: Eerdmans.

Sjöberg, Åke W., and Eugen Bergmann (eds.). 1969. *The Collection of Sumerian Temple Hymns.* TCS 3. Locust Valley, NY: Augustin.

Slomovic, Elieser. 1979. "Toward an Understanding of the Formation of Historical Titles in the Book of Psalms." *ZAW* 91/3, 350–380.

Smith, Gary V. 2007. *Isaiah 1–39.* NAC 15A. Nashville: Broadman & Holman.

———. 2009. *Isaiah 40–66.* NAC 15B. Nashville: Broadman & Holman.

Sommer, Benjamin. 1996. "Allusions and Illusions: The Unity of the Book of Isaiah in Light of Deutero-Isaiah's Use of Prophetic Tradition," pages 156–186 in Roy F. Melugin and Marvin A. Sweeney (eds.), *New Visions of Isaiah.* JSOTSup 214. Sheffield, UK: Sheffield Academic.

———. 2004. Review of Klaus Baltzer, *Deutero-Isaiah. JBL* 123/1, 149–153.

Speyer, Wolfgang. 1971. *Die Literarische Fälschung im Hiednischen und Christlichen Altertum: Ein Versuch Ihrer Deutung.* München: C. H. Beck'sche Verlagsbuchhandlung.

Stade, B. 1906. "Zu Jes. 3, 1.17.24. 5, 1. 8, 1 f. 12—14. 16. 9, 7—20. 10, 26." *ZAW* 26/1, 129–141.

Stanley, Christopher D. 1992. "The Importance of *4QTanḥumim (4Q176)." RevQ* 15/4, 569–582.

Steck, Odil H. 1997. "Autor und/oder Redaktor in Jesaja 56–66," pages 219–259 in Craig C. Broyles and Craig A. Evans (eds.), *Writing & Reading the Scroll of Isaiah: Studies of an Interpretive Tradition.* Vol. 1. VTSup 70. Leiden: Brill.

———. 1998. *Die Erste Jesajarolle von Qumran (1QIsa): Schreibweise als Leseanteilung für ein Prophetenbuch.* SBS 173. Stuttgart: Katholisches Bibelwerk.

Stegemann, Hartmut. 1993. *Die Essener, Qumran, Johannes der Täufer und Jesus.* Freiburg: Herder.

Stern, Sacha. 1994. "Attribution and Authorship in the Babylonian Talmud." *JJS* 45/1, 28–51.

———. 1995. "The Concept of Authorship in the Babylonian Talmud." *JJS* 46, 183–195.

Stokes, Ryan E. 2019. *The Satan: How God's Executioner Became the Enemy.* Grand Rapids, MI: Eerdmans.

Stökl, Jonathan, and Corrine L. Carvalho (eds.). 2013. *Prophets Male and Female: Gender and Prophecy in the Hebrew Bible, the Eastern Mediterranean, and the Ancient Near East.* AIL 15. Atlanta, GA: SBL.

Stordalen, Terje. 2015. "Canon and Canonical Commentary: Comparative Perspectives on Canonical Ecologies," pages 133–160 in

Terje Stordalen and Saphinaz-Amal Naguib (eds.), *The Formative Past and the Formation of the Future: Collective Remembering and Identity Formation*. Oslo: Novus.

Storey, Ian C. (trans.). 2011. *Fragments of Old Comedy*. Vol. 2: *Diopeithes to Pherecrates*. 2nd ed. LCL 514. Cambridge, MA: Harvard University Press.

Stott, Katherine M. 2008. *Why Did They Write This Way? Reflections on References to Written Documents in the Hebrew Bible and Ancient Literature*. LHBOTS 492. New York: T&T Clark.

Strawn, Brent A. 2006. "Excerpted Manuscripts at Qumran: Their Significance for the Textual History of the Hebrew Bible and the Socio-religious History of the Qumran Community and Its Literature," pages 107–168 in James H. Charlesworth (ed.), *The Bible and the Dead Sea Scrolls: The Princeton Symposium on the Dead Sea Scrolls*. Vol. 2: *The Dead Sea Scrolls and the Qumran Community*. Waco, TX: Baylor University Press.

———. 2007. "Excerpted 'Non-biblical' Scrolls at Qumran? Background, Analogies, Function," pages 65–123 in Michael Thomas Davis and Brent A. Strawn (eds.), *Qumran Studies: New Approaches, New Questions*. Grand Rapids, MI: Eerdmans.

Stromberg, Jacob. 2009. "The Role of Redaction Criticism in the Evaluation of a Textual Variant: Another Look at 1QIsa^a XXXII 14 (38:21–22)." *DSD* 16/2, 155–189.

———. 2011. *Isaiah after Exile: The Author of Third Isaiah as Reader and Redactor of the Book*. Oxford Theological Monographs. Oxford: Oxford University Press.

Strugnell, John. 1969. "Notes en marge du volume V des 'Discoveries in the Judaean Desert of Jordan.'" *RevQ* 7, 163–276.

Sukenik, Eliezer L. 1955. *The Dead Sea Scrolls of the Hebrew University*. Jerusalem: Magnes.

Svärd, Saana. 2013. "Female Agency and Authorship in Mesopotamian Texts." *Kaskal* 10, 269–280.

Swanson, Dwight. 2009. "The Text of Isaiah at Qumran," pages 191–212 in David G. Firth and H. G. M. Williamson (eds.), *Interpreting Isaiah: Issues and Approaches*. Downers Grove, IL: InterVarsity.

Sweeney, Marvin A. 1988. *Isaiah 1–4 and the Post-exilic Understanding of the Isaianic Tradition*. BZAW 171. Berlin: de Gruyter.

———. 1996. *Isaiah 1–39 with an Introduction to Prophetic Literature*. FOTL 16. Grand Rapids, MI: Eerdmans.

———. 2016a. "Isaiah (Book and Person): I. Hebrew Bible/Old Testament," pages 298–306 in *Encyclopedia of the Bible and Its Reception*. Vol. 13: *Integrity—Jesuit Order*. Berlin: de Gruyter.

———. 2016b. *Isaiah 40–66*. FOTL. Grand Rapids, MI: Eerdmans.

Swoboda, Sören. 2014. *Tod und Sterben im Krieg bei Josephus: Die Intentionen von Bellum und Antiquitates im Kontext griechisch-römischer Historiographie*. Tübingen: Mohr Siebeck.

Talmage, Frank. 1967. "חרם אנוש in Isaiah 8:1." *HTR* 60, 465–468.

Thackeray, John (trans.). 1926. *Josephus:* The Life, Against Apion. LCL 186. Cambridge, MA: Harvard University Press.

———. 1929. *Josephus: The Man and the Historian*. New York: Jewish Institute of Religion.

———(trans.). 1998. *Josephus: Jewish Antiquities*. LCL 242. Cambridge, MA: Harvard University Press.

Thompson, John A. 1994. *1, 2 Chronicles*. NAC 9. Nashville: Broadman & Holman.

Throntveit, Mark A. 2003. "The Relationship of Hezekiah to David and Solomon in the Books of Chronicles," pages 105–121 in Patrick M. Graham, Steven L. McKenzie, and Gary N. Knoppers (eds.), *The Chronicler as Theologian: Essays in Honor of Ralph W. Klein*. JSOTSup 371. New York: T&T Clark.

Tiemeyer, Lena-Sofia. 2011. *For the Comfort of Zion: The Geographical and Theological Location of Isaiah 40–55*. VTSup 139. Leiden: Brill.

Tigay, Jeffrey H. 1982. *The Evolution of the Gilgamesh Epic*. Philadelphia: University of Pennsylvania Press.

Tinney, Steve. 1998. "Texts, Tablets, and Teaching: Scribal Education in Nippur and Ur." *Expedition* 40/2, 40–50.

———. 1999. "On the Curricular Setting of Sumerian Literature." *Iraq* 61, 159–172.

Tov, Emanuel. 1997. "The Text of Isaiah at Qumran," pages 491–511 in Craig C. Broyles and Craig A. Evans (eds.), *Writing & Reading the Scroll of Isaiah: Studies of an Interpretive Tradition*. Vol. 2. VTSup 70/2. Leiden: Brill.

———. 2002. "Scribal Notations in the Texts from the Judaean Desert." *DJD* 39, 323–349.

———. 2012. *Textual Criticism of the Hebrew Bible*. 3rd ed. Minneapolis, MN: Fortress.

———. 2019. "Exegesis and Theology in the Transmission of Isaiah," pages 94–127 in James H. Charlesworth (ed.), *The Unperceived Continuity of Isaiah*. London: Bloomsbury T&T Clark.

Trebolle-Barrea, Julio. 2000. "Qumran Evidence for a Biblical Standard Text and for Non-standard and Parabiblical Texts," pages 89–106 in Timothy H. Lim (ed.), *The Dead Sea Scrolls in Their Historical Contexts*. London: T&T Clark.

Tredennick, Hugh (trans.). 1996. *Aristotle: Metaphysics, Books I–IX*. LCL 271. Cambridge, MA: Harvard University Press.

Tucker, Gene M. 1977. "Prophetic Superscriptions and the Growth of a Canon," pages 56–70 in George W. Coats and Burke O. Long (eds.), *Canon and Authority: Essays in Old Testament Religion and Theology*. Philadelphia: Fortress.

Tull, Patricia K. 2017. "Who Says What to Whom: Speakers, Hearers, and Overhearers in Second Isaiah," pages 157–168 in Shelley L. Birdsong and Serge Frolov (eds.), *Partners with God: Theological and Critical Readings of the Bible in Honor of Marvin A. Sweeney*. Claremont, CA: Claremont.

Tzoref, Shani. 2019. "Pesharim," pages 335–338 in George J. Brooke and Charlotte Hempel (eds.), *T&T Clark Companion to the Dead Sea Scrolls*. London: T&T Clark.

Uhlig, Torsten. 2009. *The Theme of Hardening in the Book of Isaiah: An Analysis of Communicative Action*. FAT II/39. Tübingen: Mohr Siebeck.

Ulrich, Eugene. 2000. "Isaiah, Book Of," pages 384–388 in Lawrence H. Schiffman and James C. VanderKam (eds.), *EDSS*. Vol. 1. New York: Oxford University Press.

———. 2001. "The Developmental Composition of the Book of Isaiah: Light from 1QIsaᵃ on Additions in the MT." *DSD* 8, 288–305.

———. 2017. "The Prophet Isaiah at Qumran," pages 144–166 in Donald W. Parry, Stephen D. Ricks, and Andrew C. Skinner (eds.), *The Prophetic Voice at Qumran: The Leonardo Museum Conference on the Dead Sea Scrolls, 11–12 April 2014*. Leiden: Brill.

Ulrich, Eugene C., Frank Moore Cross, Russell E. Fuller, Judith E. Sanderson, Patrick W. Skehan, and Emanuel Tov (eds.). 1997. *Qumran Cave 4.X: The Prophets*. DJD XV. Oxford: Clarendon.

Usher, Stephen (trans.). 1985. *Dionysius of Halicarnassus: Critical Essays*. Vol. 2: *On Literary Composition, Dinarchus, Letters to Ammaeus and Pompeius*. LCL 466. Cambridge, MA: Harvard University Press.

Van de Mieroop, Marc. 2016. *Philosophy before the Greeks: The Pursuit of Truth in Ancient Babylonia*. Princeton: Princeton University Press.

VanderKam, James C. 2002. "The Wording of Biblical Citations in Some Rewritten Scriptural Works," pages 41–56 in Edward D. Herbert and Emanuel Tov (eds.), *The Bible as Book: The Hebrew Bible and the Judaean Desert Discoveries*. London: British Library & Oak Knoll.

———. 2018. *Jubilees 2: A Commentary on the Book of Jubilees Chapters 22–50*. Hermeneia. Minneapolis, MN: Fortress.

van der Kooij, Arie. 1997. "Isaiah in the Septuagint," pages 513–529 in Craig C. Broyles and Craig A. Evans (eds.), *Writing & Reading the*

Scroll of Isaiah: Studies of an Interpretive Tradition. Vol. 2. VTSup 70/2. Leiden: Brill.

van der Toorn, Karel. 2007. *Scribal Culture and the Making of the Hebrew Bible.* Cambridge, MA: Harvard University Press.

van der Vorm-Croughs, Mirjam. 2014. *The Old Greek of Isaiah: An Analysis of Its Pluses and Minuses.* Atlanta, GA: SBL.

van der Weel, Adriaan. 2019. "Literary Authorship in the Digital Age," pages 218–234 in Ingo Berensmeyer, Gert Buelens, and Barysa Demoor (eds.), *The Cambridge Handbook of Literary Authorship.* Cambridge: Cambridge University Press.

van der Woude, Annemarieke. 2011. "The Comfort of Zion: Personification in Isaiah 40–66," pages 159–167 in Archibald L. H. M. van Wieringen and Annemarieke van der Woude (eds.), *"Enlarge the Site of Your Tent": The City as Unifying Theme in Isaiah.* OtSt 58. Leiden: Brill.

van Dijk, Jan J. A. 1962. "Die Inschriftenfunde," pages 39–62 in Heinrich J. Lenzen (ed.), *XVIII. vorläufiger Bericht über die von dem Deutschen Archäologischen Institut und der Deutschen Orient-Gesellschaft aus Mitteln der Deutschen Forschungsgemeinschaft unternommenen Ausgrabungen in Uruk-Warka.* Berlin: Mann.

VanDyke, Elizabeth. 2021. "The Pens of the Prophets: The Materiality of Scribal Practice in Isaiah 8." Paper presented at the SBL Annual Meeting, San Antonio, TX, November 21.

van Henten, Jan Willem. 2018. "Josephus as Narrator," pages 121–150 in Eve-Marie Becker and Jörg Rüpke (eds.), *Autoren in religiösen literarischen Texten der späthellenistischen under der frühkaiserzeitlichen Welt: Zwölf Fallstudien.* Culture, Religion, and Politics in the Greco-Roman World 3. Tübingen: Mohr Siebeck.

van Seters, John. 2000. "Prophetic Orality in the Context of the Ancient Near East: A Response to Culley, Crenshaw, and Davies," pages 83–88 in Ehud Ben Zvi and Michael H. Floyd (eds.), *Writings and Speech in Israelite and Ancient Near Eastern Prophecy.* SBL SymSer 10. Atlanta, GA: SBL.

Vanstiphout, Herman L. J. 2003. "The Old Babylonian Literary Canon: Structure, Function, and Intention," pages 1–28 in Gillis J. Dorleijn (ed.), *Cultural Repertoires: Structure, Function, and Dynamics.* Leuven: Peeters.

van Unnik, Willem C. 1978. "Die Formel 'nichts wegnehmen, nichts zufügen,'" pages 26–40 in Willem C. van Unnik (ed.), *Flavius Josephus als historischer Schriftsteller.* Heidelberg: Lambert Schneider.

van Wieringen, Archibald L. H. M. 2005. "Isaiah's Roles: The Unity of a Bible Book from the Perspective of the Sender-Role," pages 115–124 in Ulrich Berges and P. Chatelion Counet (eds.), *One Text, Thousand Methods: Studies in Honor of Sjef van Tilborg*. Leiden: Brill.

Vayntrub, Jacqueline. 2018. "Before Authorship: Solomon and Prov. 1:1." *BibInt* 26, 182–206.

Veldhuis, Niek C. 2004. *Religion, Literature, and Scholarship: The Sumerian Composition "Nanše and the Birds."* CM 22. Leiden: Brill.

Verheyden, Joseph. 2021. "All Mysteries Revealed? On the Interplay between Hiding and Revealing and the Dangers of Heavenly Journeys according to the *Ascension of Isaiah*," pages 70–87 in Igor Dorfmann-Lazarev (ed.), *Apocryphal and Esoteric Sources in the Development of Christianity and Judaism: The Eastern Mediterranean, the Near East, and Beyond*. TSEC 21. Leiden: Brill.

Vermes, Geza. 1968. "The Decalogue and the Minim," pages 232–240 in Matthew Black and Georg Fohrer (eds.), *In Memoriam Paul Kahle*. Berlin: de Gruyter.

———. 2004. *The Complete Dead Sea Scrolls in English*. London: Penguin.

Wagner, S. 1978. "דָּרַשׁ," pages 293–307 in G. Johannes Botterweck, Helmer Ringgren, and Heinz-Josef Fabry (eds.), *TDOT* 3. Translated by John T. Willis, Geoffrey W. Bromiley, and David E. Green. Grand Rapids, MI: Eerdmans.

Waltke, Bruce K., and M. O'Connor. 1990. *An Introduction to Biblical Hebrew Syntax*. Winona Lake, IN: Eisenbrauns.

Warhurst, Amber K. 2011. "The Chronicler's Use of the Prophets," pages 165–181 in Ehud Ben Zvi and Diana V. Edelman (eds.), *What Was Authoritative for Chronicles?* Winona Lake, IN: Eisenbrauns.

Watts, John D. W. 1985. *Isaiah 1–33*. WBC 24. Waco, TX: Word Books.

———. 1987. *Isaiah 34–66*. WBC 25. Waco, TX: Word Books.

———. 2004. *Isaiah 1–33*. 2nd ed. WBC 24. Grand Rapids, MI: Eerdmans.

Wee, John Z. 2015. "Phenomena in Writing: Creating and Interpreting Variants of the Diagnostic Series Sa-gig," pages 247–287 in J. Cale Johnson (ed.), *In the Wake of the Compendia: Infrastructural Contexts and the Licensing of Empiricism in Ancient and Medieval Mesopotamia*. Berlin: de Gruyter.

Weiss, Richard D. 1986. *A Definition of the Genre Maśśāʾ in the Hebrew Bible*. PhD diss.: Claremont Graduate University.

———. 1992. "Oracle, Old Testament," pages 28–29 in David Noel Freedman (ed.), *ABD*. New York: Doubleday.

Weitemeyer, Mogens. 1990. "Babylonian and Assyrian Catalogues," pages 379–390 in Egon Keck, Svend Søndergaard, and Ellen Wulff (eds.), *Living Waters: Scandinavian Orientalistic Studies Presented to Dr. Frede Løkkegaard on His Seventy-Fifth Birthday, January 27th 1990*. Copenhagen: Museum Tusculanum.

West, M. L. 1997. *The East Face of Helicon: West Asiatic Elements in Greek Poetry and Myth*. Oxford: Clarendon.

Westenholz, Joan Goodnick. 1997. *Legends of the Kings of Akkade: The Texts*. Winona Lake, IN: Eisenbrauns.

Westermann, Claus. 1969. *Isaiah 40–66: A Commentary*. Translated by David M. G. Stalker. OTL. Philadelphia: Westminster.

———. 1991. *Basic Forms of Prophetic Speech*. Translated by Hugh Clayton White. Louisville, KY: Westminster John Knox.

Weyde, Karl William. 2018. "Once Again the Term *Maśśā'* in Zechariah 9:1; 12:1 and in Malachi 1:1: What Is Its Significance?" *Acta Theologica Supplementum* 26, 251–267.

Whealey, Alice. 2003. *Josephus on Jesus: The Testimonium Flavianum Controversy from Late Antiquity to Modern Times*. New York: Peter Lang.

Whybray, R. Norman. 1975. *Isaiah 40–66*. NCB Commentary. London: Oliphants.

Wikander, Ola. 2017. *Unburning Fame: Horses, Dragons, Beings of Smoke, and Other Indo-European Motifs in Ugarit and the Hebrew Bible*. ConBOT 62. Winona Lake, IN: Eisenbrauns.

Wilcke, Claus. 1972. "Der aktuelle Bezug der Sammlung der sumerischen Tempelhymnen und ein Fragment eines Klageliedes." *ZA* 62, 35–61.

Wildberger, Hans. 1991. *Isaiah 1–12*. Translated by Thomas H. Trapp. CC. Minneapolis, MN: Fortress.

———. 1997. *Isaiah 13–27*. Translated by Thomas H. Trapp. CC. Minneapolis, MN: Fortress.

———. 2002. *Isaiah 28–39*. Translated by Thomas H. Trapp. CC. Minneapolis, MN: Fortress.

Willgren [now Davage], David. 2016a. *The Formation of the 'Book' of Psalms: Reconsidering the Transmission and Canonization of Psalmody in Light of Material Culture and the Poetics of Anthologies*. FAT II/88. Tübingen: Mohr Siebeck.

———. 2016b. "Ps 72:20—a Frozen Colophon?" *JBL* 135/1, 49–60.

———. 2017a. "Antwort Gottes: Isaiah 40–55 and the Transformation of Psalmody," pages 96–115 in Greger Andersson, Tommy Wasserman, and David Willgren (eds.), *Studies in Isaiah: History, Theology, and Reception*. LHBOTS 654. Edinburgh: T&T Clark.

———. 2017b. "Did David Lay Down His Crown? Reframing Issues of Deliberate Juxtaposition and Interpretive Contexts in the 'Book' of Psalms with Psalm 147 as a Case in Point," pages 212–228 in Mika S. Pajunen and Jeremy Penner (eds.), *Functions of Psalms and Prayers in the Late Second Temple Period*. BZAW 486. Berlin: de Gruyter.

————. 2019a. "Canonical Tamings of Suffering: On How Paratextual Activities Reshapes the Relationship between God and Human in Psalm 71," pages 176–207 in David Willgren (ed.), *God and Humans in the Hebrew Bible and Beyond: A Festschrift for Lennart Boström on His 67th Birthday*. Sheffield, UK: Sheffield Phoenix.

————. 2019b. "'May YHWH Avenge Me on You; but My Hand Shall Not Be against You' (1 Sam. 24:13): Mapping Land and Resistance in the 'Biographical' Notes of the 'Book' of Psalms." *JSOT* 43/3, 417–435.

————. 2020. "A Teleological Fallacy in Psalms Studies? Decentralizing the 'Masoretic' Psalms Sequence in the Formation of the 'Book' of Psalms," pages 33–50 in Alma Brodersen, Friederike Neumann, and David Willgren (eds.), *Intertextualität und die Entstehung des Psalters*. FAT II/114. Tübingen: Mohr Siebeck.

Willgren Davage, David. 2019. "A 'Book' of Psalms in 4QMidrEschat[a.b]?" *SJOT* 33/2, 223–243.

————. 2020a. "'As It Is Written concerning Him in the Songs of David' (11Q13 2 9–10): On the Role of Paratextual Activity in Shaping Eschatological Reimaginations of Psalm 82," pages 3–44 in Erkki Koskenniemi and David Willgren Davage (eds.), *David, Messianism, and Eschatology: Ambiguity in the Reception History of the Book of Psalms in Judaism and Christianity*. Studies in the Reception History of the Bible 9. Åbo: Åbo Akademi University.

————. 2020b. "Why Davidic Superscriptions Do Not Demarcate Earlier Collections of Psalms." *JBL* 139/1, 67–86.

————. 2021. "Sin without Grace? A Fresh Look at the Theological Significance of לרוח היום in Genesis 3:8," pages 115–137 in Blaženka Scheuer and David Willgren Davage (eds.), *Suffering, Sin, and the Problem of Evil*. Tübingen: Mohr Siebeck.

————. Forthcoming. "Stitching Psalms Together: On the Function and Use of Psalms in 4Q171." *CBQ*.

Willi, T. 1972. *Die Chronik als Auslegung: Untersuchungen zur literarischen Gestaltung der historischen Überlieferung Israels*. FRLANT 106. Göttingen: Vandenhoeck & Ruprecht.

Williams, Catrin H. 2005. "Isaiah in John's Gospel," pages 101–116 in Steve Moyise and Maarten J. J. Menken (eds.), *Isaiah in the New Testament: The New Testament and the Scriptures of Israel*. London: T&T Clark.

Williams, Ronald J. 2007. *William's Hebrew Syntax*. 3rd ed. Toronto: University of Toronto Press.

Williamson, H. G. M. 1977. *Israel in the Book of Chronicles*. London: Cambridge University Press.

———. 1982. *1 and 2 Chronicles*. NCB Commentary. Grand Rapids, MI: Eerdmans.

———. 1993. "First and Last in Isaiah," pages 95–108 in Heather A. McKay and David J. A. Clines (eds.), *Of Prophets' Visions and the Wisdom of Sages: Essays in Honour of R. Norman Whybray on His Seventieth Birthday*. JSOTSup 162. Sheffield, UK: JSOT.

———. 1994. *The Book Called Isaiah: Deutero-Isaiah's Role in Composition and Redaction*. Oxford: Oxford University Press.

———. 2005. "Isaiah, Micah and Qumran," pages 203–211 in Geoffrey Khan (ed.), *Semitic Studies in Honour of Edward Ullendorff*. Studies in Semitic Languages and Linguistics 47. Leiden: Brill.

———. 2009. "Recent Issues in the Study of Isaiah," pages 21–39 in David G. Firth and H. G. M. Williamson (eds.), *Interpreting Isaiah: Issues and Approaches*. Downers Grove, IL: InterVarsity.

———. 2012. "Isaiah: Book Of," pages 364–378 in Mark J. Boda and J. Gordon McConville (eds.), *Dictionary of the Old Testament Prophets*. Downers Grove, IL: InterVarsity.

———. 2014. *Isaiah 1–5: A Critical and Exegetical Commentary*. ICC. London: Bloomsbury.

———. 2018. *Isaiah 6–12: A Critical and Exegetical Commentary*. ICC. London: Bloomsbury.

Willi-Plein, I. 2006. "Wort, Last oder Auftrag? Zur Bedeutung von *maśśā'* in Überschriften prophetischer Texteinheiten," pages 431–438 in *Die unwiderstehliche Wahrheit: Studien zur alttestamentlichen Prophetie. Festschrift für Arndt Meinhold*. ABG 23. Leipzig: Evangelische Verlagsanstalt.

Willis, John T. 1997. "Isaiah 2:2–5 and the Psalms of Zion," pages 295–316 in Craig C. Broyles and Craig A. Evans (eds.), *Writing & Reading the Scroll of Isaiah: Studies of an Interpretive Tradition*. Vol. 1. VTSup 70/1. Leiden: Brill.

Wilson, Gerald H. 1985. *The Editing of the Hebrew Psalter*. SBLDS 76. Chico, CA: Scholars.

Wise, Michael O., Martin G. Abegg Jr., and Edward M. Cook (eds.). 2005. *The Dead Sea Scrolls: A New English Translation*. New York: HarperCollins.

Wolf, Herbert M. 1972. "A Solution to the Immanuel Prophecy in Isaiah 7:14–8:22." *JBL* 91, 449–456.

Woodmansee, Martha. 1984. "The Genius and the Copyright: Economic and Legal Conditions of the Emergence of the 'Author.'" *Eighteenth-Century Studies* 17/4, 425–448.

Wright, Benjamin G., III. 2008. "Ben Sira on the Sage as Exemplar," pages 165–182 in Benjamin G. Wright III (ed.), *Praise Israel for

Wisdom and Instruction: Essays on Ben Sira and Wisdom, the Letter of Aristeas and the Septuagint. Leiden: Brill.

———. 2011. "Conflicted Boundaries: Ben Sira, Sage and Seer," pages 229–253 in Martti Nissinen (ed.), *Congress Volume: Helsinki 2010.* VTSup 148. Leiden: Brill.

Wright, Benjamin G., III, and Eva Mroczek. 2021. "Ben Sira's Pseudo-pseudepigraphy: Idealizations from Antiquity to the Early Middle Ages," pages 213–239 in Samuel L. Adams, Greg Schmidt Goering, and Matthew Goff (eds.), *Sirach in Its Contexts: The Pursuit of Wisdom and Human Flourishing.* Leiden: Brill.

Wyatt, Nicolas. 2015. "The Evidence of the Colophons in the Assessment of Ilimilku's Scribal and Authorial Role." *UF* 46, 399–446.

Wyrick, Jed. 2004. *The Ascension of Authorship: Attribution and Canon Formation in Jewish, Hellenistic, and Christian Traditions.* Harvard Studies in Comparative Literature 49. Cambridge, MA: Harvard University Press.

Young, Edward. 1759. *Conjectures on Original Composition: In a Letter to the Author of Sir Charles Grandison.* London: A. Millar and R. and J. Dodsley.

Zahavy, Tzvee (trans.). 1989. *The Talmud of the Land of Israel: A Preliminary Translation and Explanation.* Vol. 1: *Berakhot.* Edited by Jacob Neusner. Chicago: University of Chicago Press.

Zapff, Burkard M. 1995. *Schriftgelehrte Prophetie: Jes 13 und die Komposition des Jesajabuches: Ein Beitrag zur Erforschung des Redaktionsgeschichte des Jesajabuches.* Würzburg: Echter.

Zeitlin, Solomon. 1953. "Midrash: A Historical Study." *JQR* 44/1, 21–36.

Zenger, Erich. 1991. "Was wird anders bei kanonischer Psalmenauslegung?," pages 397–413 in Friedrich V. Reiterer (ed.), *Ein Gott, eine Offenbarung: Beiträge zur biblischen Exegese, Theologie und Spiritualitat; Festschrift für Notker Füglister OSB zum 60. Geburtstag.* Würzburg: Echter.

Zgoll, Annette. 1997. *Der Rechtsfall der En-[h]edu-Ana im Lied nin-me-šara.* AOAT 246. Münster: Ugarit-Verlag.

Ziegler, Joseph. 1950. "Die Hilfe Gottes 'am Morgen,'" pages 281–288 in H. Junker and J. Botterweck (eds.), *Alttestamentliche Studien: Friedrich Nötscher zum Sechzigsten Geburtstag.* BBB 1. Bonn: Peter Hanstein Verlag.

———. 1980. *Sapientia Iesu Filii Sirach.* 2nd ed. Göttingen: Vandenhoeck & Ruprecht.

Zimmern, Heinrich. 1930. "Ein Zyklus altsumerischer Lieder auf die Haupttempel Babylonians." *ZA* 39/4, 245–276.

INDEX OF AUTHORS

INDEX OF PASSAGES

2 *Samuel,* 157–58, 162, 168, 175, 273–74

63:3	145
69:29	85
71	255
72:18	190
75:9	280
77:14	190
78	230
78:2	230
78:12	190
79	188–91, 195, 197
79:1–3	191
79:1	191
79:2	191
79:3	190–91
79:8–13	191
86:10	190
88:10	190
89:19	145–46
96:10	249
103	174
104	174
127	255
136:4	190
142	175
142:1	174–75
143:8	xii

Proverbs, 173, 254, 273, 275

1:1–6	180
1:1	180
1:22	278
22:29	145
24:32	145
26:8	94
29:18	145
29:20	145
30:4	94

Job, 272–74

4:12–16	146
4:13	145
7:14	145–46
8:17	145
9:7	94
15:17	145
19:23	101
19:26–27	145

20:8	145–46
23:9	145
24:1	145
24:16	94
27:12	145
33:14–16	146
33:15	145
34:32	145
36:25	145
37:7	94

Song of Songs, 173, 273, 275

4:12	94
7:1	145

Ruth, 273

4:7	92

Lamentations, 273, 275, 279

2:9	145
2:14	145

Ecclesiastes, 6, 8, 173, 273, 275

1:1	267
1:4–7	267

Esther, 273–74

3:12	95
8:8	95
8:10	95

Daniel, 146, 221, 270, 273–74

1:17	146
2:8	145
2:19	145–46
2:26	146
2:28	146
2:31	146
2:34	146
2:41	146
2:43	146
2:45	146
3:25	145
3:27	145
4:2	146
4:6–8	146
4:10	146
4:15	146

Septuagint

2 Chronicles

27:7	160
33:19	165

2 Maccabees

18:14	222

Psalms

26:1	176
96:1	177
142:1	177
143:1	177
151	177

Jonah

3:4	244

Isaiah

3:6	227
6:10	227
8:1	87
13:1	254

20:2	114
22:15	227
30:16	227
39:6	227
40:6	117
44:26	128
45:14	227
51:3	227
52:13	254
58:3	227

Additions to *Daniel*

Bel and the Dragon, 270
Susanna, 270

2 Esdras

2:18	222
14:21–48	270

4 Maccabees

18:14	187

Ancient Near Eastern Texts

Bit Meseri, 59
Catalogs of Incipits, 26–29
A Catalogue of Texts and Authors,
    32–33, 36–37, 40, 47, 59, 73,
    155, 290
Chronicle of Ancient Kings, 74
Chronicle of the Esagila, 74
Cuthean Legend, 37–38

177–80	38

Enuma Elish, 39–40, 43, 46–47, 82,
    290

VII, 145–62	39–40

Epic of Gilgamesh, 36–39, 49, 73,
    149, 172, 290

i, 1–2, 5–8	37
i, 25–26	38

Erra Epic, 33–36, 38, 40, 49, 73, 92,
    97, 103, 147, 290

V, 39–44	33
V, 43	34
V, 45–61	35–36

Esagil-kīn-apli's Manifesto, 41–42

Exaltation of Inanna, 27, 29–31,
    34–35, 38, 112, 147, 180, 290

51–55	30
138–44	29–30
145–47	31
151	31

Hymn ascribed to Assurbanipal, 49
Inscriptions of Esarhaddon, 171
Instructions of Shuruppak, 33
Lachish Ostraca

3	90

Ludlul bēl nēmeqi, 33, 46
Marduk's Address to the Demons,
    45–46
Mari letters, 80–81, 88, 89–90, 99

1	80
2	80
4	81
5	81
9	81
71	81

Nineveh oracles, 81, 151

Apocrypha and Pseudepigrapha

1 *Enoch*, 199, 244
91–92   199

4 *Baruch*
9:22 251

Apocalypse of Paul
40   249

Ascension of Isaiah, 236, 248–56
1–5 249–50, 252, 254–55
1:1–2   250
1:2–6   249
1:2–3   250
1:3–4   249
1:5 250
1:6 252, 254
1:7 251
1:9–10   251
1:12–13 251
2:1–6   251
2:7–11   251
2:7–10   251
2:9 254
3:1 251
3:6–7   251
3:8–10   251
3:12 251
3:13–4:22   249, 254
3:13–20 251
3:26 252
3:31 252
4:1–13   252
4:14–22 252
4:14 252
4:17 252
4:21–22 254–55
5   252
5:2 252
5:14–15 252
5:15–16 249
6–11   249–50, 252–55
6:1 250, 254
6:16 254
7:3 250

11   252
11:1 257
11:10   257
11:39–40 255
11:41   252

Ben Sira, 10, 173, 179–86, 218, 262
1:30 182
6:19–22 182
24:28   181
24:30–34 180–81
24:34   181–82
33:16   181
39   179
39:1–2   181–82
39:6–11 182
39:6 181
39:9–11 183
39:12   181
39:32   184
43:31–33 182
44:3–9   182–83
44:7–9   182
48:14   187
48:22–25 184
48:22–23 184
50:27   179–80, 182, 184

Jubilees, 187, 194, 216
4:17–19 199
8:11–12 199
10:13–14 199
12:27   199
21:10   199
45:16   199

Letter of Aristeas, 239–40
308–16   240

Lives of the Prophets, 256–57
1:8 256

Greek and Latin Works